AF333990

Chinese America

Stereotype and Reality

PETER LANG
New York • Washington, D.C./Baltimore • Bern
Frankfurt am Main • Berlin • Brussels • Vienna • Oxford

Birgit Zinzius

Chinese America

Stereotype and Reality

History, Present, and Future of the Chinese Americans

PETER LANG
New York • Washington, D.C./Baltimore • Bern
Frankfurt am Main • Berlin • Brussels • Vienna • Oxford

Library of Congress Cataloging-in-Publication Data

Zinzius, Birgit.
Chinese America: stereotype and reality: history, present, and future
of the Chinese Americans / Birgit Zinzius.
p. cm.
Includes bibliographical references and index.
1. Chinese Americans—History. 2. Chinese Americans—Social conditions.
3. Immigrants—United States—History. 4. China—Emigration and immigration—History.
5. Taiwan—Emigration and immigration—History. 6. Hong Kong (China)—
Emigration and immigration—History. 7. United States—Emigration and immigration—History.
8. United States—Ethnic relations. 9. Chinese Americans—California—
San Francisco—History. 10. San Francisco (Calif.)—Ethnic relations. I. Title.
E184.C5Z56   305.895'1073'09—dc22   2004004007
ISBN 0-8204-6744-8

Bibliographic information published by **Die Deutsche Bibliothek.**
Die Deutsche Bibliothek lists this publication in the "Deutsche
Nationalbibliografie"; detailed bibliographic data is available
on the Internet at http://dnb.ddb.de/.

The paper in this book meets the guidelines for permanence and durability
of the Committee on Production Guidelines for Book Longevity
of the Council of Library Resources.

For Tommy

Contents

List of Figures

List of Tables

Acknowledgments

The book could not have been completed without the support of many people. Their help and, in many cases, their integration into the Chinese community enabled my access to first-hand experiences about Chinese Americans and their interaction with the mainstream American community and politics.

In particular, I would like to thank Dean Du Dao-tung in Tianjin, China, for his support. Interviews with members of the Congress, Senate, and community leaders enabled me to cover broad political opinions. Thomas A. Daschle (Senator), Robert T. Matsui (Member of Congress), Nancy Pelosi (Member of Congress), Paul Simon (Senator), John D. Trasvina, James McCormick, Rolland Lowe, Thomas Hsieh, Elaine L. Ng, and Edward A. Hailes, were particularly helpful and informative.

James Fang and Patrick Anderson (*Asian Week*), Philipp Choi, Cheryl Tsui, Vernon Kato, Rose Shirinian, Kelvin Tang, (*KTSF*), Fred Brown, Serena Chen, Elaine Sit, Franklin Wong (*East West*), and Joseph Wong (*San Francisco Chinese News*) provided excellent media support.

Thomas Chinn und Daisy Chinn (*California Historical Society*), Philipp Chow (*Chinese Historical Society*), Paul Chau-Jiunn Shie, (*Chinese American Society*), Nancy Chang, Daphne Kwok, Nancy W. Huang (*Organizations of Chinese Americans*), Yvonne Lee, Harry W. Low (*Chinese American Citizen Alliance*), Harvey Wong (*Chinese Consolidated Benevolent Association*), Him Mark Lai (*Chinese Historical Society*), Gloria Tan (*Gum Moon Women's Residence*), Bill Tamayo (*Asian Law Caucus*), Henry Der, Emily Lee, Kathy Lowe (*Chinese for Affirmative Action*), and Dennis Wong (*Six Companies*) provided in-depth insight into Chinese Americans and their history.

Amado Cabezas (Asian American Studies Department; University of California Berkeley), Sucheng Chan (Asian American Studies Department, University of California, Santa Barbara), Harry H. L. Kitano (Professor of Social Welfare and Sociology, Endowed Chair, Japanese American Studies, University of California, Los Angeles), Peter Kwong (SUNY College at Old Westbury, Long Island), Betty Lee Sung (Department of Asian American Studies, Professor & Chair, City College of New York), Ronald Takaki (Professor of Asian American Studies Department at the University of California, Berkeley), Sau-Ling Cynthia Wong (Professor, Department of Ethnic Studies, Asian American Studies Program, University of California, Berkeley), and Judy Yung (American Studies, University of California, Santa Cruz), supported the work with their open and encouraging discussions. Thanks for great talks goes especially to Frank Chew Chin, Arthur Dong, Fred Ho, Gus Lee, Amy Tan, Wayne Wang, Stella Wong, and Conni Young

Yue, who provided first-hand information about the cultural awakening of the Chinese American community.

My special gratitude goes to Ling-chi Wang (Chair, Asian American Studies Department at the University of California, Berkeley). His scientific support and insights into the Chinese American community were a major source for this work.

Wei-chi Poon (Asian American Studies Collection Librarian, Ethnic Studies Library, University of California, Berkeley) was a great help and inspiration during all literature studies.

I thank Fred Brown, Jeanny Look, Elaine Sit, Chester Wong, and S.K. Wong for her friendship, and especially May Lee and her family, for treating me like a part of their family. I am grateful also to all others that have contributed, and could not been mentioned here.

Last but not least, I want to thank my family, who encouraged my path, and thus made this book possible.

Birgit Zinzius, Jakarta, January 2005

List of Abbreviations

AABDC	Asian American Business Development Council
AAFNY	Asian American Federation of New York
AAGEN	Asian American Government Executives Network
AAMA	Asian American Manufacturers Association
ABAG	Association of Bay Area Governments
ACP	Association of Chinese Professionals
API/PI	Asian and Pacific Islander/Pacific Islander
APT	Asian Pacific Triangle
CAA	Chinese for Affirmative Action
CACA	Chinese American Citizen Alliance
CADC	Chinese American Democratic Club
CAIEP	Chinese Association for International Exchange of Personnel
CAPA	Chinese American Political Association
CAPAC	Congressional Asian Pacific Caucus
CAPAL	Conference on Asian American Pacific Leadership
CASPA	Chinese American Semiconductor Professionals Association
CAST	Chinese Association for Science and Technology
CAUSE-Vision 21	Chinese Americans United for Self-Empowerment
CAVEC	Chinese American Voter Education Committee
CCBA	Chinese Consolidated Benevolent Organization
CC	Central Committee
CCC	Chinese Chamber of Commerce
CCDC	Chinatown Community Development Center
CEDG	Chinatown Economic Development Group
CIE	Chinese Institute of Engineers
CINA	Chinese Information & Networking Association
CITA	Chinese Internet Technology Association
COTN	China Oversea Talent Network
CPC	Communist Party of China
CSPA	Chinese Student Protection Act, and Chinese Software Professionals Assoc.
DPP	Democratic Progressive Party—Taiwan
EB	Employment-Based
ELL/ESL	English Language Learners/English as a Second Language
FB	Family-Based
FBI	Federal Bureau of Investigation
FDI	Foreign Direct Investment
HKSAR	Hong Kong Special Administrative Region
IA	Immigration Act
IFCSS	Independent Federation of Chinese Students and Scholars
IIRIRA	Illegal Immigration Reform and Immigrant Responsibility Act
INA	Immigration and National Amendment Act
INS	Immigration and Naturalization Service
IRA	Immigration Reform Act
IRCA	Immigration Reform and Control Act
KMT	Kuomintang (National People's Party—Taiwan)
LEAP	Leadership Education for Asian Pacific's

LEP/NEP	Limited English Proficiency/No English Proficiency
MjD	Minzhu-jinhu Dang (Democratic Progress Party)
MOFTEC	Ministry of Foreign Trade and Economic Cooperation
NAACP	National Association for the Advancement of Colored People
NACSA	National American Chinese Semiconductor Association
NCLB	No Child Left Behind Act
NECINA	New England Chinese Information and Network Association
NNIR	National Network for Immigration and Refugees Rights
OMB	Office of Management and Budget
OCA	Organization of Chinese Americans
PRC	People's Republic of China
ROC	Republic of China (Taiwan)
SCEA	Silicon Valley Chinese Engineers Association
SCOBA	Silicon Valley Chinese Oversea Business Association
SVCWireless	Silicon Valley Chinese Wireless Technology Association
WTO	World Trade Organization

Introduction

The ethnic composition of the United States has changed continuously over the last two centuries. Driven by economic, political, and social motives, millions of immigrants have arrived from all over the world. During the nineteenth century, early immigrants came mainly from Europe and Africa, followed by an increasing number of Hispanics in the twentieth century. The history and present situation of these ethnic groups, such as the Europeans, Blacks and Hispanics, is well-documented in literature and scholarly studies. Not as well documented is a smaller and less visible immigrant group, the Asians, and in particular the Chinese. Their unobtrusive, low-profile attitude does not place them in the immediate spotlight. Their number and influence seems, however, to be growing strongly, which may signal a new shift in the ethnic composition of the United States, especially in the twenty-first century.

It is thus the aim of this study to draw a complete picture of the Chinese Americans, from their early immigration in the mid-nineteenth century until the present day. The study also explains the social and political backgrounds of the Chinese emigration from China, Hong Kong and Taiwan, and analyzes the influence of the Chinese economic development on migration patterns, including the effects of the current economic boom. The main centers of Chinese immigration, California and the San Francisco Bay Area in particular, and New York, are the major focus areas of the study. Detailed statistics about immigrant figures will be presented and analyzed based on the historical, cultural, and political background, as well as economic, gender, and social factors–among others. Two centuries of United States' immigration laws will be reviewed in detail, with a particular emphasis on anti-Chinese legislation.

Based on these immigration data and the underlying legislation, a close look at Chinese settlements throughout the United States will be taken, from the mid-nineteenth century Chinatown in San Francisco to the suburban migration patterns at the beginning of the twenty-first century. An analysis of Chinese Americans in all States over the past 150 years will be presented to evaluate settlement patterns and developments over the entire historical period.

The educational and professional situation of the Chinese Americans will be studied thereafter, and compared to mainstream America and the other major ethnic groups: White, Black and Hispanic. The integration of the Chinese Americans will then be presented, from local social activities to their national political engagement, from arts to music and sports, politics to economics, a broad spectrum of activities of the Chinese Americans will be studied to draw a detailed picture about their past and present situation in the United States.

Based on the findings over the past 150 years, future trends and perspectives will be outlined, and, in particular, the role of the Chinese Americans in the Pacific Rim business sector will be discussed.

My interest in China and the Chinese began in the early 1980s, when I had the chance to take up a teaching position in Tianjin. During two years in mainland China, I met several Chinese Americans who made their first trip to their ancestors' country . They were unable to communicate in Chinese and tried desperately to understand the habits and life of their ancestors. At that time I asked myself about the story of these Chinese living in the United States, a question I have researched ever since. This book conveys the essence of two decades of research of and experiences with Chinese Americans. It provides a complete and detailed overview of Chinese America in the twenty-first century from an impartial, European perspective.

Since my first encounter in China, the situation of Chinese Americans has changed significantly and become much more diversified. The dramatic economic and political changes in China, which may well become the world's largest economy within a few decades, have had a strong influence on this change. Bilateral relations between China and the United States during the twenty-first century will therefore shape the global economy and both societies. Chinese Americans may provide a crucial interface for these two distinct cultures in the future. At only one percent of the United States population, Chinese Americans are still a relatively small minority, although one with many facets and stereotypes. This study will analyze their historic and present situation in detail, including their influence on mainstream America and the United States of the twenty-first century.

1. CHINESE EMIGRATION TO CALIFORNIA FROM 1848 UNTIL 1924

Changes within Classical Chinese Society

Dissolution of Social Hierarchies

Over millennia, the Chinese saw their country as the center of civilization. This view, as well as its solid social structures offered little potential for influence from outside or for internal changes. First, the Chinese Emperors were not interested in diplomatic contacts with the West and second, there was no substantial interest in western products, which might have equaled the extensive demand for Chinese products. In a country with silver currency, foreign currencies were in little demand (Fairbank, 1998, 141–2; Perkins, 1999, 111). From a western viewpoint, therefore, major barriers existed at the beginning of the nineteenth-century for the development of economic relations.

To understand the eventual beginning of changes resulting from foreign influence around the middle of the nineteenth-century, one must initially look at the classical structure of Chinese society. Since state and society achieve almost religious status, the following will first show the ideal and second the actual association. Results from Sinology as an important medium for understanding the primary situation of Chinese immigrants to the United States has in the past only been touched upon superficially, if at all.[1] Confucianism was the state doctrine from the beginning of the Han-Dynasty (206 B.C.–A.D. 220) until the end of the empire (1911). The reasons for this continuity are closely related to the relative stability of Chinese social structures. Family and tribe were the basic elements of state structure within the Confucian view and also the nucleus of society. The smallest element, therefore, was not the individual, but the family, which outlives its members (Levy, Marion, 1986, 47).

The value the family had within the philosophical Confucian system can be recognized from the *five virtues*, which are described in the *Book of Changes* (*I Ching*; pinyin: *Yijing*). For Confucius, a person becomes noble not by birth but through developing *five virtues*: *humanity* (*ren*), righteousness (*yi*), proper conduct (*li*), wisdom (*zhi*), and trustworthiness (*xin*).[2]

---

[1] As I state in my Magister thesis about dangerous misperceptions about the Chinese in the United States: "Any integration should be seen not only from an American but also Chinese perspective to reveal disturbances in the hosting society." Zinzius, 1988, 11.

[2] For further details see Huang, 1998. The teachings of Confucius (*pinyin*: Kongfuzi) remain influential in China and parts of Asia, especially Taiwan, Singapore, Japan, Korea and Vietnam.

Three virtues touched upon the family in the closest sense: the relationships between father and son, between elder and younger brothers, and between husband and wife. Within the non-family sector, the most important were those between Emperor and ministers, as well as those between friends. These were never relationships between equals. This was a typical phenomenon of the Confucian social order, which was patriarchal, and strictly hierarchical (Zinzius, 1996, 26).

Ownership and power within Chinese society has not succumbed to pressure to change throughout millennia, even after the downfall of the big dynasties, foreign occupation, agricultural crisis, and rural uprisings. The bureaucrat aristocracy might be seen as having taken over from the traditional hereditary aristocracy within the Han-Dynasty and having created an elite culture, which differed from that of the four classes: *literati (shi)*, *peasants (nong)*, *artisans (gong)*, and *merchants (shang)*. However, this changed little of the model function of Confucianism for all classes of society. The academic officials (*scholar officials*), who were dependant on the Emperor's Court, were always able to protect the existing system from changes within society, thereby representing an important stabilizing factor for the class system. It can be regarded as the support of state orthodoxy.

The hierarchy of the classical society consisted of five levels: The Emperor stood at the top, thanks to the unique role as mediator between heaven and earth given to him by Confucianism. In the case of severe interventions, e.g. revolution or invasion, however, he could lose this mandate by election. The bureaucrats occupied the second level and were divided into various subclasses. In contrast to Japan, China did not have a warrior caste. Officers were recruited from the bureaucrat caste, whereas soldiers were recruited from the peasant caste upon demand. The prestige of the officers was that of the bureaucrats. The soldiers returned to their fields and families after wars, since the armies were dissolved. Surprising in comparison to western standards is the fact that the traders took up the lowest level in the official hierarchy behind the artisans, although they represented the richest families in the cities. As the main support of the state, the peasants stood above the artisans who, however, created their own understanding within the city guilds. The low recognition of city trading defined the model in which he who neither produced nor worked for the state had little or no demand for social acceptance (Eberhard, 1948, 275–280). The state depended on the archaic part of the social structure—peasants and bureaucrats, who protected the country in case of war.

What was within the Chinese system only a weak, secondary, underprivileged caste, was used by the West as the point of attack. In cities, especially where western subsidiaries existed, e.g. Canton, the rich traders quickly expanded their influence.[3]

Its exceptional position in the South and at the mouth of the Pearl River made Canton the most important port in Southern China and thus, a main attraction for foreign trade and foreign ships. The first sighting of the "Empress of China" in Chinese waters in 1784 signaled the difficult entry of the United States into the lucrative trade in East Asia. Since it was forbidden for foreigners to have direct contacts with the hinterland and outside of their trading subsidiaries, a mediating class was created, the comprador class, who achieved exceptional political influence due to their special contacts with foreigners. But despite or possibly because of their influence and riches, the compradors, as traders and representatives, were hated outcasts. They were "the extended arm of imperialism" and were considered as enemies of their Chinese home due to the contact with "Whites" (Franke, 1962, 70-75). Therefore, members of the comprador class were pushed into even more intensive contact with foreigners. They used their new contacts either to expand their businesses to America or to emigrate. In contrast to their homeland, where the bureaucrats hindered their expansion, the trading caste would overseas quickly achieve a dominating role in politics and society.

Within this social scenario, a solution for the problems of the foreign trading nations was identified when the British East India Company began to expand its opium trade via the Chinese traders after the purchase of Bengal in the second half of the eighteenth century. Consumption and sale had been forbidden by imperial edict since 1729. The increasing corruption of bureaucrats by the compradors, however, indicated the downfall of imperial authority and thus supported the undisturbed expansion of opium trade. Eventually this became one of the most important factors of British trade with China. The Chinese authorities became concerned about the outflow of the already scarce silver to pay for the poison, as well as about the negative influence on the morality of society.

Even so, next to increased punishment, thoughts of legalization of opium smuggling were considered because parts of the government were rightly concerned about provoking the foreign powers. Initially, the hard line prevailed until 1839 when direct confrontation with the British arose over a shipment of 20,000 chests of opium that had been mixed with chalk (Perkins, 1999, 368–9).

---

[3] Today, Canton is known as Guangzhou. It is the capitol of Kwantung province—today known as Guangdong province.

The British traders called upon the government in London to take action. British troops and its navy occupied Canton (Guangzhou), Amoy (Xiamen), Ningpo (Ningbo), Shanghai and the mouth of the Yangtze (Yangzi) River.[4]

From the unequal situation between Chinese defense and British nautical power, the newly created "unequal contracts" basically ended the Chinese isolation policy by offering western powers far reaching rights (*Treaty of Nanjing, 1842*). Trade barriers were reduced. Opium trading which mainly flourished in southern areas, was legalized. Furthermore, China handed over Hong Kong to Great Britain. The success of the first aggressive war brought on the second, the so-called Opium Wars, which England and France subsequently fought against China and brought the *"Treaty of Tientsin (Tianjin), 1858."* This made possible the opening of European representation in Beijing where the Emperor's Summer Palace had been destroyed during the war (Fairbank, 1998, 201). The Consular Rights for all foreigners and the availability of Christian missions was introduced. Furthermore, the Chinese government had to make territorial concessions to European trade (Pu Yi, 1998). Thus the first prerequisites for long term integration of China in international relationships had been created.[5]

Comparing the previously discussed Confucian model with the actual situation in the South around 1850, clear differences appear. By the time of the Opium Wars the Emperor was far away, powerless, and completely under the influence of his consultants and court. Depending the personal power of the individual, the Emperor's Representative or the military leader led the Provinces. A "Bourgeoisie" had been created, consisting of higher gentry (bureaucrats and landlords) and lower gentry (merchants). This gentry not only included bureaucrats who had achieved their position after lengthy studies and passing of a literary state exam, but ever increasingly those who gained their position thanks to wealth and contacts. The examination became a farce, since title and position could be obtained "through the back door." Rich merchants and landlords could purchase for themselves or their children membership in the bureaucracy. The gentry maintained a certain number of privileges with regard to regular taxation and legal questions. The expansion

---

[4] Throughout the work, historic names are used in their related context; the current name–according to the mainland Chinese *pinyin*-system of romanization–is shown in brackets. The modern standard *pinyin* spelling system was approved by the Chinese Government in 1958, and adopted in 1979. Exceptions are familiar names of people, places or organizations outside mainland China, such as Dr. Sun Yat-sen, Chiang Kai-shek, and *Kuomintang*. For these exceptions, the traditional Wade-Giles system was applied.

[5] For detailed information see: Fairbank, John K. *Trade and Diplomacy on the China Coast. The Opening of the Treaty Ports 1842–1854.* Cambridge, MA: Harvard University Press, 1953. Waley, Arthur. *The Opium War Through Chinese Eyes.* London: Allen & Unwin, 1958. Eberhard, Wolfgang. *A History of China*, London: Routledge & Kegan, 1948.

of the bureaucrats was at the cost of the state (Fairbank, 1998, 235–6). Peasants were driven further into debt, due to bad crops and high taxation, but also because they would not give up certain traditions, e.g. expensive family festivities, weddings and burials. If they were unable to pay back their debts in the allocated period, they lost their land to the creditor, usually a landlord, and remained as tenant on their previously owned property. Finally, due to this corrupt bureaucracy, weak Emperor and poor peasants, the pillars of society became unstable.

Push Factors: Hunger and Revolution

The described signs of social destruction were increased by deep changes within population and social structure. The population explosion from 180 million in 1751 to 430 million in 1850 could not be curbed by natural catastrophes, which led to bottlenecks in supply (Eberhard, 1948, 273). The number of peasants without their own land increased by the end of the nineteenth century from 65% to 70%. Those with land were no better off, since their property hardly sufficed to feed their families, so they were forced to rent land from a landowner. The artisans were slightly more prosperous than the peasants, but they were also victims of the social changes. The social discrepancies and the weakness of the central government in Beijing resulted in local and regional uprisings.

The Taiping Rebellion (1850 to 1864) in Southern China was intended to distribute land ownership equally between the farming families and state government and to distribute crops. This uprising ended, however, when the rebels collaborated with the landlords at the expense of the peasants and the already weakened Qing-Dynasty.[6]

From 1850 on, the uprisings around Kwangsi (Guangxi), heavily directed against the Emperor's government, quickly expanded into the already poor coastal regions. Many poor peasants sought refuge as bandits in the mountains, and due to high unemployment the *coolie* trade with Panama, Cuba and South America bloomed.[7]

---

[6] The Qing-Dynasty, or also Ch'ing or Manchu-Dynasty, was China's last imperial dynasty (1644–1911). It was overthrown by the Revolution of 1911, which established the Republic of China (ROC) in 1912 (Perkins, 19989, 420).

[7] The *coolie trade* started in 1847, when the first Chinese contractors were shipped from Macao to Peru. The contracts made the Chinese virtually slaves and should not be confused with the *Contract Labor System*, which brought Chinese workers to the United States. Within the next 30 years, Cuba imported about 150,000 and Peru over 74,000 coolies. See Kim, 1989, 213.

Emigration in China was first legalized in 1868 when the Qing-Dynasty contractually regulated departures with the United States. Previously, illegal departure or abetting illegal departure had been sentenced by death.[8] With increasing economic and political decline in China, the number of those on the lower end of the social scale increased. This group consisted of *mean people*, e.g. nomads such as actors, artists, day laborers, cooks, and carriers. Since the Taiping Rebellion had already revealed China's weakness, the 1911 Revolution finally brought about the downfall of the Chinese Emperor.

The distribution of property, as well as the economic and political dependency upon imperial states, remained central and unsolved problems. When the Empress Dowager Tz'u Hsi (Cixi) died in 1908, the dynasties tradition was also nearing its end. She left the throne to her son, Henry Puyi, who was, however, only three years old. Thus the bureaucrats quickly took over the reins of power, but could not stop the downfall of the dynasty.[9]

Already as early as 1894, Dr. Sun Yat-sen (1866–1925) had been agitating for a republic in China and had therefore founded the *Kuomintang* (*KMT*) with the intention of creating a new political power base of the state.[10] Sun Yat-sen became the most important revolutionary in the battle against the Qing regime. After its downfall in 1912, he became the first president of the Chinese Republic. He set goals for the revolution and gave it theories of state and government.

In 1910, the first National Assembly was held. One year later, Dr. Sun Yat-sen returned from exile and became president of the provisional government in Nanjing. After 5000 years China had something like a democracy for the first time. A society which had been autocratically structured and almost continuously under the social order of Confucianism must have seen democratic principles as foreign and unobtainable. Dr. Sun

---

[8] The Law *Ta Ting Leu Lee* dates from 1712. Kim, Hyung-Chan, 1986, 505; for further information see: Tin-Yuke Char. *The Sandalwood Mountains*. Honolulu, University Press of Hawaii, 1975. MacFair, H.F., *The Chinese Abroad*, Shanghai, China, Commercial Press, 1924.

[9] The Iron Emperor, who was also called the "Old Buddha," died on November 15, 1908. Once before China had had a powerful female Emperor with Wu Zhao (627–705), who reigned from 690 to 704.

[10] The ruling party *Kuomintang (KMT)*, in *pinyin: Guomindang (GMD)*, was founded in Honolulu in 1894 under the name *Xingzhonghui (Society for the Rebirth of China)*. It is based on the Three Principles: nationalism, democracy, and peoples livelihood. In 1905, it merged with Japanese organizations, forming the *Tongmenhui (Revolutionary Alliance)*. The *Kuomintang*, which means National People's Party, got its present name in 1912, and was dissolved in 1914 by President Shikai. In 1919, it was reestablished, and Russian advisors helped to reshape it similar to the CPSU in 1923–24. The Central Committee as well as the permanent committee of the CC remains present until today. The various elements of the party cover the complete social and political life.

Yat-sen's revolution was carried off by the intellectuals and had no popular characteristics. It is most likely this fact that condemned the Chinese Republic—the first of the two modern forms of state—to failure.

From a European perspective, the continuity of Chinese society has often been seen as stagnation. The failure of the middle classes to grow hindered the creation of production and therefore a new determination of intra-social life. As the *Kuomintang* grew to be a new octopus, Chinese society could only slowly free itself from classical structures and obtained little political power. Already in 1916, China was split by military powers into regions of influence. Also a new state agreement by the *Kuomintang* could not bring any improvement in the social and political situation.

The period between 1911 and 1930 was thus one of social and political chaos. Regional warlords continuously attempted to obtain total power. Also Dr. Sun Yat-sen was unable to obtain national power during his period in office. Catastrophic hunger conditions existed in the North, causing peasant's uprisings, union strikes, and demonstrations, which were all violently crushed by those in power. Japanese and Europeans were only supportive of their own colonial interests in the country. The pressure to emigrate in the first thirty years of the twentieth century was therefore unhalting.

Family Relationships during Emigration

Family relationships within classical Chinese society continued to play an important role in the development of emigration amid the political changes in China. As with the development of the state, Confucianism was also the basis of all familial norms. Confucianism did not allow any substantial change in state orthodoxy, and only gradual differences between the sexes, which had determined the roles of men and women for over two thousand years and well into the twentieth century.

During the Han-Dynasty (206 B.C.–A.D. 220) the principles of family ideology were laid down in the so-called *Five Classics of Confucianism* (*wujing*).[11] The intra-family hierarchy was determined by age and sex. Within numerous generations, the eldest was always superior; within a generation this was also the case of its eldest member, whereby women were always lower than the men.

Women showed rare interest in emigration. On all levels women had a lower position and had to fulfill important tasks in the husband's family.

---

[11] The *Five Classics of Confucianism* are: Book of Changes (*Yijing or I Ching)*, Book of History (*shujing*), Book of Rites (*liji*), Book of Songs (*shijing*). and Spring and Autumn Annals (*chunqiu*). The Confucian canon also includes the *Four Books of Confucianism* (*sishu*): the Analects of Confucius (*lunyu*), Book of Mencius (*Mengzi*), Doctrine of the Mean (*zhongyong*), and Great Learning (*daxue*), (Fairbank, 1998, 67, Perkins, 1999, 160).

During her husband's stay abroad, she had to take care of her parents-in-law and maintain the forefathers cult, which gave the institution of the family a timelessness and transcendence. The living had to bring the dead presents and inform them of their earthly life; in return, they kept watch over the living and their heirs. This was strictly adhered to, so that the desire to continue the family tree ad infinitum came close to the wish for immortality. From its moral value, therefore, the Chinese family was the "safest foundation of the State." (Plath, 1862, 38; Berling, 1982, 5; Fairbank, 1998, 51-53). Due to her tasks within the family, the stay of Chinese women in their homeland, during emigration periods was, therefore, clearly predetermined.

The relationship between emigrants and their families had major economic importance, not only for the natural family, but also for the society in their homeland. Between 25% to 50% of males in Chinatowns were married, but separated from their partners, who had stayed in China. This split did not mean an unintentional break with the family. On the contrary, emigration was undertaken with the order to uphold the family and thus the larger society. The village often contracted young men to an arranged "blind marriage" prior to their departure. As compensation for the marriage and the resulting required support, the bride's family guaranteed her faithfulness. In the split family the rules of the Confucian system developed their full meaning. Subsequent emigration of sons or male family members fulfilled a double purpose, namely the continuation of emigration while maintaining the family in their homeland (Zinzius, 1988, 122). Some families had to sell their children due to economic hardship and the inability to feed them. While the boys and men were employed as workers overseas, many of the girls were traded into bordellos in California.

In China, prostitution was considered an out of house pleasure. Various classes of bordello existed, depending on the material situation and cultural requirements of its customers. The lack of a "spiritual and romantic view of a sexual relationship" (Fairbank, 1998, 19) in marriage was the prerequisite for the existence of a "higher" form of prostitution, which was only for the requirements and fantasies of the upper class. There were different levels of purchased love, as indicated in the various abilities of the woman and the varied forms of "courting." This higher prostitution was accepted and even norm shaping, analogous to the ideal of family and its marriage and social rules. Prostitution in Chinatown helped keep the workers who lived in simple conditions happy and compensate them for their missing families, who otherwise would have had to be looked after (Zinzius, 1988, 77). The *split Confucian family* was clearly identifiable with the working class family. In contrast, the early Chinese American family, which earned this name insofar as it distanced itself from Chinese tradition and nearing to American styles, was identifiable in the commercial circles. These traders were the only ones allowed to continue bringing their dependants into the country, after the Chinese Laws went into effect.

The discrepancy in the sexes within Chinatown heightened the position of Chinese women, but also made them the objects of even more brutal suppression than in traditional Chinese society. Higher class prostitutes maintained exceptional privileges and freedom, but the majority of young women were unscrupulously used and abused as objects of success by rivaling groups. Since no long-term, independent marriages were created, a potentially very mobile, but also very origin-bound society existed. The Confucian system upheld male dominance in California. The *split Confucian family* represented an intact and functioning unit (Zinzius, 1988, 99-100). The regard for marriage and prostitution in China play a major role in the evaluation of Chinatown society.

Geographic Derivation and Orientation of Emigration

Between 1820, when the United States Office of Immigration noted the first immigrant from China, and 1840, only eleven Chinese arrived in the United States, according to official data. In 1847, only three Chinese students, who had taken up studies at The Monson Academy in Massachusetts, are recorded (Kim, Hyuang-Chan, 1986, 579). Some sources indicate that already in the seventeenth and eighteenth centuries some Chinese sailors arriving on trading ships remained as servants.

Chinese emigration to North America in the first half of the nineteenth-century—the period of the "old emigration"—represents only a marginal portion of the mass Chinese exodus of millions of emigrants to the Philippines, Vietnam, Thailand, Malaysia, Indonesia, South America and the Caribbean (Mangiafico, 1988, 11; Pan, 2000, 60-71). The first immigration wave to the United States was only induced by the first gold rush in the Sacramento Valley in the 1850s. In the nineteenth century, most of the Chinese immigrants to California were of Cantonese origin. Canton has an independent culture; even the language is so different from the official *putonghua* (Mandarin Chinese) that communication is impossible. Next to the Cantonese, a large group in Canton are the Hakka (15%), who also have their own culture and language and suffer therefore from discrimination. Many Hakka were *boat people* without fixed abode. Furthermore, equally large groups came from the neighboring Fukien (Fujian) Province, and had settled in the Swatow (Shantou) area and the island of Hainan.

What provoked the emigration from these areas to the United States? In Canton, Kwantung province, the economically most important and most populous area of China, there were more than 28 million people in 1851, living on an area half the size of California (Lai, 1973, 13). A third was concentrated on a fifth of the area, along the opulent lands near the rivers in the Pearl River Delta. Per person only 0.2 acre of land were available for agriculture. The political and economic power base of the province Canton (Guangdong) is found in the north-eastern Pearl River Delta. From there emigrants shipped out to the United States.[12]

The emigrants to the United States mainly came from only eight districts of three different regions of Canton:

> 1. The Siyi, "four districts," (Cantonese: Sze Yup), consist of Xinhui (Cantonese: Sunwui), Xinning (Taishan, Cantonese: Toishan), Kaiping (Cantonese: Hoiping), and Encheng (Enping, Cantonese: Yanping). Originally, it was a very poor region with some agriculture and only a little fishing. Almost 70% of the Chinese immigrants to California come from the Sze Yup areas, over half of them from the district Taishan (Lai, Him Mark, 2002).

> 2. In the upper Pearl River Delta, near Canton is the Sanyi, "three districts," (Cantonese: Sam Yup) consist of Nanhai (Foshan, Cantonese: Namhoi), Punyu, and Shunde (Cantonese: Shuntak). The nearness to Canton and to the coast made it a very abundant plain and an agriculturally rich area with strong trade. Approximately 20% of the emigrants in the 1850s came from Sam Yup (Pan, 2000; 36, 235).

> 3. The third center of Chinese emigration to America were the districts of Xiangshan (Zhongshan), Chixi, and Xinan (Baoan). Xiangshang is near Aomen (Macao) in the delta mouth (Pan, 2000; 36, 235).

The central role of Canton as the place of transaction for Chinese workers bound for the United States is therefore hardly surprising. A short resume of the discussed facts: Pride and the traditional Chinese values had been severely shaken due to the presence of foreign powers and the destruction of centralized power by revolutions, which had paralyzed industry and trade. Furthermore, morale in some parts of society and in the corrupt bureaucracy had been further weakened by the continuously increasing opium consumption. A mass exodus in the nineteenth century, created by many wars in Southern China, surpassed all previous emigration movements. The most important potential for emigration in the second half of the nineteenth century that mainly affected the United States came from

---

[12] Guangdong is the strongest economic region within China. In 2002 the Pearl River Delta province had about 89 million inhabitants, accounting for 6.9% of China's population. In 2002, Guangdong generated 11.4% of Chinas GDP, 35% of its foreign trade, and 45% of its high-tech exports. Guangdong attracts about 25% of all Foreign Direct Investments in China. The provincial capital of Guangzhou has a per-capita GDP of US$1,400, almost twice the national average. Three Special Economic Zones (SEZ) operate since the 1980 and are the major economy centers of Guangdong: Shenzen (near Hong Kong), Zhuhai (near Macao), and Shantou (in the East). A recent trade agreement between Hong Kong and mainland China stimulates the investment of Hong Kong based businesses in China even more (*Asian Wall Street Journal*, September 30, 2003, A1, A4).

the economically successful, but socially despised traders, and the growing poor who had fled to the coastal towns. Young men emigrated to maintain the continuity of the family in an economically and politically unstable time. Married women stayed due to their familial obligations to their parents-in-law. Single women arrived overseas, sometimes as prostitutes.

Economic Situation in the Destination Country

Pull-Factors: Gold and Work

From 1849 until approximately 1858, California's economy depended almost totally upon gold. Without systematic upgrading of potential agricultural areas and without infrastructure, a complete development of the new state was unthinkable. The modernization processes in mining were initially not transferred to agriculture, in which most farms were only self-sufficient (*Getting Together*, 1972, 4–5).

The economic system was still mainly colonial. Only in the 1860s was there a fast phase of industrialization. The success of the Northern States in the Civil War increased the investment interest of the North in the Southern States. The rapid change required services and distribution and in the short term a large increase in the workforce, but one which could not be employed continuously, e.g. initially in competition-less garment factories and later during the construction of the railways. Solving the traffic problem with private railroads (*Union and Central Pacific*), which obtained cheap land in exchange for laying track, increased land speculation and a rigid employment policy. The most important functions in the provision of the workforce were covered by import and export traders and Chinese subsidiaries in California.

For many poor Chinese it was initially their desperation which drove them to the ships docked in Hong Kong and Macao, which would take them to an unsure future: "To be starved and to be buried in the sea are the same" (Coolidge, 1909, 17). In addition to the flight from poverty, there were also other factors that caused emigration, e.g. rumors coming from the United States promising quick riches to immigrants. In the spring of 1848, the stories of gold findings in California spread like wildfire through Hong Kong. Shortly thereafter, the first Chinese returned with visual proof of quick success. Business oriented British and American captains supported this with placards and posters (Sandmeyer, 1973, 15) to win over travelers for the trips to the United States.

Of the United States immigrants of this era, the Chinese were the only ones who could cross the Pacific directly from Hong Kong. Although 7,000 miles away and requiring almost three months travel, this trip from Canton to the North American Pacific Coast took less time than the transcontinental crossing from the East Coast or the sea routes via the Panama Canal or Cape

Horn (Hunt, 1929, 259). This meant that the transportation of larger groups could be easily accomplished in conjunction with trade between China and the United States. From 1852 on, ships arriving from Hong Kong regularly brought larger numbers of emigrants to San Francisco. Due to the hunger catastrophes and existence-threatening poverty caused by social unrest, they soon identified regular potentials in their countrymen (Lyman, 1986, 164).

Chinese immigrants to the United States in the nineteenth century are generally classified as merchants and workers. Since it was usually impossible for the poor rural population to pay the ticket upfront, a credit system (*credit-ticket system*) was initiated, whereby Chinese merchants recommended workers to companies in the United States. The debts incurred by the emigrants were covered by a labor contract that bound them for a number of years, but which did not make them "unfree," as the *coolies* were.[13]

Furthermore, they were easily controllable in the living quarters in Chinatown, which belonged to the merchants. From this form of work contract they were hardly predestined for a life in the pioneer society. Initially the Chinese had come to seek gold, but often only obtained prospecting rights in those areas, where white prospectors had already emptied the mines. The time in which one could seek his fortune, mostly by gold mining, was over by the beginning of the 1860s—only a few years after the beginning of the Chinese immigration. For the income of the Chinese workforce gold mining was therefore never really an important factor.

The distribution of Chinese according to work categories gives the following structure: In 1868 in California, traders and independent entrepreneurs represented 12.5% (5,000) of the workforce. Alone railroad and mine workers represented 58% (23,000) of the active population, and when factory workers (3,500) are added this grows to 67%. These numbers only support evidence of the division of workers into a two-class society and also of the dependency of the Chinese workforce upon economic growth periods. Surprising is the low number of peasants (5%) and the already developed service industry with laundry owners (4%) and household servants (7.6%).

---

[13] The expression *coolie* can be interpreted in various ways. *Koli* originally stands for a native crowd in western India. The Chinese term *coolie* means "hard work" or "hard life," and therefore did not directly stand for the worker. The Chinese slowly took over this expression, which was used wrongly by foreigners. In Chinese *chu-tsai*, basically means "human pig." Kim, 1988, 211. For further comments see: Irick, Robert L., *Ch'ing Policy towards the coolie trade*, 1847–1878. San Francisco Materials Center, 1982 and Barth, Gunther. *Bitter Strength*. Cambridge/Mass., Harvard University Press, 1964.

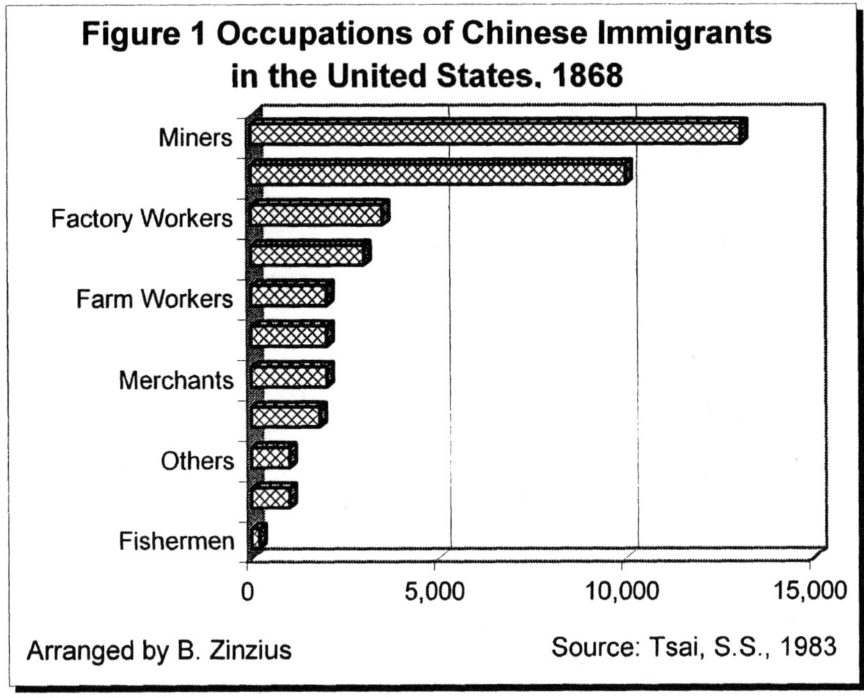

When capital and workers started to flow from the East, the Chinese workers suffered from a decline in their employment opportunities and their pay levels. For many Chinese, these developments lowered their standard of living and increased discrimination by whites. The Chinese became a favorite target for revolt against structural changes and unemployment. By 1852 at the latest, they were no longer individual travelers, but came by the thousands. That created the belief of a massive storming.

Organized by those Chinese businessmen who knew the surroundings, the poorer among them at least were an easily maneuverable reserve in workforce which could be employed in certain—and often exotic—niches, should bottle-necks or discrimination arise (Kung, 1962, 26). Due to their responsibilities toward their families in China and toward their creditors, Chinese workers were often forced to take on work at low income levels. Many of the approximately 10,000 Chinese who were initially employed in railroad construction had to be happy to find employment at lowest income levels within other emidustries, which were increasingly feeling competition from the East, due to the railroad network.

Upon the arrival of competitive workers from the East in the 1870s, the Chinese were then discriminated against as strike- and pay-breakers by the unions (*Getting Together*, 1972, 10–11). Trade qualifications in traditional jobs became less and less meaningful with the end of the gold rush, and even the clever Chinese who had adapted jobs traditionally held by women, especially in laundries, were threatened by mechanization (Coolidge, 1909, 406–407). The possibility to work in these women's jobs in service to the white society was drastically reduced since the ratio of the sexes within the whites had stabilized in the eighteen-seventies; whereas the Chinese male predomination in Chinese population had become an enduring condition. The end of the pioneer era also meant the expulsion of Chinese shops and pubs from the gold rush towns. The Chinese were stamped as outsiders whom the whites denied their little success.

From the report of a Congressional Committee 1877–79:

"Laundry work, cigar making, slippers, sewingmachine-labor, they have very nearly monopolized. They are largely employed as domestic servants and as office-boys. In assorting and repacking teas, in silk and woolen manufactories, in fruit-picking, in gardening, in harvesting, in building levees for the restoration of tule lands, in railroad-building, in placer mining, in basket-peddling of vegetables and fruits, in fishing and peddling fish are among the most noted of their industries, and from these industries I have named they have nearly driven out the white laborers." (*Joint Special Committee*, 1877, 17).

It is hard to believe that the Chinese freely entered these jobs, whose low incomes gave them little security or reputation. With regard to current social problems, one would more easily presume that these jobs were either badly paid or not well-liked. Beginning in 1889, the State of California stopped land purchases by Chinese and Japanese, which was extended to a general prohibition in 1913 (*Alien Land Act of California*). Therefore, the fear of Chinese monopolizing important or especially lucrative businesses can hardly have caused the strong regulation of their immigration. Likewise, one need not have feared America becoming Chinese, since the total number of Asian immigrants never surpassed 4.4% of total immigration.

More likely, the new Asian arrivals, with their fragile appearance, did not fit the picture of rough individuals of the "Wild West." Their ability to adapt to the loopholes within California's primitive economic system was a complete contradiction to that of the pioneers with their traditional businesses. As the pioneer society perfected itself, the Chinese flocked to the short-term boom of industrial development. The majority, however, could neither return home with a sack of gold during economic crises nor become peasants. In many free businesses, e.g. fishing, they were more heavily taxed. There remained, therefore, only industrial work and a return to the Chinatown economy. After the fall of the gold rush, such an economy existed only in San Francisco.

San Francisco Chinatown: A New Home

Life in California soon concentrated around the quickly growing cities in which the strengthening private capital chose to base itself. The regulative influence of federal subsidies and intervention had decreased everywhere in the 1850s. This explains the uncontrollable growth of a Chinese workers' quarter. The single, state-directed, mixed economic system was in the process of changing into a mainly privately-driven economy. Politically, the initiative for structural changes was left to the community authorities. This meant, for example, that San Francisco steered the development in Chinatown with its own regulations.

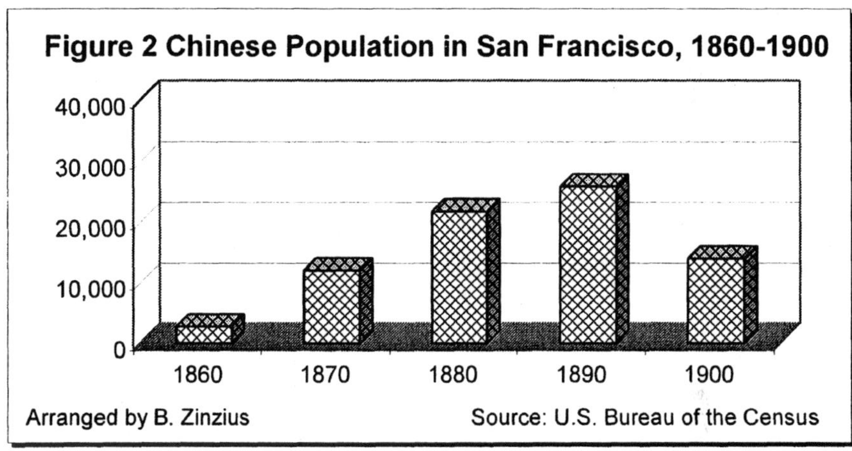

In 1860, the Chinese quarter of San Francisco already had 2,719 inhabitants, by 1880 it had grown to 21,745. The second largest Chinatown, in New York City, only had 800 at that time. Other Chinese quarters grew mainly in rural areas, but were not stable. Often they moved with gold-mining caravans and, when they were not too far from San Francisco, the workers would flock there for the weekend. The character of Chinatown was also determined by the tendency to work there. Whoever worked outside returned to its protection at night. The name "Chinatown" was first mentioned in American dailies in 1853, but its existence was already documented around 1848, at the beginning of Chinese immigration. San Francisco was and remained the most important arrival port for immigrants. In 1890, the Chinese represented 35.7% of the town's population. A similar level was to be achieved only hundred years later.

Apart from its population, to what extent was Chinatown Chinese? Dillon underlines that in 1873 only 25 of 316 large properties registered in 1904 were Chinese owned (1962, 98). The architecture of Chinatown was therefore western, because the owners of houses and shops were mainly white Americans. Imitations of Ming buildings according to American taste, as one can see today, did not exist. Chinatown, however, had its own exotic atmosphere, which must have pleasantly surprised Chinese arrivals, but left white visitors feeling foreign. Already in 1849, when the Chinese only occupied a few blocks, they renamed Sacramento Street "T'ang Yen Gai." (Barth, 1964, 110–Chinese Street). What was hidden behind this facade is differentially described in literature. Therefore, here some examples:

> "San Francisco's Chinatown became a city within a city and sufficient to itself. An invisible moat seemed to cut the Chinese off from the main stream of American life just beyond the borders. From birth to death, a Chinese found his needs met within the enclave of an area ten blocks square. He lived a life as he remembered it back in the villages in Kwangtung." (Sung, 1976, 133).

Sung's statement make a concrete argument, namely, the authentic Chinese life-cycle unfolded in a surrounding identical with that in Canton. A radically different position with regard to these basic questions is noted in the following statement:

> "In spite of their strong ties to homeland, Chinese immigrants did not establish a miniature replica of traditional Chinese society in America. They lived an abnormal society full of young males, wandering sojourners, whose dream was to put in a few years of hard labor and to return home wealthy and respected as a *Gold Mountain Guest*." (Tsai, 1983, 2).

Those scholars for whom it is clear that Chinatown was a society deviating from the norm, do not necessarily regard it in unison as an adaptation to special circumstances. Whereas Tsai sees in this as a fraudulent form or an actualization of the traditional Chinese society, Melendy believes it to be a frozen replica:

> "San Francisco's Chinatown became a city within the larger city, cut off from the encircling economic and social activities. Here Chinese residents lived following the traditions of old China. In fact, the San Franciscans lived more in the past than did their relatives in China as they became cut off from the homeland and lived with memories, not the realities, of the old life." (Melendy, 1972, 69–81).

According to Melendy, the Chinese colony in Chinatown was therefore both cut off from its direct social and economic surroundings, as well as from contact with the homeland. The belief that Chinatown had been economically cut off from its immediate surroundings can hardly be supported. Apart from the impossibility of such a situation, this interpretation would need to explain the existence of American-Chinese trade, which was both an integral part of the Chinese immigration and, to a certain extent, a product of it. The circumstantial housing of poor Chinese immigrants in Chinatown was a function and a result of intensive contacts with both the American surroundings and the Chinese homeland. As mediators for both sides, the Chinese merchants who had little prestige in traditional China had extensive influence on social structures in Chinatown. Therefore, Chinatown could not be a true copy of traditional Chinese life.

The foregoing analysis of Chinese social structures leading up to the emigration period around 1850 was undertaken to eliminate false interpretations, which would show the social structure of Chinatown simply as a compensational product of ghetto lifestyles. Returning to our original point of observation, it can be shown that the majority of Chinatown inhabitants originated from rural areas, whereas Chinatown was urban and built with western architecture. In this context, as an example of the mixture or deformation of homeland structures, one could add that the blooming prostitution in Chinatown had only been available to the upper classes in China. Lyman's analysis of social relationships in Chinatown indicates the dual function of the Chinese merchants, that of work arranger on the outside and as authority and creditor within the community.[14]

On the outside the merchants were the managers of the Chinese warehouses, supplying the Chinese inhabitants with food, herbs, clothes, and other goods from the homeland. In the backrooms, other business was conducted: lottery tickets were sold, men played Mahjong, or smoked opium. The warehouses were also banks for those employees who entrusted their employer with their income. Therefore, they sometimes differed from their primary use as warehouses, and were really centers of communication, both within the community as well as with China.

The workers lived in dorms or small flats, which were also owned by the merchants and paid for by the residents.[15] This created an unusual and situation-dependant lifestyle in which, however, relationships with the homeland played an important role.

In China, individualism as it is known in the West had never developed, since the family and not the individual was the smallest common denominator within the social structure. All holders of a family name believed themselves related. With the acceptance into a family clan, the origin and level of relation were unimportant. In the southern regions from which most immigrants originated, the number of names and clans was limited to several of dozen. This condition, as well as outside pressures, supported the organization of life within Chinatown according to clan

---

[14] "Chinatown also housed the Chinese elite, the merchants of the ghetto who acted as spokesmen for and protectors of the laborers and who held the latter in a state of political dependence and debt bondage." (Lyman, 1970, 104).

[15] "Most of the men lived in boarding houses, crowded small rooms with other members of their family or village. To save space, beds were sometimes nailed to the walls, two or three above each other. In some crowded rooms, the men slept in shifts. At the end of each year, expenses were divided among members. These fongs, or rooms, were the basic living arrangements in early Chinatowns across the country." (Chiu, 1960, 50–51).

principles. The clan provided rooms in which singles lived, as well as communal areas. The merchant who organized work and housing was usually a very influential clan member or even its leader. A clan leader was very interested in recruiting name relatives, since the increased size of the clan increased his prestige and also the number of services which could be provided and upon which he could rely on. The uptake of certain economic interests by the clan often led to the monopolization of a certain business sector or a trade within Chinatown by that specific clan.

A second organizational form was the district clan, which profited from the fact that the majority of immigrants originated from ten of the ninety districts within Kwantung province. Only in Chinese cities did the district organizations previously hold any substantial function over and above that of the family. In America however, they often had to compensate for the lacking family stability. Furthermore, they represented a strong umbrella organization in San Francisco, known as the *Chinese Consolidated Benevolent Association (CCBA)*, the so-called *Six Companies*, a type of government and spokesperson for Chinese in America. They wanted to have as little to do as possible with the "white devils" and then only via their most important representatives. The clans, however, not only covered important social and protection functions for the Chinese workers, but they also collected the debts originating from the passage, and thus made the connections tying the living and working situation to an inescapable network.

Only after having paid off the debts and having saved some money was one able to create small capital associations, so-called *hui*, with others who often shared the same abode. From these the typical Chinatown businesses have developed.[16]

Therefore, it is clear that Chinatown was not a true copy of Chinese lifestyle. In summary, one can say that Chinatown's character consisted of particular attitudes and particular social structures. These were, on the one hand, a result of the specific organization of Chinese immigration and work mediation and, on the other, a result of discrimination of the Chinese workforce in California.

---

[16] The term *hui* is used for a voluntary organization, which could be an economic, religious or criminal gang, without a strict corporate body. Although related, *hui* should not be confused with *huiguan*, similar to the German *Landsmannschaften*, a formal association of sojourning persons from the same native place (Lyman, 1977, 102; Pan, 2000, 76–77).

Immigration and *Anti-Chinese Law*: From "Free" Immigration (1848–1882) to Immigration Stop (1924)

California Law

In July 1868, the United States and China signed the *Burlingame Treaty*, named after Anson Burlingame, at that time the American ambassador in Peking. The treaty had been initiated by the Americans with the intent of breaking open Chinese isolationism—in this sense, a repetition of the *Treaty of Tientsin,* 1858. This contract allowed Americans to live and do business in so-called free trade zones (*treaty ports*). The contract allowed free entry based on reciprocity, but did not allow the naturalization of Chinese as United States citizens.[17]

Chinese immigration into the United States, the first officially accepted emigration, however, allowed various options: pleasure, business, but also permanent residency. Furthermore, China received all the rights conferred by Favored Nation Status, and the Chinese received the opportunity to use all public educational institutions freely (Chen J., 1980, 129). Federal politics, however, were in contradiction to California State Law. Although the Constitution specifically excluded the right of state sovereignty with regard to foreign states, California State Law worked against Chinese immigration.

In 1854, a section of the first California State Constitution of 1850, which prohibited Blacks and Native Americans from standing as witnesses against Whites in court, was expanded to include Chinese (Eaves, 1910, 126). With that, a period of anti-Chinese law-making was initiated. In 1855, a *Capitation Tax Ordinance* was implemented under which ship owners or captains had to pay fifty dollars for each Chinese transported to America (*California Statutes,* Sacramento, California, 1855, 194). In 1858 followed the prohibition of immigration for Chinese, a provision which held captains and whole crews responsible in the case of violation (*California Statutes,* Sacramento, California, 1858, 295). Although questions of constitutionality were raised and the Supreme Court declared both Statutes to be unconstitutional (1858 and 1870), two further anti-Chinese Statutes were adopted. These were a head tax for all persons of Chinese origin (1862) and high fines for persons aiding the immigration of Asians without prior proof of that person's "good character." (Chinn, 1969, 24).

Next to the obstruction and taxation of Chinese immigration, mainly in the eighteen-seventies, city ordinances were implemented with the primary

---

[17] For further details of the negotiations see: Bevans, Charles I., *Treaties and Other International Agreements of the United States of America, 1776–1949.* Washington, DC: 1971; Tsai, Shih-shan H. *China and the Overseas Chinese in the United States, 1868–1911.* Fayetteville, AR: 1983, Chapter 2.

intent of regulating Chinese lifestyles and working habits. In 1870, the *Cubic Air Ordinance* appeared in San Francisco, upgraded to state law as the *Lodging House Ordinance* in 1876. This ordinance, declared as hygiene protection, stated that all living quarters required a certain free area for each occupant. Naturally, Chinese dormitories did not fulfill this requirement. Those who did not pay the fines were jailed. In order to empty the jails and still obtain the fines, a new prohibition was implemented. Again, under the cover of hygiene, the *Queue Ordinance* of 1870 required all prisoners to have short hair. Rather than allow their ponytails to be removed, most Chinese prisoners preferred to buy back their freedom. The ponytail represented a symbol of loyalty toward their homeland and the Qing-Dynasty until 1911.

In 1860, with the exclusion of the Chinese from public schools in California, the explicit wording of the *Burlingame Treaty* was broken. A few years later (1866), this was "mellowed" to allow Chinese children to attend public schools, if there was no counter statement from the White population. From there, the route to race segregation at schools was not far (1870), (Kung, 1962, 72). A list of further regulations was directed against employment of the Chinese or against jobs preferred by the Chinese. Some communities, upon whose territory gold had been found, simply forbid the Chinese any mining rights (*Mariposa County Mining Regulations 1848; Columbia District Mining Regulations 1852*). Moreover, the *Foreign Miners Tax Law*, a State Law of 1850, applied a special tax to foreign miners.

Of the five million dollars obtained in the twenty years of its existence in California, 95% was pulled from Chinese pockets (Coolidge, 1909, 70).[18]

The *Laundry Ordinance* stood as a further barrier. San Francisco's City Government taxed laundries that did not employ horses to deliver the laundry with a higher tax than those that did. This was clearly directed against the Chinese, who were less accustomed to this animal. Furthermore, the traditional Chinese method of delivering laundry on bamboo carriers was forbidden in 1870 (Chinn, 1969, 24) with the reasoning that these carriers represented a traffic hindrance. The admittance to official positions and, with that, any direct influence on institutions was prohibited to Chinese. The second State Constitution of 1879 forbid the employment of Chinese in all government bodies and public institutions.

The *Burlingame Treaty* had not specified any right to naturalization, but had not specifically excluded it either. In 1878, the San Francisco Circuit Court denied Ah Yup's naturalization request with nebulous reasoning and thus created a precedent which was upheld until 1943 (Chinn, 1969, 25).

---

[18] The *Foreign Miner's License Tax* started at $3 monthly, but was gradually raised in 1852, 1853 and 1855 to $20. It was only declared unconstitutional in 1870 (Kim, Hyung-Chan, 1986, 579).

Thus, in the state with the highest Chinese population, the official Chinese American agreements could not be upheld.

Regulation of the Chinese Question at the Federal Level

Analysis of California State Law clearly shows that it is inappropriate to talk of free immigration until approximately 1882, when the first federal ruling was implemented. Initially, the Chinese did not fight the numerous forms of discrimination. In the eighteen-sixties, however, the discrimination attained a level that forced the well-organized Chinese to act. From 1860 on, various Federal Courts were forced to listen to Chinese complaints.[19]

In 1876, Chinese protests against state laws reached their summit: Federal Courts demolished a number of anti-Chinese state laws under the Provisions of the Fourteenth Amendment of the Constitution. These rulings, however, provoked strong reactions. The opponents of Chinese immigration realized that they would only be able to stop the ever-increasing number of immigrants if they transferred the debate from Sacramento, the capital of California, to Washington, DC. The chances for the California question were positive. Due to the massive population growth in the 1870s, California had for the first time achieved political relevance on a federal level.

Furthermore, in 1876, the political situation in Washington was very unstable, since Senate and Congress were dominated by opposing parties and presidential elections were approaching in the fall. Initially, a group of opponents to the Chinese was created, the *Anti-Chinese Union*, whose membership list contained names of many Senators, Members of Congress, as well as most prominent politicians in California.[20]

The California Senate called up a commission to analyze the results of Chinese immigration. This commission completed a report for Congress with the title: "Chinese Immigration: It's Social, Moral and Political Effect" (Sacramento, 1878). Furthermore, a pamphlet entitled "Upon the Evils of Chinese Immigration" was copied 10,000-fold and distributed among newspapers throughout the country.

Congress was therefore forced to create its own *Joint Special Committee*, which set off for California. The starting point and the center of its investigation was to be the productivity of Chinese. Contrary to other pioneers, it was claimed, the Asians had not made use of their special

---

[19] Precedents: United States versus Wong Kim Ark, United States versus Sing Tuck, United States versus Jung Ah Lung; further information in Konvitz, Milton R. *The Alien and the Asiatic in American Law*. Ithaca, NY: Cornell University Press, 1946.

[20] Sandmeyer, Elmer C. *The Anti Chinese Movement in California*. Urbana, University of Illinois Press, IL: 1973, 57 et seq.

abilities in their new home, in particular their abilities in rice and tea growing, in their new home. In particular:

> "Those who had expected the Chinese to cultivate rice, tea and silk in California bitterly complained that not one acre of land has yet been devoted to the culture of rice; not one shrub to the production of tea; not one single industry has been introduced, so far as I am advised, that is peculiar to the Chinese people." (*Joint Special Committee*, 1877, 17–18).

Even if these complaints concerning the lack of integration of Chinese into American society have a certain superficial credibility, in-depth research into the causes for and the situation of their immigration, including attention to the already existing discrimination of Chinese, would have led to a different opinion. For example, most Chinese were unable to purchase and toil on land because they arrived in America highly indebted to their creditors and had to accept employment in order to pay off their debts (Tsai, 1986, 7).[21] The lack of investment capital was the strongest argument of the committee leading them to denounce other economic activities (*light labor*). The committee further concluded:

> "They perform all kinds of light labor, and that particularly which requires no capital; and they are experts in that which requires dexterous manipulation of the fingers - as the assorting of wool, working in silks, the rolling of cigars, and such matters as that." (*Joint Special Committee*, 1877, 17).

This specialization in "light labor" was by no means a genetic predisposition, which this formulation would lead us to believe. Chinese laundries were the best example—such businesses did not exist in China at that time. On the contrary, between 1850 and 1880 the Chinese were pushed out of certain industries and systematically discriminated against in others. The work of the commission, no matter how biased, still found its way into law. In 1879, upon recommendation of the committee, the *Fifteen Passenger Bill* was initially vetoed by President Hayes after it had passed both houses (*Congressional Record*, 45th Congress, 3rd Session, 2275).

This law stipulated that a maximum of fifteen Chinese passengers were allowed to be transported at one time on American ships or to disembark at an American port. Since the Chinese traveled individual only infrequently, it was hoped that their entry could be severely obstructed. Since the president perceived a conflict with the 1868 agreement with China, a delegation was sent to Beijing to negotiate a regulation of Chinese immigration (*House of Executive Documents*, 47th Congress, 1st Session, Vol. 1). The American

---

[21] The efforts to exclude the Chinese from purchasing land had been issued by law in 1889, as seen in California. Only in 1948, the Supreme Court declared this discriminating act unconstitutional.

delegation obtained acceptance of a suspension of Chinese immigration. In conformity with the clause concerning special recognition factors, all Chinese, with the exception of workers, would continue to be able to immigrate to the United States. This change of the basis for the *Burlingame Treaty* of 1880 put the suspension of Chinese immigration in the hands of Congress.

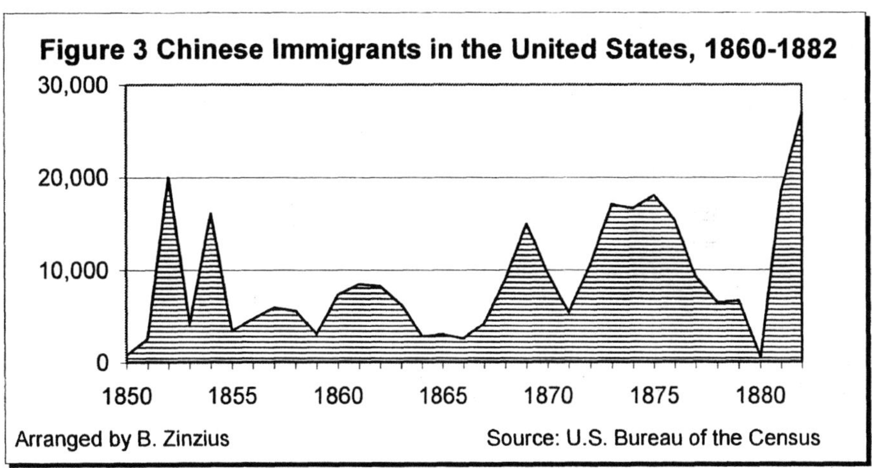

Subsequently, no fewer than seven so-called *Exclusion Bills* were entered into the 1st Session of the 47th Congress. Eventually, a proposal was accepted which instituted the exclusion for a period of twenty years. This was reduced to ten years upon the veto of President Arthur who again saw such a lengthy period as a violation of the previous agreement.

On May 6, 1882, the *Chinese Exclusion Act* was ratified which forbade the immigration of all skilled and unskilled labor, as well as the wives of those residing in the United States, and prohibited naturalization of Chinese. Only workers who had been residing in the United States prior to November 17, 1880 and wanted to return after a period overseas were not hit by this extremely harsh regulation.[22]

This law was explained as follows: the United States wanted to maintain diplomatic relations and trading contacts with China, but eliminate the transfer of Chinese workers into the structurally problematic American economy. The immigration of students, merchants, traders, pleasure and business travelers, government employees, diplomats and their aids thereby remained untouched. From a Chinese point of view, one should not forget,

---

[22] 22 Statutes at Large of the United States of America, Washington, DC, 58, as well as 23 Statutes at Large of the United States of America, Washington, DC, 115.

legal emigration was by far the exception, so it was not very difficult to submit to changes in such agreements, and thereby pacify the United States.

The *Exclusion Act* of 1882 (*Act to Execute Certain Treaty Stipulations relating to Chinese*) was the first break with liberal immigration policy by the United States. It did not, however, end a period of free immigration, but was in fact the final act in the long-standing discrimination of Chinese in California and an ongoing tug-of-war between the Legislative and Executive branches in Washington. This in-depth analysis thus strongly questions the labeling of the period up to 1882 as a generally friendly phase of free immigration that was destroyed when the *Exclusion Act* arrived like an unexpected storm. Furthermore, the massive number of eastern invaders who were too little adept to change contradicts any claim that the natural equilibrium between immigrant groups needed to be readjusted.

Exclusion Acts: *From 1882 until 1924*

Obviously, in the period following the ratification of the law in 1882, the results of the *Exclusion Act* were insufficient. In response, an amendment was introduced on July 5, 1884, which defined the title "merchant" more strictly and expanded the definition of Chinese to all members of the Chinese race.[23] The background for this more precise specification was the fact that, although the barriers had been introduced, immigration had increased, since members of the excluded working class simply declared themselves as merchants.

The clan organizations smuggled the papers of returnees out, thereby making use of confusing name analogies or fraudulent copies, which were sold in Chinatown.[24] In the western States in 1885, heavy racial uprisings and actual pogroms were initiated, during which in many Counties (Bloomfield, Redding, Boulders, Cleek and Eureka) more than 50 Chinese were killed, many hundred injured and Chinese property valued at 140,000 dollars was destroyed.

Upon pressure from many, especially union-organized anti-Chinese meetings and from a petition to Congress in the election year 1888, the *Scotts Act* was introduced, which forbid the return of any Chinese who had left the country and declared all return certificates void.

---

[23] 23 Statutes at Large of the United States of America, Washington, DC, 118.

[24] See Taft, William, *The United States and Peace*. New York, 1914, 59; Gulick, Sidney L., *American Democracy and Asiatic Citizenship*. New York, 1918, 37; 49th Congress 1st Session.

As a direct result, more than 20,000 Chinese who had left the country in a hurry were stranded abroad.[25]

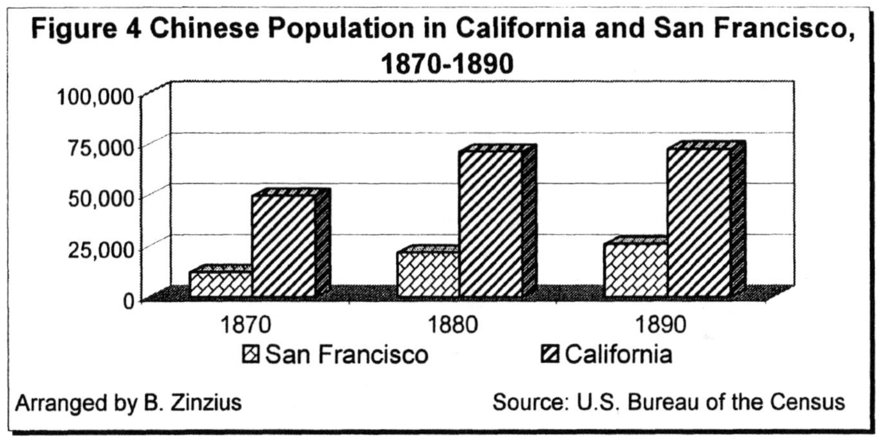

The first expiration of the *Exclusion Act* in 1892 was extended in the *Geary Act* by a further ten years. Additionally, however, this required all Chinese workers to register and obtain residential permits within one year, so that all illegal aliens could be documented. Many Chinese did not follow through with this requirement out of fear of losing group protection and in the hope of cancellation by the Supreme Court.

Therefore, upon confirmation of this act by the Supreme Court, only 12,200 of approximately 85,000 Chinese residents in the United States had been officially registered.[26] The strongest supporters of the *Exclusion Act* were now hoping for mass deportation of the Chinese. Upon evaluation of the costs for such an undertaking, however, the idea was discarded (Eaves, 1910, 195). The *McCreary Amendment* to the *Geary Act* therefore extended the period for obtaining the residence permit by a further six months in 1893.[27]

At this point, the story took an unintended turn from the view of the anti-Chinese supporters. This short-term threat to the Asian immigrants had uncovered the level of discrimination and induced a paradoxical

---

[25] *Act* of October 1, 1888, *25 Statutes at Large of the United States of America*, Washington, DC, 504; an exception was only granted for re-immigrants who had their wives, children, parents or at least $1,000 in capital in the United States.

[26] The Supreme Court confirmed the law—eleven days after expiration of the period of registration—on May 15, 1893 in the case of *Fong Yue Ting versus the United States of America* the *Geary Act* as legal; *House Executive Documents*, 53rd Congress, 2nd Session. Vol. 1, 234; *Supreme Court Reporter 13*, 149 U.S. 689, 1893, 1016–41.

[27] 28 Statutes at Large of the United States of America, Washington, DC, 7.

solidarization effect: The anti-Chinese campaign transpired into a pro-Chinese campaign, mainly lead by social and religious organizations.

Public opinion softened during this period due to the initiation of an eastward movement of Chinese. The crossfire also shifted toward Japanese immigration, which increased at the same level as the Chinese immigration was stagnating. The inverse population development of Chinese and Japanese between 1890 and 1930 in California is shown in the following table:

Table 1 Chinese and Japanese Immigrants in California, 1890–1930		
1890	72,472 Chinese	1,147 Japanese
1900	45,743 Chinese	10,151 Japanese
1910	36,248 Chinese	41,356 Japanese
1920	28,812 Chinese	71,952 Japanese
1930	37,367 Chinese	97,456 Japanese

Arranged by B. Zinzius   Source: U.S. Bureau of the Census

The pressure directed at Chinese immigration was reduced as more humanitarian aspects came into play. The *Gresham-Yang Treaty* of 1894 brought about a relaxed interpretation of the *Scott Act* in compensation for the strict provisions against emigration of Chinese laborers. Therefore, Chinese whose return had previously been guaranteed in their papers, but prevented under the *Scotts Act*, were now allowed to return to America. Transit visas were also accepted (Kim, Hyung-Chan, 1986, 522).

Since the *Geary Act* had been extended by a further ten years in 1902, the United States took it upon itself to reintroduce the *Exclusion Acts* in 1904 after China had unilaterally disregarded the *Gresham-Yang Treaty*.[28] More and more, a general dislike of foreigners became apparent in the United States, which ebbed only for the short period of Wilson's presidency. The quickly growing exodus from Southern Europe alarmed large parts of the population at the beginning of the twentieth century. It was feared that mass immigration from Italy, Russia and Austria-Hungary would push the racial and cultural homogeneity of the so-called *old immigrants* from the North and West of Europe out of equilibrium.

The bad economic cycle from 1870 until 1910 also stimulated fear. A concentration of immigrants in industrial areas gave the impression that America could no longer sustain such a large volume of immigrants.

---

[28] Further information in Konvitz, Milton R. *The Alien and the Asiatic in American Law.* Ithaca, NY: Cornell University Press, 1946; Tung, William L. *The Chinese in America.* 1820–1973. Dobbs Ferry, NY: Oceana Publications, 1974; Wu, Cheng-Tsu. *"Chink!".* New York, NY: World Publishing, 1972.

Therefore, a general reduction of immigration levels was demanded, especially by the unions.

In 1913, the so-called *Dillingham Bill*[29] was presented to President Taft for signature, and, four years later, the *Immigration Act* was presented to President Woodrow Wilson. Both vetoed the acts due to their *literacy clauses*, which would have regulated immigration on the basis of language capabilities.

The political discussion on this matter had a long history. Already in 1896, Senator Henry Cabot Lodge had stood for such a regulation in the Senate. President Cleveland had however, vetoed this. Further attempts to make immigration dependent upon the ability to read and write also failed.[30] In this restrictive situation, the Chinese found a form of illegal immigration, possibly due to their lengthy painful experiences. They turned to the clauses permitting the transfer of nationality for those born overseas from 1855 until 1934.

Due to the exclusion of naturalization, Chinese born in America prior to the *Burlingame Treaty* (1868) were the only ones with American citizenship. Upon return from visits to their homeland they indicated that they had children whom they did not really have. The documents prepared by the American authorities were then sold in Hong Kong, so many young men arrived with false names as sons of false fathers (*paper sons*).[31]

This *paper business* system, practiced for decades, was outstandingly successful. The number of American-born Chinese jumped for the first time after the San Francisco earthquake of 1906, because many municipal records were destroyed in the fires and many Chinese declared themselves American. Many Chinese residents used the opportunity to forge themselves birth certificates and became *paper citizens*. An elaborated system of *paper merchants* and *paper stores* completed the illegal entry scheme. Whereas in 1900, only 6,657 men were registered as American-born, the number had increased to 11,921 in 1910.[32]

---

[29] Named after William Paul Dillingham, Head of the first major immigrant Commission.

[30] See Scott, Franklin D. *The Peopling of America: Perspectives on Immigration*. Washington, DC, 1972. AHA Pamphlets No. 241, 51–52.

[31] *Paper Son* is a remarkable memoir about the life of a Chinese American living under false pretenses during the exclusion era (1882–1943) in the United States. (*Paper Son: One Man's Story*. Chin, Tung P., Chin Winifred. Philadelphia, PA: Temple Univ. Press, 2000).

[32] In 1934, a continuous residency of ten years in the United States was necessary to be able to let the children follow later to the United States. The *Act from September 11, 1957* restricted the deportation of *paper sons* in all cases where a spouse, parent or child of U.S. citizen or foreigner had permanent resident status. In 1959, a call for these *paper sons* by the *Immigration and Naturalization Service* revealed 8,000 cases, which were later granted permanent resident status for revealing their identity. *Time*, January 20, 1958, 17 et seq.

How often Chinese traveled to China for marriage or to "create paper sons" can be seen from records of the Immigration Service (1915), which indicate that not less than 61% of all entrees between 1899 and 1910 had previously entered the country. Some did so to such an extent that they were recognized by the immigration officials. The "market value" of male heirs was far higher than that of females. Therefore, returning Chinese Americans mostly registered births of male heirs. For every four-hundred male births registered came one female birth registered (Sung, 1976, 99).[33]

After the beginning of World War I, Congress took up the population's fear of a new wave of immigration and presented a new law to the Senate that contained both a literacy test and a planned Asian Barred Zone, i.e. a return to language and geographic discrimination. This law was implemented on December 14, 1916. The presidential veto was overturned by Congress (Kim, Hyung-Chan, 1986, 306–307).

In the subsequently implemented *Immigration Act* of 1917, an exclusion zone was created from which immigration was to be totally excluded: Burma, Thailand, Indochina, India, Malaysia, Asian areas of the Soviet Union, Polynesia and East Indies.[34]

The *Immigration Act* of 1921 was only a provisional step toward the *Second Exclusion Act* of 1924. This act introduced the principle of quota ruling and thus it was the most important new regulation until 1965. The quota was, in contrast to the provisions of the 1921 act, reduced to only 2% of the existing population per nationality—based on the census records of 1890. This percentage set the cap at 200,000 immigrants per year and was reduced in 1927 to 150,000. The minimum level for every nationality was set at 100 immigrants per year (Kim, Hyung-Chan, 1986, 309). The United States had become a less immigration friendly country. Four years later, the *National Origins Quota Act* of May 19, 1921 was quickly introduced as a provisional measure to reduce the post-war exodus from Southern Europe.

With few exceptions, immigration from all countries was reduced to 3% of the number of residents of 1910 from each country. Further, a cap was set at 357,803 persons in total.[35]

Only this last addition is perceived by Euro-centric research as the real beginning of isolation and anti-foreigner sentiment. Restrictive regulations,

---

[33] In 1864 were exactly 193,418 immigrants, 313,339 in 1874, already 518,592 in 1884 and 1,285,349 in 1907 (Kung, 1962, 81).

[34] According to the Webster's Dictionary, Indochina consists of Cambodia, Laos and Vietnam, an area also named French Indochina. The expression Indochina is also sometimes used for South East Asia, e.g. including Burma, Thailand and Malaysia (Webster's Dictionary, 1993).

[35] See Auerbach, Frank L., *Immigration Laws of the United States.* Indianapolis, Bobbs-Merrill Company, 1955, 47 et seq.

therefore, appear as a consequence of disappointment in idealistic United States intervention abroad and especially as a protection against the import of political instability from Europe.

Such an interpretation of American immigration policy contradicts the lessons taught by the history of Chinese immigration. The emigration from the southern coastal provinces of China beginning in the mid nineteenth century was strongly influenced by colonial policies. Their intervention caused the destruction of the traditional power base in China. The rumors of gold findings in California strengthened the pressure factors in China to such an extent that a heavy emigration flow to America materialized until the anti-Chinese laws of 1882 stopped it.[36]

The *Exclusion Act* was the final straw in an enduring discrimination of the Chinese in California and was the result of a temporary subordination of Washington to this upwardly mobile Western State. This interpretation also runs counter to the idea that this era was the clear moment of change in a long-term policy. Already in 1894, a loosening of the particularly anti-Chinese regulations within *Immigration Law* became apparent (*Gresham-Yang Treaty*), as the Chinese population growth was strongly declining and the Japanese population dramatically increasing. Further discrimination of Chinese immigration has to be regarded, on the one hand, as a secondary effect of general Asian immigration policy and, on the other, as a departure from anti-Chinese regulations into more generally restrictive regulations, as expressed in 1921.

It becomes therefore clear that any attempt by research to equate the Chinatown phenomenon with abnormality is in fact an unnecessary authentication of anti-Chinese laws. It is now time to describe Chinatown in an unbiased manner: Chinatown society did not reconstruct Chinese society, but developed new, original relationships between the social classes. These relationships grew out of the way the Chinese pursued their interests during the industrialization process of Californian society, while also desiring to maintain the relationships within the Chinese family structure.

---

[36] *Closing the Gate: Race, Politics, and the Chinese Exclusion Act* details about the instruments that enacted the *Chinese Exclusion Act* and the impact of this movement on United States immigration (Gyory, Andrew. University of North Carolina Press, 1998).

2. BETWEEN 1924 AND 1965

Development of Chinese American Relationships

To understand the drastic changes in the constitution of the emigrant waves, as well as the communities abroad in the United States, it is necessary to recapitulate the socio-politico changes within China in the first half of the twentieth century. The complicated political development of the years between 1924 and 1965 can only be generally described and oriented according to the thematic requirements of this study. After the decline of the Empire, in the era of the first Chinese Republic (1912–1949), two rivaling political ideologies eventually emerged.[1] The *Communist Party of China* (*CPC*) was founded in 1921. Until the nationalists led by Chiang Kai-shek, the successor of Dr. Sun Yat-sen, split in 1927, these two—the Communists and Chiang Kai-shek's supporters—formed a coalition in the *Kuomintang* (*KMT*). Peasants without property had become tenants on the land, or moved to the cities to become industrial workers in national and foreign companies. Therefore, in the 1920s, a new class of industrial workers and a class of capitalists were formed. The bloody suppression of the workers' movement in Shanghai in 1927 proved the end of the initial successes of the *CPC*.[2] Because of the overpowering imperialistic state and the nationalistic *Kuomintang* in the cities, in combination with the fact that land-reform presented the largest social problem in such an agricultural state like China, the *CPC* was forced to retire to the rural areas and into the mountains and to build up the peasants' movement. A major role in this new orientation of the party line was taken by Mao Zedong who became sole party leader in 1935.

After the war with Japan (1937–1945), the Chinese had two leadership figures to choose from. Chiang Kai-shek who had been supported by the United States had not been able to bring peace to China. During his twenty years in government, he had concentrated on the destruction of communism and underestimated the Japanese.[3]

---

[1] See Fairbank, John K. *The Great Chinese Revolution 1800–1985.* New York, 1987.

[2] Significant changes emerged in China due to the victory of the October-Revolution and the political swing of the Soviet Union towards China, on the one hand, and the unfortunate result of the conference of Versailles, which gave the former German concessions in Shandong province to Japan, on the other. Following the demonstrations on May 4, 1919, a small part of the progressive Chinese intelligentsia changed from Western ideals to Marxist ones. With the help of delegates from the International Communist Movement, Communist cells rose in various cities, which founded the *Communist Party of China* (*CPC*) in July. Until 1930, the *CPC* concentrated on the working class, as this class was assumed to bear the strongest revolutionary potential—following strict Marxist theories.

[3] In 1935, the Japanese colonized the Manchuria, and created the small state of Manchukuo by appointing the former Emperor, Puyi, Henry. See also Pu Yi, 1998. Today, the historical region in northeastern

The Agricultural Revolution (distribution of property among peasants and farm workers) and the National Revolution (achievement of total independence from abroad) were the central ideology of the campaign of the *CPC* campaign under Mao Zedong. After a lengthy guerilla war in 1949, the Communists were able to succeed against the *Kuomintang*, who fled to Taiwan where Chiang Kai-shek finally installed the seat of government of the "Republic of China."[4]

The transfer of power to the *CPC* in 1949 brought with it a complete change to the old social structure: The ruling classes of bureaucrats, landowners and compradors were removed from their positions, and the enormous social discrepancy within agriculture and townships was heavily reduced by in-depth redistribution. In place of the old upper class stepped the *CPC*, which took over all leading positions of state and economy by inserting its members into these key positions.[5] The consequences of the communist reforms for the emigration movement were also revolutionary. First, the land reform bound the rural population more strongly to its traditional surroundings, rural migration was strongly reduced. Second, the lengthy civil war had left both the population in China, as well as the communities abroad, split into two groups—even before Mao Zedong came to power.

In 1937, the *Six Companies* in San Francisco, the umbrella organization of all Chinese American organizations, established the *China War Relief Association of America*. During the eight year Sino-Japanese conflict, 25 million dollars were made available for the Chinese war effort. Not only was money organized for the Chinese nationalists, but boycott appeals were issued against Japanese businesses and demonstrations against Japan. The United States' support for Chiang Kai-shek improved the image and lifestyles of Chinese Americans. After the attack on Pearl Harbor in 1941, the United States and China became allies in the Pacific. The American cooperation with the military leadership in China also elevated Chiang Kai-shek to the status of trustworthy ally.

China consists of the three modern provinces Liaoning, Jilin, and Heilongjiang, one of China's most important industrial areas. "Manchuria." *Britannica Concise Encyclopedia*, Encyclopædia Britannica Premium Service, <http://www.britannica.com/ecb/article?eu=396445> March 10, 2003.

[4] See also Chapter 3 "Immigration Between 1965 and 2000," under "Taiwan: Democracy without Freedom."

[5] Through this shift, the *CPC* controls today almost every industrial and governmental institution. The increasing privileges of party officials, total exclusion of criticism, as well as the control of party and state by the population led to a ruling class of government bureaucrats, which has a hierarchy similar to that of the governmental officials in the empire.

The initiation for the Taiwanese- or *Kuomintang*-orientation of the overseas Chinese[6] communities was the United States' support of the Generalissimo whose brutal methods of suppression were equally misinterpreted by the United States government, as were the uses of the free-flowing monies to the *Kuomintang* regime. The Soong Clan, the family of Chiang Kai-shek's wife Soong Mei-ling, enriched itself so much that the government of Taiwan was able to buy political sympathy and was able to make substantial capital investments in the United States.[7]

A few years ago in 1986, T.V. Soong (Soong Tse-wen) died in New York as "the richest man in the world." The Harvard-educated banker, member of the Soong Clan, and brother of Soong Mei-ling, financed Chiang Kai-shek's move to power. During World War II, he and his sister cleverly convinced President Roosevelt of the necessity to support "their" China—initially against the Japanese and then against the Chinese Communists—with vast sums of money. With Roosevelt's support, Madame Chiang Kai-shek who had attended the Wellesley College in Massachusetts became one of the most popular figures in the United States. The exceptionally broad and positive media coverage of her visits to the United States improved the prestige of the Chinese population.[8]

Chinese Americans were upgraded to the level of Madame Chiang Kai-shek, who had received from the media praiseworthy descriptions such as "modern, intelligent, proud, tolerant and Christian."[9] The accolades to Madame Chiang Kai-shek by the Americans gave the war ally China sufficient support within society. Also the discrimination of the Chinese minority, which was abused by Japan for propaganda purposes, was reexamined due to the influence from Madame Chiang Kai-shek.

---

[6] In 2003, more than 61 million Chinese lived overseas, mainly in Asia (see Chapter 8 for details). The perception of the term *overseas Chinese* varies widely, depending on the country or scholar. In the Chinese language, *hua ren* means Hua people (e.g., Chinese); *hua qiao* means overseas Chinese (*qiao* means "to stay away from home somewhere else," and is frequently translated as *sojourner*). *Hua qiao* dates back to the nineteenth century and was long used for all Chinese abroad, but the term has negative connotations (Pan, 2000, 14). Four major categories of overseas Chinese are generally described: *Hua shang* (trader), *hua gong* (coolies), *hua qiao* (sojourner), and *hua yi* (descendents) as the most recent one. The *hua shang* type is the most elementary one and is predicted to be prevalent in the future (Poston, 2003, 4). These overseas Chinese are also a major source of foreign investment in China, Hong Kong, and Taiwan (Yen, 2002; 320, 345 et seq.); see also Chapter 8.

[7] Oversea Chinese support the *Kuomintang*. See Seagrave, Sterling. *The Soong-Dynasty*. Harper & Row, New York, 1985.

[8] Madame Chiang Kai-shek died in 2003 in New York at the age of 105 years.

[9] See articles in *San Francisco Examiner*, March 29, 1943 and *Los Angeles Times*, January 31, 1943.

Immediately, after her visit to the Capitol in February 1943, the *Committee for Immigration and Naturalization* in Congress began a debate over the revision of the anti-Chinese *Exclusion Acts.*[10] The respective proposal (H.R. 3070), which will be subsequently evaluated, was supported by the following words from President Roosevelt: "We must correct the historical mistakes and eradicate the misleading Japanese propaganda."[11]

The period between 1937 and 1944 has also been called the *Age of Admiration* due to Sino-American affinity. After the final loss of the *Kuomintang* at the end of a horrible civil war in China, most of the 77,500 Chinese in the United States had to decide for or against the new government: traditional values were mostly identified with the *Kuomintang* or Taiwan, but there were also many who believed in a strong China under socialist rule.

When, however, Washington denounced the communist government as a pawn of Moscow and an instrument in the plan for worldwide dictatorship by the proletariat, the Mao supporters came under strong pressure, both by the *Kuomintang*, as well as the United States authorities. During the 1950s and 1960s, the overseas community came under the total authority of the *Kuomintang.*[12] The period immediately after the *Age of Admiration*, which ended with the Communists coming to power, was known as the *Age of Disenchantment* (1944–1949).

---

[10] For further explanations see Lee, Rose Hum. "Social Attitudes Towards Chinese in the United States. Expressed in Periodical Literature from 1919 to 1944." in Isaac, Harold. *Images of Asia: American Views of China and India.* New York, NY: Harper & Row, 1972, 120 et seq.; Riggs, Fred. *Pressures on Congress: A Study of the Repeal of Chinese Exclusion.* New York, NY: Kings Crown, 1950.

[11] *"Message from the President of the United States Favoring Repeal of the Chinese Exclusion Laws,"* House Executive Documents 333, 78th Congress, 1st Session, Washington, DC, 1943, Serial 10793, 1–2.

[12] Also in the 1980s, this topic was current. In June 1985, the Taiwanese Justice Ministry announced an official investigation against a Taiwanese Parliament member. The announcement declares suspicion against Government members in the murder of the American journalist Henry Liu, who wrote critically about Taiwan. The journalist was of Chinese descent, but an American citizen. Due to the renewed protest by Taiwanese Parliament members as well as by the American Press, the accusation was reissued that Taiwanese Government did not deter from intimidating American citizens. Thus, it was requested to stop all weapon sales to Taiwan. Henry Liu had been found dead in front of his house in Daly City, California, on October 15, 1984, and the FBI took over the investigation shortly thereafter. On November 13, 1984, Chen Chi-Li—a Taiwanese criminal—was arrested. In January 1985, the Taiwanese Government announced that Li confessed to the killing and to the involvement of two Taiwanese security agents. The motive and further details never were revealed. Liu had talked critically about the Chiang-Family, which had headed the Taiwanese ruling party for decades. Sutter, Robert G., *Taiwan and the Killing of*

The return to American sobriety after war finally lead to the *Age of Hostility*, which lasted until President Nixon visited China in 1972 (Isaacs, 1972, 72 and Daniels, 1988, 301).[13]

The elimination of discrimination against Chinese immigrants (*Age of Admiration*) came about under conditions that were diametrically opposed to the future political developments and the future political relationship between China and United States. After the establishment of the Communist power-base on the Chinese mainland, the newly democratized Japan obtained from the United States occupational forces the position of a counterweight to Beijing in a new Far East *Balance of Power-System*.[14] After the loss of the western ally, Mao Zedong was able to unify the huge empire with Soviet support (1954–1957). The USSR was declared a model. Polytechnic and Technical Universities according to the Soviet model brought about a new orientation of the previously Christian-humanitarian orientation of higher education introduced by the colonial powers. When Moscow demanded that revolutionary socialism be achieved by the industrial proletariat and not by the rural masses China broke the connection. The USSR was charged with revisionism. One result was the return of the Soviet aids and technicians in 1960.

Social reconstruction was oriented toward traditional examples. The basic structure of Maoist society was the empire. The hierarchical pyramid ranged again from the nation-supporting peasants to the irrevocable power of the "great helmsman." His authority and popularity was easily equated to that of the Emperor. Although not guaranteed by godly decree, he was nevertheless legitimized by an omnipotent cult. The *Great Leap Forward* (1958–1960) was an attempt to achieve quick economic growth and to introduce the "change to communist society" via political mobilization of the masses, while compensating for the generally lacking economic and technical prerequisites. Natural catastrophes and the beginning of the Sino-Soviet conflict brought this attempt to an end. From 1961 until 1965, the more moderate wing of the *CPC* took political control. With the aid of liberalized economic policies, material encouragements, and a politics that emphasized production over ideology, i.e. social harmony instead of class war, an improved political and economic situation was achieved.[15]

Henry Liu: Issues for Congress. Congressional Research Service, Report No. 85–42F. February 1, 1985.

[13] See further discussions under Chapter 2, "Immigration Law 1924 until 1965," as well as Tsai, 1986, 115.

[14] For further details of the Balance of Power System see Waltz, 1967.

[15] For a detailed analysis of the political development between 1949–1969 see: Shinde, B.E. *Mao Zedong and the Communist Policies. 1927-1978*. South Asia Books, 1991; Fairbank, *China. A New History*. 1998, 343 et seq.

Due to the ties with Taiwan, the United States missed the opportunity to build up relationships with the People's Republic. Its relationship to communist China came under pressure because of incidents in the Straits of Formosa, which led Washington repeatedly to offer guarantees to Taiwan. The Eisenhower Domino-theory saw in the PRC a Soviet-guided spearhead of communism with its proxy war in Vietnam—a false analysis which the subsequent break between the USSR and PRC, as well as the subsequent conflict between North Vietnam and PRC would show (Eisenhower, 1954).

Exactly in these years, however, mainly due to inner domestic policy rather than foreign policy, a revision of the immigration law caused a boom in Chinese emigration.[16] The opportunity to gain support for the liberal *CPC* fraction was soon lost. Mao's intensive battle against liberal policies, which meant a return from capitalism to him, led to the counter-offensive with the Army HQ in 1966. The *Great Proletarian Cultural Revolution* (1966–1969) brought the fall from power of those supporting a capitalist trajectory, Liu Shaoqi and Deng Xiaoping. The consequences were again civil war and mass exodus. As before, after 1943, the United States found itself confronted with a totally new political situation in China immediately after the revision of the immigration laws in 1965.

Immigration Law from 1924 until 1965

Since Chinese immigration had been systematically cut off by legal restrictions between 1882 and 1924, a lengthy phase of small compromises and regulations followed which finally ended in a complete revision of the immigration laws in 1965. In the following pages these individual steps will be discussed to identify the results of this contradictory political development.

The *National Origin Act* of 1924 strengthened the 1921 Quota ruling in such a way that Asians, and in particular, Chinese, Japanese and Koreans, were discriminated against, although it had been introduced to hinder mass exodus from South and Eastern Europe. Although the calculation figures for new immigrants were based on the year 1890, in which the Chinese immigration had achieved its summit, the level was, as previously shown, reduced from 3% to 2%. This favorable year, only eight years after the immigration stop in 1882, therefore, was of little consequence for the Chinese. Additionally, applicants for whom subsequent naturalization was not intended, e.g. immigrants from Asian countries like China and Japan, were simply denied immigration. These practices entailed a general prohibition of immigration.

---

[16] See Chapter 3 "Immigration between 1965 and 2000."

The humanitarian situation of those already in the country was also difficult: Only the direct heirs of United States naturalized citizen of Asian origin were allowed to immigrate, since even their wives had been excluded by 1924. This regulation was directed against Japanese picture-brides chosen from catalogues, but hit Chinese immigration considerably. The number of female Chinese immigrants had escalated after the earthquake of 1906 and also dramatically increased between 1922 and 1924.[17] This was, as was with the so-called *paper sons*, a result of the burnt immigration documents. Many men were able falsely to declare themselves United States citizens and subsequently have their wives legitimately immigrate until 1924.[18]

In 1930, the *Immigration Act* was loosened, since the cap introduced in 1929, which set the total at 150,000 immigrants had not been met due to the beginning economic depression. The restrictive regulations in the 1920s, which were induced by the fear of new waves of immigrants, which had initially washed up more than one million people annually on American shorelines after World War I, had therefore lost all foundation. Chinese women who had married prior to May 26, 1924, were allowed to immigrate after 1930. This was only the first step in the rehabilitation of Chinese immigration. During the Sino-American honeymoon in 1943, under President Roosevelt the *Exclusion Acts* of 1882 were abolished and the annual quota for Chinese immigrants was set at 105 people.[19]

This new law also allowed the naturalization of all Chinese according to the generally valid naturalization regulations. Previously, this right had only been given to those Chinese who had served in the American Forces during World War I. With that, for the first time, Chinese born outside the United States could become Americans.[20]

---

[17] 1922: 1,050, 1924: 1,853 women—in comparison of 12 to 145 women between 1900 and 1906.

[18] See Takaki, 1989a, 235.

[19] 75% of the total quota were reserved exclusively for Chinese immigrants from China, the remaining places were for Chinese emigrating from other countries into the U.S. *Act to Repeal the Chinese Exclusions Act*, to establish quotas and for other purposes, December 13, 1943; the corresponding *Magnusson Bill* was ratified on December 17, 1943. Warren Magnusson, Washington, Edward Gossett, Texas and Walter Judd, Minnesota led the strong majority supporting this law in Congress.

[20] Song, Alfred. *Politics and Policies of the Oriental Community*. Palo Alto, California Politics and Policies, 1966, 398.

In real terms, the new regulations brought no substantial development in Chinese immigration. The Chinese quota (105 people) was based on the 1920 Census and only represented 0.6% of the Chinese population in the United States at that time, e.g. a lower quota and a worse calculation basis than in 1924.[21] This figure, therefore, was still very unfavorable for the Chinese. It was, as Robert Cleland suggests "just a gesture," especially if the higher rate of emigration from the United States back to the homeland during this period is taken into account (1944, 104).

Progress may be seen in the decline of discrimination against the Chinese in comparison to other immigrants and, more so, the Chinese being the first Asians to attain the legal right to immigration and naturalization.[22] Nevertheless, there were still barrier-creating criteria that indicated a presence of colonial views: First, the determining criterion for nationality was race, and not the citizenship based on place of birth, as with all other immigrants; Second, a 100 person quota for racially non-Chinese immigrants from China also existed, giving an equally high quota for Chinese and non-Chinese.[23]

The formulation of the decree which abolished the *Exclusion Acts* of 1943 brought the expansion of the terminology "Chinese" used as the statistical basis until recently: Members of the Chinese race, irrespective of country of origin and with at least 50% Chinese blood, fell under this ruling and were subsequently a part of this quota.[24]

---

[21] The Chinese population in the United States reached an absolute low of 61,639 in 1920, in comparison to 105,456 in 1890. However, the Republic of China had already a population of 600 million in 1943. Thus, the extremely small percentage gave the Chinese Government little reason to take interest in the immigration to the United States. It was, however, important for the Communistic Government to enable an intellectual elite studying in America.

[22] For further information on the problematic of race in the United States see the Report of the Advisory Board to the *President's Initiative on Race* (Franklin, 1998, 42–3), and Fredrickson, 2002. Since the mid-1990s, a completely new era regarding race was initiated, when the population in California and Washington approved public propositions to restrict the use of "race" (Zelnick, 2002, 405 et seq.). For further discussions see Chapter 6 "*Affirmative Action* or Multicultural Society?" and Chapter 7 "Family Structures."

[23] Riggs, Fred W. Pressure on Congress: *A Study of the Real Chinese Exclusion*. New York, 1950, 126 et seq.

[24] U.S. Congressional Record, 78th Congress, 1st Session 1943, Vol. LXXXIX, 8583 and 8595. To enforce miscegenation laws in America, since the early nineteenth century, the one–drop blood rule defined especially the race Black (Davis, 1991, 4; Wright. 1994). The standardization of the racial and ethnic data in 1977 did not address the minimum percentage of blood (Office of Management and Budget, 1977). See also Chapter 4 "Habitat," for detailed explanations about racial categories.

The revision of the standards for Census 2000 abolished the minimum blood-ratio: "Observer do **not** establish criteria or qualifications (such as blood quantum levels) that are to be used in determining a particular individual's racial or ethnic classification."[25] Also, Chinese were defined as, "A person having origins in ... China." (Office of Management and Budget, 1997b, pp. 58785, 58787)

This definition of Chinese immigration has far-reaching significance: The term "Chinese" could now be applied to countries whose population has only tenuous connections to the history and culture of China and to the Sino-American relationships. Today for example, economic refugees of Chinese race are predominantly Cambodian, Hmong,[26] Laotian, and Vietnamese.[27]

Therefore, for the following discussion of Chinese immigration in the context of Sino-American relationships, only the categories of China, Taiwan, and Hong Kong will be included, which were separated mainly as a result of World War II. The end of the war brought further changes. In 1946, in respecting the preferences of allies and military personnel, Chinese wives of American citizens were declared non-quota immigrants. This was also the case for the resident Chinese who had had the opportunity to immigrate after 1943.[28]

---

[25] As recently as 1986, the United States Supreme Court refused to review the case of a Louisiana women, whose genetic heritage was 1/32 *Black*, and, thus, had been categorized as *Black* ("One Drop of Blood," Wright, *The New Yorker*, August 3, 1994).

[26] The Hmong, or Miao, are aboriginal peoples of China. About seven million live in Southern China, and about one million in Thailand, Laos, Vietnam, Burma, the United States and Australia. During the Vietnam War, the Hmong supported the American Army, which is one of the reasons that over 195,000 Hmong have been admitted as Refugees and Asylees to the United States (*South East Asian Refugee and Action Center, SEARAC.* "Laotian & Hmong refugees." <http://www.searac.org/laoref.html> (*SEARAC*, 2003).

[27] A recent study about Chinese neighborhood populations showed, that APA immigrants from Cambodia, Laos, and Vietnam live in isolated communities. Employment rates, poverty levels, school education, and linguistic isolation are among the most adverse of all Asian groups, yet, the conditions are far better than in their native homelands. "Asiantowns," such as in St. Paul (Hmong), Long Beach ("Little Pnom Phen," Cambodian), Orange County ("Little Saigon," Vietnamese), Stockton ("Manilatown," Filipinos), and Lowell (Cambodian) are examples of a new kind of ethnic Chinese economic immigrant. (Ong, 2002a, 4; Waldinger, 1996, 10–11).

[28] A large number of Chinese had to join the Army. Over 40% of the Chinese recruits were foreign–born. In some cases the citizenship—which was necessary for joining the army—was postponed, in other cases it was granted prior to the call. The need for soldiers during the war was obviously so large that even the prohibition to grant American citizenship to Asians was bypassed. According to Thomas Chinn, 15,000 to 20,000 Chinese served in the American army, of which 25% served in the Air Force. Chinese were recruited in the 3rd and 4th Infantry Division in Europe as well as in the 6th, 32nd and 77th Infantry Division in Asia. Chinn, 1989, 147–150 and Chan, S., 1991, 122, 76 et seq.

Amendments such as the 1945 *War Bride Act* and the 1946 *Alien Fiancée Act* allowed a larger number of women to immigrate.[29]

According to Chinn, 6,000 women are thought to have immigrated as wives of Chinese American servicemen (1989, 141). Differentiating between quota and non-quota immigration therefore becomes critical, since non-quota immigrants represented the largest portion of the immigrants in the 1950s, as we will see. One of the most noteworthy results of the period between 1846 and 1953 was that, due to the various exceptions for female immigration, almost 10,000 women immigrated, an important factor in allowing the Chinese American society to stabilize.[30]

The end of the nineteen-forties brought with it the end to the positive swing in Sino-American relations which had significantly reduced pressure on the Chinese. Thereafter, any relaxation of immigration laws was no longer based on the positive relationship between the two nations, but more on support for victims of the communist regime and opponents of the People's Republic of China.

1948 to 1959: Emergency Laws and Stranded Students

Without additional measures, the immigration quota for 1943 would have been totally unacceptable, both with regard to the social requirements of the Chinese in the United States, mainly the repatriation of families, as well as with regard to the large number of political refugees from China and Indochina. Post-war poverty was extreme, and the American economy was booming.

The *Displaced Persons Act* of 1948 allowed the immigration of a further 205,000 people into the United States. Originally, this law was intended to support Europeans, but its expansion (*China Aid Act*, June 16, 1950) allowed resident Chinese who did not intend to return to communist China to stay. 15,000 Chinese profited from this ruling with life residency status.[31] In addition to refugees and political outcasts were a substantial number of students. Chinese educational emigration had its beginnings in the 1920s.

---

[29] *1945 War Brides Act of December 28*, 1945, *59 Statutes at Large of the United States of America*, Washington, DC, 659, handed in by Samuel Dickstein, New York, "Allowing alien wives, children, and husbands of the members of the U.S. armed forces to come as non-quota immigrants, and eliminating provisions concerning mental and physical defectives." *1946 G.I. Fiancées Act of June 1946, 60 Statutes at Large of the United States of America*, Washington, DC, 339.

[30] In the 1950s, the number of female immigrants amounted to between 50% and 90%. Chinn, 1989, 147.

[31] Further information at: Kung, 1962, Tsai, 1986, Kim, Hyung-Chan, 1986, 225.

Between 1925 and 1949, the Chinese represented the largest group of foreigners at American universities.[32] The majority of those students, however, could not be categorized as immigrants, since, in contrast to the relatively low level of employment in the United States, these researchers were looking forward to lucrative and socially acceptable jobs back home in China.[33] The so-called *stranded students*, who had immigrated during 1945 until 1949 and constituted practically all of the English speaking elite of the country, had to stay after the power struggle which enabled the communists to take power and which created a new kind of Chinese intelligentsia.

In total, this number was about 4,000 of which a few hundred emigrated to Hong Kong and Taiwan.[34] A number of the student arrivals in the United States became renowned persona in American research or industry, e.g. the philosopher Wang Hao at the Rockefeller University, the physicists and Nobel Price Laureates Chen Ning Yang and Tsung-Dao Lee, the chemist and Nobel Price Laureate Yuan T. Lee, or the computer expert and inventor An Wang.[35] So, what had originally been intended to educate the scientific heirs in their homeland had become new riches for American research and industry.[36]

These young scientists also represented for the first time cultural pluralism among Chinese immigrants. They were fluent in English, but spoke Chinese at home. Their work and prestige lifted their self-esteem and the recognition of Chinese society. Both public, as well as private sponsors supported this Chinese elite, whose future seemed initially destroyed by the downfall of the nationalistic government in Beijing. The *China Area Aid Act of 1950* allowed the President to expand all financial support to any area within China, which was not under communist rule. In total, the government

---

[32] China Institute of America (Ed.). *A Survey of Chinese Students in American Universities and Colleges in the Past One Hundred Years.* New York, 1954, 17–19.

Table 2 Number of Chinese Students in the United States, 1943-1949

1943–44:	706	1946–47:	1,678
1944–45:	823	1947–48:	2,310
1945–46:	1,298	1948–49:	3,914 (of total 31,122, e.g. 15 %)

[33] Further information in: *Senate Report 1515*, Table 14, 898; Kung, S.W. *Chinese in American Life.* Seattle, WA: University of Washington Press, 1962, 76.

[34] In total 3,465 refugees, including students, scientists, diplomats, journalists, priests, as well as a group of rich Chinese, received *permanent resident status.*

[35] Dr. An Wang started his company, Wang Laboratories, in 1951 with $600. The company grew to $3 billion sales in 1986, but later failed because it did not recognize the importance of personal computers. Dr. Wang died in 1990 of cancer, and the company was subsequently sold in 1999 to Gentronics, Netherlands (Kenney, Charles, 1992).

[36] On the *brain drain*—the exodus of scientists, see Chapter 6 "Education," and "The Influx of Chinese Intelligence—*Brain Drain*."

set out 40 million dollars for general aid and 8 million dollars for humanitarian measures.

Between 1949 and 1955 alone, the State Department spent $7.9 million on support, assistance, and medical aid for Chinese students. Furthermore, the students were allowed to take up paid employment in the United States, if they received permission from the Immigration and Naturalization Commission.[37] Among the private supporters of Chinese students, one must mention the publicist Henry R. Luce who made his New York home, today called the "China House," available to Chinese students.[38]

The Catholic cultural organization, *Sino-American Amity*, founded by Cardinal Yu Bin in Washington in 1943, supported more than 4,000 Chinese students in the 1950s and 1960s. Also, the China Institute opened a service-center for stranded students in Berkeley, California, and in New Jersey.[39]

After the founding of the People's Republic of China in 1949, emigration from the country was no longer allowed. The liberal immigration policy in the United States, however, attracted many highly qualified students from Hong Kong, Taiwan and Southeast Asia who ever increasingly found work in the United States subsequent to completing their studies. The relatively special circumstances of 1943 until 1952 principally underline the fact that during this period the United States was frequently confronted with situations which showed their immigration regulations to be inadequate immediately after their implementation. This was particularly the cases with the abolition of the *Exclusion Acts in 1943*, the subsequent "female quotas" between 1944 and 1946, as well as with the *Displaced Persons Act of 1948* and its expansion in the *China Area Aid Act of 1950*.

The McCarran-Water Act *and the Period between 1952 and 1965*

The *McCarran-Water Act* of 1952, which was introduced in response to the anti-communist isolationist policies, introduced the principle of family reunification into the immigration system.[40]

The still valid quota systems of 1921 and 1924 were made more precise through a preferential system built on the following four criteria:

---

[37] *U.S. Statutes at Large*, 64 Stat. 202, 22nd United States Congress; Public Law 535, 81st Congress.

[38] Henry Luce, Editor and Owner of *Time* magazine, the child of American missionaries in China, was on the side of Chiang Kai-shek and the Soong family, who received, therefore, wide publicity in his publications.

[39] For history of the China Institute see Robert Lee. *Guide To Chinese American Philanthropy and Charitable Giving Patterns*. Brisbane, Pathway Press, 1990.

[40] The conservative Senator Patrick McCarren from Nevada commented on his draft of the law as follows: "If this oasis of the world should be overrun, perverted and contaminated or destroyed, the last flickering light of humanity will be extinguished." Kim, H.C., 1986, 311.

1. 50% of the quota was delegated to persons with higher education, technical education, specialist abilities, or long-term experience in trades in high demand on the American market. The dependants of these *professionals* were also included in this regulation.
2. 30% was delegated to the parents of Chinese Americans, with residency in the United States and above the age of 21.
3. 20% was delegated to the dependants of *permanent residents*.
4. Any unused quota of the above mentioned categories could be used, up to a maximum of 25%, by siblings and children of Chinese Americans, as long as they did not qualify as non-quota immigrants by marriage or by having passed 21 years of age.

Additionally, this new regulation eliminated race as a criterion for immigration and naturalization and implemented a new principle of nationality. Relevant for Chinese immigration was also the new determinant of *APT* (*Asia Pacific Triangle*), to which 23 Asian nations, including China, belonged. The minimum quota for each country of APT was 100. However, the total number of all immigrants could not surpass 2,000 per annum. Thus, the world was divided into zones and the Asian one was not especially favored.

China received a double quota, but according to the following principle: 100 places were delegated to Taiwan, the only diplomatically-recognized China. 105 places were delegated to other Chinese of all nationalities, which included all those already living abroad in other nations (Bass, 1990, 86). Regardless of this regulation, 27,000 Chinese immigrated to China between 1952 and 1960 (US Census, 1960, 127) of which approximately 3,000 fell under the *Refugee Acts of 1953, 1957 and 1959* (Chan, S., 1990, 141).

The refugee movement maintained its relevance for the Chinese immigration: President Kennedy reacted in May 1962 to a mass exodus of Chinese to Hong Kong by issuing additional approval for 15,000 refugees to enter the United States—mainly women, children and students. As previously indicated, the majority of the Chinese influx fell under the female non-quota immigration: in 1952 and 1953, immediately after implementation, the ratio was higher than 80%, approximately 16,000 women (Daniels, 1988, 307). These figures for Chinese immigration, however, follow generally accepted tendencies, e.g. between 1952 and 1965 more than two-thirds of all immigrants were non-quota immigrants (Bass, 1990, 198).

Population Development as a Result of Push and Pull
from 1850 until 1965

In the following section, the development of population for the whole period will be fully analyzed in terms of the most important *push* factors in the originating country and *pull* factors in the recipient country, as well as in terms of migration-reducing factors on both sides, in order to use these results to investigate the latest tendencies.

Excluding prostitutes, the Chinese population in California was a purely male society at the beginning of the "free immigration" phase (1850 to 1882). In the literature it is often referred to as a *bachelor society*, since it consisted mostly of newly-arriving, young single males. The data on the development of the bachelor society show both the reasons for and the results of American immigration law throughout the whole period, but they have never been disclosed in their combined entirety. Chinese immigration between 1852 and 1870 increased strongly, reaching as high as 4.4% of total immigration, but due to ever increasing restrictions, it sank initially to 1.2% in 1890 and further to 0.33% in 1905.

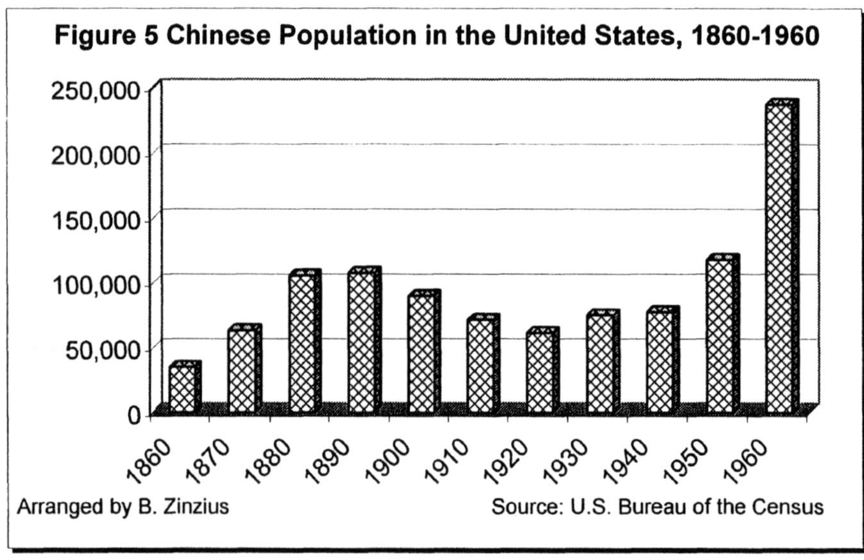

The State of California, the main target of immigration, saw an immense increase in the Chinese population in the decades between 1850 and 1880. By the time the *Exclusion Act* was introduced in 1882, the Chinese population had achieved a level of 92,600.[41]

---

[41] In 1860, 34,933 Chinese lived in the U.S., 63,199 in 1870, 105,465 in 1880. As a result of the *Exclusion Act,* a recession began with 89,863 in 1900, only 71,531 in 1910 and reaching a low of 61,639 in 1920. Until 1930, this figure grew back to 74,954. U.S. Census, 1930–1960.

Up to 1880, the number of immigrants, who remained almost exclusively male, had grown continuously.[42] The *Exclusion Act of 1882*, which was discriminatory insofar as it was directed only against Chinese, ended the previously steady influx of a willing Chinese workforce into California. Between 1890 and 1940, the *Age of Exclusion*, the bachelor society of early immigration developed into a family society, as the number of new immigrants stagnated. This impression is at least indicated by the data.

At the beginning of this period only 10% were native-born, whereas toward the end their number represented 52%, an even higher percentage than today. This structural change within the group, previously ignored in literature, is astonishing, since immigration regulations seemed to oppose such a development: While it seems logical that a group cut off from its reinforcement would substantially increase the number of native-born members within one or two generations, it is hardly expected in this case, since the ratio of women at the point of implementation of the *Exclusion Acts* was relatively low. Did the Chinese marry outside of their group, or, contrary to the existing regulations, could more women than men immigrate? Did Chinese women conceive exceptionally vast numbers of children?

The quota regulation of 1921 resulting from the isolation policy should not have favored the Chinese situation, since the basis for the quota determination was the number of resident population, which had already been reduced. One could have expected dramatic results from the *National Origins Act* of 1924 which in all practicality introduced an official reduction of immigration for the wives of Chinese businessmen who had previously been excluded from the regulations of 1882.[43] Numerous hypotheses may help explain the unusual qualitative change within the Chinese American group.

The 1924 practice suggests possibly that, via the loophole permitting entry of wives of Chinese businessmen, enough young women of childbearing age were entering to maintain the existing age structure among females. Statistical data reveals a strong increase in the female population between 1906 and 1924. In 1940, of the 39,566 Chinese immigrants, 12,225, or 30%, were women. The total Chinese population at this time was 77,504 people of which 20,115, or 26%, were women. The number of foreign-born women evidently increased between 1910 and 1940, namely by approximately 35% to 50% per decade. Crosschecking the figures shows that, at the beginning of the century, the proportion between men and women was opposite with regard to their origin—native-born versus foreign-born, e.g. many men born in the country and many women coming from abroad.

---

[42] 1860: 94.9% male, 5.1% female; 1880: 95.5% male, 4.5% female. U.S. Census, 1860–1880.

[43] See Chapter 1 "Chinese Immigration to California." *National Origin Act.*

Whereas the immigration quota for women remained stable and high, the percentage of local-born men grew by over 10%.[44] During the period between 1900 and 1940 and prior to the end of the racial discrimination of Chinese, the Chinese population reached its lowest point.

Nevertheless, the percentage of immigrating women grew, even if the absolute number of men immigrating was larger.[45] In addition, the average age of women was significantly lower. Based on this data, the rapid increase of American-born Chinese is obvious. In 1910, only a few of the women who had immigrated before 1880 could bear children, since 80% were between 15 and 35 years in 1880. Between 1880 and 1910 not many immigrated. In 1920, however, almost 50% of the female population was less than 14 years old, which means that beginning in 1920 there was a large group of women reaching child bearing age. After 1882, a large number of immigrants kept the overall number of Chinese in the country high, despite death and emigration.

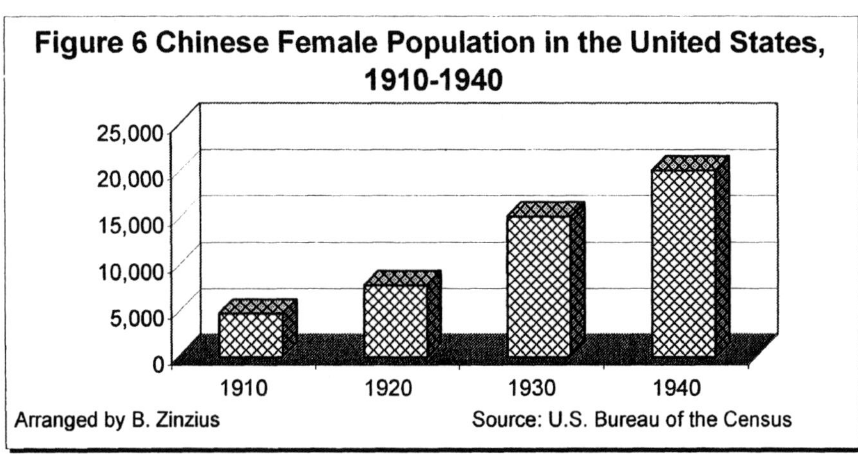

Figure 6 Chinese Female Population in the United States, 1910-1940

More than a few "merchant women" fall under that category.[46] In addition, many of the illegal immigrants, as well as residents, requested to be registered as native-born after the great earthquake or 1906 destroyed all immigration documents. One researcher calculated that some Chinese women would have had to have had over 800 children in the United States, if all claimants of native-born status had been born there (Takaki, 1989a, 424).

---

[44] Male: 1920 24.7% American-born versus 75.3% foreign-born
        1930 34.6% American-born versus 65.4% foreign-born
        1940 44.8% American-born versus 55.2% foreign-born, U.S. Census, 1920–1940.

[45] 1920: 41.8% female under 14 years old and 9.7% male under 14 years old.

[46] Many Chinese claimed to be merchants, since the *Exclusion Act* did not prohibit this group. Many of their "wives" were even prostitutes. From 1910 to 1920, the number of merchants'

The real change of the American Chinese society into a family-based society happened, therefore, between 1920 and 1940, as the figures of the native-born Chinese show. Nevertheless, one has to keep in mind that many of these were probably foreign-born.

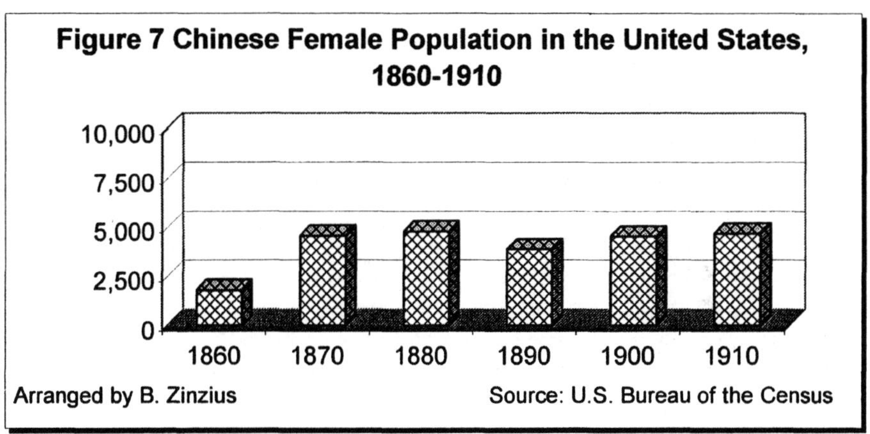

How can the change in the proportion between men and women from 1920 to 1940 be interpreted? The Chinese population in the United States doubled between 1930 and 1940. In 1910, there were 1,430 men per 100 women, while in 1930 the proportion had already reached 395 to 100 (U.S. Census 1930–1960). In addition, beginning in 1930 women were allowed to follow their husbands if they had been married for over six years. The growth of the female population between 1920 and 1940 shows no decline, and out of the American-based Chinese women, with at least twice as many American-born as foreign-born.[47]

The economic crisis in the nineteen-thirties deterred immigrant workers, and is expressed in the very high rate of unemployment (25% as compared to 11% for the American urban population in 1925). The close connection between the different Chinese businesses started a kind of chain reaction: the

wives increased from 275 to 1,104. In total 24,345 immigrants were admitted between 1921 to 1930, out of which 1,469 were female—in spite of their exclusion between 1924 and 1930; between 1931 and 1940, out of 3,989 immigrants 607 were female, e.g. almost every sixth. See also Zinzius, 1988.

[47] **Table 3 Chinese Population in the United States by Gender, 1910–1940**

	Male	**in %**	**Female**	**in %**	**Total**
1910	66,881	93.5%	4,650	6.5%	71,531
1920	51,852	86.9%	7,748	13.1%	59,600
1930	59,813	79.8%	15,152	20.2%	74,965
1940	57,250	74.0%	20,115	26.0%	77,365

Arranged by B. Zinzius   Source: U.S. Bureau of the Census.

closure of restaurants led to the breakdown of many importers. Whereas the percentage of the working Chinese population was at 80% in 1870, it declined to about 47% in 1940. The traditional workers' group, which was composed of 67% of all workers in 1870, was virtually eradicated in 1940. The migration to the East as well as the concentration in Chinatowns was the most obvious sign of change within the Chinese community, showing the adaptation towards the crisis.

New immigrants had balanced re-migration to China as well as the natural decline in the population in the early years. During the Depression, this was no longer the case. Between 1930 and 1940, the Chinese male population decreased by 2,500, whereas the female population increased by 5,000.[48] The strict control measures directed at the so-called *paper sons* were finally responsible for the decline of the Chinese male population. Between 1910 and 1940, this group was kept under almost inhumane conditions in the refugee camp on Angel Island in the San Francisco Bay.[49]

A strong indicator of the deterring effect this camp had on the potential Chinese immigrants is their number: Whereas in 1892 a total of 6,327 Chinese had been rejected at the borders, between 1935 and 1940 only 894 were rejected.[50]

With a careful interpretation, the increase of the female population in the period between 1900 and 1940 can be seen as a compensation for the stagnating male population. Especially important is the characteristic change in the employment and living structures. The high level of female immigration continued after the war, e.g. the number of immigrating women remained always higher than that of men.

---

[48] Between 1910 and 1920, the number of the male foreign-born Chinese in the United States decreased from 54,000 to 40,000, and the number of female foreign-born Chinese increased similarly from 2,500 to 5,000 in 1930. In 1940, 100 female Chinese of foreign descent had 295 male counterparts, in 1950 just 190 and in 1960 only 133.

[49] Angel Island, the largest island in the San Francisco Bay, was first mentioned in 1769. Until 1910, it has been used as military reserve and quarantine station. It is probably best known as *Angel Island Immigration Station*, for which it was used from 1910 to 1940. In contrast to Ellis Island, where the vast majority of immigrants were processed immediately, annually thousand of immigrants–most of whom were Chinese–were detained at the station for weeks or month. Only a fire in 1940 and the end of the exclusion laws in 1943 ended the painful arrival process. Further details and Chinese poetry from Angel Island have been compiled by Him Mark Lai, Genny Lim, and Judy Yung in: *Island: Poetry and History of Chinese Immigrants on Angel Island, 1910–1940.* 1999.

[50] Between 1930 and 1940, only 398 persons immigrated per year, whereas between 1925 and 1930 it had been 1,400. Between 1915 to 1943, about 3,000 Chinese had been expelled from the United States, whereas between 1892 and 1928 expulsions had been about 9,000 according to a U.S. Marshall; Statistical Abstract of the United States, 1957, Table 107, Statistical Abstract of the United States, 1960, Table 1113; Senate Report 1515, Table 5; Immigration and Naturalization Service, "Annual Report," 1928, Table 104.

In 1946, many young women of Chinese American GI's were able to enter under the terms of a special regulation, which finally stabilized the gender situation. And, in the period between 1948 and 1952, the number of immigrating women was almost ten times as high as that of men.[51] In 1960, the ratio of men and women was almost normal, e.g. 133 to 101.

This trend towards a family-based society also affected relations with the Chinese mainland. Newly founded or immigrated families set up a new life in the United States, and contacts to the homeland grew less frequent. This fact is indicated in the decline of private money transfers between the United States and China. Chinese immigration thus does not exemplify a *sojourner-mentality*, as is often stated in scientific publications, but rather a tendency to set up a family-based society.[52]

Beginning with the indefinite extension of the *Exclusion Act* in 1910, which included the cessation of home visits, an increased immigration of women as well as a decreased immigration of men can be noted. The strengthened female immigration was simultaneously a condition and an expression of the growing decay of the sending Chinese society, as well as an increased naturalization of the receiving Chinese American society. The decrease of the Chinese population since 1890, the distribution within the United States as well as the increase of other nationalities, such as Japanese or Southern Europeans, resulted in a normalization of the relations between the Chinese and the White population. Xenophobia, especially towards the Chinese, decreased significantly. Individual incidents, such as the pursuit of the *paper sons*, as well as the unemployment during the Depression hit men especially hard, whereas the Americans realized that the increasing number of women led to a better integration of the Chinese into the American society. The traditional dominance of the men was thereby broken, and women gained more and more confidence. The lack of diplomatic relations between the United States and the People's Republic of China made it almost impossible for the Chinese Americans after 1949 to visit their homeland or family in China.

> "Not once have I swept my parents graves. I sent them money, but how can I even think of myself as filial? Now? Now it is too late for me, I am too old to travel."
> (*Asian American Women United of California*, Ed. 1989, 12).

The United States had all reason to help the Chinese, who were very cooperative. The role of women as well as the possibility to follow the husband was strongly improved in China. Thus in the 1950s 32,000 Chinese

---

[51] See statistics at Daniels, 1988, 199.
[52] See discussion in Meissenburg, Karin. *The Writings on the Wall*. 1987, 31–33.

immigrated who did not fall under the quota regulation—57% of those were women (Daniels, 1988, 306).

The result was a shift of the gender distribution towards women, a tendency, which has not decreased since then. This means that the stabilization of the Chinese society in America was not just a result of the civil rights movement of the 1960s as well as the legislation of 1965.[53]

The American legislation totally misjudged the described developments, most probably because of the unequal gender distribution. It is interesting to recognize that special regulations between 1945 and 1965 led to a selection of immigrants, especially women, students, and more highly educated people, which nobody had foreseen. The highly educated population within the Chinese rose from 2.8% in 1940 to 7.1% in 1950 and reached an astonishing 17.9% in 1960. Beside service professions, this category was the strongest. These figures also show that between 1940 and 1960, a radical change in the Chinese society occurred, especially when compared to the traditional Chinatown society.

The hypothesis that the development of the immigrants outpaced the legislative restrictions can be seen in a further analysis of the population. In 1943 the legislative aim was to avoid a discrimination of the Chinese after World War II and in 1952 an anti-foreign and anti-communist fear triggered the encouragement of family reunions. Nobody followed, however, the qualitative and quantitative changes of the Chinese community during this time. In addition, it has to be mentioned that the immigrants coming from Taiwan and Hong Kong since the 1950s found an at least partially consolidated Chinese community.

---

[53] See also Chapter 3 "Changes in the Situation in the Countries of Origin."

3. IMMIGRATION BETWEEN 1965 AND 2000

The Regulations of 1965

Reasons for New Regulations

In the last third of the twentieth century, almost every second immigrant to the United States has come from Asia. From 1965 to 2000 the Asian population in the United States has grown from one million to twelve million. This 35-year period has thus seen the arrival of 8.4 million Asian immigrants, seven times as many as the 1.2 million during the whole historical period between 1850 and 1960.[1]

The *Immigration and National Amendment Act* of 1965 (*INA*) initiated the second massive wave of Asian immigration and thus, a new era in the history of Chinese Americans. Still, it would be misleading to conclude that 1965 brought about a quantitative and qualitative development of the Asian American population and, more specifically, the Chinese American population. As shown, the number of Chinese immigrants had increased considerably in the decade between 1940 and 1950, not as a result of substantial changes in domestic policy and society, as in 1965, but because of short-lived political changes in the relationship between China and the United States. Skepticism with regard to the turning point 1965 is supported by the results of the previous chapter's analysis. The same caution applies when analyzing the 1965 laws, in which the painful history of the *INA*'s development will be of particular interest. In the first instance, it is important to outline the social coordinates for the revision of immigration law. Thus, the importance of the time, 1965, should become more understandable.

Whatever the role played by domestic policy during the revisions of 1965 and 1968, the importance of foreign policy in the period cannot be disregarded; both are interdependent, irrespective of which was more determinant. At the height of the Cold War, a government crippled by the Vietnam War and increasing poverty wanted, or even needed to profit from the idea that the United States provided leadership in the "free world." Discriminatory immigration policy would have befitted the United States

---

[1] Between 1820 and 2000, over 66 million immigrants were admitted by the United States, making it the largest immigrant country worldwide. Prior to 1950, 90% of all immigrants came from Europe, after 1950 the ratio changed completely. In 2000, the highest number of American immigrants came from Mexico (171,748), followed by the Soviet Union (43,807), China (41,861), the Philippines (40,587), and India (39,072; U.S. Bureau of the Census, 2001); less than 10% came from Europe. The ethnic composition of America is thus drastically changing, driven by the strong growth of Hispanic and Asian immigrants.

neither internally nor externally. The political goal to obtain a more equal society and a widespread consensus on the necessary reforms in all areas of society required the support of the ethnic minorities, which until then had been neglected. Kennedy and Johnson were the first presidents to show a distinct interest in the vote of non-Whites. With regard to solidarity, captured under the idea of the *great society*, President Johnson sponsored programs to counter poverty, and leant his support to the Civil-Rights Movement. On various levels, domestic majorities supported the rights of minorities. In 1965, a strong democratic majority dominated Congress. Private aid organizations, civil initiatives, and pressure groups supported the implementation of a humanitarian immigration law in which the repatriation of families, often split for decades, lay at the forefront.

The *Civil Rights Act* of 1964, established to enforce the reach of the Fourteenth Amendment of the Constitution from 1868, and the *Executive Order* of 1965, represented nationwide success of the new political and social coalition over the remaining discriminating laws and regulations of the States.[2] A flourishing economy required that its backers, including the unions, stand behind an influx of foreign workers. The Labor Department formulated requirements for certain businesses and proposed trade preferences for the selection of immigrants. Asian groups had hardly any political clout in Washington at that time. They supported no particular party, but were interested in increasing the relatively small number of Asian voters.[3] With the successes of the Black Civil Rights Movement under Martin Luther King, Jr., though, all legal discrimination of minorities was abolished. However, the different political agendas of the interests groups involved in the further shaping of the law, which had started well before 1965, hindered its progress, as their political goals were too far apart.

Immigration and National Amendments Act

The immigration regulation of 1965 came close to a rehabilitation of President Truman's "Commission on Immigration and Naturalization" of 1952, which had reported to the 83rd Congress on January 1, 1953.[4]

---

[2] *Executive Order* 11246 (1965): "Affirmative Action Requirements of Government Contractors and Subcontractors." *History of Civil Rights Laws.* <http://www.withylaw.com/history.htm> December 12, 2002.

[3] See also in *"registering to vote"* about the efforts of Chinese organizations to get registered. Strokes, Bruce. *"Learning the game."* National Journal, October 22, 1988, 2649–2654. Eckrich, Teresa, Lew Catherine, and Treisman, Joel. *A Pilot Assessment of Voter Registration in San Francisco's Community.* San Francisco, Coro Foundation, 1986.

[4] President Truman used his veto against the ratification of the *McCarren-Walter Act* on June 25, 1952, and also set up a commission to establish counter bills, however none of those was successful.

In its recommendation under the heading "Whom We Shall Welcome" it had discussed abolishing the quota system according to nationality and the implementing a general cap of 250,000 immigrants per year. Flexibility could be upheld via special visa contingencies given out in special political situations, in response to difficulties in other countries, or in answer to American demand for particularly qualified workers were required. These guidelines remained the most important until the recent *Immigration Law* of 1990. Before 1965, however, they did not achieve a congressional majority.

In a speech before Congress on July 23, 1963, President Kennedy recommended a widespread revision of the quota system. Only one day later, New York Representative, Emanuel Celler, drew up most of Kennedy's suggestions and demands in a legislative proposal.[5] These had, however, previously been conceptualized under Truman in 1952. The resulting *Celler-Hart Act* required the elimination of the APT provisions, in other words, the discrimination of Asian countries by strict adherence to the quota regulations in the *McCarran-Walter Act*. The bill was, however, defeated by Congress.[6]

President Johnson promised to continue his predecessor's policies after Kennedy's assassination in November 1963. His proposals to ease the regulations on immigration were blocked by the senators from the South.

In September of the following year, Celler and Hart brought up in the Senate the previous year's proposal with the addition of one amendment: Instead of being processed according to their nationality, immigrants were to be processed according to their vocational qualifications. This time they were successful (89th Congress, 1965).[7]

The conflict of interest between the supporters of vocational qualification and the supporters of family repatriation was to become the central focus of all future legislative initiatives. President Johnson signed the *Immigration and Nationality Act* on October 3, 1965, during a ceremony at the Statue of Liberty on Liberty Island, New York. The new law implemented the following categorization of caps and preferential regulations:

First, 170,000 visas per annum were delegated to the Eastern Hemisphere with a maximum of 20,000 visas per national origin. National origin now meant the country of origin and no longer membership of a particular race, e.g. ethnic Chinese. Thereby, it became possible to adjust the maximum level per country, should that be required. Due

---

[5] Senator Phillip Hart of Michigan introduced the counterpart bills.

[6] The *McCarren-Walter* Act introduced the possibility for Asians to obtain American citizenship (naturalization), after cessation of the status "non-eligible for citizenship" for Chinese in 1943. Nevertheless, a strict quota system was implemented for Asians, depending on their national origin (National Origin System).

[7] The law passed the Congress with 318 to 95 votes on September 15, and the Senate accepted it with a vote of 76 to 16 one week later (Kim, 1986, 311 et. seq.).

to the lack of diplomatic relations with the PRC, the Chinese quota fell in practice to Taiwan. Hong Kong, as a British crown colony, obtained the quota reserved for dependant territories, namely 1% of that of the metropole. 120,000 visas were allocated to the Western Hemisphere, however, without any cap per country. For the first time, a quantitative cap had been introduced for the Western Hemisphere.[8] The regulations in the *Celler-Hart Law* were introduced as the *Amendment to the Immigration and Nationality Act* in 1968.

Second, the preferential system within the given quota regulations was applicable for both Eastern and Western Hemispheres. It differentiated immigrants according to vocational and relationship criteria, whereby the latter was of greater importance. Excluded from the quota regulations and numeric caps were immediate relatives of American citizens, e.g. children, spouses, and parents. The group which had the most immediate relatives wanting to immigrate would therefore have profited the most within the first few years after the law, especially since there existed a special, additional quota for the relatives of *permanent residents*.[9] 74% of the total quota—a great success for the supporters of the minority-humanitarian solution—was allocated to the repatriation of families, 20% was allocated for vocational preferences, and the rest to refugees.

The preferences functioned as follows:

1st Preference: a maximum of 20% of the visas were allocated to unmarried sons or daughters of United States citizens over 21 years of age.

2nd Preference: a maximum of 20%, plus any unused quota from the previous preference (hereafter QPP), were allocated to spouses or unmarried sons and daughters of foreigners with permanent resident status.

3rd Preference: a maximum of 10% were allocated to professionals, scientists and artists, including their spouses and children.

4th Preference: a maximum of 10%, plus QPP 1–3, were allocated to married sons and daughters of United States citizens, including their spouses and children.

5th Preference: a maximum of 24%, plus QPP 1–4, were allocated to siblings of United States citizens over the age of 21, including their spouses and children.

6th Preference: a maximum of 10% were allocated to skilled or unskilled laborer, lacking in the United States, including their spouses and children.

7th Preference: a maximum of 6% for refugees for whom limited immigration or change of status was approved, especially for those fleeing Communist-dominated countries.[10,11]

---

[8] Between 1961 and 1970, only 3.3 million people immigrated, 97,000 thereof from the People's Republic of China and Taiwan, 26,000 from Hong Kong.

[9] Aliens residing in the United States can receive the status of permanent resident aliens if they have been living for five years in the United States, are at least eighteen years old, vow to respect the American Constitution and are able to speak, read, and write basic English. *CRS Report for Congress.* "Immigration Legislation – Questions and Answers." Joyce C. Vialet. Specialist in Immigration Policy, Education and Public Welfare Division. June 4, 1991, 18.

[10] *Reports of the Visa Office*, 1968, Bureau of Security and Consular affairs. Department of State, 65, with additional comments in special publications. See also the following footnote.

[11] The source: *U.S. Immigration Policy and National Interest, Staff Report of the Select Commission of Immigration and Refugee Policy*, April 30, 1981, 372 does not include Preference 7 nor the "non-preference status." In addition, the non-used quota of the previous

Further Developments of the Laws of 1965

Between 1975 and 1980, the *Immigration and National Amendments Act* (*INA*) of 1965 underwent a number of adjustments, none of which brought any significant change, but which made it more difficult to determine the exact results of the law and to determine specific problems. The *Immigration and Nationality Act* of 1976 extended the quota per country to 20,000 visas and included the Western hemisphere in the preferential guidelines. The quota for Hong Kong Chinese was increased from 200 to 600. The *World-Wide Ceiling Law* of 1978 united the quota for the Western and Eastern hemispheres in a cap of 290,000 immigrants per annum. In 1980, it was reduced to 280,000.

The *Refugee Act* of 1980 allocated 50,000 visas per annum to so-called "Normal Flow Refugees" (political refugees). Refugees could now improve their legal situation after one year. It also authorized the president to increase the quota in special cases, subsequent to congressional approval. For example, President George H.W. Bush's measures in 1989 to offer ten thousands of Chinese students permanent resident status fell into this category.[12]

The support measures for refugees remained of great importance for the Chinese contingent. Subsequent to the implementation of the *Indochina Refugee Act* of 1978, between 1981 to 1988, 282,000 refugees from Vietnam entered the country of which at least 30% were ethnic Chinese (*Statistical Abstract*, 1991, No. 10).

---

preference is also not included. Sucheng Chan specifies as criteria for preferences 1–4 an age of at least 21 years, which is probably correct, since this excludes an overlapping with the non-quota regulation for children of United States citizens (Chan, 1991, 146). Luciano Mangiafico includes adopted children and stepchildren of United States citizens under the first preference, as well as special immigrants such as priests (*minister of religion*) and former employees of the United States government (Mangiafico, 1988, 122). One reason for the different interpretations could be the continuing parliamentary discussions as well as various changes and additions to the law in the following years.

[12] The *Chinese Temporary Protected Status Act* of 1989 allowed all Chinese students in the United States during the Tiananmen Square Massacre to stay for a period of three years. The Act was later replaced by the *Chinese Student Protection Act* (*CSPA*) in 1992, which admitted 52,826 students until 1996 (1993: 26,915; 1994: 21,297: 1995: 4,213; 1996: 401; *Statistical Yearbooks of the Immigration and Naturalization Service*, U.S. Bureau of the Census, 1995 and 1996). See also Chapter 3 "Definitions."

The large number of accepted refugees—231,000 in 1980 and 122,326 in 1990—were only possible, because the *Refugee Act* extracted the refugees from the preferential system and from the worldwide cap.[13]

In the 1980s, a widespread evaluation with its corresponding legislative consequences was finally implemented, initially striking at illegal immigration (1986) and eventually at the revision of legal immigration (1990). Already in the early 1970s, it had become apparent that the preference and quota system of 1965 had by no means covered total immigration equally. Certain groups, in particular Hispanics and Asians, had over-proportionately profited. In addition to the non-quota immigration came a swell of illegal immigration. That it took over twenty years to react can be explained by the difficult birth of the Immigration Laws of 1965. Widespread revisions were postponed by both houses. Furthermore, Hispanic groups were lobbying very effectively. They were able to postpone restrictive measures against illegal immigration until 1986, which already existed as a legislative proposal in 1982 (*Simpson-Mazzoli Bill*).

Their reluctance stemmed from the fact that Hispanics, and in particular Mexicans, were profiting from a large number of job vacancies for illegal immigrants in agriculture (in 1991, 921,000 legalizations of illegal immigrants in the agricultural sector resulted from the *Special Agriculture Worker Program*).[14] Their success must be recognized in their support of democratic presidential candidates in 1984. The exact background must be discussed later. With the *Immigration Reform and Control Act* (*Simpson-Rodino Bill*) in 1986, it was attempted to overcome illegal immigration by providing an amnesty for those already resident and by forcing the employers to register their employees. The success of this regulation, however, proved to be short-lived. In 1986 alone, 1,767,400 illegal border crossings were documented, covering nearly all nationalities.[15]

The *New York Times* reports in January 1991 of a flourishing flesh trade to New York in which Chinese in particular participated (January 3, 1991). Even after extremely restrictive legislative measures, immigration to the United States has, therefore, only become more nebulous. The market for illegal immigrants on the other hand has expanded, not only into the traditional agricultural sector, but into the urban services sector, an area in which Chinese are predominantly found: the urban services sector.

---

[13] *CRS Report for Congress*. "Immigration Legislation–Questions and Answers." Joyce C. Vialet. Specialist in Immigration Policy, Education and Public Welfare Division. June 4, 1991, 10.

[14] 12. Ibid., 8.

[15] From implementation of the new law until 1989, the number of registered but not authorized frontier crossings fell to 954,243 but increased to 1,169,937 in 1990. 12. Ibid., 13.

According to more recent estimations, illegal aliens are currently believed to be between 3.5 and 12 million people (*Close Up Foundation*, 1998: 5 million; Immigration and Naturalization Service, 2002: 7 million).

Law of 1986 (IRCA 1986)

The bill to control illegal immigration (*IRCA 1986*) was initially proposed by Simpson and Mazzoli[16] in 1982 and contains four main components:

1. Amnesty in the form of back-dated legalization of millions of illegal aliens in the country as of a certain date.
2. Sanctions against employers who knowingly employ illegal aliens.
3. Introduction of a national identification system (Identification Card).
4. Revision of family repatriation by elimination of the 5th Preference (siblings of United States citizens) and by reduction of the 2nd Preference (spouses and unmarried children under 21 years of age of permanent residents).

The *Simpson-Mazzoli Bill* was introduced in the biennium of the Reagan presidency, at a time the nation was deep in recession and thousands were being laid off. New immigration had to be slowed and the potential cause of unrest, illegal aliens, had to be integrated. Mass lay-offs in the auto industry in 1981 and 1982 provoked protests against Japanese imports and so-called *Japan bashing*.

At the same time, all anger was directed against immigrants from the East, who were supposedly taking away jobs from Americans. The murder of Vincent Chin, a 27-year-old Chinese American, by two unemployed Whites who had believed him to be Japanese represents one of the ugliest episodes.[17] Discrimination of Chinese Americans continues, and a recent study indicated that "25% of Americans reflect strong negative attitudes and stereotypes against Chinese and Asian Americans." (*Committee of 100*, April 25, 2001)

---

[16] Senator Alan K. Simpson was Member of the Select Commission on Immigration and Refugee Policy from 1979 to 1981; he retired from the Senate in 1996. Congressman Mazzoli was chairman of the *House Subcommittee on Immigration and Refugee Affairs*; he retired in 1995.

[17] Vincent Chin was killed in Detroit as the result of a dispute with two Whites, one of whom had been laid off. Both were convicted of manslaughter, but received only probation terms. The lenient sentences outraged and mobilized the Asian community (Ho, Christine, 2003).

Only two months after the implementation of "Operation Jobs"[18] by the Immigration and Naturalization Service (INS),[19] the racial upheaval declined. The government had to send a signal opposing illegal immigration, even if more was not possible without the introduction of "unfakable" general identification system.[20]

As clear as the regulations of the bill were, equally clear was the response. Mainly conservative groups and the unions turned against the legalization process for illegal aliens because they feared greater competition and disadvantages for the national workforce. According to a survey from *Newsweek*, 60% of those questioned really believed that illegal aliens were taking jobs away from Americans (June 13, 1983).

Political activists on the Chinese American side criticized the Simpson-Mazzoli Bill mainly due to its intended amendment to the 5th Preference. A special committee was founded with the name *To Retain the 5th Preference.*

Whereas other minorities, like Latin Americans and Haitians, as well as Civil Rights organizations, also criticized the problematic sanctions of employers, the Chinese activists concentrated solely on the pending reduction of family repatriation.[21]

The leader of the *House Judiciary Committee*,[22] Peter Rodino (D-NJ), a trusted congressional veteran and a renowned liberal, spoke out in favor of maintaining the 5th Preference and thus obtained support from the Chinese group. The *Committee to Retain the 5th Preference* was finally successful. The corresponding article was struck from the bill. With that, a major portion of the resistance to the bill was broken. Congress superficially brushed aside the defense of the 5th Preference by defining it as an *Asian concern.*

Other Asian groups, however, did not agree. The Filipinos, for example, who had to expect a lead time of twelve years for family repatriation via the

---

[18] During the "Operation Jobs," 5,000 illegal workers were arrested in April 1982. The Immigration and Naturalization Service used these arrests for publicity, announcing that for each arrest a job for an American citizen had been created.

[19] The Immigration and Naturalization Service, which deals with all immigration questions within the United States, is under the Justice Department. For consular matters abroad, specially granting of visas, the Bureau of Consular Affairs in the State Department is responsible. See *CRS Report for Congress.* "Immigration Legislation – Questions and Answers." Joyce C. Vialet. Specialist in Immigration Policy, Education and Public Welfare Division. June 4, 1991, 13.

[20] U.S. Commission on Civil Rights, *Recent Activities Against Citizen and Resident of Asian Descent.* Clearing House Publication No. 88, 1988.

[21] Detailed report in: *Asian American Policy Review*, Spring 1981, 70; see also "Census Slashes Estimate Illegal Aliens." *Los Angeles Times*, May 7, 1983.

[22] The Judiciary Committee and the Subcommittee on Immigration and Refugee Affairs are the main bodies drafting immigration laws to be presented for the Congress.

preference system, had given up their interest in this regulation and sought alternatives to reduce the backlog of willing immigrants.

Because they were mainly able to enter the country on limited resident permits, they were particularly non-supportive of the sanctions against employers who knowingly employed illegal aliens. Their pressure groups aligned themselves, therefore, with those of the Mexicans, who were also notably increasing their number of illegal aliens. Their fear was that among employers a preconception concerning the danger of employing dark skinned, Spanish speaking employees would develop. After the introduction of the *Immigration Reform and Control Act* of 1986 (*IRCA*), 40% of employers believed it to be more risky to employ Hispanics whereas 39% felt it more risky to employ Asians.[23]

These statistics appeared in a survey in 1989, prepared by a number of Asian groups and brought before the Senate in support of a resolution to eliminate sanctions against employers. They had learned from the one-sided support of family repatriation. For the Hispanics, Asians suddenly became desired partners. Whereas, on the one hand, the lobbyists had to tone down their resistance in order not to provoke even stricter regulations, on the other hand, as a consequence, they expanded their interest group base to be prepared for future actions. From 1986 on, a coordination system for Hispanic and Asian groups was created in the *National Network for Immigration and Refugees Rights* (*NNIR*).

Their joint goals have since become the reduction of preferential waiting lists, resistance toward a general identification system, a new preferential list based on lingual criteria, and, finally, a halt to extradition for those trying to become legal under provisions of *IRCA 1986*.[24]

In the future, it will become more difficult for Washington to buy off the well-organized Chinese with liberalization of certain articles of law, thus dividing and conquering the Asians and Hispanics who are the major beneficiaries of the laws of 1965.

Since the implementation of *IRCA 1986*, approximately 2.6 million illegal aliens have profited from the amnesty, which legalized all illegal immigrants that had arrived before January 1, 1982. This has, however, left the unsystematic immigration policy in the United States unchanged. It remains a combination of two almost equally strong elements, namely legal

---

[23] Public Research Institute Report, San Francisco State University, 1989, brought into the Senate on April 20, 1990; supporting organizations are the *Asian American Legal Defense and Education Funds*, *Asian Law Caucus* and the *Organization of Chinese Americans*.

[24] See Frank D. Bean, George Vernez and Charles B. Keely. *Opening and Closing the Doors: Evaluation Immigration Reform and Control.* Santa Monica, Washington, DC: 1989.

and illegal immigration, which is mainly possible due to political maintenance of the "soft border" with Mexico.

The INS, which clearly requires better control measures, is powerless in the battle against illegal immigration due to the "liberty syndrome" existing in the American public. The sensitivity toward a "controlled state" sets enormous barriers against effective immigration policy and continues to make the introduction of a general identification system, as demanded by Simpson-Mazzoli, impossible. President Reagan had described the situation years earlier as follows: "This country [America] has lost control of its borders, and no country can sustain that kind of position." (Reagan, 1983).

Immigration Act of 1990 (IA 1990)

Driven forward by his success in 1986, Senator Simpson (R-ID) promptly laid before the 1987–88 Congress a bill for legal immigration, which would eliminate the 5th Preference and limit the 2nd Preference. Single sons and daughters over 26 years old of permanent residents were to be eliminated from the preferential regulation. A consensus could not be found in Congress since it was obviously tired of long debates. The Asian lobby immediately attacked the tendencies of such a bill, since family repatriation was to make space for vocational qualifications. Senator Edward Kennedy who became a co-sponsor the following year said, "One's skills should be the principle determinant."

The direction of Simpson's initiative was turned around. Congress was pushed to redefine the term "family" in the sense that spouses and under-aged children of permanent residents were to be considered "immediate relatives" and therefore no longer fell under the guidelines of the quota regulations.[25]

In Congress of 1989–90, Simpson launched a counter-offensive. He warned that should, the quotas be liberalized, then the *family backlogs* for Asian countries and Mexico would be greatly reduced. On this basis it would be difficult to maintain an equal system of immigration policy, especially toward those already discriminated against by *INA* 1965, the Europeans and Africans. As a counter-argument against "family repatriation," Simpson claimed that, generally speaking, the level of education and productivity was lower than that of "vocational immigrants" and that there was insufficient recruitment of a skilled workforce.

---

[25] Estimates state that in 1990, 1.5 million people were on the waiting list for family re-unification, thereof 600,000 Asians (Johnny Ng, "Houses pass the Bill," *Asian Week*, November 5, 1990, 27).

Simpson, who had previously been an ardent supporter of strict limitations on the extent of exclusion, had suddenly presented himself as a clever tactician, supporting "inclusion" and "balance."[26]

An elimination of the 5th Preference was hardly possible. Technical reasons spoke against this proposal. Eleanor Chelimsky, Assistant Comptroller General, GAO, explained to the *Senate Subcommittee on Immigration and Refugee Affairs* on March 3, 1989, "A limitation (of the 5th Preference) to unmarried brothers and sisters would reduce the number of new applicants, but it would still take 75 years to reduce the existing waiting list to an acceptable level." The question was whether a general limitation could be achieved which would, at least indirectly, hit the strongest immigrant groups.[27] Simpson and Kennedy, who had become the Head of the *Senate Immigration Committee*, favored a solution in which all categories, including the previously excluded family preference, would fall under the worldwide cap of 590,000.

Actual annual immigration levels had, however, reached a multiple of this capping level, which therefore questioned the validity of this figure. The fears of Simpson and Kennedy seem valid. The geographic analysis of the immigration figures of 1985 indicates a turning point. Since 1980, the total number of immigrants had been declining. In 1985, however, it began to grow considerably.[28]

If the family preferences could not be broken, then at least the vocational preferences had to be upgraded. Congress expanded the *Simpson-Kennedy Bill* with one factor, which was to end the privilege of family preference once and for all: An increase in the number of visas for the vocational preferences and an introduction of a special contingency for previously discriminated countries. The majority (25 of 34) were European nations. It was further planned to introduce stricter measures concerning the extradition of illegal aliens.

All this seemed to run counter to Asian interests. A strong opposition, however, had already been set up in both Houses. In the Senate, amendments were introduced which guaranteed a minimum of 216,000 visas based on family preferences. Even more liberal was the idea of the new Head of the *House Immigration Subcommittee*, Bruce Morrison: Unlimited immigration

---

[26] See also Chapter 5 "Business Structures and Income," under "Law and Age Structure."

[27] Quota in October 1991: 270,000; number of total issued visas including legalized aliens: 1.5 million (1990).

[28] See *CRS Report for Congress.* "Immigration Legislation–Questions and Answers." Joyce C. Vialet. Specialist in Immigration Policy, Education and Public Welfare Division. June 4, 1991, 3.

of members of the immediate family of permanent residents, along with a general increase of the visa quota of the other family preferences.

The orientation of immigration toward the labor market was to be maintained, but in such a way that open positions could be quickly filled by foreigners. All this lead to nothing more than a substantial increase in the annual visa contingency. Finally, a compromise was found that integrated the restrictive *Simpson-Kennedy Bill* into the more liberal *Morrison Bill* (H.R. 4000) and adhered to the Asian demands.[29] The bill (H.R. 4300), also known as *Family Unity and Employment Opportunity Act* of 1990, already shows in its title the desired equilibrium between the two focal points, family and vocation. It was introduced step by step, as the following describes:

1. A new worldwide cap was introduced that included all immigrants and refugees and lay slightly above that of the previous years (700,000 until 1994, thereafter 675,000).

2. A maximum of 480,000 visas (initially 465,000) were set aside for family preferences, whereby immediate relatives did not fall under the country quotas, but were deducted at a minimum of 226,000 from the total cap at the end of the year.[30] The annual cap, therefore, was the sum of family preference limit (480,000), vocational preference limit (140,000), and two new categories for Diversity Immigrants (55,000), and Refugees and Asylees[31] (variable quota, authorized by the president) to be discussed below.

3. Within this new upper limit, the number of visas for vocational preferences was increased from 54,000 to 140,000 where the majority was to be reserved for specialists, scientists, and managers (80,000), skilled laborers (40,000) and 10,000 each for the two small categories, unskilled laborers and investors ($1 million).[32]

4. The types of non-immigrant visa have been reorganized. Currently there are 43 different non-immigrant visa categories, categorized A-1 to R.

What are the concrete results of Simpson's originally anti-Asian and anti-Hispanic, respectively, anti-family preferences, proposal H.R. 4300 (*IA 1990*)?

---

[29] Congressman Morrison proposed an expansion of the visa quota of 100,000 to reduce the backlog. In addition, he proposed an "immediate relative status" for wives and minor children of permanent residents. Furthermore, a stop of deportations was proposed for those illegal immigrants who had been granted amnesty under the IRCA in 1986, as was a limited residency permit for aliens with a job.

[30] Four *Family-Based* categories for the allocation of immigrant visa quotas were established (FB-1 to FB-4). FB-1 equals the 1st, FB-2 the 2nd, FB-3 the 4th, and FB-4 the 5th Preference of the *1965* of *INA*.

[31] The Refugees and Asylees category equals the 7th Preference of the *INA* of 1965.

[32] Five *Employment-Based* categories for the allocation of immigrant visa quotas were established, EB-1 to EB-5. EB-1 and EB-2 equal the 3rd Preference, and EB-3 equals the 6th Preference of the *INA* of 1965. EB-5 is the category "investors."

Initially, it is interesting to note that the importance of the vocational preference in the Kennedy Bill stemmed from many senators' original belief that it would mainly attract highly educated Whites. In the final proposal, of the 140,000 visas for vocational preferences, 80,000 are allocated to academics, scientists, and managers.[33] Exactly in these categories, however, Asian countries have greater and emigration-willing potential than Europe, and in particular the three Chinas, the Philippines, and India.[34]

Additionally, a new investment category was introduced which seemed to be ideal for a certain group of Chinese: The new immigration law offers millionaires a fast track on the road to the promised land. Annually, 10,000 visas are to be prepared for those non-Americans who are willing to invest one million dollars and create at least ten new job positions. If the immigrant is willing to invest in an economically poor region, he only needs to pay half that amount; 30% of all investor visas are marked for these poor regions.

The United States government referred to similar programs in other countries: Since 1986, Canada had thus imported more than three billion dollars with which more than 40,000 new jobs were created. Similarly, approximately 10,000 immigrants had brought $1.3 billion to Australia the years before. The Washington economic experts believed to be able to earn ten billion dollars during five years through this form of *green card* sale.

This was a high goal when compared to the levels of investment needed in Canada (US$220,000) and Australia (US$535,000) to obtain the residential documents. Optimism, however, succeeded. California State Officials believed that the majority of investments would also remain in the preferred immigration state of the Chinese: California. It was no secret that with this portion of the law America has been eyeing the financial strength of Hong Kong Chinese. And this is not the only fact giving the impression that "America is selling itself to the highest bidder."

In the decade leading up to 2001, however, the *IA 1990* has attracted only 5,452 "investor" immigrants, about 5% of the targeted number.[35] The majority of these investors were Chinese: 28% come from Taiwan, 24% from mainland China, and 4% from Hong Kong.[36]

Furthermore, over half of all "investor immigrants" were family members. The program did not result in the expected number of investors, and, therefore, standards were gradually eroded to enable more people to

---

[33] *CRS Report for Congress.* "Immigration Legislation – Questions and Answers." Joyce C. Vialet. Specialist in Immigration Policy, Education and Public Welfare Division. June 4, 1991, 5.

[34] See Daniels, 1991, 402.

[35] *1995–2001 Statistical Yearbooks of the INS.* U.S. Department of Justice, table 6.

[36] The term mainland China is used to distinguish geographically between the Chinese mainland, Hong Kong, and Taiwan.

apply. Thus, a peak was reached in 1997 with 1,361 investors, 64.4% of which were Chinese.

The Chinese used a loophole, which allowed them to deposit far less money, on average less than $50,000 per investor, and provide promissory notes for the balance.[37] The General Attorney's Office stopped this practice in 1999.[38] Since then, the annual number of investors has receded to less than 200, about 40% of which are Chinese (U.S. Department of Justice, *INS*, 2001).

Some Asian and Chinese Civil Rights Movements, e.g. *Asian American Legal Defense and Education Fund, Asian Law Caucus* and *Overseas Chinese American Organization*, had continuously supported the maintenance of family repatriation and an increase in the visa quota according to the *Berman-Morrison Bill*, but were strictly opposed to the more restrictive parts of the original *Simpson-Kennedy Bill*.[39]

Generally, the lobbyists for the new immigration legislation in Washington believed that the Asian groups would not oppose the new law as long as family repatriation was upheld. This calculation was finally successful, although the influence of these groups was much stronger than during the introduction of *IRCA 1986*.

Interestingly, not only the increased influence of Asian lobbies could be felt, but also the unification among all Asian groups in their approach and support for the *Morrison Bill*, which thus overrode their political differences. Previously, similar unification had shown itself only during and after the Tiananmen Square Massacre, 1989.

Special committees of Asian American groups had organized and coordinated reports and calls in the Asian media.[40] The Chinese American minority paper *East West* printed a letter campaign supporting the *Berman-Morrison Bill*; pre-formulated letters were printed and the readers were requested to send as many as possible to their respective congressmen. A typical format was:

---

[37] "Abuses Are Cited in Trade of Money for US Residence." Eric Schmitt. *New York Times*, April 12, 1998.

[38] Firms that had benefited from investor visa promotion lost their appeal in the 9th Circuit Court in California 2001, a decision that may even lead to the invalidation of earlier approved visas. *Federation for American Immigration Reform (FAIR)*. "Investor Visas." August, 2002. <http://www.fairus.org/html/04155806.htm> (February 8, 2003).

[39] The Republican Congressman Howard Berman held a fundraising banquet for "Fairness in Family Immigration" by the *Committee for Immigration Justice* and the *Chinese Consolidated Benevolent Association*. This was a "$100 plate event" from an advocate for family reunion. "Rep. Berman Due in San Francisco Chinatown for Immigration." Judith A. Lyons, *Asian Week*, September 22, 1989.

[40] *Organization of Chinese Americans, Chinese Citizen Alliances, Committee for Immigration and Justice, Asian Law Caucus* et. al.

> "Dear Congressman, I urge you to support Congressmen Berman and Morrison's bill on immigration. Family values and strength are central to our American way of life and must remain the foundation of our immigration policy. Sincerely, ..."

Congressman Robert Matsui (D-CA) believes this law to be a major part of one of the most important American traditions, namely worldwide family repatriation under the protection of and to the benefit to American democracy: "If this country does continue to advance economically, politically and culturally, we must not fear the talents and intelligence of those to come to this country and contribute their skills."[41] In support of the *Spouse Bill* (H.R. 4275) which allows the wives of permanent residents limited residency—an area in which the waiting lists are particularly long—is the following: "... the purpose of the Spouse Bill is not to award special advantages for foreign aliens, but to preserve family unity within the American society."[42] Cleverly, the Chinese lobby differentiates between the maintenance of the Chinese American family and the arrival of the foreign family.

Senator Paul Simon (D-IL) was one of three members of the *Senate Committee for Immigration and Refugees*. Since his presidential candidacy in 1988, he has been vying for the support of the Asians and makes everything possible available to them. In return, he has received their support, especially from the financially well-equipped who hold large *fundraising banquets*. A 1990 letter from the *Organization of Chinese American Women* praised him in particular for his efforts on behalf of the Chinese cause, but also mentioned areas in which more is expected of him. They are especially concerned about the reduction of the immigration quota for unskilled laborers to 10,000 per annum, which is equal to the investment quota of the super rich, which seems to end once and for all the ideal that America is a refuge for the poor and persecuted. Many Chinese are, at least during the first years of residence in the United States, among those especially found in the less qualified service jobs.[43]

---

[41] Congressman Robert Matsui from Sacramento is a Japanese American of second generation, who experienced imprisonment in a concentration camp during World War II. With a keen eye on potential voters potential and the aim to become Senator, he strongly supports *Asian Americans* and also receives strong financial support from this group.

[42] Speech of Sam H. Chang during the seminar *Asian and Pacific American Issues* in May 1992 in Washington. Chang also proposed additional quotas for brothers and sisters of United States citizens, which could be taken from unused quotas of other preferences. In addition he proposed a new *Student Protection Act*, which should grant *resident status* to the over 52,000 Chinese students which were admitted under President George Bush.

[43] Open letter of the *Organization of Chinese American Women* to Senator Paul Simon, October 22, 1990. Senator Simon died in December 2003 at the age of 75 years.

Also Senator Daschle from South Dakota—a State with increasing Chinese population[44]—received support from the Asian population. He lost, however, his re-election in 2004 against Senator Thune, despite the support of minority groups. He is aware of the influence of Chinese Americans and of the financial prowess of new immigrants, especially those from Hong Kong and Taiwan.

Since 1994, the family category has also been expanded by a further category that benefits those countries with strong new immigration levels and relatively few United States residents: 55,000 additional visas are allocated annually to wives and unmarried children of permanent residents.[45] Furthermore, the country quota has been expanded from 20,000 to 25,620, and Hong Kong received its own country quota in 1996. The country quotas have mainly been filled by Asian and Latin American countries.[46]

Beginning in 1995, up to 55,000 visas for *Diversity Immigrants* have been annually allocated to those previously underrepresented who could not immigrate using the family preferential quota. Northern Ireland has its own quota.[47] The countries that have filled the country quotas of 20,000 annual visas are China, Korea, the Philippines, India, Mexico and the Dominican Republic. The new diversity categories possibly offer more places to Europeans, but only in addition to other categories, thus increasing the total level of immigration, but not reducing the family preference category.

The preferences for permanent residents, as well as the new categories, cultural exchange program aliens (students), and religious occupations (mainly Christian scholars from Hong Kong and Korea) will undoubtedly benefit the Chinese, whose immigration has increased substantially in recent years. The *Morrison Legal Immigration Bill* (H.R. 4300) has subsequently been seen by the Asian American press as a success of strong Asian lobbying. The Asians can finally feel satisfaction. Family repatriation has been maintained and at least some Asian groups will benefit over-proportionately from the new academic preferences. This will need to be analyzed further, especially with regard to the Chinese group.

---

[44] See Chapter 4 "Habitat."

[45] See also the footnote on the speech by Chang, previous page.

[46] *CRS Report for Congress*. "Immigration Legislation – Questions and Answers." Joyce C. Vialet. Specialist in Immigration Policy, Education and Public Welfare Division. June 4, 1991, 9.

[47] Senator Edward Kennedy, who is of Irish descent, is one of the initiators of this bill. He wanted, perhaps, to convert 100,000 illegal Irish immigrants into legal United States citizens and new voters. The temporary program allocated 55,000 immigrant visa to disadvantaged states and regions, and became known as "Irish lottery." The program failed to attract Irish immigrants, mainly because of the prosperous Irish economy, while the majority of immigrants came from central African nations (Joppke, 2003, 8).

Since the beginning of the 1990s, several factors increased the pressure on immigration. The economic slump during the early 1990s, combined with a massive wave of illegal immigrants, especially Mexicans, provided a strong basis for strict, and thus controversial new immigration laws, which will be discussed in the next chapter. Advocates of liberal legislation have been able to prevent stricter regulations, such as the implementation of a national identification system, despite the political climate and support by President Reagan, Senator Simpson (R-ID) and Congressman Frank (D-MA), among others. The discussion of such regulations has thus been continuous since the early 1980s, when it was first introduced in the *Simpson-Rodino* Bill.

The tragic events of September 11, 2001 added completely new aspects to the immigration discussions and changed the general perception about an ID-system. Senator Tom Ridge (D-PA), the *Secretary of Homeland Security*, is in favor of a national ID-card, which obviously will have consequences for immigrants.[48] Since the end of 2001, an increased emigration of foreign students and workers can already be seen.

Immigration Reform Act of 1996 (*IIRIRA 1996*)

Since the 1990s, about 900,000 legal and 300,000 illegal immigrants come annually to the United States, and the total number of illegal immigrants is estimated at about seven million (U.S. Department of Justice, *Statistical Yearbook of the Immigration and Naturalization Service*, 2003). This situation, together with the economic roller coaster of the 1990s, has made immigration in general, and immigration policy issues in particular, a current and controversial issue throughout American society. The discussion centers on several major issues, ranging from national identity to the economy, including constitutional rights and social benefits for illegal immigrants.

Pro-immigration advocates claim that immigration is a basic pillar of the United States, as inscribed at the base of the Statue of Liberty.[49] They further assert that low-wage workers, who fill undesirable jobs, as well as multiculturally and multilingually versed employees are essential for the American economy to stay globally competitive.

---

[48] Senator Tom Ridge was sworn in on January 24, 2003 as *Secretary of Homeland Security* by President Bush. In earlier speeches, Secretary Ridge proposed to "study ways to set national standards for driver's licenses that would assist in preventing fraudulent identification and expose aliens who overstayed their visas." *The Washington Times*, May 2, 2002.

[49] America has always been an immigrant country, as the inscription at the base of the Statue of Liberty indicates: "Give me your tired, your poor, Your huddled masses yearning to breathe free, The wretched refuse of your teeming shore. Send these, the homeless, tempest-tost to me, I lift my lamp beside the golden door!" (Emma Lazarus, 1883). Since the

Immigration hardliners argue that illegal immigrants take low-skilled and skilled jobs away from Americans. Furthermore, the discussion touches national identity, e.g. whether America should keep its dominant European culture or accept cultural change. Pat Buchanan's support of the eurocenteric position during his 1996 presidential campaign, for example, resonated strongly with a portion of conservative voters. Other aspects of illegal immigration include the provision of social benefits or financial and medical support, and deportation, especially of criminals.

In 1995, the *Immigration Reform Act* was rejected, and a modified version, the *Illegal Immigration Reform and Immigrant Responsibility Act* (*IIRIRA*) was signed by President Clinton in August 1996. The bill had a broad impact on immigration control and immigrants' rights. It strictly penalized illegal immigration, including the overstay of any type of visa. The border guards were doubled to 10,000, and illegal immigrants lost many rights and social benefits. HIV-positive and criminal immigrants can be deported. INS officials were given much broader judicial authority, and worksite enforcement was strengthened.

IIRIRA had a clear effect on immigration, especially on immigrants from Central and Latin America, who were the focal point of the debate. Chinese immigration, however, was hardly affected and grew continuously. With 414,119 legal immigrants in the 1990s, and with 110,696 Chinese studying in America in 2002–2003, the Chinese Americans are continuously expanding their presence in the United States.

In 1999, the liberal Congressman Frank (D-MA) introduced the *Family Reunification Act* to soften the harsh laws of 1996, which have torn apart thousands of American families and stripped long-term legal immigrants of basic rights. The post-September 11, 2001 climate provides, however, a challenge for the bill, which was reintroduced in 2003. It would bring a strengthening of family-oriented immigration laws, adding benefits especially for Chinese Americans, who use their Confucian extended family structure as a main basis of immigration, rather than employment-based preferences.[50] With the continuous flow of immigrants into the United States, especially from China, India, and Philippines, the ethnic composition of America will continue to diversify and thus further open up discussions on immigration. Chinese Americans will be an increasingly important part of immigration.

---

seventeenth century, European and African immigrants formed the majority of American society. Since the 1960s, however, Asian and Hispanic immigrants increase the racial diversity of United States significantly towards a multicultural society.

[50] 70% of all Chinese immigrants used family-based preferences in 2000. *INS Statistical Yearbook 2000*, 2002.

Definitions

The complicated nationality definitions on which the new immigration laws are based require further analysis before any interpretation of their effects on Chinese Americans can be formed. Because a number of definitions seem to overlap, clarity can only be achieved with reference to the questionnaires of the 1980 census, when six separate response categories for Asians were introduced, e.g. Asian Indian, Chinese, Filipino, Japanese, Korean and Vietnamese.[51] It must be noted, however, that, since the questionnaires were completed by the people themselves, they contain some inconsistencies in how the people defined themselves. Thus we must take into account the imprecision in the actual figures for the different ethnic groups who fall in the Asian and Chinese categories. According to the official language, *Asia* geographically included China (without further specification), Japanese Territories as of 1860, India, Turkey, and "other Asia." Since 1952, the Philippines has also been included (Cabezas, 1989, 89). In total, twenty nations were affected by the *Asian Pacific Triangle Provision* of the 1952 *McCarran-Walter Act*. This provision was removed in 1965, thus abolishing 100 years of anti-Asian discrimination in matters of immigration. The definitions, however, largely remained in place.

The following nationalities are included in the definition of Asians, according to Him Mark Lai, president of the *Chinese Historical Society*, San Francisco:[52] Chinese, Filipinos, Japanese, Asian Indians, Koreans, Vietnamese, Laotians, Cambodians, Pakistanis, Indonesians and Hmong. The largest groups are the Chinese, Asian Indians, Filipinos, Japanese, Koreans and Vietnamese. Since 1980, in the statistics of the U.S. Census Bureau, *Asians and Pacific Islanders* (*API*) are grouped together. Since the Census 2000, however, Asians and Pacific Islanders were split again in *Asian* and *Native Hawaiian and Pacific Islanders*.[53]

---

[51] In general, terms used in the study refer to the definitions for the Census 2000. The term *Black* is used as it is preferred by a plurality of the Black population in the United States, although, since the Census 2000, the term *Black or African American* is official. However, the term *African American* is sometimes confused as it could exclude Caribbean Blacks, or include African Whites (OMB 1997a, 6.1.13). The terms *Hispanic*, *American Indian*, and *White* are the expressions preferred by a majority of these populations and were thus used in the study. See also Chapter 4 "Habitat," under "Countrywide Characteristics of Asian Communities" on definitions of race and ethnic groups by the U.S. Census.

[52] Him Marc Lai. "Chinese Americans, Who Defines Us?" *Amerasia Journal*, 1988, vii-x, and interviews 1990 to 1992.

[53] "Pacific Islanders" are Polynesian, Hawaiian, Samoan, Tongan, Micronesian, Guamanian, Melanesian and Fijian by definition since 1980. The largest group are Hawaiian, Samoan and Guamanian. "All other Pacific Islanders" include Tahitian and inhabitants of the

The undefined usage of the term Chinese causes particular problems with regard to immigration: Chinese was previously used as a nebulous racial term. Since 1943, Chinese were defined according to biological criteria, i.e. whoever was of at least 50% Chinese origin (see *Exclusion Acts*, 1943). However, since 1965, the geographic determination of the country of origin is important (U.S. Census, 1980). Within the definition of Asians, the term Chinese is used as an undifferentiated term. Therefore, despite recognition of the three separate countries, people from mainland China, Taiwan, and Hong Kong are still treated as one group (Mangiafico, 1988, 121). In general, the total number of immigrants from these three countries is counted as Chinese Americans, as well as other ethnic Chinese groups, such as the large number of Chinese Vietnamese, which immigrated especially in the 1970s.

The quota rulings for Chinese, therefore, require fuller analysis: The first quota ruling, between 1921 and 1924, applied to the Chinese as a race. After 1949, the more precise nationality terminology was applied, and after 1952 the quotas for Chinese were included within the totals and exceptions mentioned in the APT provisions. In 1952, Taiwan was initially allocated 105 visas annually; whereas all other Chinese, irrespective of origin, received a total of 100. From 1957 until 1979, Taiwan was included in the figures for China whereas Hong Kong had 1% of the English contingency (*U.S. Commission on Civil Rights*, 1988, 30). With the acknowledgement of China in 1979, the People's Republic of China, the Republic of China (Taiwan), and Hong Kong received separate quotas.

As such, this new regulation must be considered revolutionary since the People's Republic, which had been previously ignored, now received its own special quota (20,000 visas) which, however, was only the same as Taiwan.[54] The Hong Kong quota was initially increased to 500 in 1976, but, in preparation of its rejoining the People's Republic of China, it received 5,000 in 1986, so that it was no longer bound to the colonial quota.

The country quotas were increased in 1990 and since October 1, 1991, independent states are allocated 25,620 visas annually, whereas dependant territories receive 7,320 visas annually. Until 1993, the Hong Kong quota was increased to 10,000; thereafter, the dominion received the same quota as independent countries. Until 1990, therefore, 45,000 Chinese could immigrate, although each country only received a maximum quota of 20,000. The reunification of Hong Kong with mainland China was agreed upon in

---

Marshall and Turkesian Islands, which are registered as "Pacific Islanders." (OMB, 1997a, 58786)

[54] Prior to 1979, the majority of Chinese quota immigrants came from Taiwan, and this quota remains despite improvements in relations between China and Taiwan. Beginning in 1949, no legal emigration from China was possible, only the escape via Hong Kong.

1989, and finally implemented on July 1, 1997, meant a combination of the previously separate quotas. The anticipated increase and over-proportional representation of Hong Kong immigrants in the Chinese immigration figures as a result of the reunification, however, did not materialize. A further group, which should not be forgotten, are the immediate relatives of United States residents, as well as refugees who no longer fall under the 7th Preference.

Since 1980, refugees are excluded from the non-quota immigrants and treated separately. Furthermore, the quota also excludes special cases, like the tens of thousands of students, who fell under the *Chinese Student Protection Act* (*CSPA*) authorized by President Bush in 1992.[55] Until 1998, the annual quota of worldwide *Refugees and Asylees* authorized by the president has been increased to 83,000, and about 90% of this quota is regularly used.[56]

Effects of the Laws since 1965

Quota and Non-Quota Immigrants

The laws of 1965 resulted in a strong increase in Asian and Hispanic immigration, combined with a decrease in European immigration. Analysis of the data, in particular that concerning Chinese immigration supplies the following picture: In each decade since 1950, the Asian portion of immigration in the United States more than doubled.

In the 1950s, Asians represented 6%, in the 1960s 12.8%, and in the 1970s already 26.6% of the total immigration figures. By 1990, the Asian figure had grown further to 37.3%, approaching the level of Latin American immigrants of 47%. The most recent figures released in 2002 show Asians as the second largest immigrant group with 30.1% of all immigrants, compared to Latin American immigrants with 44.2% (*2000 Statistical Yearbook of the INS*, U.S. Department of Justice, 2002). Chinese immigrants represented on average 20% of all Asian immigrants, and thus were the largest Asian immigrant group.[57]

---

[55] In total, 52,826 Chinese students were admitted based on the *CSPA*. See Chapter 3.

[56] "Refugees and Asylees are persons unable or unwilling to return because of a well-founded fear to be persecuted because of race, religion, nationality, membership in a particular social group, or political opinion." *U.S. Immigration Policy.* Close Up Foundation, July 1998.

[57] Between 1820 and 2000, 8,814,852 Asians immigrated into the United States, 13.3% of all immigrants. The Chinese with 1,745,499 (19.8%) are the largest immigrant group among the Asians. The majority of the Asians immigrants arrived between 1950 and 2000, 7,702,898 people. During this period, the Chinese were the second largest immigrant group with 1,346,617 (17.5%), surpassed only by Filipinos with 1,525,379 (19.8%). Koreans and Asian Indians both accounted for 10.5% of all Asians in this period. The Chinese regained the position as the largest Asian immigrant nation in the 1990s, surpassing the high numbers of

In 1950, 117,629 Chinese were living in the United States. In 1960, this number grew by 101.7% to 237,292, and in 1970 by 86.2% to 441,853. In the 1970s, the ethnic Chinese population grew by 83.8% to 812,178; in the 1980s it grew even stronger (101.6%), so that by 1990 1,645,472 and by 2000 2,432,858 Chinese Americans were living in the United States (47.9%).

Already in 1988, Mangiafico showed that the number of Chinese immigrants quadrupled in both the 1960s and 1970s, although the total immigrant population had not even doubled during each period (Mangiafico, 1988). The massive increase in the Asian, and especially the Chinese population surprised all supporters of the regulations, since they had based their expectations on a small percentage of the total population (1%), and thus only a small increase (Reimers, 1985, 94).

They expected a development similar to that of African immigration. Lack of studies, for example, on the single Chinese sojourners or on the strong family ties were definitely major reasons for their misunderstanding of the immigration potential. Thus, the basis of few family ties between Africans and African Americans led to the belief of little family repatriation. This proved to be correct for the African American immigration, however not for some Asian groups (Morrison, 1982, 27). The potential Chinese population growth-rate was based on incorrect criteria.[58]

Official calculations had originally projected that in 1990 1,259,038 Chinese would live in the United States, 1,683,537 by 2000, and that the figure would reach 2,457,046 by 2020 (Bouvier, 1987). The current figures show how wrong the official assumptions were: In 2000, already 2,432,858 Chinese Americans lived in the United States (U.S. Bureau of the Census, 2002). The most recent prediction by the *Center for Immigration Studies* indicates that the Asian population will more than triple before 2100, e.g. grow from 4% to 13% of the American population (Kolankiewicz, 2000). Thus, about 75 million Asians and over 25 million Chinese Americans are predicted to live in the United States by 2100.

According to the Population Reference Bureau, the actual figure of 2000 should have only been reached in the year 2020. Obviously, it is important to identify how these miscalculations occurred, and why the growth-rate of the Chinese population was and remains so large, especially with regard to future development. At the same time, the effects of the laws of 1965 can be

---

Filipinos from the 1970s and 1980s. (*2000 Statistical Yearbook of the Immigration and Naturalization Service*, U.S. Departmt. of Justice, 2002, 9).

[58] For further details see: David Reimers. *Still the Golden Door. The Third World Comes to America*. New York, Columbia University Press, 1985; Thomas K. Morrison. "The Relationship of United States Aid, Trade and Investment to Migration Pressures in Major Sending Countries." (*International Migration Review* 16. 1982).

correlated in association with each special case. Initially, it must seem surprising that the number of Chinese grew from 812,178 in 1980 to 1,645,472 in 1990, and 2,432,858 in 2000, although the quota system would only have allowed an increase of a maximum of 450,000 (total of all annual quota for China, Taiwan and Hong Kong).

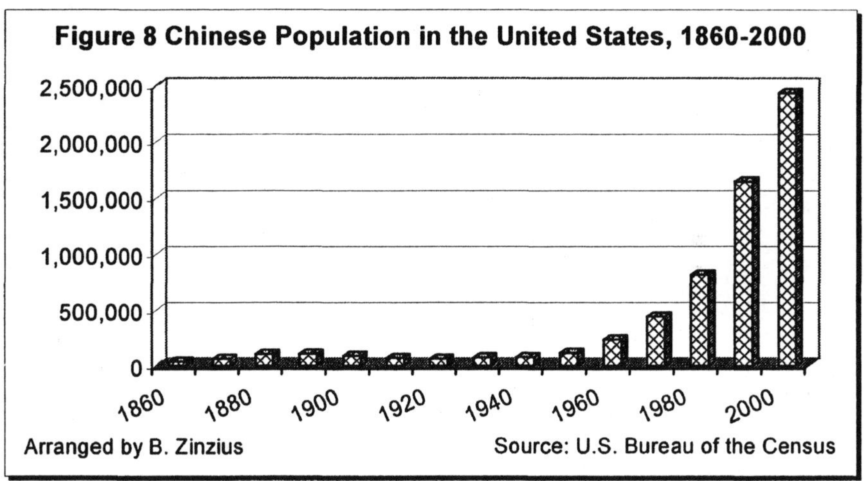

A possible explanation, as its historic development would indicate, could be a high number of immigrants under the special or non-quota immigrant regulations, especially wives. An alternative could be a high birth-rate and low death-rate.[59]

The perception that Chinese women bear many children had already become apparent in the United States during the 1920s due to the large number of *paper sons* who, however, were not real heirs. A low death-rate, along with a high birth-rate, could also be expected from a relatively young population like the Chinese.[60] Starting with the birth-rate, approximately 120,000 children would have been born during the 1980s, based on the known birth rate of 1980 (1%) and an average population of 1,200,000 for the decade (1980: 800,000; 1990 1,600,000).[61]

---

[59] The important aspect of birth-rates, which helps identify multiple child families driven to immigration by poverty, shall be covered later in the investigation of the Chinese American family. At present, only the overall birth-rate is of interest.

[60] See Chapter 7 "Family Structures."

[61] As a brief exemplary calculation, one could assume that if only those women who immigrated between 1970 and 1980 gave birth to 3,250 children per year, e.g. 32,500 per decade, this would represent already more than a quarter of the total number.

From this figure a small number of deaths must be subtracted. For persons over 65 years of age, the Asian community has a death ratio of only 5.9%, in contrast to the total United States ratio of 11.9%. The difference between births and deaths, at a death ratio of 1.15%, would result in a population growth of 70,000 (120,000 births minus 50,000 deaths). Thus, in the 1980s, approximately 65% (520,000 people) of the Chinese population growth can be explained with quota immigration and natural population growth.[62] Approximately 38.5% (280,000 of 730,000) of the immigrants would have arrived under the preferences of United States residents, *special immigrants*, *refugees* or *non-quota immigrants* in the widest sense.

Finally, the legalized illegal aliens must be added. The creation and development of the 1986 laws show that this factor should not be overlooked. This calculation is backed up by the official Visa Report[63] of 1983 wherein of 25,777 People's Republic of China immigrants, 6,651 (25.8%) were immediate relatives or special immigrants.[64]

A quota of 12% to 13% for legalization is not unrealistic with regard to the *IRCA 1986* regulations. In 1986, nearly 479,000 illegal immigrants, of which 70% were Mexicans, fell under the amnesty. Similarly, if only 5% of those receiving amnesty for the decade 1980 to 1990 were Chinese, then this figure in combination with those above would give us the total population growth for the 1980s (*San Francisco Chronicle*, January 5, 1990). Thus, legalization is considered a hidden form of non-quota immigration. Further analysis will show whether these initial results can be confirmed.

Use of the Preferential System

A preliminary initial insight concerning immigration and particularly potential Chinese population growth is offered by the tendencies related to quota immigration. Which preferences are most frequently used and what effects do they this have on non-quota immigration? According to the visa statistics of 1985, the majority of immigration fell under the family preferences system. Only a few immigrants entered under the vocational preference, which requires particular qualifications meeting the demand for particular capabilities (until 1990 only 54,000 visas annually). Of the total number of 602,000 immigrants from all countries in 1985, only 24,000 occurred under the vocational preference, i.e. 4% (U.S. Department of Justice, *1985 Statistical Yearbook of the INS*).

---

[62] For the basic assumptions see: Statistic of the *1980 Census of the Population*. U.S. Census Bureau, U.S. Summary. Washington, DC: Government Printing Office, 1981.

[63] *Visa Office of the United States Department*, unpublished report, Feb. 1985. Mangiafico, 1988, 123.

[64] In 1983, 42,475 Chinese immigrated. U.S. Bureau of the Census.

The immigration data for 1985 clearly shows that next to the 90,000 applications under family preference, only approximately 3,000 for vocational preference were put forward. The absolute majority of Chinese immigrants fell under the 5th Preference, i.e. immigrants entering as siblings of United States residents and/or as their spouses or children.

The latter has had a strong effect on the processing time. In 1985, only those applications from Chinese from the People's Republic falling under the 5th Preference category prior to February 8, 1979, were processed. For Hong Kong only those prior to June 23, 1973, and for Taiwan only those prior to March 22, 1981 were processed. Only applications from People's Republic of China and Taiwan falling under the 1st Preference (single sons and daughters) and the 4th Preference (single and married sons and daughters over the age of 21) were processed immediately. All other applications have lead times of one to seven years. The new regulations of 1990, however, relieve the 2nd Preference, since 50% of unused quota of the 1st Preference are added.[65]

The data, up to the present, clearly indicates that family reunification plays the most important role for the Chinese. It is, therefore, fair to assume that this is also the case in the non-quota area, although the subsequent immigration of immediate heirs seems to be of secondary importance, since the quota for these seems sufficient. Contrary to Europeans, Chinese seem to have siblings, and subsequently the whole family, follow of the first immigrant. This is documented in the strong interest in the 5th Preference and will be analyzed in the following section.

Nationality and permanent residence status play an important role in the opportunity to have the whole family immigrate. The next question thus becomes, how long on average do Chinese remain in the United States, how many are United States citizens, and how many intend to become citizens? The answers will demonstrate the importance of family repatriation in the future. United States citizens can have immediate relatives immigrate under the non-quota regulations.[66]

---

[65] *CRS Report for Congress*. "Immigration Legislation – Questions and Answers." Joyce C. Vialet. Specialist in Immigration Policy, Education and Public Welfare Division. June 4, 1991, 4. **Table 4 Chinese Immigration by Ethnicity and Preferential Class, 2000.**

	China		Hong Kong		Taiwan	
Family sponsored	11,332	27.1%	4,521	62.8%	4,443	46.9%
Employment based	12,350	29.5%	889	12.4%	2,603	27.5%
Immediate relative	17,688	42.2%	1,558	25.6%	2,399	25.3%
Total	41,861	100%	7,199	100%	9,478	100%

Arranged by B. Zinzius   U.S. Department of Justice, *INS Statistical Yearbook 2000*. 2002.

[66] Parents of U.S. citizens, spouses and minor children, see Chapter 3 "Immigration and National Amendments Acts."

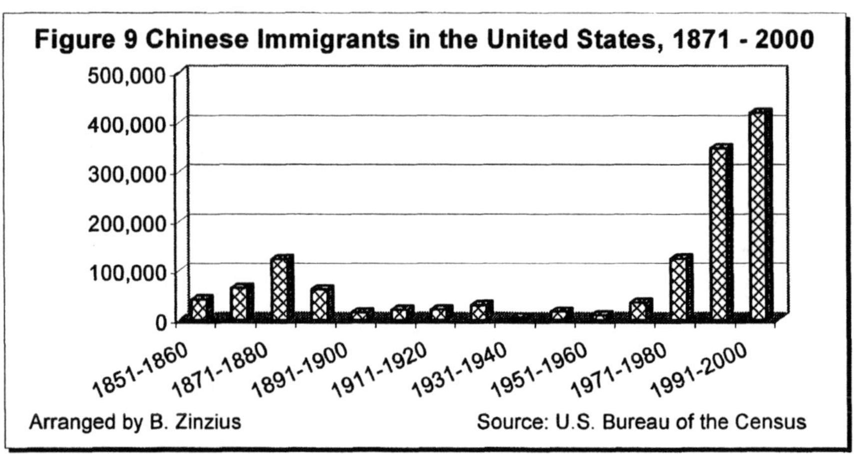

Since 1990, at least some of these non-quota immigrants are included in the cap for total immigration figures.[67] United States citizens can use the 1st, 4th and 5th Preferences, as can resident aliens who have transferred their status to that of permanent residents after five years of continuous residency. This group can then also use the 2nd Preference to have spouses and single children follow.[68]

Of the Chinese Americans in the United States in 1980, 54.8% were foreign-born from China, Taiwan and Hong Kong. 6.6% had been in the United States twenty years or longer, 50.3% of the mainland Chinese had been naturalized (1964: 76.8%), 28.9% of the Taiwanese (1964: 90%) and of the Hong Kong Chinese 38.3% (1964: 76.6%). Thus, in 1965, the mainland Chinese were the most stable group with the lowest subsequent foreign contingency. The high level of foreign-born within the total group, however, makes the family preference into a continuous problem.[69] Irrespective of the small portion of United States citizens and permanent residents within the total group, their preferential quotas have always been completely filled.

Whereas the increases were apparent for the mainland Chinese in the first half of the 1980s, subsequent to the opening in 1979, a similar development occurred during the second half of the decade for the Taiwanese

---

[67] U.S. Bureau of the Census, "Foreign-Born Chinese Immigrants. Tabulations from the 1980 Census of the Population and Housing," mimeographed report, Washington, DC: Oct. 1984. See also under Chapter 3 "Immigration Act of 1990 (IA)."

[68] See under Chapter 3 "Law from 1986 (*IRCA* 1986)."

[69] Of the total group of Chinese in 1980, 64.8% came from the People's Republic, 17% from Taiwan and 18.2% from Hong Kong (Mangiafico, 1988, 124). 25% of the mainland Chinese stayed already longer than 25 years in the United States, over 50% came in the 1970s. Out of the Taiwanese, less than 2% came prior to 1960, but 80% in the 1970s. More than two-thirds of the Hong Kong Chinese arrived in the 1970s.

who had had a relatively minor portion of United States citizens in 1980. After five years of permanent resident status, citizenship can be obtained.

In 1983, 6,257 Chinese living in the United States changed their status to that of permanent residents, thus receiving unlimited residency, which, when calculated for the decade 1980 to 1990, would mean a total of approximately 60,000 new permanent residents. The *IA 1990* allows limited non-quota immigration for permanent residents.[70] Hence, the United States citizenship ratio within the group remains relatively low, while new immigration is increasing. With the increase in citizenship during the 1980s, the non-quota, family-based immigration will also continue to increase.

This race for the quotas, which is particularly beneficial for United States citizens, is definitely increasing rather than decreasing. This situation is putting pressure on legislature, as the discussions regarding the 1990 regulations have shown. The non-relative, non-quota immigration is also high. Sucheng Chan estimates that since 1965 at least as many non-quota as quota immigrants have arrived, namely two million in each category. Since 1975, many hundreds of thousands of refugees of Chinese descent from Laos, Cambodia and Vietnam have found their way to the United States. Furthermore, approximately 800,000 students, tourists, and non-immigrants from China, Taiwan, and Hong Kong have obtained permanent resident status. If one adds the subsequently legalized aliens, it is clear why the quota for family repatriation were never sufficient for the Chinese.[71]

The quota and preferential systems are thus losing their importance. According to McKee in 1981, more than 50% of all immigrants did not fall under these regulations (McKee, 1985, 26). Between 1978 (*Indochina Refugee Act* 1978) and 1986 (first new regulations after 1965), however, there must have been a large portion of non-quota immigrants. In 1976, 24.3% of 597.289 immigrants did not fall under the quota regulations; in 1978, already 41.7% of a total of 625,442 did not. In 1981, 31.2% were refugees and 21.7% were other non-quota immigrants out of a total of 697,000.

From 1980 until 1990, quota immigration was capped at 270,000 annually; however, the total immigration figures stood between 500,000 and 600,000 annually. The figures for Chinese emigrants are equally split between 1981 and 1988, with 295,000 from Taiwan and mainland China and 43,900 from Hong Kong (U.S. Department of Justice, Immigration and Naturalization Service, *Statistical Yearbook, 1991*). Their strong family

---

[70] See under Chapter 3 "Immigration Act of 1990 (IA)."

[71] See Sucheng Chan. *Asian Americans: An Interpretive History*. Boston, Twayne Publishers, 1991. See also in *1979 Statistical Yearbook of the INS*. In Humanity on the Move by Jesse O. McKee, U.S. Department, U.S. Immigration Policy, 1981.

bonds, as well as their over-proportional presence let them appear as *special immigrants*.

The strong increase in population (1980 to 1990: 127%; 1990 to 2000 47.8%) within the Chinese group has mainly occurred due to the filling of immigration quotas and strong non-quota immigration and, only to a small extent, due to natural population growth.[72] Of 750,000 immigrants, 280,000 were non-quota immigrants. Quota immigration and natural population growth represent 65% of the increase in Chinese American population. Non-quota immigration and the legalization of illegal aliens, therefore, made up approximately 38.5% of the total figure for 1980 until 1990—as previously calculated—is therefore analytically and comparatively proven.

Chain Migration

What led to the increase in new immigration among the Chinese? If Chinese relatives exceptionally often follow an immigrant, then one must look at those who are either have resided the longest in the United States or who were separated the longest from their families. Did the supposed bachelors have their wives follow between 1965 and 1968, and thus start an avalanche?

This is probable. The Chinese population doubled for the first time between 1970 and 1980, after their immediate relatives and spouses were permitted to follow without giving a specific reason. At the same time, the ratio of the sexes improved significantly in favor of women.[73] This proves that a large potential group of non-quota immigrants—wives of United States citizens—existed. Non-quota immigration has not been only a side-effect of regular quota immigration, but has actually initiated it.

Chinese students played an increasingly important role in stimulating this chain reaction, as proved by the countless family histories over the last 25 years, which tell a consistent story of family repatriation within the Chinese American population. In an interview, the editor of the minority paper *East West* explained, "My brother-in-law left his wife back in Taiwan when he came here as a student to complete his PhD in Engineering. After completing his studies, he was offered a job in San Jose. Initially, a sister and his wife followed who subsequently had one of our brothers and me follow." (Interview with Simon Lee, September 18, 1992).

In the 1960s, a large number of students who intended to complete their studies followed the stranded students of the 1950s. The American system supported the integration of foreigners holding American degrees.

---

[72] See also Chapter 7 "Family Structures," under "Mixed Marriages."
[73] See also Chapter 7 "Family Structures," under "The Change in the Ratio of Sexes."

In 1980, already 50% of the 300,000 foreign students in the United States were from China and other Asian nations.[74]

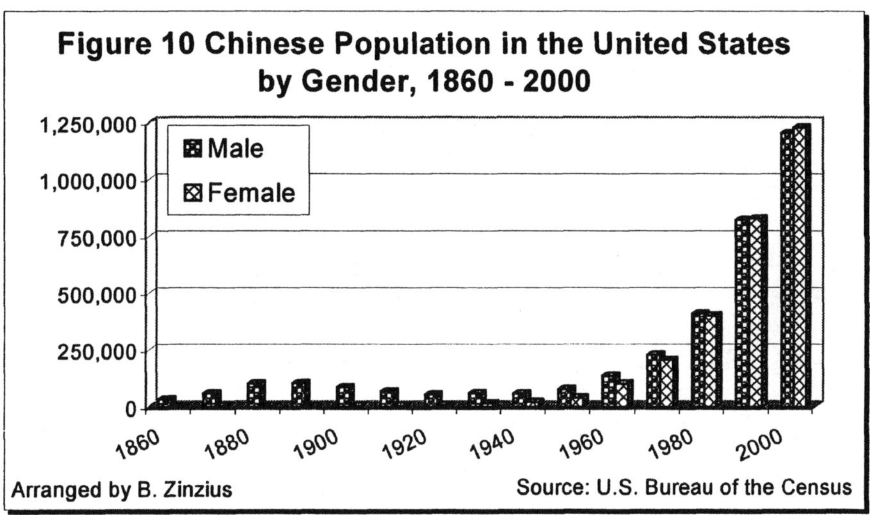

Figure 10 Chinese Population in the United States by Gender, 1860 - 2000

Arranged by B. Zinzius   Source: U.S. Bureau of the Census

Thousands of students have been able to find jobs after completing their studies, thereby fulfilling the requirements for academics according to the vocational preferences. As resident aliens they can start the family repatriation process. After five years of continuous residency, they can then obtain American citizenship and invite other relatives to immigrate under the quota and non-quota regulations. Once brother and sister have immigrated, this system can be perpetuated by their spouses immigrating. Reimers has termed this phenomenon *chain migration*.

Even without the snowball effect, from a purely numerical view, student immigration has grown in importance. According to a report by the International Institute of Education, Taiwan and mainland China hold first and second slots in the contingency of foreign students in United States. In 1987, 67,000 students from China, Taiwan, and Hong Kong, were matriculated at American colleges and universities, whereas, in 1955, only 10,000 from all Asian nations were matriculated. In 2003, the number of Chinese students, including those from Taiwan and Hong Kong, had reached 110,696. In 2004, the number had fallen to 95,296 students, but Chinese remained the largest ethnic group of students in the United States.[75]

---

[74] See also Chapter 6 "Education," under "The Influx of Chinese Intelligence—*Brain Drain.*"
[75] See also *Open Doors Report*, 2003 and 2004.

In addition to this steady growth of Chinese immigrant students, the *Chinese Student Protection Act* endorsed by President George H.W. Bush in 1992 triggered a further immigration wave. Subsequent to the Tiananmen Square Massacre, Congresswoman Nancy Pelosi (D-CA) in proposing new conditions for the preference clauses for mainland China, stated: "The aging despots who had students run over by tanks belong to the past, the students who protested at Tiananmen, to Chinas future" (Interview, 1990).

The Act was strongly supported by a sophisticated campaign of the *Independent Federation of Chinese Students and Scholars (IFCSS)* and granted automatic green cards to 60,000 Chinese students. Opponents of the Act, including Sidney Jones, then Executive Director of *Asian Watch/Human Rights Watch*, criticized the law as unnecessary because only few students needed real asylum, and they could have used regular asylum channels as well.[76]

In addition to all these immigrant categories, adoption as an additional cause of Chinese immigration is increasing in significance. Between 1990 and 2002, more than 30,000 Chinese children were adopted by United States citizens, the majority of them girls (Donaldson, 2003). In China, girls are often given to orphanages as a consequence of China's male-oriented one-child policy.

In 2000, 5,716 children under five years old immigrated from China into the United States, 593 boys and 5,123 girls, confirming this fact (U.S. Department of Justice, *Statistical Yearbook of the Immigration and Naturalization Service*, 2000). This trend is further increasing, 6,638 orphan children immigrated in 2003 from China, 95% thereof girls (Homeland Security, 2003 Yearbook of Immigration Statistics, Sept. 2004, table 10).

Changes in the Situation in the Countries of Origin

Economic, political, and social factors were the historic causes for Chinese emigration, and they will continue to be its major source in the future. Socio-economic aspects in the countries of origin must, therefore, be analyzed in detail to understand current and future trends of Chinese immigration into, and emigration from, the United States.

---

[76] Norman Matloff, Professor at the University of California, Davis, is a specialist on immigration issues and questions recent immigration policies. For further information see his article under: "Family reunification—Just a Passport to Jobs." *Los Angeles Times*, July 10, 1995.

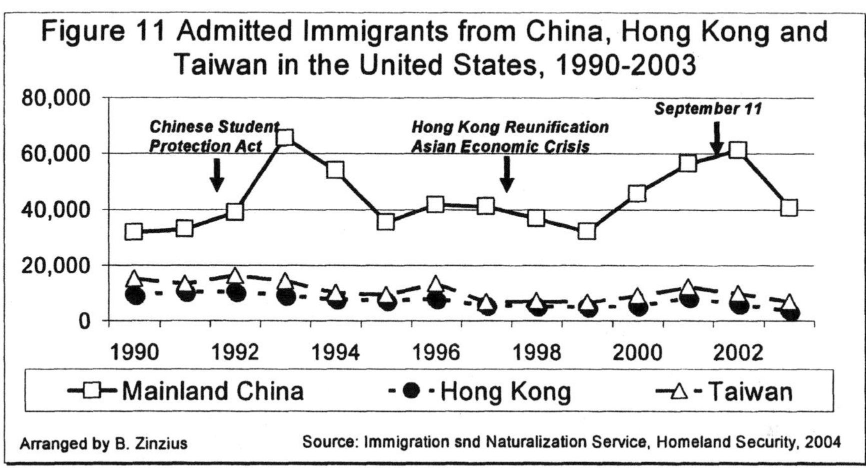

The historical, political, economical, and social conditions in the three Chinese territories differ significantly. The reunification of Hong Kong with mainland China on July 1, 1997, the economical and political changes between Taiwan and China, and the booming economy of the last few decades in all three territories have changed the local situations considerably.[77]

The most recent immigrants figures from mainland China to the United States show continuous growth after the Asian economic crisis. A decline in immigration can only be seen in the much smaller numbers from Hong Kong—despite, or even because, the return to mainland China—and from Taiwan. At the same time, an increasing return of overseas Chinese to mainland China can be seen. These figures will be analyzed in the context of the actual political, social, and economic situation in all three territories.

People's Republic of China: Market Economy without Democracy

The Chinese people suffered under the conflicts between the revolutionaries known as the "Gang of Four," led by Mao's last wife, Jiang Qing, and the moderates following Zhou Enlai who wanted Western-style modernization.

---

[77] **Table 5 GDP data in Purchasing Power Parity for Selected Countries, 1952, 1978, and 2002.**

US$	1952		1978		2002	
	GDP (bio)	GDP per capita	GDP (bio)	GDP per capita	GDP (bio)	GDP per capita
China	305	537	935	979	5,700	4,400
Hong Kong	5	2,377	94	9,277	186	26,000
Taiwan	9	1,063	43	5,542	406	18,000
USA	1,625	10,316	4,089	18,373	10,400	37,008

Arranged by B. Zinzius   Source: OECD, governmental data.

See also Chapter 6 "From *Brain Drain* to *Brain Gain*-Returning to the Homeland."

During this ten-year period following the mid-1960s, the wheels of progress stopped in China. The country fell technologically, scientifically, and militarily behind in comparison to the United States, Japan, and the USSR. When Mao Zedong died on September 9, 1976, the power of the "Gang of Four" was crushed in the center and the provinces. The battle between Maoists and revolutionaries, which had been raging for a decade, developed into civil war.

The "Four Modernizations" program in agriculture, industry, national defense, and science and technology, was supposed to help China grow into a new world power. The course of the Third Plenary Meeting of the XI Central Committee (CC) and the *Communist Party of China* (*CPC*) in December 1978 claimed this to be the "major task of the current epoch." Economic growth was considered the major priority, and class frictions were thought to have ended.[78] After cleaning out the Maoist supporters at the XII CC in 1982, the XIII CC of 1987 finally brought further strengthening of personnel for the market-oriented reformers, strongly encouraged by Deng Xiaoping's slogan "to get rich is glorious."[79]

The long-term, continuous political change in China, which encourages entrepreneurial activities, provides a more stable basis for the much-needed economic and social restructuring of the country. Jiang Zemin's political doctrine, the *Three Represents*, aims to "represent the fundamental interest of the greatest majority of the people."[80]

---

[78] The People's Republic of China covers a total area of 9.56 million square kilometers with 1.272 billion inhabitants. In 2002, real GDP was $1,116 billion (+7.5%), per-capita GDP was $878, and the GNI per capita at purchasing power parity was $4,260. Major export products are garments, shoes, plastic products, toys, and sporting goods; major import items are primary plastic, steel, crude oil, machinery, and paper. The official unemployment figure in 2002 was 3.6%, unofficial figures claim over 10%. The capital is Beijing. 92% are Han-Chinese, 8% are minorities, comprised of 15.5 million Zhuang, 9.8 million Manchu, 8.6 million Zhui, 7.2 million Uiguri, 6.5 million Yi, 6 million Miao, 4.8 million Mongolian, 4.6 million Tibetan, 2.5 million Buyi, 2 million Korean, and 1.5 million Hakka. Mandarin (*putonghua*, the Beijing dialect) is the official state language, Cantonese is the major language in the south, in addition to many dialects and the languages of the minorities. The school attendance rate is 73%, average living expectancy is 70 years, urbanization is 24%. Segal, *Asian Wall Street Journal*, October 28, 2002, R1-R12; Asian Pacific Market Handbook, Synovate, 2003; Zinzius 1999a.

[79] Deng voiced his famous phrase in 1982 (Zinzius, 1999a).

[80] The *Three Represents* theory was delivered during Jiang Zemin's inspection tour of Guangdong Province in early 2000. He pointed out: "The key to handling Chinas matters well lies within our Party. As long as our party unswervingly represents the development trend of advanced productive forces, the orientation of advanced culture and the fundamental interests of the overwhelming majority of the people in China, it can remain invincible, win wholehearted support of the people of all ethnic groups and lead the people to make progress steadily." (Jiang Zemin, 2000).

In 2002, private entrepreneurs were elected to the Central Committee, including Zhang Ruimin, president of *Haier*, one of the world's largest electric appliance maker, and Ms. Wu Yi, the former Chinese trade minister, as the first women ever to serve in the Central Committee. These political changes prove that, although, the Party's structure is still Marxist-Leninist, it embraces the market economy much more strongly and, thus, paves the way for further economic growth. The highly visible accession to the WTO on September 17, 2001, is a further event that has changed China significantly. It brought immense market opportunities and growth for China's well-established industries in the coastal regions, but also massive economic dislocation for the uncompetitive state-owned enterprises and the outdated agricultural sector ("rust belt"), which still employs over 60% of all Chinese. With the unavoidable shutdown of uncompetitive and unprofitable state-owned enterprises, unemployment is a major source of unrest and eventually a trigger for emigration. On the other hand, the strong economic growth of the last twenty years, fuelled by the largest *foreign direct investment* in the world (over US$52 billion in 2002), will be a major driver of employment, growth, and the modernization of China's economy, providing a more stable domestic environment and social structure.

It is very likely that China's economic growth will continue, acting as a engine for political and social change. The growing number of American companies that are investing in China, the increasing number of Chinese companies that are setting up operations in the United States, and international events, such as the Olympic Games in 2008, and the World Expo in 2010, are strong indicators for China's growth and globalization.[81]

Since the 1950s, almost one million people from China, Hong Kong, and Taiwan have studied abroad since the 1950s, many thereof in the United States. China's globalization will generate further needs and desires to study, work, and live abroad. At the same time, the Chinese government encourages overseas Chinese to return to China and participate in the economic boom.[82]

---

[81] *Haier* is the number one producer of refrigerators in the United States, having surpassed General Electric in several categories. Haier manufactures electric appliances in its American subsidiaries for companies such as *Office Depot*, *Target*, or "Kitchen Chef" for *Wall Mart* (Yi. *The Haier Way*, 2002, 223–4).

[82] Since the end of the 1990s, many overseas Chinese, including Taiwanese and Hong Kong Chinese, have returned to mainland China. Their return, temporary or permanent, is fuelled by the booming economy. It is estimated that about 13,000 mainland students return annually, and the number of returning long-term overseas Chinese is even higher. In 2003, the Chinese government introduced a new permanent resident permit ("green card" system) to attract skilled overseas Chinese. These skilled professionals can maintain their residence status elsewhere, a service that targets especially Hong Kong and Taiwan citizen. See also chapter 6, "From Brain Drain to Brain Gain-Returning to the Homeland," and Chapter 8 "The New Global Entrepreneurs."

Taiwan: Democracy without Freedom

Due to the lost battle at Shimonoseki in 1895, Taiwan was ceded to Japan. The Japanese colonial masters used the agriculture and industry to their own benefit and neglected the interests of the inhabitants.[83] The Chinese population was discriminated against in both work and public life. During World War II, Taiwan was Japan's most important base for the Southeast Asian conflict. After the Japanese capitulation in 1945, China took back the island as a province (*Cairo Edict*, 1943, and *Potsdam Agreement*, 1945).

A positive result of fifty years of Japanese occupation was the development of the education system and the island's infrastructure. In 1949, the *Kuomintang* government under Chiang Kai-shek (Jiang Jieshie, Tschiang Kai-shek) lost the Chinese mainland to the Chinese communists during the civil war and fled to the island. Approximately two million Chinese, among them the elite technocrats and their capital, left the mainland for Taiwan. Under the elite officers of Chiang Kai-shek and with strong financial support from the United States, a new country sui generis was created, which guaranteed its existence with economic success. Major factors were the hands-on development projects of companies from Shanghai and Southern China and a successful agricultural reform.

There was substantial political change in Taiwan during the 1990s, which has influenced the Chinese-Taiwanese relations. The second presidential election in Taiwan brought a narrow victory for President Chen

---

[83] Taiwan comprises an area of 36,000 square kilometers and has 22.5 million inhabitants. The main ethnic group are Han-Chinese (98%), the remaining 2% are indigenous people from eleven aboriginal tribes, and 60 other minorities from the mainland. In 2002, real GNP was $286 billion (+3.5%), per-capita GNP was $12,876. Major export products are electronic, information and communication products; major import products are electronic products, machinery and chemicals. The official unemployment figure in 2002 was 5.3%. The capital is Taipei, and, since the arrival of the *Kuomintang*, the official language is Mandarin (*guoyu*), trading language is English. Southern Fujianese—a subdialect of Xiamen, often called Taiwanese—is natively spoken by 70%, less than 20% speak Hakka. The school attendance rate is 99.9%, and life expectancy is 76.8 years. Urbanization is 74%. Historic background: the history of Taiwan was formed by various influences of different cultures, especially related to its geographical position between the East-Asian mainland, the Malay-Polynesia and Japan. Already in the seventeenth century, Chinese and European colonialists arrived. Portuguese shippers named the Island Ilha Formosa (beautiful island), by which it was mainly known in the western world. Under the rule of the East-Indian Company (1624–1661), the Netherlands established Taiwan as their major trade center in East Asia. Although they could not prevent Chinese immigration, they could force them to plant sugar cane and were able to implement per-capita taxes. The Qing-Dynasty conquered the island in 1683 and later made it a Chinese province (1886). Taiwanese Government Information Office, July 2000; Segal, 2002; Li Li, 2002; Asian Pacific Market Handbook, Synovate, 2003; Zinzius 1999a.

Shui-bian, the candidate of the opposition party *DPP* in March 18, 2000. His victory ended five decades of rule by the conservative *Kuomintang* and toppled its last President Lee Teng-hui.

President Chen was reelected in March 2004 amid controversy over an assassination attempt and his strict opposition against China's "one country" concept. Although the *DPP* aims for a separate nationality, it also opened the way for a subtle, more pragmatic policy towards the mainland, which becomes increasingly visible. This ambivalence can be seen in the official policy towards mainland China. Various new laws and regulations increase the cross-Straits cooperation and open relations between the two countries, while political statements and the push for a new constitution increase tensions considerably.[84] It remains to be seen whether Deng Xiaoping's "one country–two system" concept will be a suitable model for Taiwan, or if the Taiwanese will reject it. The Taiwanese question is, however, of paramount importance for the development of China in the twenty-first century.

Economically, Taiwan is possibly the most dynamic and multi-structured member of the four small dragons (Hong Kong, Singapore, South Korea and Taiwan), ranking number twenty in terms of GDP in the world. The cooperation between Taiwan and China looks strongly focused toward a mutual future: In 2002, 40.2% of Taiwan's economic activity was in bilateral trade with its Asian neighbors—most of it with mainland China; 19% with the United States.

Many Taiwanese companies seek cheap labor and market potential in the mainland, setting precedents that narrow the political gap between both systems. World-leading Taiwanese semiconductor companies, such as Taiwan Semiconductor Manufacturing (TSM) and United Microelectronics Corporation (UMC), have invested heavily in China. Lite-On Technology, which supplies companies like Dell and Hewlett Packard, employs 3,000 workers in their Taiwanese headquarters, and 300,000 in their 18 mainland factories. In 2003, 50,000 Taiwanese companies produce already in China, and more than 300,000 Taiwanese work the mainland; Taiwanese companies account for more than 60% of the mainland's information technology exports. For China's future as an economic superpower, a recent headline in Asian Week prophesies: "The United States of China. How Business is moving Taipei and Beijing together" (Chen, Allen, 2001).

---

[84] "Chen Declares Taiwan Will Walk 'Own Road'." *Asian Wall Street Journal*, October 7, 2003, A1, A6.

Chinese companies are matching their Taiwanese counterparts and invest significantly in Taiwan. The famous Tsingtao brewery, China's largest beer maker, which is partly owned by Anheuser-Bush, plans to build a brewery in Taiwan.[85] *Haier,* the largest Chinese appliance maker, is forming a strategic alliance with Sampo to increase its Taiwanese presence (Yi, 2003, 196-7). The increasing economic links between China and Taiwan are paving the road for a closer political cooperation in the next decades.

Much of this economic development and technology transfer is based on Taiwan's cooperation with the United States, including more than one hundred thousand students since 1950.[86] The need for well-educated staff to run the Taiwanese high-tech companies, including their Chinese entities, will continue to stimulate Taiwanese immigration to and return from the United States.

Hong Kong: Freedom without Democracy

Since the nineteenth century, Hong Kong has been the center of friction between competing British and Chinese powers.[87] Its position as a deep sea, typhoon-protected port, a trading post and transshipping point, were vital for its foundation as a crown colony, in 1842. At the beginning of the nineteenth century, Hong Kong had already been used for opium transshipments. After the first Opium War, 1840–1842, China ceded Hong Kong Island to Great Britain "forever" (*Treaty of Nanking,* 1842).[88]

---

[85] Anheuser-Bush plans to increase its stake in Tsingtao from 9.9% to 27% until 2010. Lee, Jane L. "Investors in Chinese Brewers May Find Patience Pays Off." *Asian Wall Street Journal,* August 8-10, 2003, M1.

[86] Immigrant and population figures for Taiwanese Americans, or people with Taiwanese ancestors, are included under China. In 1990, 73,778 Taiwanese immigrants were living in the United States. Until 2000, this number had grown to 118,048 (*Taiwanese alone*), respectively 144,795 (*Taiwanese alone or in combination with one or more races*).

[87] The former crown colony Hong Kong comprises an area of 1,070 square kilometers and has 6.72 million inhabitants, mainly Chinese. In 2002, the real GDP was $166 billion (+1.5%), per-capita GDP was $24,187, GNI per capita at purchasing power parity was $26,050. The official unemployment figure was 7.6%. Major trade products are electrical machinery, apparel and clothing accessories, telecom equipment and office machines. 1% of the population is European, and 0.8% of other Asian nationalities. The local language is Cantonese, and official and trading language is English. The school attendance rate is 94%, and the life expectancy 78.8 years. The urbanization is 93%. 68% of the total GDP is produced by the service sector, 31% by industry and mining area, and 1% by agriculture. The territory comprises the island Hong Kong itself ("scenting harbor"), the peninsula Kowloon ("nine dragons") and the "new territories", which reach far into the mainland; Segal, *Asian Wall Street Journal* October 28, 2002, R1-R12; Li Li, 2002; Asian Pacific Market Handbook, Synovate, 2003; Zinzius 1999a.

[88] See Chapter 1 "Chinese Immigration to California 1848 until 1924."

In 1860, Great Britain incorporated peninsular Kowloon, which was formerly agreed to in the *Peking Convention* in the same year. After the loss of the war against Japan in 1898, Great Britain secured the New Territories for 99 years (approximately nine-tenth of the crown colony as it was known until 1997). In 1938, the Japanese occupied the northern part of Hong Kong and then in 1941 the island. The Japanese occupation lasted until 1945. Great Britain then took back the Colony. Recommendations from the United States to hand back Hong Kong to China at that time were vehemently rejected. In the nineteenth century, the expanding British colonial power confronted a domestically weak China. This status quo only changed during the twentieth century.

After 1949, China made it clear that the previously unequal agreements were no longer acceptable. After lengthy, intense negotiations, Great Britain and China signed an agreement on December 19, 1984, whereby the whole territory was returned to China on July 1, 1997. Many Chinese throughout the world view the British occupation as a humiliation, and the return in 1997 as the end of 150 years of colonial occupation. The Western view, however, often portrays the handover as a human rights disaster: "a prosperous free city [...] being thrown over to the Chinese wolf." (Wang, Ling-chi, 1997) Although Hong Kong has become one of the worlds most prosperous nations during the British occupation, democratic structures had never been fully developed. After the handover, western politicians nevertheless demand the full democratization of Hong Kong more than ever before. The Chairman of the Asia-Pacific Subcommittee of the U.S. Senate stated in 2004 "The U.S. government has an historical and vested interest in the development of democracy in Hong Kong." (Senator Brownback, 2004)

Even with its traditionally undemocratic structure, Hong Kong has remained relatively politically stable. Prior to World War II, it was usually just a temporary destination for most of its population. Since 1945, however, a feeling of connectedness and an interest in political activity has developed among Hong Kong Chinese. China has promised to maintain Hong Kong as a Special Zone (*Hong Kong Special Administrative Region—HKSAR*) after the handover in 1997, with immediate representation under the People's Government in Beijing. It will maintain with its own constitution, economic, and social structure for a further fifty years, a setup called "one country—two systems."

During the first few years of the HKSAR, the "one country-two systems" approach functioned well, maintaining a delicate balance in a political triangle of a colonial governed (yet entrepreneurial and free) past, a central and socialist supervised (yet market-oriented) present, and an increasingly democratic and pluralistic future during a time of rapid globalization. There are frequent political tensions between democracy movements and the administration selected by Beijing (Pottinger, 2003, A1, A5). Many examples, however, demonstrate the pluralistic status of Hong Kong, such as the continued legal presence of *Falun Gong*, organizations like the *Center for Human Rights in China*, the critical opinions of publications at newsstands, and the effective and uncorrupt civil service. This is in line with the aspiration of the Chief Executive, Tung Chee-hwa, to develop Hong Kong into the "most globalized city in Asia." The then-U.S. Consul General for Hong Kong, Michael Klosson, formulated Hong Kong's status during a luncheon of the American Chamber of Commerce on June 6, 2002 as follows:

> "Above all, Hong Kong in its new status remains a work in progress. These remain early days for a novel arrangement that provides Hong Kong's way of life to remain unchanged for fifty years. ... Hong Kong has been a stimulus for the mainland's dramatic transformation. As a window on China's potential future, (China's richest city) Hong Kong shows a way forward toward prosperity, tolerance, the rule of law and corruption-free dealings." (Klosson, 2002)

Hong Kong's future democratic, legal, and economic development is an important milestone for China as an example for a possible reunification of Taiwan. Current trade relations between the three territories show already today the strong economic interaction.

Since the 1970s, many Hong Kong Chinese went to the United States for studies or employment. Since the reunification in 1997, not only the ties between Hong Kong and China have become closer. Hong Kong is the largest investor in mainland China with over \$215 billion, representing 48% of all foreign direct investment. Overseas Chinese are increasing their investment activities in China, often using Hong Kong as a base, including Richard Li, son of Li Kashing, Asia's richest tycoon, who also studied in the United States. Charles Zhang, the founder of *Sohu.com*, is another example: he studied at the Massachusetts Institute of Technology in Boston and was able to attract investments from *Intel* and *Dow Jones* for his company *Sohu.com*, one of China's largest Internet search engines.[89] Technical and management capacities are required for these new investments–often in the high-tech sector, a gap that is increasingly filled by Chinese Americans that return to China; they are thus an important link in the Pacific Rim trade.

---

[89] California, and San Francisco in particular, were especially favored destinations of Hong Kong Chinese during the 1980s and 1990s. Investors from Hong Kong prefer San Francisco due to the similar starting situation. In San Francisco, property prices are relatively low in comparison to Taipei, Singapore, Tokyo, and Seoul—the other important trading centers of the Pacific Rim. At the beginning of the 1990s, economic growth remained greater in Korea and Taiwan than the United States, but the general political situation and greater social stability have given the advantage to San Francisco. Smaller businesses and two to four apartment properties are preferred by medium-sized investors from Hong Kong. Confirming

Organizations such as the *Silicon Valley Chinese Wireless Association* (SVC Wireless), or the *New England Chinese Information and Network Association* (*NECINA*), promote exchange and cooperation in the Pacific Rim, especially with China. The close economic cooperation between mainland China, Hong Kong, and Taiwan is therefore an important stimulus of Chinese emigration to, and return from the United States and other countries; these returnees are also very important for the Chinese economy.

In the first chapters, we have established a statistical background and reasons for Chinese emigration to the United States, including the conditions in their homeland. How are the conditions of these Chinese immigrants in the United States, especially their socio-economic environment? Where do the Chinese live, how are their social standards, and to which extend are they integrated in the American society? Are the Chinese Americans assimilated, or rather excluded? These are some of the questions that will be answered in the next chapter.

---

the strong demand for property by immigrants in San Francisco, George Devine, an independent real estate agent, explained that his clients were more asking him to find real estate that was not only to be considered as an investment, but to have future function as living space for the investor (Interview with G. Devine, 1992).

Table 6   Federal Anti-Chinese Legislation in the United States

1790   *Naturalization Rule Adopted*: Two year residency to become citizen
1844   *Wang-Hea Treaty*: Peace, amity and trade agreement with China
1858   *Sino-American Treaty of Tientsin*: Revision of the *Wang-Hea Treaty*
1868   *Burlingame Treaty*: Guaranteed religious and educational freedom
1879   *Congressional Act:* Limited the number of Chinese on one ship
1882   *Chinese Exclusion Act*: Suspended immigration of Chinese laborers
1886   *14th Amendment of the Constitution*: Protection of basic civil rights
1888   *Scott Act*: Prohibited Chinese re-entry after temporary departure
1889   *Act of July 7*: Chinese were prohibited from entering Hawaii
1892   *Geary Act*: Prohibited Chinese entry, excluded bail and habeas corpus
1894   *Gresham-Yang Treaty*: Repeal of *Scott's Act*, allowing re-entry
1898   *Supreme Court*: Full constitutional rights for Chinese Americans
1902   *Chinese Exclusion Act*: Extended and widened to all States
1906   *Anti-Miscegenation Law*: Prohibited Chinese from marrying non-Chinese
1913   *Dillingham Bill (Alien Land Act)*: Prohibited foreign land ownership
1917   *Immigration Act*: Introduction of the *Asia Barred Zone*
1921   *National Origins Quota Act*: Prepared the *Second Exclusion Act*
1924   *National Origins Act (2nd Exclusion Act)*: Excluded naturalization
1943   *Magnusson Bill*: Repeal of *Exclusion Acts* of 1882 and 1924
1945   *Alien Fiancée Act (War Brides Act)*: Non-quota for Chinese wives
1948   *Displaced Person Act*: Allowed 205,000 Europeans into the U.S.
1950   *Chinese Area Aid Act*: *Displaced Person Act* expanded to the PRC
1952   *McCarran-Walter Act*: Allowed 15,000 political refugees from China
1953   *Refugee Act ['57, '59]*: Admission of political Communist-refugees
1954   *Taiwan Support Act*: Economic and military support of Taiwan
1955   *Confession Program*: Political Immunity for true identity of Chinese
1964   *Civil Rights Act*: Prohibited discrimination based on race, sex or origin
1965   *Immigration Reform Act (Celler-Hart Act)*: Vocational immigration
1976   *Health Professions Act*: Doctors removed from preferential list
1977   *Eilber-Act*: Required equal salary for foreign employees
1978   *Indochina Refugee Act; World Wide Ceiling Law*
1979   *Taiwan Relations Act;* Start of direct relations with the PRC
1980   *Refugee Act*: Grants special rights to Refugees and Asylees
1982   *Simpson-Mazzoli Bill*: Proposed the revision of the 5th Preference
1986   *Immigration Reform and Control Act (IRCA, Simpson-Rodino Bill)*
1990   *Immigration Act (IA)*: Legalization of illegal immigrants
1992   *Chinese Student Protection Act*: Admission of refugee students
1996   *Immigration Reform Act (IIRIRA)*: Control of illegal immigrants
2002   *Family Reunification Act (FRA)*: Reversed provisions of the *IRA* '96
Arranged by B. Zinzius

Table 7   Regional Anti-Chinese Legislation in the United States

1850-5 *Foreign Miners Tax Law*: $20 monthly tax for Chinese miners
1852   *Bond Act*: required all arriving Chinese to post $500 as bond
1854   *California Supreme Court Decision*: Chinese ineligible to testify
1855   *Capitation Tax Ordinance*: $50 tax for every Chinese (voided 1957)
1858   *Act to Prevent further Immigration of Chinese and Mongols*
1860   *Fishing Tax*: $4 monthly tax on Chinese fishing (repealed 1864)
1862   *California's Anti-Coolie Tax*: $2.50 monthly tax for Chinese laborers
1870   *Act to Prevent Importing of Chinese Criminals*: Proof of character
1875   *Shrimp Net Law*: Regulated the size of Chinese shrimp-catching nets
1879   *California State Constitution*: Prohibition to hire Chinese workers
1880   *Fishing Act*: Prohibited Chinese from any fishing activity
1880   *Act to Prevent Licenses to Aliens:* Chinese ineligible for business visa
1882   *California Legal Holiday:* Public anti-Chinese demonstrations
1885   *Political Codes Amendment*: Chinese prohibited from public schools
1887   *Penal Code:* Fishing license tax aimed at Chinese fishermen
1889   *Alien Land Act of California*: Prohibited land purchase by Chinese
1891   *Act Prohibiting Immigration of Chinese Persons into State*
1893   *Fishing Games Act*: Prohibited use of Chinese methods of fishing nets

Local Anti-Chinese Legislation in the United States

1848   *Mariposa County Mining Regulation*: Prohibited Chinese Mining
1852   *Columbia District Mining Regulation*: Prohibited Chinese Mining
1870   *Act to Stop Hiring Chinese*: No Chinese to be hired in San Francisco
1870   *San Francisco Sidewalk Ordinance:* Prohibited Chinese pole-baskets
1870   *San Francisco Cubic Air Ordinance*: Health tax on Chinese housing
1873   *San Francisco Laundry Tax*: High tax on laundries without vehicle
1875   *San Francisco Anti-Queue Law*: Cutting queues of all arrested
1880   *San Francisco Anti-Ironing Law*: Closing Chinese nighttime laundries
1882   *San Francisco Laundry Licensing Law*: Mandatory Chinese License

Major Court Decisions Concerning Chinese Americans

1889   *Chae Chan Ping vs. U.S.*: Denial of re-entry and habeas corpus
1893   *Fong Yue Ting vs. U.S.*: Deportation without certificate of residence
1898   *Wong Kim Ark vs. U.S.*: Guarantees citizenship to US-born Chinese
1922   *Ho vs. White*: Congress entitled to deport illegal aliens
1967   *Loving vs. Virginia*: Anti-miscegenation laws ruled unconstitutional
1974   *Lau vs. Nichols*: Prohibition of language-based discrimination
1978   *Bakke vs. UC California*: Race permissible as admission criteria
1999   *Ho vs. San Francisco*: Cancellation of race-based school admission
2003   *Gratz/Grutter vs. Bollinger*: Race permissible as admission criteria
Arranged by B. Zinzius

4. HABITAT

Nationwide Characteristics of Chinese American Communities

According to Henning and Mangun, a habitat is the sum of all surrounding characteristics of a particular place that is occupied by an organism, a people, or a community, in which the organism lives naturally (Henning, 1989). This definition is broad enough to use as foundation for the following analysis of the current life of Chinese Americans.

In this chapter, we will analyze in detail Chinese habitats in the United States, first by looking at them as part of demographic changes in Asian and particularly Chinese American settlements during the past several decades, and second by investigating the specific phenomenon in San Francisco and the Bay Area, the nucleus of Chinese America.

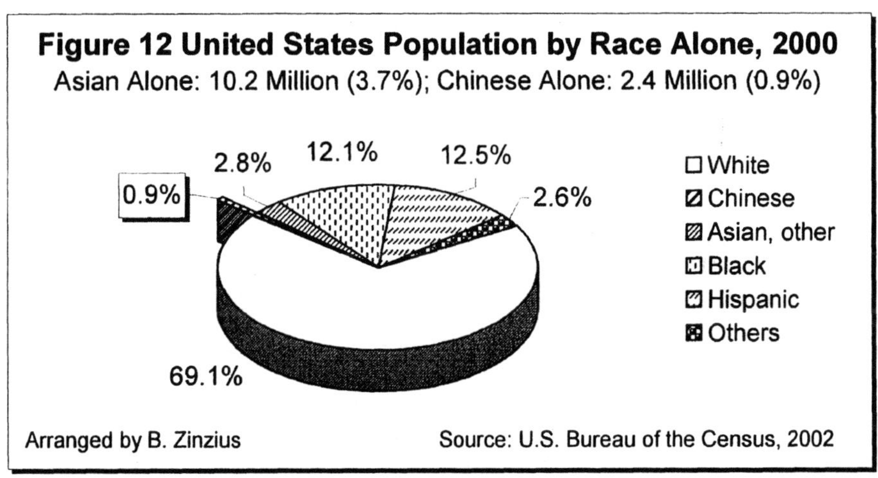

In 2000, 3.7% of the American population, or 10.2 million people, were Asians, of which the Chinese constituted the majority with 2.4 million (0.9%).[1] This number has risen rapidly since the 1965 immigration legislation, after which the second wave of Chinese immigrants brought a massive increase in the Asians population as a whole and radically shifted its composition towards Chinese predominance.

---

[1] The census of 2000 added a multiracial category (*one or more races*), which makes earlier census data not directly comparable. The U.S. Office of Management and Budget (OMB) is, therefore, currently working on "bridging methodologies" that can be used to provide better comparability between new and old censuses. (U.S. Bureau of the Census, Census 2000 Brief, C2KBR/01-16 and C2KBR/01-1, March 2001). Unless stated otherwise, throughout

In 1960, the number of Chinese in the United States was 237,000, only half the total of the Japanese Americans. Just twenty years later, however, the Chinese totaled 806,040 and had surpassed the Japanese in population. From 1980 to 1990 the Chinese again doubled to 1,645,472, and until 2000 continued to grow by almost 50% to 2,432,858.

Table 8 Asian and Pacific Islanders Alone in the United States, by Ethnic Groups, 1990 and 2000

	1990	% of Pop.	2000	% of Pop.
API Alone and Other Races	–	–	11,866,949	4.2%
API and Other Races	–	–	1,655,830	0.6%
API Alone	7,273,662	2.9%	10,211,119	3.7%
Asian Alone	6,908,638	2.8%	9,581,098	3.6%
Chinese	1,645,472	0.7%	2,432,858	0.9%
Filipino	1,406,770	0.6%	1,850,314	0.7%
Japanese	847,562	0.3%	1,678,765	0.6%
Asian Indian	815,447	0.3%	1,122,528	0.4%
Korean	798,849	0.3%	1,076,872	0.4%
Vietnamese	614,547	0.2%	796,700	0.3%
Laotian	149,014	0.1%	168,707	0.1%
Cambodian	147,411	0.1%	171,937	0.1%
Thai	91,275	0.1%	112,989	0.0%
Hmong	90,082	0.1%	169,428	0.1%
Pacific Islanders	340,929	0.1%	353,509	0.1%

Arranged by B. Zinzius   Source: U.S. Bureau of the Census, 2002

After 1965, the percentage of foreign-born among the Chinese increased significantly, from 39.3% in 1960, to 46.9% in 1970, 63.3% in 1980, and 69.4% in 1990. This increase clearly indicates that the immigration laws of

this work, the number for *Asian alone* and for *Chinese alone* was used to assure data consistency. The figure for *Asian in combination with one or more races* (or *Chinese*) is about 16% higher, e.g. *Asian in combination with one or more races* represent 4.2% of the United States population (instead of 3.7%), and *Chinese in combination with one or more races* represent 0.95% (2,734,841 persons) instead of 0.85% *Chinese alone* (2,432,858 persons). This new category will have strong political and social consequences for Asian Americans (Hahn, 2000, 56 et seq.). Furthermore, definitions of races and ethnic groups, e.g. Asian, Black, and Hispanic, differ significantly. People predominantly of Asian descent were categorized as Asian, whereas people with traces of Black ancestors were categorized as Black. This rule, regarded as the *one-drop-of-blood* rule, still exists today (Davis, 1991, 4 et seq.). Since the census of 1970, *Hispanic* are categorized as an *ethnic group*, not as a *race*, and *Hispanic/non-Hispanic* has been separated from *race*. Thus, people of *Hispanic origin* can be racially classified as *White* or *any other race*. Since the census of 2000, race is also determined by self-determination, whereas previously, race was determined by the interviewers (*Office of Management and Budget*, 1997b, chapters 3, 4).

1965 formed the main impetus for the growth of the Chinese population. Between 1990 and 2000, the percentage of foreign-born receded to 62.4%, something not caused by an absolute decline of Chinese immigrants but by an increase of American-born Chinese. The majority of all Chinese immigrants are mainland Chinese, who represent about 60%; whereas Hong Kong Chinese represent about 15%, and Taiwanese about 25% of all Chinese immigrants.[2]

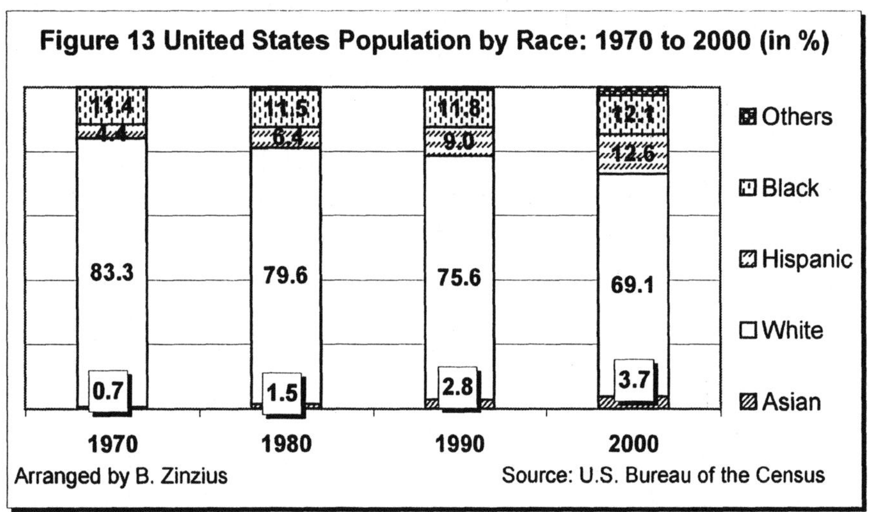

In addition to noting developments among different countries of origin, it is interesting to record the changes in historical and regional migration within the United States since 1965. Approximately 60% of this second wave of Chinese migrants found new homes in California or New York, thus rejuvenating the old Chinatowns.[3] California and New York have always been the most important states for Chinese immigration, followed distantly by Texas, New Jersey and Massachusetts. Since 1990, with 56,600 Chinese (4.7%), Hawaii seems to be the only state with a decreasing Chinese population. According to the newly introduced multiracial categories, however, there are 170,803 *Chinese alone or in combination with other races* in Hawaii (14.1%), over three times the number of *Chinese alone*, indicating a high number of mixed-race Chinese (1990: 6.2% for all Chinese).

---

[2] In 2000, 62.5% of all Chinese immigrants came from the People's Republic of China, 23.4% from the Republic of China (Taiwan), and 14.1% from Hong Kong. The Chinese figures do not include ethnic Chinese, who emigrated from other countries, such as Cambodia, Indonesia, Laos, Malaysia, Vietnam, or the Hmong (U.S. Census 2000, PCT19).

[3] Between 1996 and 2000, 31.1% of all Chinese immigrants settled in California, 23.5% in New York. During the same time, 49.9% of all Taiwanese chose California, and 7.6% New

Between 1980 and 1990, the strongest growth period of Asian Americans, California's Asian population increased to 2,845,695 (+116%), of which 704,850 were Chinese, indicating a growth-rate of over 127%.[4] In the same period, New York accounted for 693,760 Asians (+115%), of which 284,144 were Chinese (+92%), and Hawaii for 685,236 Asians (+12.6%), of which 68,804 were Chinese (+22%).

Table 9 Chinese American Alone Population in Selected States, 1970-2000[5]

	1970		1980		1990		2000	
	Chinese	% of pop.	Chinese	% of pop.	Chinese	% of pop.	Chinese	% of pop.
California	170,131	0.8%	322,309	1.4%	704,850	2.4%	980,642	2.9%
Hawaii	52,039	6.8%	56,285	5.8%	68,804	6.2%	56,600	4.7%
Illinois	14,474	0.1%	28,597	0.3%	49,936	0.4%	76,725	0.6%
Massachusetts	14,012	0.2%	25,015	0.4%	53,792	0.9%	84,392	1.3%
New Jersey	9,233	0.1%	23,369	0.3%	59,084	0.8%	100,355	1.2%
New York	81,378	0.4%	148,105	0.8%	284,114	1.6%	424,774	2.2%
Texas	7,635	0.1%	25,461	0.2%	63,232	0.4%	105,829	0.5%
United States	**435,062**	**0.2%**	**806,040**	**0.4%**	**1,645,472**	**0.7%**	**2,432,858**	**0.9%**

Arranged by B. Zinzius   Source: U.S. Bureau of the Census

Between 1990 and 2000, the absolute number of Asian Americans continued to increase strongly, while the growth-rate receded to 39% (Chinese: 48%). The census of 2000 accounts for 3,697,513 Californian Asians, of which 980,642 were Chinese. New York's Asian population totaled 1,044,976, of which 424,774 were Chinese. Since 1990, other states have also gained in importance for the Chinese, especially Texas with 105,829 (+67.4%), New Jersey with 100,355 (+69.8%), and Massachusetts with 84,392 Chinese Americans (+56.9%).

York as their places of residence. From 1850 to 2000, at least 75% of all Chinese settled in six states: California, Illinois, Massachusetts, New Jersey, New York, and Texas. For historical population data of all States for Asian and Chinese, see Chapter 10, "Appendix."

[4] The *State Population Research Units* predicted an Asian growth-rate of 136% between 1980 and 2000. Thus, they adequately pointed to Asians as the fastest growing group, but still underestimated the pace of their growth, as the real growth-rate was 192% (US Census, C2KBR/01-16, 2001). A projection of the *Center for Immigration Studies* in 2000 predicts that the Asian American community in the United States will grow from 4% to 13% in 2100, whereas the White population will fall below 40% (Kolankiewicz, 2000).

[5] Since the census of 1990, Taiwanese have been accounted for in some census questions. In 1990, 73,778 Taiwanese Americans lived in the United States. The number grew by 60% to 118,048 in 2000. 62,317 of these Taiwanese live in California (52.7%), 7,095 in New York (6.0%), 6,931 in Texas (5.9%), 5.879 in New Jersey (5.0%), 3,427 in Illinois (2.9%), and 2,364 in Massachusetts (2%; U.S. Bureau of the Census, 2000). In reality, these figures could be significantly higher, as some Taiwanese may not reveal their origin for political

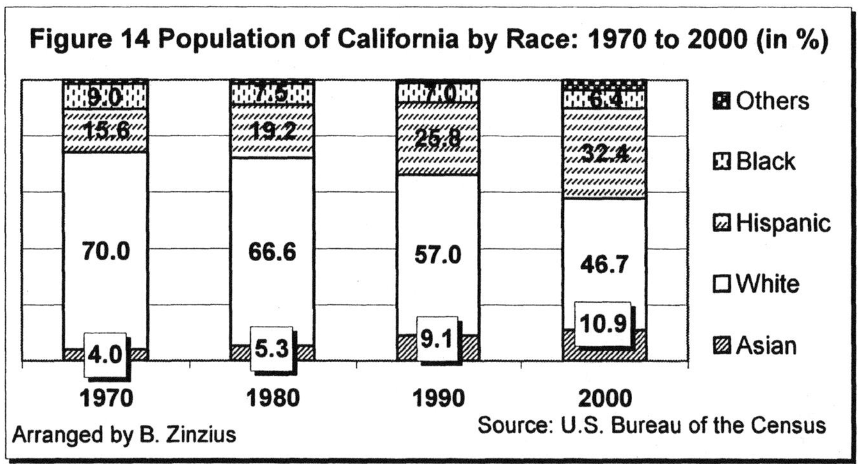

It is important to determine why, for over 150 years, Chinese immigrants focused on a limited number of states, with almost two-thirds of all Chinese Americans living in California and New York alone. Specific labor market conditions, educational chances, social and ethnic infrastructures, and entrepreneurial opportunities, among other factors, have to be evaluated as possible bases for Chinese American settlement patterns.

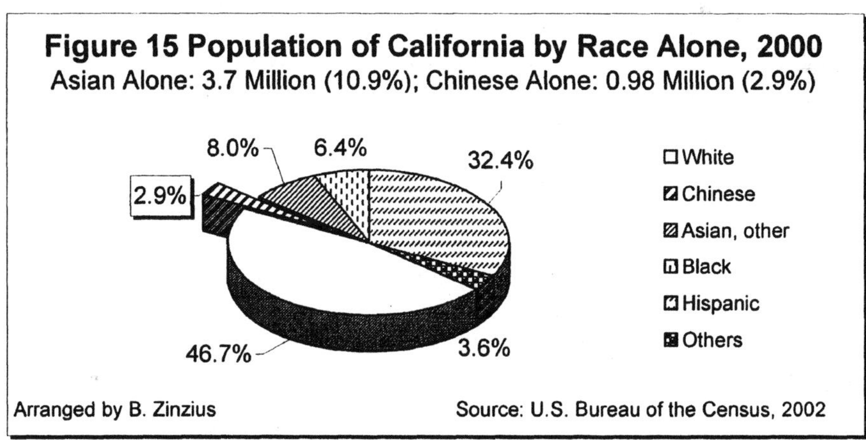

General employment data and nationwide economic trends over the past few decades, such as the stimulation of the service sector by massive tax-cuts in the 1980s, and the high-tech boom of the 1990s, do not explain the specific Chinese American habitation patterns. In order to understand

reasons (*Chinese American Data Center*, 2002). For further demographic details about Chinese American in the United States see Chapter 10, "Appendix."

Chinese American settlement patterns, it is necessary to look at housing and population details over the past several decades. A special focus should be on the evolution of Chinese settlements in their primary regions, California and New York. Specifically the old and new Chinatowns of San Francisco, followed by the larger Bay Area, will be analyzed. These data will be compared with the development in New York City and other regions of the United States.

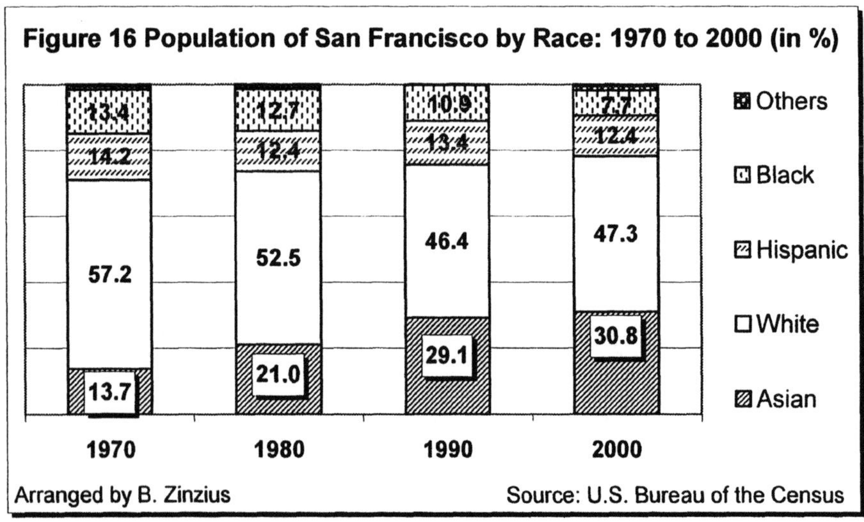

It is important to note that the majority of Chinese immigrants (over 90%) live in metropolitan areas.[6] The largest number of Chinese Americans in any state live in California. The San Francisco Bay Area is therefore an ideal region to analyze trends of the Chinese American population.

In 1980, 147,426 (21%) Asians lived in San Francisco, of which 82,244 were Chinese (12.1%). By 1990, the Asian population reached 210,876 (29.1%), including 130,753 Chinese (18.1%), and by 2000 the Asian population reached 239,234 (30.8%), with 152,620 (19.6%) of the total population being Chinese, or better: *Chinese Americans*. Thus, the Chinese represent 63.8% of the Asian population in San Francisco, compared to 23.8% nationwide.

---

[6] A study by Lo and Wang details living patterns of various ethnic Chinese groups in America (Lo, 1997, 71–72). Schwartz also describes high urban residential rates among Asian and Pacific Islanders (Schwartz, 2002).

According to the figures from 2000, outside of San Francisco, the Chinese account for just 6.9% of the Bay Area population. A detailed analysis shows that their habitation pattern is quite heterogeneous. In cities like Cupertino, Hillsboro, Milbrae, and Milpitas, the center of Silicon Valley, Chinese make up as much as 24% of the population.[7]

Table 10 Chinese American Alone Population in the Bay Area, 1970-2000

County / City	1970 Chinese	1970 % of pop.	1980 Chinese	1980 % of pop.	1990 Chinese	1990 % of pop.	2000 Chinese	2000 % of pop.
Alameda	**20,072**	**1.9%**	**32,205**	**2.9%**	**68,184**	**5.3%**	**112,006**	**7.8%**
Fremont	569	0.6%	2,391	1.8%	15,136	5.7%	29,240	14.4%
Hayward	790	0.8%	1,528	1.6%	3,285	2.9%	3,998	2.9%
Oakland	11,335	3.1%	15,325	4.5%	27,922	7.2%	31,834	8.0%
Contra Costa	**3,088**	**0.6%**	**10,381**	**1.6%**	**22,519**	**2.8%**	**28,948**	**3.1%**
Concord	281	0.3%	1,474	1.4%	2,952	2.7%	2,632	2.2%
Marin	**873**	**0.4%**	**2,097**	**0.9%**	**2,962**	**1.3%**	**3,523**	**1.4%**
Napa	**323**	**0.4%**	**710**	**0.7%**	**644**	**0.6%**	**537**	**0.4%**
San Francisco	**58,696**	**8.2%**	**82,244**	**12.1%**	**130,753**	**18.1%**	**152,620**	**19.6%**
San Mateo	**5,379**	**1.0%**	**16,624**	**2.8%**	**34,118**	**5.0%**	**48,996**	**6.9%**
Daly City	1,108	1.7%	5,391	6.9%	11,444	11.3%	14,063	13.6%
Hillsboro	–	–	–	–	–	–	1,973	18.2%
Milbrae	–	–	–	–	–	–	3,427	16.5%
South SFO	–	–	–	–	20,448	7.3%	4,739	7.8%
Santa Clara	**7,817**	**0.7%**	**22,745**	**1.8%**	**65,924**	**4.4%**	**115,781**	**6.9%**
Cupertino	–	–	937	5.2%	5,245	15.2%	12,031	23.8%
Milpitas	–	–	–	–	–	–	8,098	12.9%
San Jose	2,595	0.6%	9,802	1.6%	65,801	4.5%	51,109	5.7%
Sunnyvale	1,273	1.3%	3,360	3.2%	6,349	5.4%	12,597	9.6%
Solano	**770**	**0.5%**	**1,184**	**0.5%**	**3,178**	**0.9%**	**3,318**	**0.8%**
Vallejo	323	0.5%	333	0.4%	1,310	1.2%	1,032	0.9%
Sonoma	**448**	**0.2%**	**826**	**0.3%**	**2,207**	**0.6%**	**3,007**	**0.7%**
Santa Rosa	145	0.3%	300	0.4%	792	0.7%	1,118	0.8%
Bay Area	**97,466**	**2.1%**	**169,016**	**3.3%**	**328,858**	**5.5%**	**468,736**	**6.9%**

Arranged by B. Zinzius   Source: U.S. Bureau of the Census, 2003

In Contra Costa, Napa, and Solano, the Californian wine region, the Chinese constitute less than 1% of the population. This pattern is clearly distinct from other Asians, such as the Filipinos, who represent 20.7% of the population in Vallejo, 31.6% of Daly City, and 18.8% of Union City.

---

[7] Silicon Valley, the center of high-tech America, consists of several cities in San Mateo and Santa Clara Counties, including Cupertino, Milpitas, San Carlos, and Sunnyvale. The percentage of Hong Kong Chinese in these cities is disproportionately high, e.g. 25% of all Chinese immigrating to Daly City after 1983 came from Hong Kong (Luu, 1999).

San Francisco Chinatown

In addition to offering the possibility for historical comparison, San Francisco—with 19.5% Chinese Americans—stands at the center of this analysis because of its current place at the heart of a changing and expanding Chinese immigration. Furthermore, multicultural California has often been a role model for many social and political changes in the United States, signaling future developments in the American society.

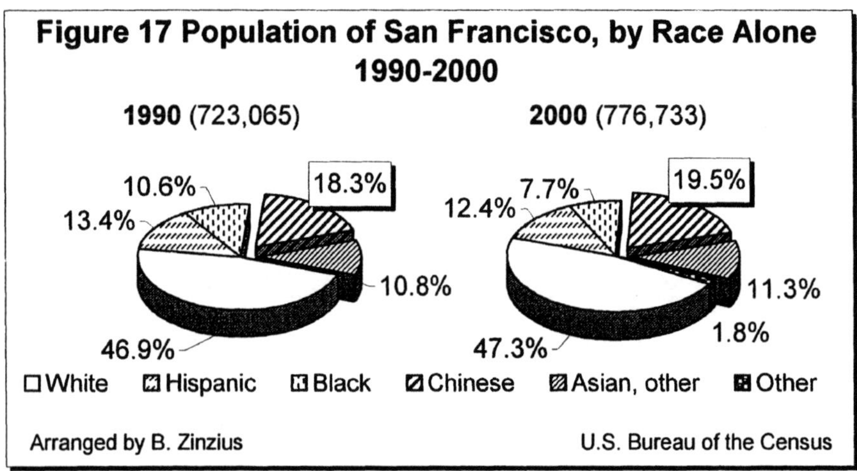

Asian, and specifically Chinese, immigration to San Francisco has changed dramatically over the past several decades.[8] The ghetto-like structures of Chinatowns have long been the sole habitat of the Chinese (Zinzius, 1988). Today, Chinatowns are no longer necessarily pure Chinese quarters, but still have Chinese majorities and Chinese controlled infrastructures.[9] The growth no longer affects only the classical areas of Chinese population—such as Chinatown. The surrounding towns and cities of the entire San Francisco Bay Area already have large Asian communities, although contact to San Francisco itself remains important. Ghettos and the traditional form of Chinese migration—move to the big city—are nevertheless becoming increasingly obsolete.

---

[8] The figures for 1990 and 2000 were calculated from census tract data provided by the *Association of Bay Area Governments* for 2000, and the census of 1990. The census tract allocation of San Francisco districts was also obtained from *ABAG* (ABAG, 2002). Census tracts 113, 114 and 118 are used here as the basis for all Chinatown-figures.

[9] Since the 1970s, Filipinos have strongly increased their presence in the Bay Area, Asian Indians and Vietnamese since the 1980s.

In 2000, only 24 of 101 cities in the Bay Area had already a White population of less than 50%, whereby East Palo Alto and Oakland showed the largest decreases. In counties where until the mid-1980s the majority were rich Whites, we now have increased migration of Asians, especially Chinese. The percentage is still relatively small, but is increasing rapidly. Hillsboro, for example, used to be a favorite area of the upper class Whites, but has become the preferred domicile of rich Hong Kong Chinese.[10] Already in 1991, the *San Francisco Examiner* estimated that in 2003, based on the population growth-rates of the 1980s, the White population in California would be less than 40% (*San Francisco Examiner*, April 14, 1991). This prediction does not appear to have come true since in 2000 there were still 46.7% Whites living in California, compared to 10.9% Asian and Pacific Islanders. Its failure to occur may partially be due immigrants from Eastern European. In 2000 alone, over 1,000 Russians came to the Bay Area. Nevertheless, assuming the continuation of current growth-rates, the prediction of the *Examiner* may well come true within another decade.

From 1980 to 1990 the Asian population in San Francisco grew by 53% to 29.1%, the Chinese American grew 58.9% to 18.3%, while the percentage of Whites decreased by 11.7% from 52.5% to 46.4%, and the Black by 14.2% to 10.9%. From 1990 to 2000, this trend continued: the Asian population grew by 21.6% (Chinese: 16.7%), whereas the White (-4.2%) and Black populations (-24.1%) decreased compared to all other ethnic groups.[11] Over the past two decades, four important tendencies of change in San Francisco's macro-structural population, composition, and characteristics can be identified:

1. Between 1990 and 2000, old Chinatown decreased its population by 4%. The Whites grew 13.7% to 8.2%, a tendency contrary to their general development. Chinese Americans increased 10% to 85.9%, whereas the other Asians lost considerably.[12]

---

[10] 18.2% of Hillsboro's population are of Chinese descent, many of which are from Hong Kong.

[11] In 2000, *Asian and Pacific Islanders* represented 30.8% of the population, non-Hispanic Whites 47.3%, Hispanic 12.4% and Black 7.7%.

[12] Population counts of minorities have a high degree of uncertainty, as the example of San Francisco Chinatown shows. The data from the census of 2000 indicate 7,976 inhabitants for San Francisco Chinatown. The *Chinatown Economic Development Group* (*CEDG*, 2000) states 14,230 inhabitants, whereas Ong and Miller refer to 26,710 (Ong, 2002a, 9). Other sources indicate up to 40,000 inhabitants (*San Francisco Examiner*, August 17, 1987). Census results of ethnic minorities are frequently too low, resulting in distorted statistics and insufficient funding (Ong, 2002b, 9). An estimated 6.1 million people, predominantly minorities, were not accounted for in the census of 2000, and California's minorities could

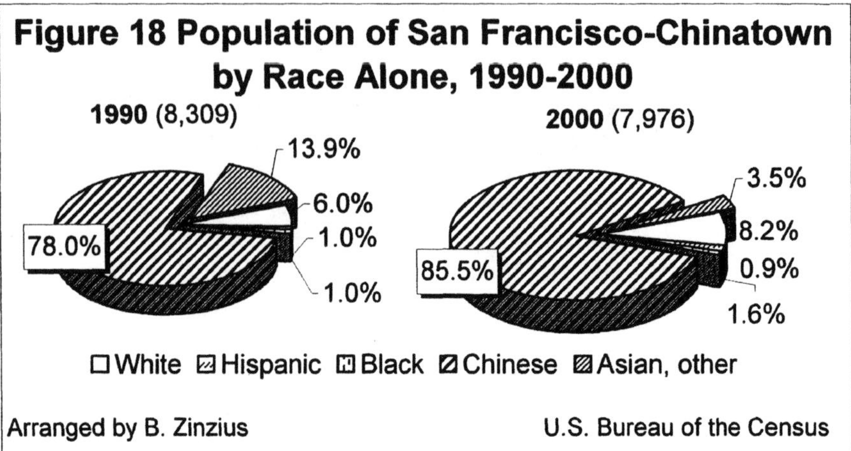

2. Impressive was the large increase of Asians during the 1980s in the areas surrounding Chinatown: North Beach 25%, Downtown Financial District 26%, Tenderloin 93%, and Nob Hill 8%. Between 1990 and 2000, however, Asians (particular Chinese), moved further out into middle-class suburbs, their population in Nob Hill decreased -16.4% (Chinese: -20.2%), Downtown -6.1% (Chinese: -30.5%), and in North Beach -18.9% (Chinese: -24.7%).

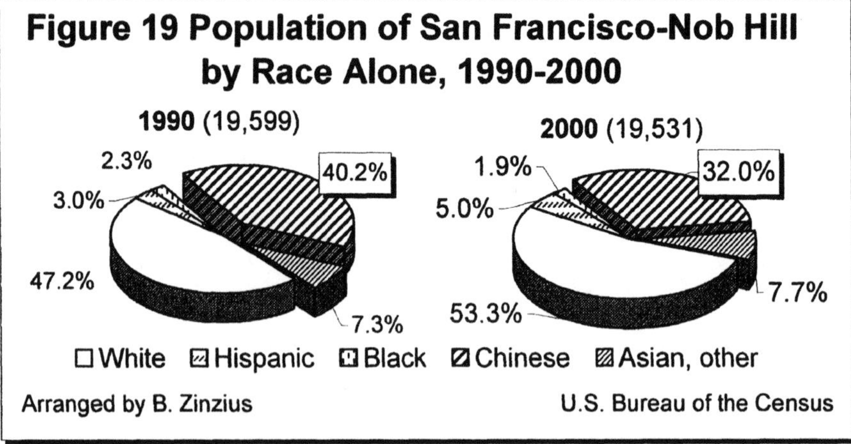

3. In other parts of town the Asian population is quickly becoming the strongest group. In upper class White areas, e.g. Marina and Presidio Heights, they have been rising since the 1980s. Previously

be as high as 76%, instead of the official 43% (*Asian Week*, January 26, 2001). Furthermore, the new multiracial categories of the census of 2000 make comparisons difficult.

White middle-class areas like Richmond and Sunset are already established Chinatowns with an Asian population of 44% (Chinese: 31%) and 46% (Chinese: 34%), (Census 2000).

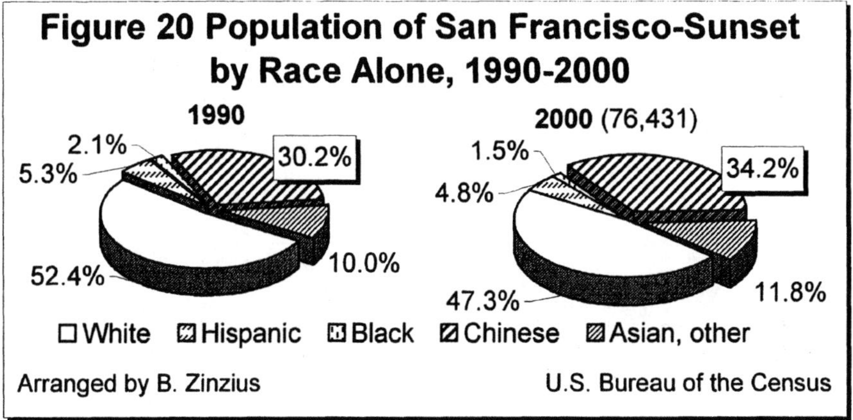

4. In areas with a previously small Asian population, their growth is increasingly visible. New Chinatowns are developing in Bayview, Crocker Amazon, Ingleside, and Oceanview. Here, new compositions of the ethnic groups stand out, e.g. between 1990 and 2000 in Bayview Blacks decreased 25.2% to 46.7%, Hispanics grew 106% to 16.5%, and the Asians grew 25.3% to 26.8% (Chinese: 54% to 18.4%). In Oceanview, Blacks decreased by 42.8% to 24.7%, while the Asian grew by 60.9% to 44% (Chinese: 106% to 31.1%).

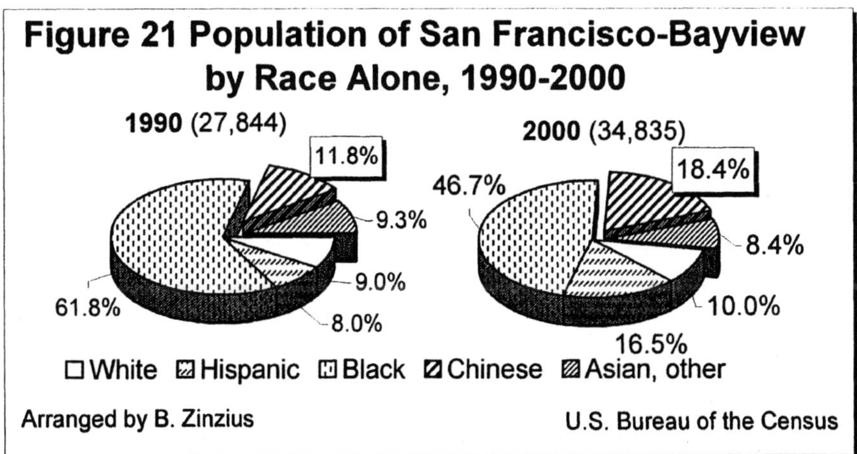

We may, therefore, conclude that Asians are entering all the neighborhoods and thus breaking down the ghettos. In 2000, 11% Asians constituted 11% of the population in the traditional Hispanic neighborhood of Mission. In South San Francisco the Whites have been increasingly displaced, as the drastic increase in areas such as Crocker Amazon and Oceanview show.

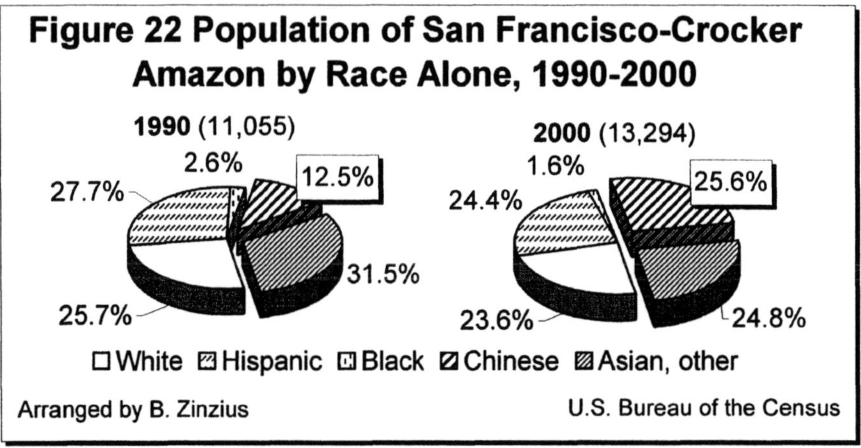

During the 1980s, in Portola and Crocker Amazon, the growth-rates for Asian groups reached 66% to a total of 39% while the number of Whites decreased by 22%. Between 1990 and 2000, the Chinese in Crocker Amazon grew by 117% to 25.6% (Asians overall grew "only" 21.9%), and became the largest ethnic group, surpassing the 23.6% of Whites. The White community, excluding the Hispanic American group, represents the majority in 28 of 36 districts, and in 18 already every third resident is Asian.

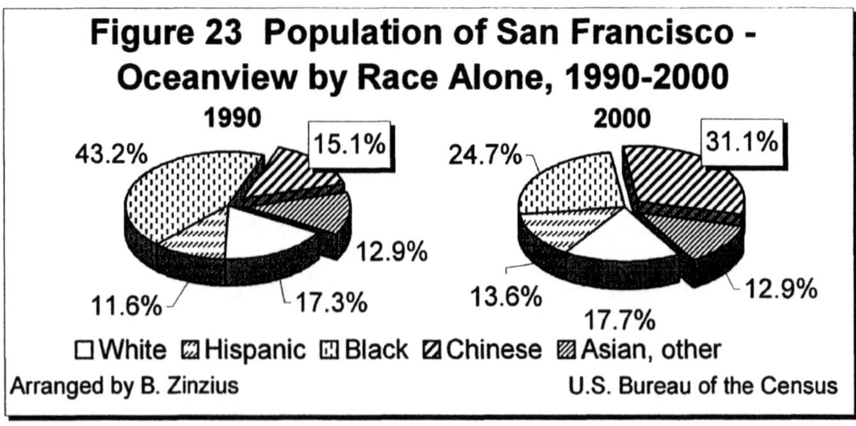

In addition to the quantitative increase in the Asian community in all districts, a qualitative change is noticeable. To put it simply: Asians are moving into higher income areas, which used to be the domain of Whites, who in turn occupy lower class areas or move towards suburbs. This phenomenon is caused by the continued growth through immigration, and by a general gentrification of the population, causing districts to change their social and economic structure significantly over just a few decades. "There is something remarkable about San Francisco and New York, the first and second densest cities in the country," says Mitchell Schwarzer, Professor of Architectural History in San Francisco. "... Wealthy, educated people from all over the world have flooded into San Francisco over the past couple of decades. The landscape, vibrant economy, and tolerant social climate attract immigrants from Russia, China, Mexico, [and] Latin America. ... San Francisco's [housing] problems are those of success. Here, people are less pulled toward the suburbs than pushed out of the expensive and desirable central city." (Schwarzer, 2001, 3, 5). White residents frequently complain about this phenomenon, for example in Los Angeles: "They lived in their own neighborhoods and moved into ours after they learned English. ... Today, the Chinese come right in with their money and their ways. We are the aliens." (*AsianWeek*, May 24-30, 1996; Horton, 1995, 20-21).

Table 11 Inhabitants in Selected Districts of San Francisco by Race/Ethnicity, 2000

	Total Population	Chinese	Growth '90–'00	Asian incl. Chinese	Growth '90–'00	White	Hispanic	Black
Chinatown	7,976	**85.5%**	9.6%	89.3%	-2.8%	8.2%	0.9%	1.6%
Excelsior	32,890	**18.3%**	49.2%	35.0%	26.9%	27.0%	29.9%	7.6%
Haight Ashbury	25,921	**2.6%**	14.4%	7.9%	-5.6%	78.2%	7.3%	10.8%
Lakeshore	13,554	**8.6%**	74.6%	23.4%	50.9%	63.7%	6.3%	6.3%
Marina	22,457	**5.6%**	-3.2%	10.0%	14.5%	88.2%	4.0%	0.5%
Mission	60,202	**4.7%**	-9.8%	11.2%	-16.9%	52.4%	50.1%	3.5%
Outer Mission	23,528	**12.4%**	89.0%	35.2%	29.6%	32.0%	29.0%	3.7%
Parkside	14,578	**40.3%**	20.4%	53.5%	21.9%	43.8%	5.5%	1.0%
Presidio Heights	9,907	**10.5%**	-25.4%	16.4%	-11.0%	78.3%	4.4%	3.5%
Potrero	10,542	**3.8%**	-4.2%	8.2%	-21.0%	68.5%	11.8%	17.1%
Richmond	65,365	**31.4%**	-9.1%	46.4%	-5.6%	50.3%	4.7%	1.7%
South of Market	15,651	**7.5%**	84.9%	25.3%	29.1%	55.9%	10.4%	12.5%
Sunset	76,431	**34.2%**	13.6%	45.8%	14.5%	47.3%	4.8%	1.5%
Upper Market	17,302	**3.3%**	-17.1%	7.2%	0.7%	85.4%	9.7%	3.1%
Visitation Valley	14,241	**31.3%**	18.3%	59.4%	16.5%	13.7%	7.4%	14.2%
San Francisco	**751,477**	**19.6%**	**8.6%**	**30.8%**	**7.5%**	**47.3%**	**12.4%**	**7.7%**

Arranged by B. Zinzius   U.S. Bureau of the Census, 1990, 2000

A further interesting aspect is that the White population is decreasing in many American cities, primarily due to gentrification. The decrease is, however, reversed in some districts, mainly in the less affluent areas of San

Francisco, e.g. Hayes Valley, Western Addition, and South of Market, and usually at the cost of the Black population. These Whites are often new immigrants from Eastern Europe, e.g. Russia, which represent already 12% of the White population in San Francisco (U.S. Bureau of the Census, 2000).

From these demographic trends arise interesting questions with regard to property ownership. A survey of the United States population shows that the Chinese possess less property than the average American. 54% of Chinese (Asians 53%) live in their own homes, whereas the overall average is 71%. The average property value of Asians is, however, far higher than that of the national average, since they are concentrated in the expensive West or around big cities. In 2000, the median home value in the United States for White, non-Hispanic was $123,400, whereas for Asians it was $199,300.[13] Looking at California alone, the difference in value is reduced, but still shows a benefit for the Asians. Until 1947, Asians were prohibited from owning property, thus all current ownership stems from purchases within the last fifty years.

In order to differentiate the Asian community from other ethnic groups, the following specific questions need to be answered: How do the Chinese live in San Francisco? Where do the rich live, where do the less privileged live? How does the property ownership change the face of the town?

It will be furthermore necessary to identify how changes in living quarters have influenced on the lifestyle of Chinese Americans, and business and educational opportunities have developed in comparison to other groups, or, still more important, what kinds of social development have encouraged penetration into more expensive residential areas. Before asking these questions, however, the old Chinatown and reasons for the migration to the new living areas need to be established.

The Old Chinatown

"Forget it, Jake. It's Chinatown!" said the cop to Detective J.J. Gittes as the drama reached its bloody climax. *Chinatown* from Roman Polanski's film is a synonym for mysterious darkness, for crimes that happen at night and for which there is no solution (Eaton, 1998). "Incorrect," says the Chinese American author, Amy Tan. Her Chinatown is "like a big family, including

---

[13] **Table 12 Median House Value in the United States, 1990 and 2000**

	United States		**California**		**San Francisco**	
	All	Asian	All	Asian	All	Asian
1990	$79,100	$148,548	$195,500	$217,250	$298,900	$282,419
2000	$119,600	$199,300	$211,500	$256,700	$396,400	$361,800

Source: U.S. Census, tables H023-H026 for 1990; HCT-42A, D for 2000
In 1980: United States, $47,200; Asian and Pacific Islanders $83.900; Chinese $89,600.

all of its social problems. Everyone knows everyone. The quarter has something special about it, but also something claustrophobic. It is a ghetto." Tourists plough along Grant Street, the main thoroughfare of the twenty blocks of San Francisco's traditional Chinatown. In the shop windows, they see jade Buddhas and eat dim sum lunches in the booths of the *Far East Café*. At the street market on Stockton Street, the Chinese women bargain for black mushrooms, fresh ginger, and watermelons. At the stone chessboards of Portsmouth Square, in the shade of the pines, old men in black fill their days with chess, Chinese chess. Amy Tan mentioned that chess is a game of secrets in which one shows ones knowledge, without giving oneself away (Interview 1991). The bustling Chinatown of San Francisco is the springboard into the New World and also the last haven from it. This description could be a picture in the mind's eye of a visitor to Chinatown. The reality behind the exotic facade is probably the most important secret of old Chinatown. Up to 50,000 people live in this small area, making Chinatown's 24 blocks the most densely populated area after Central Manhattan.[14]

Table 13 Social Characteristics of San Francisco-Chinatown

	1990			2000		
	U.S.	SFO	Chinatown	U.S.	SFO	Chinatown
Age >60 Years	16.8%	19.0%	38.5%	11.2%	21.1%	41.5%
Foreign-Born	7.9%	34.0%	77.2%	11.1%	36.8%	76.3%
Family Income	$35,225	$40,561	$20,126	$50,046	$63,545	$25,295
Capita Income	$14,420	$16,409	$11,695	$21,587	$34,556	$14,776
Gross Rent	$447	$653	$298	$602	$928	$413
Homeowner	52.2%	43.3%	5.7%	53.2%	46.2%	4.7%
Poverty Rate	13.1%	12.7%	25.2%	12.4%	11.3%	20.8%

Arranged by B. Zinzius   Source: U.S. Bureau of the Census, 1990, 2000

Up to 30,000 live in the actual center of old Chinatown between Powell, Kearny, Bush, and Broadway. The other 20,000 live on the surrounding streets, also known as Greater Chinatown. Nearly all the buildings in the center were built after the earthquake of 1906 and had to survive that of 1989. They are early pioneer architecture, although most facades have Chinese shingles (sinocized). They are generally known as "un-reinforced masonry buildings (UMB)," which means there is no anti-seismic reinforcement. In the centers of each block are numerous small units, which remind one of the bachelor society: multiple families share one kitchen and bathroom. These apartments have no central heating and 80% are considered

---

[14] The *San Francisco Examiner* reports 40,000 (August 17, 1987). See also the earlier discussion in Footnotes 8, 11, and Chapter 4 "Chinatowns Outside San Francisco."

to be "substandard" according to city guidelines (Ling-chi Wang, Interview, 1990).

The income level and especially the age structure in Chinatown shows the great demand for Council Housing. The population is aging, and in 2000, 41% of the population was over 60 years old. 76% of all Chinatown inhabitants were foreign-born. One must guess that only the elderly and the newly arrived live in this dense and overpopulated area. The level of hygiene and the level of medicinal support of many Chinatown inhabitants are questionable. Many seniors live alone. The living space is still small for them and also decrepit. For example Ms. Lena Chao paid a monthly rent of $340 for her apartment in 1991.[15] She left Hong Kong in 1950 and worked as a waitress until her retirement, and has lived in Grand Avenue since 1968. The roof of her housing is not sealed, and the door must be boarded against mice. The old lady who lives in her ten square meter room has to battle with 24 others for a place in one of the three bathrooms. In the 1970s, 60% of all apartments in Chinatown did not have their own bathroom facilities (Interview with Henry Der, 1991). Up to today, not much has changed regarding the social characteristics of Chinatown inhabitants. They face similar problems in San Francisco and New York, such as linguistic isolation, low-wage employment, gentrification, inadequate healthcare, and lack of housing (Ong, 2002a, 33).

Thomas Hsieh, a former San Francisco mayor and first supervisor of Chinese origin, says that several of the houses in which these old people live are inadequate, since some owners do not believe that repair is of value. The buildings do not always comply with construction, fire and safety, or health guidelines and could be dangerous for the occupants in the case of a stronger earthquake (Interview with Thomas Hsieh, 1990). The *Ping Yuen Housing Projects* were the first council housing developments for Chinese. They were built by the city between 1950 and 1961, but are still considered "new." Regarded as one of the best housing units in Chinatown, the crime and turnover rates are very low and the rent is based on level of income.

The upper level of income for a single person for 1991 stood at $4,000 and for a family of eight at $7,300. Council Housing has created 555 new units, which is countered by a waiting list of 5,000.[16] The Chinatown Doctor and local activist, Dr. Rolland Lowe says: "Vacancies seldom occur!" (Interview in 1991).

---

[15] The median rent in San Francisco increased 452% between 1979 and 2000. In the same time, the Consumer Price Index only increased 178% (Grubb, 2002).

[16] Qualification for *affordable housing* is based on the *Area Mean Income* (*AMI*). Persons considered low income earn below 80% of the *AMI*, very low income below 50%. The high

Apart from the inability of the elderly, the property market also suffers under the hectic actions of the Chinese business people. The existing building substance erodes, since they, especially the Hong Kong Chinese still subscribe to the strategy of the quick resale. They describe this as frying real estate in a wok. Thus, the prices for real estate far outrun regular price increases by far. So, the short-term owners try to improve the temporary value with short-term rental agreements causing the rents to escalate at each change by 200%–300% and thus forcing the elderly population out (Interview with Peter Kwong, 1991). The International House, the last bastion of Manila Town before entering Chinatown, is an example of concentrated community action to oppose the release of cheap living space. The Thai real-estate company, *Four Seasons Corp.*, which intended to develop a new business and office building, purchased the Boarding House. The protest was led by Asian students from Berkeley, who were able to achieve the restoration of the hotel and hinder its demolition until 1972 (Nee, 1986, 389–391; *Asian Women United*, Ed. 1989, 477).

In a survey of Chinatown inhabitants, the author, Chalsa Loo, described the Chinese living situation as "Bitter Homes and Garbage," an ironic reversal of the magazine title *Better Homes and Gardens*. Only 13% of the inhabitants were also owners of the property (Loo, 1982a, 105). Today, this percentage has decreased even more to 4.7% (Census 2000). There are further differences between the Chinese and social norms: 87% of the population do not possess an automobile (Census 2000); a third works more than five days a week; the highest suicide rate in San Francisco is in Chinatown (Interview with Benjamin Wong, 1989). Thus, Chinatown inhabitants are a far cry from the middle-class ideal of America.

From Chalsa Loo's questionnaire it could be determined that 78% live in Chinatown, because they want to live among Chinese, very often because of the language barrier.[17] The community has introduced a number of bilingual institutions. Thus, care has been taken for the newly arrived who do not speak English. In Chinatown, everything is Chinese: banks, telephone companies, residences for the old and poor, kindergarten, religious institutions, vocational training programs.

Since 1977, the *Chinatown Community Development Center* (*CCDC,* formerly known as *Chinatown Resource Center, CRC,* and *Chinese Community Housing Corporation, CCHC*) aims to enhance the quality of life

---

income level in San Francisco allows many to qualify for *affordable housing*, especially in areas such as Chinatown. *Affordable housing* units are scarce in San Francisco, and the government has initiated various programs to increase their number (Amoroso, 2001).

[17] In 2000, the linguistic situation of Chinatown inhabitants is identical to 1980: 78.9% speak an Asian language, and 63.4% are linguistically isolated (Census 2000, table P20).

of San Francisco residents. So far the *CCDC* has created over 2,200 new or rehabilitated *affordable housing* units, and manages more than one thousand housing units and ten commercial spaces for small businesses, primarily in Chinatown, North Beach and Tenderloin. The 34-unit *Namiki Apartments* is an example of an *affordable housing* project that expired in 2001 and was taken over by the *CCDC*. Others include the 72-unit *Golden Gate Apartments* in Western Addition, and the 204-unit Notre Dame Apartments on Broadway and Van Ness, the largest expiring use project in San Francisco.[18] The *CCDC* provides, thus, a needed support for the housing market in San Francisco, where *affordable housing* is in a severe crisis. In cooperation with the *Chinatown Alleyway Improvement Association*, CCDC has also supported activities such as the *Chinatown Alleyway Master Plan*. The *Chinatown Alleyway Tours* is a youth-run program of the *CCDC*, created to educate people about Chinatown, attracting tourists and locals.[19] Another organization providing support specifically for newcomers, is the *Chinese Newcomer Service Center (CNSC)*, which has served as a cultural bridge and support for new immigrants since 1969. These Chinatown development programs are closely supported by the city administration. In 1996, San Francisco Mayor Brown appointed a 21-member task force, called the *Chinatown Economic Development Group (CEDG)*, to implement economic development activities in the historic Chinatown. The non-profit organization aims to improve the image and attractiveness of Chinatown, and has so far created various projects to attract tourists and visitors.

These developments demonstrate the city's recognition of Chinatown's importance as a top tourist attraction. Other cities are initiating similar activities, and in 2000, members of the *Los Angeles Chinatown Business Council* launched a concerted effort to rejuvenate its Chinatown, especially the historic district to stimulate local businesses and attract tourists (*Los Angeles Times*, May 26, 2000). Following September 11, 2001, New York also started a major program after to support Chinatown, in order to recoup tourism and revive ethnic businesses.[20]

---

[18] "Tenants and Chinatown Community Development Center Save Affordable Housing for Seniors." (Vodak, 2002).

[19] In 1998, *CCDC* received the *Fannie Mae Foundation Sustained Excellence Award*. Congresswoman Nancy Pelosi honored the *CCDC* for its accomplishments in the U.S. Congress at this occasion. In 2000, *CCDC* was awarded with the *Metropolitan Life Foundations Award for Excellence* in affordable housing.

[20] 24,500 jobs were lost in Manhattan's Chinatown because of the terrorist attacks on September 11, 2001, mainly in the garment and tourist industry. Several organizations, including the *Asian American Business Development Council (AABDC)*, and the *Asian American Federation of New York (AAFNY)*, have started initiatives to revive businesses and

In 2003, the Severe Acute Respiratory Symptom (SARS) was another setback for Chinatowns in the United States. In total, thirty-six probable cases were reported, six in New York, and nine in California. Despite these low numbers, 84% of all Chinatown businesses experienced declining revenues of up to 25%. The public had connected SARS to the Chinese because it had originated in Southern China (*Los Angeles Times*, May 4, 2003). Only several months after the infection was contained, Chinatown businesses are back to normal.

For the remaining, elderly Chinatown residents, the major concern has been health care. Until the mid-1980s, there was only one Chinese hospital, built in 1924, with 60-bed capacity. Even in 1970, only 30 doctors were available for the treatment of 50,000 inhabitants of the greater Chinatown area.[21] Only in 1985 was a new hospital erected next to the old, which had been built by the *Six Companies* from donations collected on a grand scale by Chinese American organizations.[22]

Reservation about western medicine is a historical phenomenon, but they are slowly decreasing. In the past, it was problematic for the Chinatown inhabitants to accustom themselves to the unusual diet in town hospitals or to visit health centers outside Chinatown. Since oriental medicine supports psychosomatic relationships, physical sickness was considered a sign of moral sickness, and thus admitting its presence was to be avoided whenever possible.[23]

Since then, Chinatown inhabitants are more aware of their choices: Chinese and western medicine is requested. In case of sickness the doctor or school doctor is consulted rather than the acupuncture specialist or homeopath, naturally presuming that he is Chinese (Interview with Thomas Chinn, 1990; Interview with Dr. Rolland Lowe, 1989).

---

attract tourists, recognizing Chinatown as an important part of New York's society. "Chinatown after September 11th." (Sim, 2002, 1).

[21] This meant 1,000 persons per physician; in 2000, the number is 781. For comparison: Germany–293, United States–341, European Union–450, Japan–610, United Kingdom–611, China–648, Mexico–800, Taiwan–802, India–2,460, Indonesia–7,030, Philippines–8,120 (World Health Organization, 2001).

[22] All cases are traditional solidarity communities, which emerged at the turn of the century: *Chinese Consolidated Benevolent, Chinese Chamber of Commerce, Chinese American Citizen Alliance, Chinese Christian Union, Shiu Hing Benevolent Association, Chinatown YMCA.*

[23] See Satcher, David. *Report of the Surgeon General, 2001. Mental Health: Culture, Race, and Ethnicity.* Office of the Surgeon General, 2003.

Today, mainly Chinese doctors versed in both western and oriental medicine practice in Chinatown. In 2001, 64 physicians practiced in Chinatown, 26 of which advertise even in Chinese.[24] Health and senior citizen centers, childcare programs, neighborhood and merchant organizations offer additional social services.[25]

So, in Chinatown, health and safety regulations have not been a priority. Who is responsible? A shadow government still stands between inhabitants and city authorities. Clans and family organizations possess approximately 80% of all property, e.g. the *Six Companies, Chinese Consolidated Benevolent Association (CCBA)*, who abuse the living requirements of newly arrived countrymen (Interview with Him Marc Lai, 1989). Especially district organizations and *tongs* profited from the vast immigration of the 1960s (*East West*, 1960–1979). Today, the *Six Companies*, once a powerful head of the family and district organizations with multiple functions, survives solely from rental income. 32% of Chinese Americans, however, mostly young, American-born have a desire for change in lifestyle and are prepared to leave the old Chinatown (Loo, 1982b, 105). A growing factor of conflict is on the one hand the increasing demand for public housing for aged and newly arrived, versus the business interests of large real-estate companies from Pacific Rim countries.

The New Chinatowns

In Richmond and Sunset, two better districts in the West of San Francisco, one finds the third, fourth and fifth generation Chinese. This is where the Asian middle-class goes shopping. They were the first to profit from the abolition of the special law prohibiting the purchase of property by Chinese. Living space in old Chinatown became insufficient after the families reunification had started. The living space grew too small. Rejoined families developed greater initiative in the choice of area of living than the single early immigrants who intended to live economically.

From acupuncture to Chinese videos, everything a Chinese family desires can be found in Richmond. St. Clement Street is sprawling with Chinese restaurants and bakeries. It is no longer necessary to travel to Chinatown. Prices for food and a visit to the restaurant are just as cheap and the variety is as vast. A trip through the established districts reminds the foreign visitor more of Hong Kong than the old Chinatown.

---

[24] *San Francisco Medical Society*, <http://www.sfms.org/doctor.htm> (January 17, 2003).

[25] *NICOS Chinese Health Coalition* is one example for social Chinatown organizations. It is a collaboration of more than 40 health and human service related organizations.

A good example for the new migration of Chinese Americans is the Bayview district, which has a high Asian growth-rate. Between Felton and Woolsey Street there are approximately fifty small shops, banks, and restaurants. Chinese Americans run more than a third of them. Several years ago there were many empty shops. In an area of only four blocks on San Bruno Ave., two new Chinese restaurants, an ice-cream parlor, and a video shop—all with Chinese owners—have opened. An additional two businesses were taken over by Chinese.[26] How can this be explained?

Chinese are occupying districts in which the opportunities for business activity are still good. In Richmond and Sunset this is already no longer possible since the squarefoot prices have escalated. Especially small entrepreneurs use the neighborhood supply niche, e.g. provision of small demands to the neighborhood. In Bayview's San Bruno Ave., the rents are still lower than in better districts, e.g. 1 sq. foot costs approximately $1–2 per month, which results in an average shop rent of $1,000–2,000 monthly. In Richmond the monthly rent is already $2–3 per sq. foot, whereas in Chinatown it is $15 per square foot. Also, apartments are affordable and thus attractive to newly arrived. Apartments with two bedrooms cost $300 less than in Richmond and Sunset, as can be seen in the local newspaper ads.[27]

Value increase, however, is very high, e.g. in 1990 it was 20% on average, and between 1990 and 2000, property values and rental cost in Bayview increased by 80% on average. The good infrastructure, especially public schooling and public transport, supports this. The MUNI-Express-Bus service which connects Bayview with Chinatown and the Downtown districts very quickly. The buses are full of Asian commuters. This is all rounded off with mild temperatures and a clear view of the Bay with little fog. It will remain to be seen if Bayview grows into another Sunset.

Chinatowns Outside San Francisco

Can the habitation patterns of Chinese Americans in San Francisco be generalized for the United States? Are the developments in other cities similar? Over 90% of all Chinese Americans live in urban areas, primarily in California, Illinois, Massachusetts, New Jersey, New York, Texas and Washington. Chinatowns exist in all these states, and beside San Francisco, New York City plays an increasingly important role in the Chinese American community, a fact which suggests to compare the two cities. Since 1965, the Asian, and especially Chinese, populations show a strong growth in New

---

[26] For further details see also Kwong, Peter: *The New Chinatown*, 1996.

[27] In 2000, the Median Household Income in Richmond was $44,626, compared to $33,563 in Chinatown, $57,792 in Richmond, and $61,463 in Sunset (Grubb, 2002).

York. In 1970, 123,809 Asians were living in New York, of which 65% were Chinese. Between 1970 and 1990, Asians were the fastest growing minority, quadrupling in two decades (Chinese growth: 249%). Between 1990 and 2000, Asians grew by 60% from 489,859 to 783,058, and the Chinese by 53% to 357,243. Since the 1980s, New York has remained the largest Chinatown in America.[28]

In addition to the growth, further parallels between both Chinatowns are apparent. In the nineteenth century, hand laundries and other services also provided the predominant occupations of the Chinese in New York. At the turn of the century, New York Chinatown was a *bachelor society* of 7,000 Chinese with less than 150 women. Internal political structures were similar to San Francisco, the *Chinese Consolident Benevolent Association, CCBA,* ruled Chinatown throughout the early twentieth century (Waxman, 1998). Second and third generation Chinese started to move out into the suburbs, especially after 1965, starting new Chinatowns outside their original area.

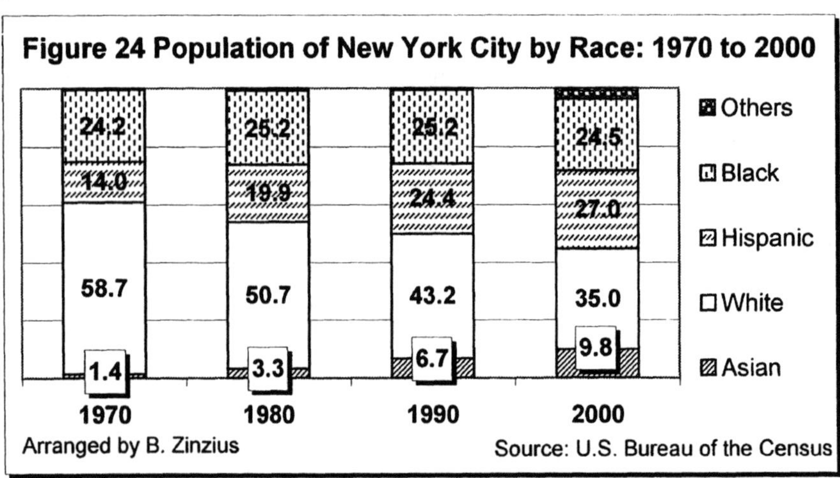

Today, between 70,000 and 150,000 Chinese are estimated to live in the Chinatowns of New York. Their residents have an important role in the local community, working in low-wage jobs, e.g. sweatshops and restaurants. Chinatown inhabitants are likely to have low earnings, a lower educational attainment, face linguistic barriers and live in below average housing

---

[28] In 2000, 66,053 people live in Manhattan's Chinatown, and 29,487 in Queens's Chinatown, Jackson Heights (Ong, 2002a, 9). Thus, since the 1980s, New York has the largest Chinatown and the largest number of Chinese outside Asia. New York City has, however, ten times the population of San Francisco. When comparing the Bay Area with New York—both areas have a similar population size—San Francisco Bay Area has the largest population of Chinese in the United States. New York's population data are derived from *Historical Census Statistics* (U.S. Bureau of the Census, 2002).

standards. They lack sufficient *affordable housing* units, similar to many other Chinatown-communities in the United States (Ong 2000a, 16).

New York and San Francsico are the two most densely populated cities in America, and the socio-economic characteristics of Chinatown inhabitants are basically equal. Furthermore, urban migration patterns of the Chinese population are similar to those in San Francisco. Today, over 60% of the Chinese in New York City live outside of Chinatown in middle-class areas, such as Manhattan and Brooklyn, where they have established new Chinatowns (Min, 1998; Zhou, 1995). Monterey Park emerged in the 1980s as the nation's first suburban Chinatown, developed by Fred Hsieh, a Chinese-born real estate developer (Waldinger, 1996, 19). The park is a suburban Chinatown in Los Angeles, and another example of a growing number of Asian middle- and upper-class suburbs. It is also called "Asian Beverly Hills," or "Little Taipei," because of its predominantly Taiwanese population. Since the middle of the 1990s, the number of mainland Chinese in Monterey Park is increasing, and newer nicknames are "Little Beijing" or "Little Shanghai." (*Los Angeles Times*, August 12, 2003). Other studies confirm this trend, showing an increased migration of Chinese Americans into wealthy suburbs of large cities (Luu, 1999; Lopez, 2002, 13-14).

Table 14 Chinatowns in the United States, 1990–2000

Chinatown	Since	Population 1990	Population 2000	Chinese in %	% API Renter	% Low Income	Pop. Density
Chicago	1870s	16,011	18,751	63%	62%	30%	11,535
New York	1880s	62,859	66,053	93%	93%	54%	88,290
Sacramento	1870s	16,566	18,739	16%	33%	62%	6,154
Seattle	1860s	6,251	6,260	20%	61%	30%	3,980
San Francisco	1850s	27,517	26,710	90%	90%	29%	53,240

Arranged by B. Zinzius   Source: Ong, 2002a, 9

Are the Chinese, especially those living outside of the traditional Chinatowns in middle- and upper-class districts, integrating into the American society, or do they live in ghettos? To answer this question, residential segregation patterns in the United States are analyzed.

Since the 1950s, residential segregation has been studied extensively as a measure for racial integration versus isolation. Although this measure depends on the definitions and statistical methods used, it is a helpful tool to study the assimilation and integration of an ethnic group within a society. The residential segregation statistics in the United States show that: [29]

---

[29] "Residential segregation describes the distribution of different groups across units within a larger area. The two most widely used dimensions of residential segregation are evenness,

1. The Asian and Pacific Islander population is much less isolated than the other large minorities, Blacks and Hispanics. The dissimilarity index for Asians was 0.411 in 2000, far below that of the Black (0.640) and the Hispanic (0.509) populations. Similar results appeared for the isolation index, which was 0.306 for Asians, compared to 0.552 for Hispanics and 0.591 for Blacks.

2. During the past two decades, however, the dissimilarity gap narrowed. In 1980, the dissimilarity index for Asians was 0.405, growing to 0.411 in 2000. For Hispanics the index was stagnant, and for Blacks it decreased from 0.727 to 0.640. Similar results appeared for the isolation index, which grew from 0.233 to 0.306 for Asians, whereas for Blacks it decreased from 0.655 to 0.591.

Table 15 Residential Segregation in the United States, 1980–2000

	Dissimilarity Index		**Isolation Index**	
	1980	**2000**	**1980**	**2000**
Black	0.727	0.640	0.655	0.591
Hispanics or Latinos	0.502	0.509	0.454	0.552
Asian and Pacific Islanders	0.405	0.411	0.233	0.306

Arranged by B. Zinzius   U.S. Bureau of the Census, 2002, CENSR-3

These examples and figures confirm the migration of Chinese Americans into mainstream American neighborhoods. The Chinese are spreading more equally among all racial groups and neighborhoods than other ethnic minorities. This allows the Chinese to assimilate or adapt better, and also influence the White majority better than Blacks and Hispanics.

Social Differentiation of Chinatown Inhabitants

In the current analysis, we must emphasize the following:

Since the immigration laws of 1965, not only the number of Asian immigrants, but also their geographic distribution and their socio-economic composition has changed. New immigration of the Chinese group is concentrated in areas of economic success, especially where the service industries play a major role.

San Francisco and New York are the major areas of attraction for Chinese immigration. Next to the old Chinatown, however, new ones have

represented by the *dissimilarity index*, and exposure, represented by the *isolation index*. The *dissimilarity index* ranges from 0 (complete integration) to 1 (complete segregation). The *isolation index* varies also from 0 to 1, and describes the extent to which minority members are exposed to only one another." The data were calculated based on the *Residential Segregation* data of the U.S. Bureau of the Census, 2002.

grown, giving new opportunities to a developing middle class. In addition, an economically successful group within the Chinese American population is pushing the Whites from the more affluent living areas. Lastly, the Chinese and other Asian businesses are continuously operating in districts that used to be considered off-limits to Asians. Among Chinese a typified picture is:

> *ABC Chinese* (*American-born Chinese*) tend to have college education, White collar jobs and choose to live outside of urban (old) Chinatowns.

> *FOB Chinese* (*fresh-off-the-boat Chinese*) have little education, speak little English, live in Chinatown and work in the lowest income bracket service industries or in the sewing industry.

> *FOP Chinese* (*fresh-off-the-plane Chinese*) are direct relatives of earlier immigrants benefiting from family reunification, and well-educated students. They live predominantly in the new Chinatowns or in the multicultural environment of top-level Universities.[30]

An initial differentiation among the new immigrants shows the majority of the Taiwanese to belong to the first and third category and the mainland Chinese (including some Hong Kong Chinese) to belong to the second and third.[31] A further hypothetical differentiation stems from knowledge of the situation and emigration tendencies of the countries of origin:

From Hong Kong approximately 50% are rich and intellectual, from Taiwan the majority are middle-class and intellectual, and from the People's Republic of China most are from the poorer population (Interview with Ling-chi Wang, 1991). A more intense analysis of employment should give further information. Thus we have defined a necessary and interesting point of focus.

For the emigration out of the old Chinatown, the change from the Chinese bachelor society to the family-oriented society has played a fundamental role. A short look at the current problems within the Chinese American family offers a preview of some important factors. Chinese children in Chinatowns are more often educated bilinguals. In the morning they are taught in English, whereas in the afternoon they attend Chinese schools where they learn either Cantonese or Mandarin, since the books, etc, are funded mainly by Taiwanese groups. Some little Chinese Americans even believe Taiwan's head of state to be their "President." (Interview with Wing Chung, 1991). Some parents embrace *ethnic diversity*, bilinguality, and multicultural surroundings, since this is closer to reality than the sterile, White communities. Others prefer to evade the confrontation with their own differences, by moving to Lafayette and Moraga, e.g. wealthy suburbs of White majority, where few other Chinese live. There the opportunity exists to

---

[30] See Chapter 6 "Education."
[31] See Chapter 3 "Changes in the Situation in the Countries of Origin."

give the children a singular, White identity and to improve the social status of the family on a long-term basis.

History and current developments indicate the increasing role that Asian and in particular Chinese immigration will play in the United States. Predictions suggest that in 2100, the Chinese will account for 3.1% of the American population, e.g. 25 million (Kolankiewicz, 2000).

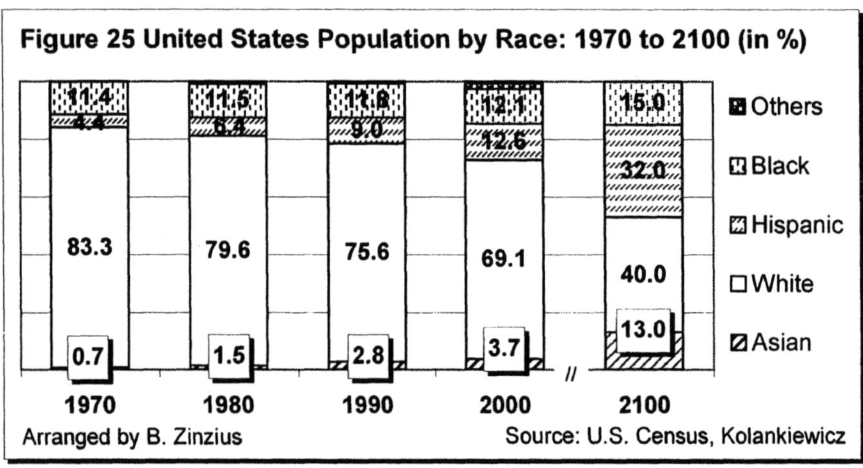

Family and family life are probably the most severe changes in comparison to the earlier Chinese American society, and many of the current and future immigrants come based on family reunification or as direct relatives. Therefore, they shall receive further analysis in the course of this work. The importance of bringing families together after immigration has been shown. In closing this chapter, it must be remembered that the settled family in the United States has become a clear impulse for leaving the ghetto. The value of the family as an economic and cultural unit is evident. The economic determination of its social forms still requires further analysis of employment and income structures. The family in its current appearance, including all most recent trends regarding partnerships and cohabitation, is therefore seen as the result and not as a determinant for education and production within the group. The living situation is an important indicator for the economic situation of the Chinese Americans. The sociologically simple combination of housing and work should not be torn apart.

5. BUSINESS STRUCTURES AND INCOME

In the 1960s, a de-industrialization began in the United States that destroyed employment and increased the competition among ethnic groups in the labor market. Supply-side, trickle-down economics, commonly known as Reaganomics, was predominant in the 1980s. President Reagan's *Economic Recovery Tax Act* of 1981 initiated massive tax cuts and, thus, created a hospitable environment for entrepreneurs, investors, and families. President Reagan always claimed that many new jobs were created either in the highest or lowest service sectors. In the *Annual Report to Congress* in 1982, he emphasized the importance of minority owned businesses and the service sector: "Small business has also played an important role in providing economic opportunities for minorities and women, both as employees and as entrepreneurs. [...] Given our nation's economic difficulties we cannot afford to ignore the resources and potential contributions of small business enterprises." (Reagan, 1982). President Reagan's tax cut policies started two decades of high growth and rising employment. At the same time, poverty rates were constantly high, and hourly wages falling, especially in the service sectors, which created the need for multiple jobs in the low-income brackets, a factor of special importance for minorities (Mack, 2000).

The widespread accommodation of the Chinese in the Bay Area, especially since 1965, indicates a far greater differentiation of employment structures than was historically the case. In analyzing immigrant employment, therefore, we must choose a perspective that accounts for the immigrant type and length of stay. The following questions thus arise: What opportunities for employment do the Chinese have in California upon arrival? Which jobs and what income have those who stay in Chinatown? What income level allows Chinese to move out of Chinatown and into better quarters? Which jobs are taken by American-born Chinese? Do the Chinese Americans establish businesses, and if so, which kind? These aspects have never been examined systematically on a broader base.

The evaluated data for the period up to 1970 already show a social differentiation of the classical two-class society with merchants and workers, indicating the decrease of the merchants' group. The number of professionals was growing strongly, whereas the working class in the classical sense had almost disappeared. Employment and income must be evaluated in further detail with regard to the newest developments. The mosaic of the Chinese American business world needs to be reconstructed with a focus on new immigration since the immigration laws of 1965 took effect, in order to prove identified tendencies or to show changes. In addition to the individual task of feeding the family, the collective component will be taken into account. Is there still, or maybe again, a Chinese business sector in the United States with typical characteristics, such as the steaming irons and smelly tobacco shops of the past, or have the Chinese merged into the general business world?

Active Population

First we shall examine the general employment rate of Chinese American groups. Throughout the recent censuses, the foundation for the following analysis, Asians and Pacific Islanders had a higher employment rate than the total population. In 1980, 66.5% of the Chinese above sixteen years old participated in the labor force, compared to 63.8% of the total population.

Table 16 Percentage of Chinese Immigrants over 16 Years, by Period and Race, 1980

	Total	'75-'80	'77-'75	'65-'70	'60-'65	before '60
Mainland-Chinese	66.5%	58.5%	73.6%	74.4%	74.7%	62.0%
Taiwan-Chinese	59.6%	50.3%	66.2%	73.7%	74.8%	75.6%
Hong Kong-Chinese	65.1%	54.7%	68.1%	68.4%	71.9%	76.7%

Arranged by B. Zinzius   Source: U.S. Bureau of the Census, 1980

This gap narrowed to 65.9% for the Chinese and 65.3% for the total population in 1990. By comparison, for Chinese women the rate was 58% in 1980 compared to 51.5% of the total female population, and in 1990 59.2%, compared to 57.5% of the total female population.[1] The Chinese not only offer a younger population, but also have a lower unemployment rate among those of working age. In 1980, of this employable Chinese group, 96.5% of mainland Chinese, 79.6% of Taiwanese, and 75% of Hong Kong Chinese are employed.[2] For mainland Chinese, the rate of those who were previously categorized in the high-income bracket is lower than that in the low-income bracket. In 1980, the unemployment rate for Chinese Americans was at 3.7% in contrast to a national average of 6.5%.

The figures for 1990, as shown in the table, evidence this claim. The unemployment figure for the general population was at 6.3%, whereas it was at 4.7% for all Chinese Americans. This high rate of employment of the whole group, the origin-specific differences in income, and the social differentiation will be examined closely.

---

[1] "Economic Report of the President, 2002." Table B-39. February 7, 2003. <http://w3.gpo.gov/eop> (March 7, 2003).

[2] Statistic: "Labor Force Participation of Chinese Immigrants over age 16." U.S. Bureau of the Census. "Foreign-Born Immigrants: Chinese." 1980 and 1990 U.S. Census of the Population and Housing. Washington, DC.

Table 17 Labor Force Participation of Chinese Immigrants, 1990 in Percent

	Total	Male	Female
United States (all)	65.3%	74.4%	56.8%
Chinese (all)	65.9%	72.9%	59.2%
Native-born Chinese	69.5%	73.6%	65.2%
Foreign-born Chinese	65.1%	72.8%	57.8%
Taiwanese	59.4%	68.9%	50.0%

Arranged by B. Zinzius   Source: Chinese American Data Center, 2002

In addition to differentiating immigrants according to country of origin, it is necessary to analyze fundamental differences between earlier immigrants and new immigrants. It must be taken into account whether the resulting differences are due to general economic development. The unemployment rate of foreign-born in 1980 was 3.7% for mainland Chinese (3% men; 4.6% women), 3.6% for Taiwanese (2.1% men; 5.4% women), and 3.9% for Hong Kong Chinese (3.8% men; 4% women). In 1980, the employment status of native-born men between the ages of 25 and 64 was very favorable, with an unemployment rate of 1.4%, in comparison to 4.0% for Whites. Even at its highest unemployment rate, the group of native-born is still below that of the total population (Cabezas, 1988, 62).[3]

Table 18 Unemployment Rates of Chinese Immigrants, 1990 in Percent

	Total	Male	Female
United States (all)	6.3%	6.4%	6.2%
Chinese (all)	4.7%	4.5%	5.0%
Native-born Chinese	3.7%	4.2%	3.2%
Foreign-born Chinese	5.0%	4.6%	5.4%
Taiwanese	5.1%	4.3%	6.1%

Arranged by B. Zinzius   Source: Chinese American Data Center, 2002

Interestingly enough, the rate for the native-born, who are no longer part of the employment pool, is also lower than that of Whites. Are new immigrants less active than native-born, e.g. children of earlier immigrants?[4] In contrast to all other groups and generations, including those immigrating before 1974, the employment rate of immigrants from 1975 to 1980 is lower than the national average.[5]

Is a long-term decline in employment of Chinese on the way? The comparative figures seem to indicate that initially upon arrival the Chinese have a larger rate of non-participants in the workforce, but their ability to

---

[3] The unemployment rate nationwide: 1970, 4.5%; 1980, 7.1%; 1982, 9.7% (recession); 1990, 5.6%; and 4.0% in 2000. U.S. Department of Labor, Labor Statistics, 2001.

[4] See Chapter 6 "Education." The older immigrants invest in the education of their children.

[5] Statistic: *"Foreign-Born Immigrants: Chinese."* 1980 U.S. Bureau of the Census, Washington, DC, 1984.

integrate is very pronounced. For the group staying 6 to 15 years in the country, the unemployment rate drops from 24.6% to 6.7%, whereas for Whites it declines from 16.4% only to 8.2% (U.S. Census of 1990).

Income, Occupation, and Working Women

Examining the average income helps locate the Chinese within the general socio-economic order and determine deviation within the group. Further information broadens our picture of the ability of new immigrants to integrate. A table of average incomes segregated according to working members of a family indicates that in 1980, in all areas where at least one and at most two family members were employed, the Chinese had higher incomes than comparable families within the total population (Cabezas, 1987, 19–20). The proportion of families in which more than one, and in particular those where more than two family members were employed, was higher than the national average. For immigrants arriving before 1979, the proportion was even higher than that of all Chinese Americans.[6] This higher proportion explains why the employment level among the higher income group, predominantly Hong Kong and Taiwan Chinese, is lower than the Chinese average.

The high income makes the employment of additional family members superfluous. This claim is only valid for the Chinese Americans as a whole, whereas the income for those new immigrants under ten years' residency was far lower in 1980. The mean income of all Chinese American families in the West was at $24,663 in 1974 and $28,377 in 1980.[7]

The next question focuses on the respective income distribution among Chinese Americans. The 1990 census shows that between 8% and 16.5% of all Chinese Americans were living in poverty, depending on their origin. Native-born Chinese showed the lowest level of poverty with 8.4%, whereas foreign-born immigrants had the highest poverty level with 16.5%. Immigrants from Taiwan and Hong Kong, however, were earning high incomes, and 50% were in the middle class comprised of new immigrants and second to fourth generation Asian Americans.

---

[6] Families with double incomes: Chinese Americans, 46.8%; United States average, 41.6%; new Chinese immigrants, 46.2%. Triple family income: 18.7%, 12.6%, 20.6 %. Statistic: "Workers per United States," "Ethnic Chinese American and Chinese Immigrant Family and the Median Income: 1979." U.S. Bureau of the Census. 1980 census of the Population. See also Chapter 7 "Family Structures."

[7] The average income of *Asian Americans* in other regions in 1980: East, $27,426; North-Central, $26,139; South, $24,934; West, $26,671. See also "Asians in America" 1990 Census. *Asian Week*, San Francisco, 1991.

In his assessment, Wang conspicuously relates immigrant generation and land of origin to certain income categories and particular the high number of people living in poverty (Interview, 1990). The high participation of women in the workforce allows conclusions concerning size of the families and average family income. If the Chinese family income stands above the national average for the norm family, one can conclude that the Chinese work more to earn more money than other American families and, in order to do so, deviate from traditional models, e.g. women in the kitchen. If, however, it is not be above the average, one can conclude that Chinese women must more often work than in other families, to obtain an income that allows an average standard of living.

The figures for 1990 indicate that the incomes of the Chinese Americans during the 1980s were starting to exceed the national average, especially for foreign-born Chinese. In 1980, the per-capita income of the Chinese was $13,309, compared to $14,186 of the national average. In 1990, on a per-capita basis, the Chinese group was slightly above the national average ($14,877:$14,420), and the mean family income of Chinese Americans had clearly surpassed the national average ($51,931:$43,803).

Thus, our earlier hypothesis can be substantiated: In Chinese families more members are employed than in other families to achieve an above-average income. In 2000, the estimated average income of Chinese Americans was $65,000, compared to the national average of $42,000. (*Businessweek Online*, September 25, 2000; US Census, Historical Income tables H-5). What special situation causes this extra work? During Ronald Reagan's presidency, a general tendency first became noticeable, whereby women in middle class families were required to work in order for the family to maintain a certain standard of living. A similar development among the Chinese, who are further confronted with integration difficulties, is therefore not a far-fetched conclusion. Studies show that Chinese Americans have a certain social mobility, since unemployment decreases with the length of stay, and after ten years a substantial increase in income is achieved. In order to achieve their family income, since 1974, more Chinese family members have had to work than the national average. Do Asian Americans individually earn less than their fellow countrymen? Amado Cabezas, Professor of Ethnic Studies at Berkeley, believes that most Asians, excluding Japanese, are still discriminated against due to race, sex, or origin (1988, 145). Taking the White population as the average (100%), then male, native-born Chinese in Oakland-San Jose earned 90.7% of that of their White colleagues and foreign-born earned only 76.5% of Whites' incomes. According to Cabezas's data, however, the difference between 45-year-old Chinese and White males during the 1980s was only slight. Until the 1990s, the young, long-term immigrants surpassed the national average.

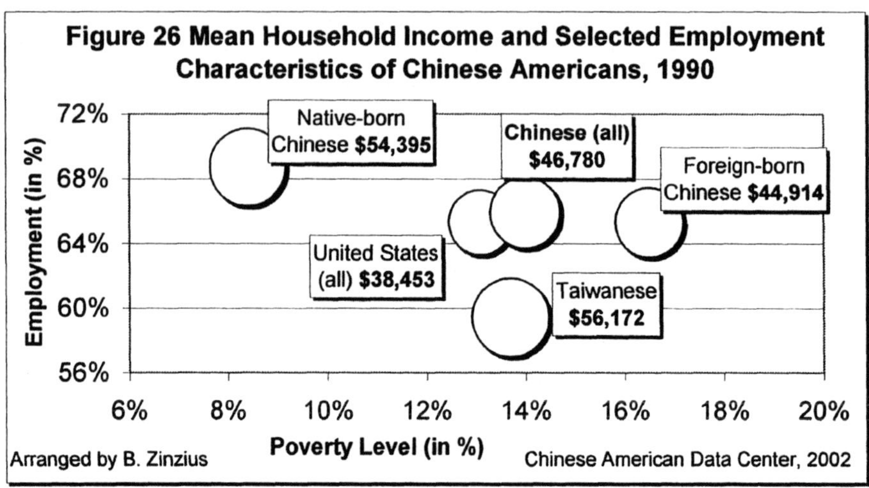

American-born Chinese men over 45 years of age improve their position in the income table from 90.7% to 94.3% in comparison to White men. This proves that second generation families establish themselves well and are upwardly mobile, thus reducing the necessity of the wife to seek employment (Cabezas, 1988, 145). The figures of the Taiwanese group strongly support this claim. What might be initially surprising, but substantiates the indicated tendency, is that Chinese American women under 45 years of age have an income (measured against that of White males) higher than their White counterparts (56.7%:44%), whereas the averages for older women are almost the same. Into this picture fits the fact that Chinese women have a higher percentage of highly educated members than Whites do. This has been a continuous development since 1950.[8]

A detailed analysis of the different Chinese groups confirms that all Chinese Americans, including foreign-born, have an above-average family and household income (Census of 1990). Native-born Chinese have the highest employment rate, the lowest poverty level and highest family income, despite the low per-capita earnings.[9]

---

[8] See also Chapter 7 "Family Structures" for income levels of women.

[9] **Table 19 Mean Income of Chinese Americans in the United States, 1989:**

		U.S. (all)	Chinese (all)	Native-born Chinese	Foreign-born Chinese	Taiwanese
1989	Per Capita	$14,420	$14,877	$11,698	$16,285	$16,079
	Family	$43,803	$51,931	$65,586	$49,345	$62,010
	Household	$38,453	$46,780	$54,395	$44,914	$56,712

Arranged by: B. Zinzius   U.S. Bureau of the Census, Historic Income Tables H-5, 2002

Taiwan-born Chinese have the highest household income of all groups ($56,172), despite the fact that they have the lowest rate of employment—due to the low employment level of Taiwanese women.[10] Foreign-born Chinese have the highest poverty rate (16.5%), due to the difficulties of the adaptation process, but still have higher incomes than the national average. In contrast, the average income of Hispanics is only $30,301, and 21.1% live below the poverty limit. African Americans have an average income of $25,872, with 22% living in poverty.

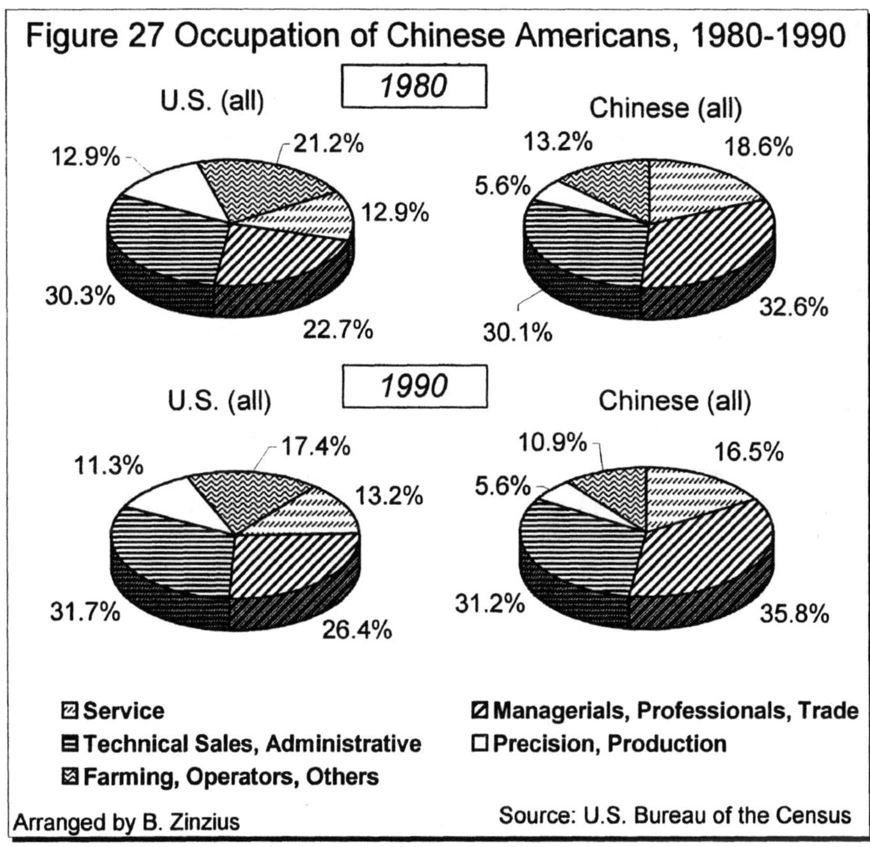

These above-average income figures are frequently used as an example for the Chinese American *model minority*. They should, however, be taken with some caution as they do not reflect the situation adequately, excluding factors such as age, education, and habitat. The majority of Chinese live in

---

[10] *Labor Force participation by Chinese-Americans, 1980-1990.* Chinese American Data Center, 2002.

California and New York, two of the most expensive areas, which results in above-average incomes. Studies taking these factors into account rarely find many differences between Asians and the national average (Sakamoto, 2002). However, they either fail to address all variables, such as regional income levels, or see Asians as one group, without differentiating among ethnicities. To evaluate the relative income of Chinese Americans, further details will be analyzed using San Francisco Bay Area as an example. First, occupation categories of Chinese Americans will be studied as another basis for income.

In 1980, 32.6% of Chinese Americans worked as managers (national average: 22.7%), 30.1% in sales and administration (national average: 30.3%), 13.2% worked in farming (national average: 21.2%), and only 5.6% in production (national average: 12.9%). This gap remained during the 1980s, although the ratio of "blue collar" jobs in all groups increased. In 1990, 35.8% of all Chinese Americans worked as managers (national average: 26.4%), 10.9% in farming (national average: 17.4%), and only 5.6% in production (national average: 11.3%). Chinese Americans have higher positions than the national average, a reason for their income levels.

An analysis of the different Chinese groups explains further details, especially for the Taiwan-born. The Taiwanese have the highest percentage of managers (48.3%) and the highest income of the Chinese Americans. All Chinese Americans have an above-average percentage of managers, thus generating higher incomes. Furthermore, 19% of all Chinese American families have three or more workers, the national average is just 13.4%.

Table 20 Economic and Social Characteristics of Chinese Americans, 1989

	US (all)	Chinese (all)	Native-born Chinese	Foreign-born Chinese	Taiwanese
Median Age	33.0	32.3	16.3	36.7	31.0
3 or more workers	13.4%	19.0%	14.4%	19.9%	14.2%
Person per family	3.27	3.65	–	–	–
Person per household	2.6	3.1	2.5	3.3	3.5
Income per Capita	$14,420	$14,877	$11,698	$16,285	$16,079
Poverty Rates	13.1%	14.0%	8.4%	16.5%	13.7%

Arranged by B. Zinzius   Source: Census 1990; Chinese American Data Center, 2002

The Chinese groups differ significantly in various economic and social parameters. It is interesting to note that the median age of native-born Chinese is only 16.3 years old, caused by a high percentage of children, which also results in a low per-capita income of this group.

Their poverty rate is nevertheless the lowest among all Chinese groups, and they have the highest family income.[11] Taiwanese have the lowest number of workers per family (14.2% have three or more worker), but the highest per capita and household income. It is also interesting to note that the differences between Asian ethnicities and the Chinese are larger than those among the Chinese themselves. Chinese per capita and family income is higher than the Asian average. Asian Indians, however, have an even higher income, whereas the Vietnamese, Laotian, and especially the Hmong have far lower ones. Therefore, data of Asians as a whole should not be taken as representative for the different ethnicities, as these figures do not reflect the vast differences of the Asian ethnic groups.[12] Factors that influence these figures are, among others, education, occupation, the ratio between foreign and native-born, the percentage of students, and the length of their stay in the United States.[13]

The occupational and social details of Chinese Americans in the San Francisco Bay Area show their broad spectrum of income and habitations. In 2000, 6.9% of the Bay Area population was Chinese, 43.7% worked as managers, and 12.8% in the service sector. The table demonstrates that Chinese Americans are more frequently found in areas with high income, high percentages of managers, and a lower percentage of service occupations.

The concentration of Chinese in Silicon Valley, the heart of Americas high-tech industry, is remarkably high, resulting in a new synonym for the term IC (Integrated Circuit) industry: "Indian and Chinese industry." The mean family income in Hillsboro exceeds $200,000, and 72% of all workers are managers. At the same time, 18.2% of the Hillsboro population is Chinese. Similar in Cupertino (23.8%), Milbrae (16.5%), Milpitas (12.9%), and Sunnyvale (9.6%). Daly City seems to be an exception with a high level

---

[11] It is important to note that the high percentage of native-born Chinese-American children does not lead to a large family size. In 1990, 69.4% of all Chinese Americans were foreign-born, whereas all their children born in the United States are naturally native-born.

[12] **Table 21 Economic and Social Characteristics of Asian Americans, 1989**

	Asian (all)	Chinese (all)	Filipino	Japanese	Asian Indian	Vietnam.	Laotian	Hmong
Median Age	30.1	32.3	31.1	36.3	28.9	25.2	20.4	12.5
>2 workers/family	19.8%	19.0%	29.6%	15.3%	17.8%	21.3%	18.9%	6.7%
Persons per family	3.8	3.6	4.0	3.1	3.8	4.4	5.0	6.6
Income/Capita ($)	13,806	14,877	13,616	11,970	17,777	9,032	5,597	2,692
Poverty Rates	14.4%	14.0%	6.4%	7.0%	9.7%	25.7%	34.7%	63.6%

Arranged by B. Zinzius   Source: Census 1990; Chinese American Data Center, 2002

[13] In 1979, Chinese Americans had an annual capita income of $7,946 for immigrants within five years of arrival, $11,797 within five to ten years, $14,333 within ten to fifteen years, and $16,663 after 20 years of immigration (Barringer, 1995, 237).

of Chinese and a lower than average percentage of managers (29.4%), but the high number of Filipinos working in the service sector distorts the pattern.

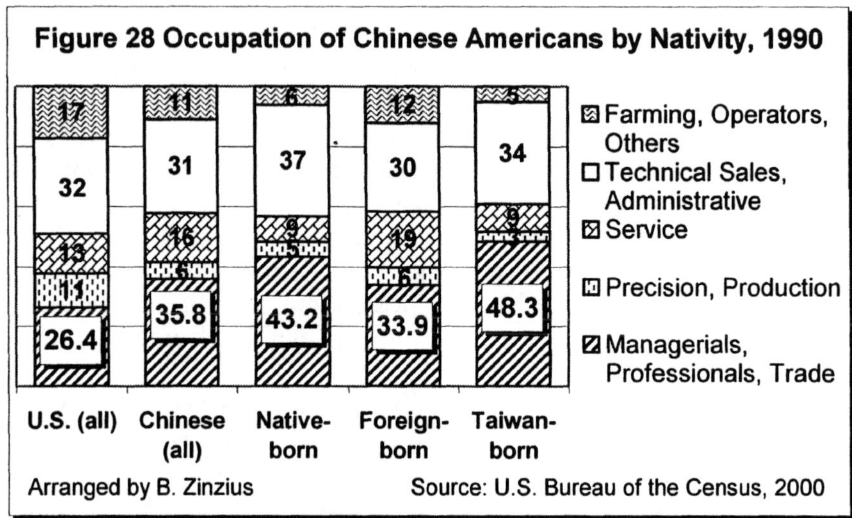

In contrast, fewer Chinese Americans are living in areas with less than average income, such as Napa County (0.4%), Solano County (0.8%), and Sonoma County (0.7%). The social and economic details of San Francisco, the county with the highest concentration of Chinese Americans, are less conclusive as a whole. In 2000, 48.3% of San Francisco's population worked as managers, and 14.3% in the service sector; the income per capita was $34,556, the mean family income $63,545, thus, all socio-economic figures for San Francisco are far above the national average, somewhat distorting the picture of the Chinese Americans nationwide. The different classes and social development of the Chinese Americans are well reflected in their preferred neighborhoods. New immigrants move to Chinatown, where they find low-wage jobs.

Among all districts, Chinatown, with 85.5% Chinese, has the lowest income levels (per capita income is 42.7% of the city average), the lowest percentage of managers (19.6%), and the highest percentage of service occupations (29.9%). A second group of districts surrounding Chinatown, which includes Bayview (Chinese: 18.2%), Crocker Amazon (Chinese: 27.2%), and Oceanview (Chinese: 31.6%), offer Chinese Americans entrepreneurial opportunities for small ethnic businesses, as well as service jobs. Although these districts have rather low per-capita incomes, the family incomes reach that of the city average. Between 1990 and 2000, growth-rates of the Chinese in some of these districts reached 165%.

Table 22 Chinese American Alone Population in the Bay Area, 2000

County / City	Total Population	Chinese	% of Pop.	Income / Capita ($)	Income / Family ($)	Poverty Rate	Managm. Jobs (%)	Service Jobs (%)
Alameda	**1,443,741**	**112,006**	**7.8%**	**26,680**	**65,857**	**11.0%**	**42.3%**	**11.9%**
Fremont	203,413	29,240	14.4%	31,411	82.199	5.4%	49.8%	7.8%
Hayward	140,030	3,998	2.9%	19,695	54,712	10.0%	26.7%	13.5%
Oakland	399,484	31,834	8.0%	21,936	44,384	19.4	39.2%	15.8%
Contra Costa	**948,816**	**28,948**	**3.1%**	**44,962**	**88,934**	**6.6%**	**52.5%**	**12.0%**
Concord	121,780	2,632	2.2%	24,727	62,093	7.6%	34.0%	17.8%
Marin	**247,289**	**3,523**	**1.4%**	**44,962**	**88,934**	**6.6%**	**52.5%**	**12.0%**
Napa	**124,279**	**537**	**0.4%**	**26,395**	**61,410**	**8.3%**	**34.6%**	**18.0%**
San Francisco	**776,733**	**152,620**	**19.6%**	**34,556**	**63,545**	**11.3%**	**48.3%**	**14.3%**
San Mateo	**707,161**	**48,996**	**6.9%**	**36,045**	**80,737**	**5.8%**	**42.7%**	**13.5%**
Daly City	103,621	14,063	13.6%	21,900	68,365	7.1%	29.4%	16.9%
Hillsboro	10,825	1,973	18.2%	98,643	200,000+	2.8%	72.2%	3.8%
Milbrae	20,718	3,427	16.5%	33,193	82,061	3.4%	41.4%	11.7%
South SFO	60,552	4,739	7.8%	23,562	66,598	5.2%	30.1%	14.5%
Santa Clara	**1,682,585**	**115,781**	**6.9%**	**32,795**	**81,717**	**7.5%**	**48.5%**	**10.5%**
Cupertino	50,546	12,031	23.8%	44,749	109,455	4.8%	71.0%	4.2%
Milpitas	62,689	8,098	12.9%	27,823	84,827	5.0%	45.5%	8.3%
San Jose	894,943	51,109	5.7%	26,697	74,813	8.8%	40.8%	12.3%
Sunnyvale	131,760	12,597	9.6%	36,524	81,634	5.4%	59.5%	9.0%
Solano	**394,542**	**3,318**	**0.8%**	**21,737**	**60,597**	**8.3%**	**30.9%**	**16.4%**
Vallejo	116,760	1,032	0.9%	20,415	56,805	10.1%	29.3%	17.9%
Sonoma	**458,614**	**3,007**	**0.7%**	**25,724**	**61,921**	**8.1%**	**35.0%**	**15.1%**
Santa Rosa	147,595	1,118	0.8%	24,495	59,659	8.5%	34.1%	15.9%
Bay Area	**6,783,760**	**468,736**	**6.9%**	**30,934**	**71,333**	**8.6%**	**43.7%**	**12.8%**

Arranged by B. Zinzius   Source: U.S. Bureau of the Census, 2002

A third group includes districts with high incomes and high percentage of managers. In these districts, such as Diamond Heights (Chinese: 11.3%), Noe Valley (Chinese: 3.0%), Richmond (Chinese: 31.4%), Sunset (Chinese: 34.2%), and Twin Peaks (Chinese: 7.6%), the per-capita and family incomes exceed the average, and the Chinese growth-rates approach 25%. The move of Chinese Americans from Chinatown into middle and upper-class districts shows their advance into higher levels of society. Nevertheless, this does not imply that Chinese Americans were able to reach top management positions, thus breaking the glass ceiling. The above-average income could result from double-income, entrepreneurship, or be purely based on the higher wages in their preferred areas.

Do Chinese American women contribute to the high family incomes of the Chinese, and do they earn more due to their education? This seems plausible. The difference in income between Chinese and Whites is higher than the difference in the rate of employment would justify. Discrimination against women as a whole exists, but it is less for Chinese than for White women. For Chinese women the employment rate has been higher than the average since 1950. In 1980, it was 58.3% versus 49.9%, and in 1990 59.2% versus the national average of 56.8%. Another possibility would be that a relatively high number of high-income women would counter the incomes of low-wage recipients (Yung, 1986, 124).

Table 23 Social Characteristics of Chinese Americans in San Francisco, 2000

Area	Total Population	Chinese	% of Pop.	Income / Capita ($)	Income / Family ($)	Poverty Rate (%)	Managm. Jobs (%)	Service Jobs (%)
San Francisco	**776,733**	**152,620**	**19.6%**	**34,556**	**63,545**	**11.3%**	**48.3%**	**14.3%**
Bayview	34,835	6,351	18.2%	16,771	48,791	21.8%	28.4%	23.3%
Chinatown	7,976	7,060	85.5%	14,776	25,295	20.2%	19.6%	29.2%
Crocker Amazon	13,294	3,617	27.2%	18,126	54,128	7.1%	27.7%	20.2%
Diamond Heights	8,019	903	11.3%	52,479	95,716	5.6%	63.3%	8.1%
Nob Hill	19,531	6,240	31.9%	42,904	49,563	10.2%	50.8%	13.3%
Noe Valley	17,597	524	3.0%	55,785	101,354	5.4%	68.2%	6.6%
North Beach	14,234	4,641	32.6%	55,618	73,407	10.9%	57.0%	9.7%
Oceanview	22,800	7,204	31.6%	19,602	60,959	8.6%	25.5%	22.8%
Parkside	14,578	5,689	39.0%	26,963	69,399	5.8%	40.9%	13.5%
Presidio Heights	9,907	775	7.8%	75,429	133,109	4.8%	64.5%	7.4%
Richmond	65,365	20,522	31.4%	32,194	68,146	7.8%	50.1%	12.2%
Sunset	76,431	26,117	34.2%	32.705	76,200	8.4%	53.3%	13.5%
Twin Peaks	10,116	767	7.6%	50,113	93,324	8.1%	63.6%	7.7%

Arranged by B. Zinzius   U.S. Bureau of the Census, 2000

The graphic shows that in 1940, women professionals represented only 8%, while women in domestic services represented 29%, and those in white and blue-collar jobs represented 18%.[14] Even in 1960, the proportion was still 17% in professional employments to 10% in domestic services.[15] In 1980, 25% of all women were in managerial or professional positions, which underlines the high education level of Chinese women, whereas technical and sales positions were the highest with 40% (U.S. Bureau of the Census, 2000). By 1990, the distribution had changed considerably and with 40.6%, the managerial or professional positions had become the largest category, whereas technical and sales positions had fallen to 33.2%. Other categories, such as production and services, also receded (U.S. Census 1990). This employment structure shows therefore a strong change towards higher positions with more responsibility and better payment.

---

[14] Throughout the twentieth century, classification of occupational categories has changed constantly as a reflection of industrial developments. Using the occupational categories of the Census 2000 as a basis, the above-mentioned graph was compiled from present and older Census data (for correlations between categories see Dean, 2002).

[15] In 1980, this category was merged under *services* (14%), *clerical and sales* were the most important group, occupying 38%. In the intermediate phase of 1970, 37% of women were

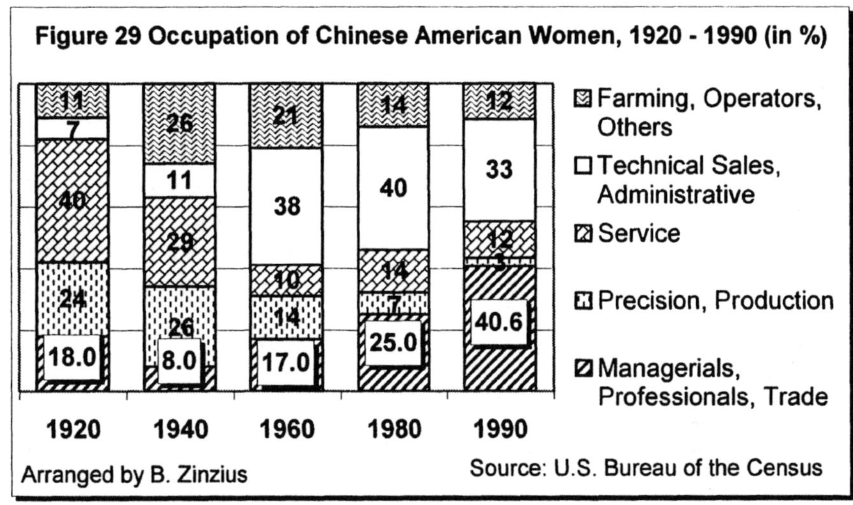

The number of married employed Chinese women is also far higher than that of Whites (70%:61%), hardly surprising regarding all the previous information.[16] Only the Japanese surpass their proportion with 76%. With regard to the integration phase and the subvention of the family income, the role of the Chinese American woman in business is at least as important as it is for the social mobility of those better off. The importance of an additional family member's income cannot be taken up here, but will be addressed later.

Some intermediate and important results can therefore be identified. Social mobility in this group is strong and upward-tending, whereas unemployment is low. Furthermore, generally speaking, the Chinese American family as a source of additional labor helps overcome the difficult integration process. Initial financial difficulties, some discrimination against race, and being in low-wage groups can play a role. An increasing number occupy highly paid managerial positions, especially native-born, Hong Kong and Taiwan Chinese, a fact that will be further examined in this chapter.

employed in the category *sales and clerical*, where 23% were *professionals* and 24 % *craftswomen and operatives*. "Major Occupations of Chinese Americans 1950 and 1970." Chen, J., 1980, graph 2.

[16] **Table 24 Percentage of Married, Employed Women in the United States, 1988:**

	Chinese (all)	Filipino	Japanese	Asian Indian	Korean	Vietnamese	White, non-Hispanic
Native-born	70%	66%	76%	48%	72%	-	61%
Foreign-born	65%	83%	27%	51%	61%	54%	52%
Arranged by B. Zinzius						Source: U.S. Bureau of the Census, 1990	

Career Opportunities

Careers and Legal Barriers

The previous results can be integrated in new questions. Does the Chinese group obtain the relatively crisis-safe position in American society after a number of years due to their original careers or education, due to the immigration regulations, or due to their career choices in the recipient country? Or are mental and cultural factors, the Confucian model, e.g. attitude towards career, education, and family, responsible for a relatively easy integration process?

From 1966 until 1975, 43% of Chinese immigrants were blue-collar workers, clerks, craftsmen, and service employees, 49% were managers, professionals and technicians. Substantially high and clearly differentiable from all other ethnic groups is the number of Chinese in service trades. In 1980, almost half of all foreign-borns Chinese were in this sector.

This figure declines, however, to 25% for the immigrants from 1975 to 1980, and for the native-borns, again by half, to 12%. The same data shows that the group of managers, professionals, and executives is generally large among Chinese. The largest proportion exists among native-borns, implying that the number of professionals increases with the length of stay.[17] The data for 1990 show a continuing trend among Chinese groups, and an overall shift to the managerial and service sectors can be seen due to general changes in the labor market. Professional and technical jobs are the most desired. Thus, in 1980, twice the number of Chinese is employed as technicians than the national average (6.3%:3.1%), and the Taiwanese represent the majority of them (11.4%:3.1%).[18]

Federal laws, however, have restricted exactly these preferred areas, since the mid-1970s. The number of scientists and engineers from Hong Kong and Taiwan living in the United States grew from 36 in 1964 to 1,164 in 1970. The number of these highly qualified Chinese has been declining since the mid-1970s. In some careers, quotas were installed due to union pressure. The *Health Professions Educational Assistance Act* of 1976 reduced the number eligible to provide health services and removed doctors and surgeons from the preferred A list. Since this regulation required testing of the applicants by the National Board of Examiners and the introduction of

---

[17] Interesting is the low number of Chinese in the security sector, alongside the high number of other clerical jobs, specially for immigrants from mainland China (10.8% of all ethnic groups in the U.S. compared to 23.5% of mainland Chinese). In the sales sector, Chinese are somewhat less represented than the national average (8.6%:10.0%), which is the same for all three groups–Taiwanese, Hong Kong and mainland Chinese.

[18] See Chapter 5 "Average Family Income, Middle Class and Working Women."

oral and written language aptitude tests, the number of immigrants in the professional medical services declined drastically. This change affected Asians in particular. Chinese doctors and medical assistants entered into the country via family reunification (Chan, S., 1991, 147). The tendency to immigrate via career preference has been declining due to the economic recession since the Carter administration. Since 1976, only one-fifth of Chinese immigrants *come under the* career preference, the rest enter under the family reunification preference. As shown, the economic slump between 1975 and 1980 meant a longer unemployment period in contrast to the national average. With the closing of this valve (immigration via career preference) in the face of continuous pressure from the existing per country quotas, Chinese immigrants turned naturally to the valve still open to them, that of family reunification.

The extreme thus far has occurred among mainland Chinese. In 1981, 456 visa applications were made for higher qualified positions (3rd Preference) and 2,653 for workers understaffed positions (1st and 2nd Preferences). These were opposed by 72,990 applications for the 5th Preference of sibling reunification, alone. During the 1990s, however, employment-sponsored immigrations have increased considerably.[19] For specialists with special abilities, artists, and scientists the waiting time is becoming shorter. For workers and tradesmen in understaffed trades, especially from Taiwan and mainland China, however, it is becoming longer due to the increasing numbers.

The *Eilber Act* of 1977 required from all potential employers of professionals that they prove that in employing immigrants they had not overlooked any United States residents and that they were paying them equal incomes. In the higher income brackets, the opportunity of financial discrimination against Chinese must be redundant. The tendency of qualified specialist immigration has been declining, while this category is growing in accord with the length of residency. This can be interpreted as follows: The

---

[19] 1985: 251 for all Chinese; see Visa Office of the U.S. Department of State, Feb. 1985.

Table 25 Chinese Immigrants by Nativity and Immigration Preference, 2000

Country of Origin	Total	Employment Based Preference	Family Sponsored Preference	Immediate Relative
Mainland China	41,861	12,350	11,332	17,688
Hong Kong	7,199	889	4,512	1,558
Taiwan	9,478	2,603	4,443	2,399

Arranged by: B. Zinzius   U.S. Bureau of the Census, 2000.

Only between 3% (1991) and 34% (1999) of all Chinese immigrants entered the United States based on employment-based preferences, the majority thereof under the 1st and 2nd Preference, e.g. as highly skilled professionals. About 70% of all immigrants entered using family ties (Immigration and Naturalization Service, *Statistical Yearbook 2000*, 2002).

education of highly qualified specialists is increasing, especially among the native-borns. The declining number of Chinese in the service sector, which was above average for Chinese Americans in 1975, offers a number of possible explanations: Among the long-term residents, a number could have moved up into the category of professionals, although the route remains to be identified. Other groups will have become members of the increasing unemployed. Between the poles of professionals and service workers, however, the opening of the group of lower qualified workers, including self-employed ones, must be considered.

Law and Age Structure

In Senator Simpson's 1982 and 1990 initiatives for the reduction of the 5th Preference,[20] the argument that family reunification increases the proportion of unproductive or less productive population played a major role.[21] Does this explain or underline the previously proposed hypotheses?

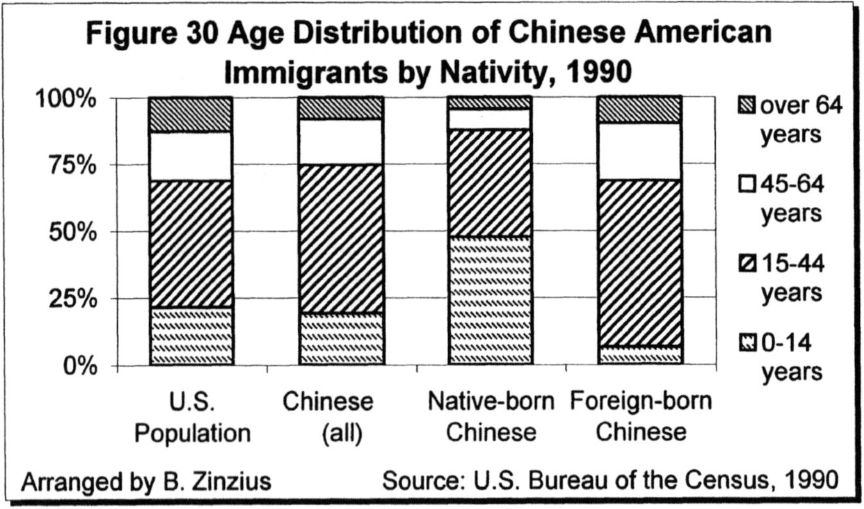

---

[20] See Chapter 3 "Immigration between 1965 and 2000."

[21] See also: Yochum. "Permanent Labor Certifications for Alien Professionals, 1975–1982." *International Migration Review* 22, 1988, 265–281.

At this point in the analysis, we only know that the unemployment level of immigrants within five years of their arrival is exceptionally high, but so was the ability to integrate over this period. Fundamentally, there are two reasons for declining productivity within a group: aging and lack of qualification. Regarding qualification, we have already seen that the level is exceptionally high for Chinese managers, specialists, and women. The age group from 25 to 34 dominates the categories of native and foreign-born Chinese Americans, and their median age is below the national average, although the gap narrowed.[22]

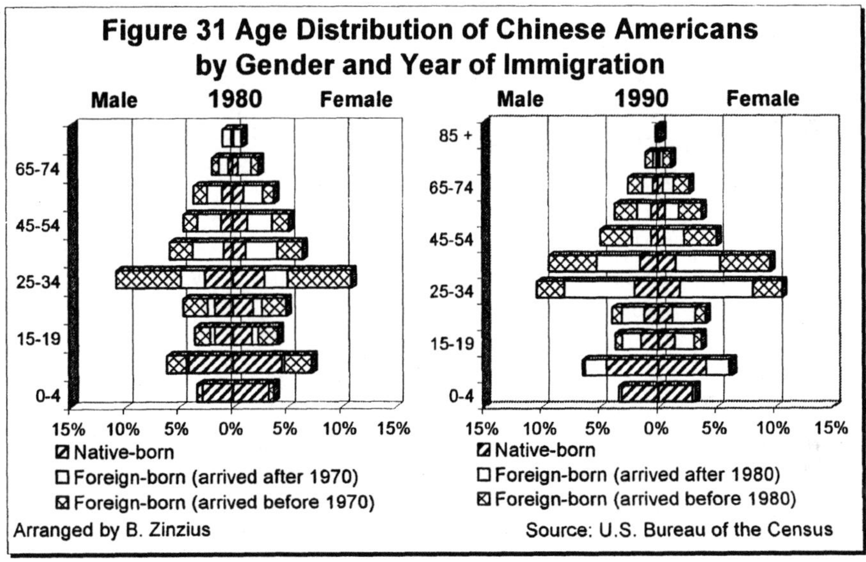

Furthermore, the most productive age group (20 to 64) is over-represented both among men and women, due to the high number of mainland immigrants. Native and foreign-born Chinese Americans represent basically two different generations: in 1990, over 57% of native Chinese Americans were below 20 years of age, compared to just 28.9% of the national average, whereas 77.2% of all foreign-born were between 20 and 64 years. Thus, the Chinese—at present—counterbalance the aging process

---

[22] **Table 26 Age Distribution of Chinese Americans, 1980 and 1990**

	U.S. (all)		Chinese (all)		Native-born		Foreign-born	
	1980	1990	1980	1990	1980	1990	1980	1990
Median Age	30.0	33.0	29.6	32.3	–	16.3	–	36.7
Below 20 years (%)	32.0%	28.9%	29.3%	26.7%	52.0%	57.2%	16.5%	13.2%
20-64 years (%)	56.7%	58.7%	63.7%	65.3%	44.8%	38.5%	75.1%	77.2%
Above 64 years (%)	11.3%	12.5%	6.9%	8.0%	3.1%	4.3%	8.4%	9.6%

Arranged by: B. Zinzius   U.S. Bureau of the Census, 1980, 1990.

within the United States, and the foreign-born immigrants are a strong resource for the labor market. Based on their age structure, the Chinese are an active part of the productive population.

Among the foreign-born Chinese, the proportion of elder mainland Chinese is still not exceptional in comparison to the total population, but it is exceptional in comparison to Chinese from Hong Kong or Taiwan, who tended to come from a young, productive group (15 to 44 years), with 76.1% and 77.1% in 1980. 25.2% of all mainland Chinese arrived before 1960, but only 6.6% Hong Kong Chinese and 1.9% Taiwanese. That means that among the mainland Chinese it was not the elders and thus more retirees who immigrated.[23] Furthermore, the Taiwanese had no quota until 1979 and the People's Republic of China only allowed emigration after 1979.

Hong Kong only had a relatively small quota as a British Colony since 1965.[24] The suspicion is that, among mainland Chinese the statistics only represent those who were early immigrants, but not those who came via Taiwan or Hong Kong. The relative aging of the mainland Chinese is thus explained. From 1970, the Chinese immigrants have increased their proportion in the age groups 15 to 39 substantially,[25] whereas the native-borns only represent a substantial proportion for the youngest groups (0 to 9 years). Of all Asian immigrants, the Chinese have the most equally distributed and most developed population structure, including a relatively high proportion of native-born and immigrants prior to 1970. In comparison to the total population, the Chinese have a lower median age.[26]

All these data indicate that the high proportion of active population among Chinese will not increase due to aging. One cannot support Simpson's first impression that productivity is reduced due to immigration via family reunification, even with regard to the age composition. But, in addition, identify that the strong Chinese presence in the most productive age group (up to 44 years) is a further explanation for the high employment rate of the group.

---

[23] "Median Ages of U.S. White, Black, Hispanic and Asian American Populations: 1980." The average age for Chinese was 29.6 years. "Age-Sex composition of the Six major Asian American Groups by Period of Immigration, and the total U.S. Population: 1980." Gardner, R., 1985, statistics 5 and 6.

[24] See Chapter 3 "Immigration between 1965 and 2000." The quota was raised in 1986 from 600 to 5,000.

[25] Even more extreme is the growth in this age group for Filipino immigrants.

[26] Between 1980 and 1990, the median age of Chinese Americans increased from 29.6 to 32.2 years old, whereas the national median age grew from 30.0 to 33.0 years old, thus the gap widened. The future development of the age pyramid of Chinese Americans depends on the balance between their birth–death ratio, but also their immigrant–emigrant ratio, a factor gaining increasing importance. See also Chapter 7 "Fertility–Children–Birth Rate," and Chapter 8 "Economy: The New *Global Entrepreneurs*."

The social data for the Chinese, e.g. employment figures, poverty rates, and household income, and the high integration ability hardly allow the conclusion of lower productivity. Moreover, not only employment, but also consumer activity, is important for the economic role of a group, especially in a country like the United States, where a strong consumption-oriented society makes the economy dependent on the production of consumer goods. Due to their age structure alone, Chinese not only work hard, they spend hard, too. Recently, they have been becoming ideal consumers. Their average age is 32.3 years old (national median age is 33.0 years old) and most have higher education.[27] They spend a long time in the large family prior to moving out, so they have a lot of money available for consumption.

According to a survey of advertisements for Asians by the *Wall Street Journal*, 66% live multiple income households (national average 53.1%) and they value quality above price. Business people in the Bay Area are slowly adjusting to a new consumer type. They are still not sure whether higher income Asians react to ethnic attributes or more to success symbols. Styles and sizes are already being adjusted to Asian purchasers.

In 2002, the purchasing power of Asians in the United States was estimated at $296.4 billion, a 152% increase over 1990, and is expected to exceed $450 billion by 2007.[28] Since the 1990s, an increasing number of advertising, consulting, and market research companies, such as *Kang & Lee Advertising* or the television channel *KTSF*, are therefore focusing on Asian American consumers, and the Chinese in particular. Corporate America is increasingly realizing the importance of Asian customers, and ethnic marketing is gaining importance in the United States.[29]

With their Asian models and main stories about Asian success managers, magazines, such as *AsiAm, aMagazine*, and *Rice* (this particular title unites all Asians), were particularly directed at Asian "yuppies," a group which is thus attaining an ethnic status symbol for the first time. The editors of *Rice* were aware that ethnic newspapers do not necessarily reach out to their readers, so they called their paper the "Premier Asian American/Pacific Rim Magazine" in order to remove the ghetto smell from the Asian touch. "Tapping the Yuppies" was a title of a newspaper article on the subject and was subtitled, "Magazines targeted at young Asian professionals hope to exploit their buying power and their cultural pride." (*San Jose Mercury*, June 27, 1988). Typical readers were Asian Americans of the third to fifth generations and couples around 30 with an annual household income of $100,000 and few, if no, children.

---

[27] Population of Asian Pacific Islanders, 1990. U.S. Bureau of the Census; See Chapter 6.

[28] Anderson, Kay. "Asian Tsunami." *Home Accents Today*, September 2002.

[29] See also Chapter 8 "Chinese Breaking the Ceiling," under "A Model Minority?"

During the 1990s, a large number of magazines targeted the Asian American community, especially young consumers. Not all exist today, including *aMagazine* and *AsiAm*.[30] More successful were Internet-based journals, like the websites *Goldsea* and *AsianNation*,[31] which both these middle- and upper-class Asian Americans.[32] Television stations, such as *KTSF, KCNS, KQED* or the *Jade Channel*, are another medium specifically for Chinese Americans, offering news, education and information in various languages, such as Cantonese and Mandarin. Radio Stations, such as *KVTO* and *Sing Tao Radio*, complete this service.

The fear of stereotyping that usually puts off Asians has not only been substituted by a clear option for ethnic marketing, as done by the editors of *Rice*, but also by many companies, such as the *Bank of America* in San Francisco, which issues advertisements and brochures in Chinese and has TV spots in Chinese style. Marketing specialists at *Remy Martin* believe that even strongly assimilated Asians of the third to fifth generations still react to ethnic signals in advertising. In the next years, advertising will, to some extent, define the form that assimilation takes or whether any particular Asian assimilation model will arise. This possibility is probably an important reason for the caution on the part of the advertisers.

Glass Ceiling and Occupational Downgrading

Subsequent to the discussion on Asian yuppies, questions arise about the Asian upper class. How successful are Chinese American entrepreneurs, managers, and scientists? Do their average short stay and high family incomes represent an exceptional vocational success?[33]

Asian professionals are divided from the top positions by a *glass ceiling* through which they can look up from their middle management positions, but can never surpass. In this context, the *Wall Street Journal* mentioned that often those companies, which advertise for Asians as technical professionals do not want them in management or leadership positions (Wu, 1985, 16).[34]

---

[30] Lai, Eric. "Click2Asia and aMagazine Shutting Down." *AsianWeek*, 8–14 March, 2002.

[31] See <http://www.goldsea.com/>, and <http://www.asian-nation.org/>.

[32] The number of printed media for the Chinese American population changed dramatically during the 1990s, including publications in Cantonese and Mandarin. *China Press, Chinese Times, Chinese American Daily News*, or the *St. Louis Chinese American News* are Chinese newspapers. Magazines include *aMagazine, Cyanide, Flicka*, or *Yolk*, and e-Magazines such as *Generation Rice* and *Generasian*.

[33] See Chapter 8 "Chinese Breaking the Ceiling," under "Model Minority?" and Chapter 5 "Business Structures and Income" for examples about extremely successful and wealthy Chinese Americans.

[34] Further information with Winfried Wu. "*Asian Americans* Charge Prejudice Slows Climb to Management Ranks," *Wall Street Journal*, September 1985. U.S. Equal Employment

Examples can be found everywhere. Of 29,000 managers in the 1,000 largest American corporations, only 159, or 0.5%, had an Asian name (*Asian Week*, 1989). Of a few dozen Asian American managers interviewed by *Fortune* magazine, very few are in top management positions. Ronald Takaki, Professor for Ethnic Studies at University of California, Berkeley wrote in 1989 that, in contrast to the number of Asian students at Berkeley, Asians were totally underrepresented in the university administration with only one of 102 top positions (1989a, 476). Difference in sex is a further criterion. "What is a glass ceiling for men becomes cement for women," said Shirley Hune in 1991, former Vice Chancellor of City University, New York, and one of few Asian women with political clout in the early 1990s.

The glass ceiling still underlines the current White majority in the leadership of the country, but it could be surpassed by reality, as will have to be shown. So-called occupational downgrading is a more difficult problem for new immigrants than the glass ceiling for long-term immigrants. Especially among mainland Chinese, many doctors, teachers, engineers, and bookkeepers initially have to take a janitor's or service job.

A few examples from a series of interviews with Chinese Americans from 1990 to 1992 support this claim: Ms. Wei Chi Poon was a biology professor prior to her emigration in 1967, her husband, Boon Pui Poon, a renowned architect. During their first years in the United States, both had to take jobs below their qualifications. The *Comprehensive Employment Training Act* allowed her to work as a librarian; she is now Head of Asian American Studies Library at Berkeley, where both their children graduated (Interview, 1991).

Further examples show more clearly social demotion experienced after immigration: In Canton, Winnie Wu was a mathematics teacher and her husband professor of Sinology. In San Francisco, she works as a simple office clerk and he is a janitor in a hotel. Ma Sit was a professional with a college degree in physics and now works on the production line of a factory. She says, "We are all college graduates, but work as seamstresses or in factories that manufacture electronic products." (Interview, 1990). Other immigrants, however, mainly from Hong Kong and Taiwan, who bring in money do not undergo economic decline. It is not unusual for engineers or professors to become restaurant or shop owners. Such is the case for Simon Lee, a graduated electronics engineer from mainland China, who now works as a waiter in a Chinese restaurant, because he could not find an equivalent occupation due to missing language skills.

Opportunity Commission report summary in Laird Harrison: "U.S. Study Finds Few Asians in Management" *Asian Week*, May 13, 1988. For glass ceiling see further in *Asian Week*, September issues 1991.

Poverty and Riches

We have thus far only analyzed average incomes among the Chinese group and vocational opportunities in connection to age, sex, origin, and length of stay. In this section, we place the social homogeneity in the spotlight. Deductions from social security in 1991, and the 1982 recession increased poverty in general. Since the Chinese were strongly affected by the crisis years, it remains to identify the effects of the economic boom after 1982.

For the period before 1965, we identified a high employment rate within the group and the tendency only to make infrequent use of federal support during crises.[35] In 1979, 6.6% of Chinese households used public assistance, e.g. child support, special pensions for handicapped, etc., and 13.9% took social security, in other words, "normal" pensions. Also here, the high rate of employment and the age structure comes to the forefront. There are less pension takers among Chinese than among Whites or Blacks. This is a clear and typical characteristic for a population not long settled. Chinese who cannot fulfill their vocational expectations due to the difficulties in the land of immigration do not remain in one place.

Instead of receiving social security, they prefer to take seasonal jobs or low-income jobs for a period of time.[36] In the last few decades, the poverty rate of Asian Americans has almost always remained below the national average, in contrast to the other large ethnic minorities.[37] A more differentiated analysis of the different Chinese ethnic groups shows that the foreign-born have a poverty level of over 16%, whereas native-born show only 8%.

These figures are based on individuals. The inclusion of the family as a comparative parameter would provide interesting results, since traditionally, single elders make up the majority of those living below the poverty level, especially among the mainland Chinese. Also, we identified that in Chinese families more than one member is usually employed.[38]

---

[35] See Chapter 1 "Chinese Emigration to California from 1848 until 1965."

[36] See Chapter 5 "Career Opportunities," and Chan, Sucheng. *Asian Americans.* Boston, Twayne Publishers, 1991, 161.

[37] **Table 27 Poverty Levels in the United States by Ethnicity, 1978 to 2000**

	1978	1980	1987	1990	2000
Total population	11.4%	13.0%	13.6%	13.6%	11.3%
White	8.7%	10.2%	10.3%	11.0%	9.4%
Black	30.6%	32.5%	33.1%	31.1%	22.0%
Hispanic	21.6%	25.7%	28.2%	27.3%	21.2%
Asian	6.7%	na	17.1%	12.1%	10.7%

Arranged by B. Zinzius. (Adams, Statistical Abstracts 1990, table 743; U.S. Bureau of the Census, 1990 in: "*We, the Asian and Pacific Islander Americans.*" Census 2000).

Thus, wealth is more unequally spread among the Chinese group than the national average and yet, even with this relatively high number of people living below the poverty level, the per capita and median household income level is higher than the national average.[39] A concession must be made here: The household income of all Asians and Asian Pacific Islanders is equal to the national average. The majority of Chinese Americans live in cities, e.g. San Francisco, New York, Honolulu, Los Angeles, or Chicago. In these cities one earns more, but the cost of living is equally higher (Chan, 1991, 168). While the Chinese have above-average incomes, their actual spending power may be well below the national average. This is confirmed when looking at house values of Asian Americans. Whereas the nationwide average price of a house is $119,600, it is $199,300 for Asians. Since the Chinese are not among the high-income top executives of international companies, due to the glass ceiling effect, we must search for the high incomes in specific businesses.

Ethnic Business and Racial Labor in Chinatown

Sweatshops and Restaurants

The inhabitants and simple workers of San Francisco's old Chinatown are definitely an underprivileged part of California's Chinese community. On the other hand, behind the large properties and trading centers of Chinatown, one finds the rich and influential Chinese. A law originating in 1957, which determined the use of lands by zoning the districts into residential, industrial, and commercial areas, declared that within Chinatown no more than 25 employees are allowed in a single business and that only sewing machines can be installed. Thus, tailors remained dependant on larger companies, but their number has increased dramatically. The owners have the cuts sewn in their shops and then deliver the finished garments to their customers. The large businesses suppress the prices as much as possible with their Chinese subcontractors, who, in turn, transfer this pressure to their employees in the form of low wages.

The Chinese American textile industry and dependent service industries are major sources of Chinese American income. Alone in the Bay Area, the garment industry has a sales volume of $3.5 billion.

---

[38] The U.S. Bureau of the Census defines a family as two or more persons living together and being related by birth, marriage or adoption.

[39] See Chapter 5 "Average Family Income."

Apparel production is the largest manufacturing industry in San Francisco.[40] 80% of production stems from small Chinatown tailors of which 90% are Chinese owned. The garment industry grew with the Chinese. Whereas in 1960, there were only 300 such businesses, in 1975 it was already 700 and in 1990, 1,100 (Interview with Ling-chi Wang, 1991). During this period, the garment industry was in a crisis due to lack of professionals. Immigration in general dropped beginning in the early 1960s. European immigrant women had retired without successors, and the Puerto Ricans and Blacks showed no interest due to the bad working conditions and the better social security support. Thus, an important step for the blooming of this Chinese business was the transfer from a bachelor society to the family-oriented society, a process that was accelerated by the relaxed laws of 1965. 75% of women arriving after 1965 were in an age group of 16 to 45, and the employment rate remained respectively high.

Chinese arrivals can inform themselves about vacancies in Chinese language newspapers or find employment via Chinese agencies. The tailor shops are the most important for the women. A manager of one in Chinatown told me: "I guess all the Chinese immigrant women who want to work come to the sewing shops." 72% of the Chinese women in Chinatown work as seamstresses. They take home a slim second income, which the family, however, desperately requires. The advantage for the women is that working hours are flexible. In many cases, the children can be brought to work or the women can go home to cook. Working at home has subsequently been banned. The seamstresses do not receive holiday or sick pay, social security is not supplied, and overtime is not paid. The working environment equals that of the standard of a developing country. Many sweatshops are located in dark, moist cellars; the air is bad and an unhygienic environment abounds. Some have no windows or heating, a welcome spot for rats and other creatures (Interview with two workers, 1991).

Increasingly, women are no longer able to perform this double function with work and family and they cannot fulfill the traditional mother role. Parents have little time to occupy themselves with their children.[41]

---

[40] In 1990, 25,000 people worked in textile manufacturing in the San Francisco Bay Area, of which the majority are Asians. During the end of the 1990s, the number of employees dropped considerably because of the *North American Free-Trade Agreement* (*NAFTA*), which caused the loss of over 115,000 jobs, which moved from California to Mexico. In 2000, over 70% of all apparel imports into the United States came from Asia, especially China. For further details of the apparel industry in California, see Chapple, 1998, 72–102.

[41] According to a questionnaire of Chalsa Loo and Paul Ong in 1982, over 75% of all garment factory workers in San Francisco were depressed about their working conditions, but glad about the opportunity to generate a second income (Loo, 1982b, 82).

The children are self-dependent, do not become whiz kids, but more often dropouts, participate in the drug scene, and often join youth gangs. The lack of knowledge of laws and language inabilities further make Chinese women a safe and cheap working potential for this business sector.[42]

Until 1967, *Levi-Strauss* had its production in Chinatown. The jeans giant withdrew its production there once it became known that the sewing personnel were oppressed. But still today, many of the large American textile companies, e.g. *Fritzie's, Lilie Ann, Esprit, The Gap, Suzie Thomkins, North Face, Macy's, Ralph Lauren, Foxy Lady, Byers* and *Twin Peaks* can still be found among the sweatshop customers. *Fritzie's* alone has approximately 50 subcontractors in Chinatown. Until the early 1990s, all of these previously named companies did not contract with union-run sweatshops, excluding *Koret of California*, whose work is done by union shops. Chinese immigrant women produce 50% of San Francisco's garments. Union organization within the Bay Area is exceptionally low at only 20% of the companies (Woo, D., 1989, 186).[43]

The incomes in the sewing shops are so low that a single income would not suffice to live. From the autobiography of a Chinese worker, the typical life of many immigrant women from the 1940s onward can be identified. Sui Sin Tom Lee began sewing immediately upon her arrival in 1955 and earned 75 cents an hour but could only survive by doing much overtime. In 1978, after 25 years in this industry, she earned $2.50 an hour. The average annual income of a seamstress was $9,000 (Wong, M., 1983, 361). Today, many are members of the *International Ladies Garment Workers Union*, but fundamentally their position has not changed. Employers continue to disregard union agreements, e.g. the 40-hour week, health requirements, and safety ordinances.

A minimum piece price of $5.25 is not being upheld. In the 1990s, there were still many seamstresses only receiving $2.00 per piece.[44] Possibly, the growing success of this special Chinatown business lies not only in the described work-sharing and its effects on income levels, but also in the market segment itself for which it produces.

---

[42] "Dirty air, long hours, from eight in the morning to eight at night, six days a week. They are paid by the piece and only a few can make good money. They don't protest because they don't know the law." Interview with Louis Ng, 1991, manager of a garment factory.

[43] In comparison, 95% of all garment workers are organized in New York. *Asian Women United of California*, 1989, 161.

[44] Check clock cards are often faked to avoid minimum wages. Tsai, 1986, 159.

Namely, low-income households in the United States have an advantage over low-priced imports from Asia, due to the low transport cost and the possible time saved to adjust to changes in trends and fashion.[45]

The sewing shops also brought along a boom in the supply services. The workers have little time and little money. Chinese restaurants in Chinatown offer fast service at acceptable prices, with take-out meals for the family at home. While in the garment industry the majority of employees are women, the opposite is the case in restaurants. The small restaurants need little starting capital. Personnel are trained on the job or consist of cooks and waiters who bound together to become self-employed. Additionally, there is an increasing number of restaurants catering to guests from outside, e.g. office personnel from the Financial District. These, too, can be cheaper, since they often employ cheap non-English speaking personnel or family members. Few waiters are trained and often they work six days a week, ten hours a day without holiday, sick, or overtime pay. Pay is low: In 1990, a salesperson in a food store earned $600 a month, a waiter $200. Even in large restaurants, the personnel live off tips, with a base wage below the minimum wage for restaurants. The owners offer the explanation that the low wages stem from the extreme competition, which does not allow higher salaries or higher prices. Nearly every day a new restaurant opens in the Bay Area. Many employees receive no health or social security, and there have even been cases where the employee not only had to provide coverage during sickness, but also had to pay from his income, in order to maintain his employment (Kwong, 1987, 64).

Chinese American Entrepreneurs: Breaking the Ceiling

The slightly expansive subtitle "The Premier Asian American/Pacific Rim Magazine" of *Rice*, which plays on the eastern business connections of Asian Americans, is, by no means, wishful thinking aimed at attracting publicity. The trading balance within the Pacific Rim shows a continuously growing deficit for the United States toward Southeast Asian countries. Expensive consumer items, e.g. designer clothes, electronic devices, computers, and antiques, are imported.

---

[45] The pressure is growing, and often pieces are offer below $2. China alone produced garments for almost $50 billion in 2000. In 1998, the average hourly wage in the garment industry in mainland China was 26 cents, in Indonesia 15 cents, in Thailand 65 cents, and in Mexico 85 cents (*Sweatshop Watch*, 2001).

In Chinatown, where only a third of all financial institutions are American, a number of Chinese banks are opening that solely provide importation services. Many of these can be identified as exclusively Chinese when considering their source of capital.[46] They have sprung up out of the ground to provide investors from Hong Kong and Taiwan the opportunity to secure their money and circumvent capital export barriers. In addition to financial and trading services, Chinese Americans are also increasing their activities in production-related businesses. According to a survey of minority-owned enterprises in 1997, Asian and Pacific Islanders owned 4.3% of all American businesses, compared to their 3.5% share of the population.

Of these total 912,960 companies, 252,577 were Chinese (1.2% of all United States companies, compared to their 0.9% share of the population), 166,737 Asian Indian, 135,571 Korean, 97,764 Vietnamese and 85,538 Japanese.[47] The income structure is slightly abnormal in comparison to the national average: The proportion of individual-owned businesses is very high at 92%, standing 8% above the national average. Subsequently, companies and corporations represent a lower proportion (companies 2%:5%; corporations 6%:11%).

Between 1992 and 1997, the number of Chinese American firms grew from 7.6% to 8.3%, and the revenue from 14.3% to 18.0% of all minority owned businesses in the United States. Chinese employed 691,757 employees, and paid $12.6 billion in wages. Chinese American-owned companies generated 49.3% more revenue than all Black-owned businesses, and 56% of the revenue of Hispanic-owned businesses, despite the fact that the Chinese have less than one-tenth of the Black and Hispanic population.

This makes Chinese Americans the most successful ethnic minority in the United States. In 1997, the Chinese American group not only had the highest number of enterprises, they also achieved the highest income of all minority-owned businesses in America, e.g. $106 billion. This represents 17.9% of all minority-owned, and 34.5% of the Asian and Pacific Islander-owned businesses, and is more than 2.4 times that earned by Japanese American enterprises.[48]

---

[46] Chinese banks in San Francisco are for example: *Bank of China, Nationalist Chinese Bank, First Nationwide, Bank of Canton.*

[47] Statistic: Participation of Chinese in Businesses, U.S. Census Bureau, *"We, the Asian and Pacific Islander Americans"*, 1988; U.S. Bureau of the Census, 2002.

[48] Statistic: *"1997 Economy Census. Minority- and Women-Owned Businesses."* U.S. Department of Commerce. Bureau of the Census, 1999.

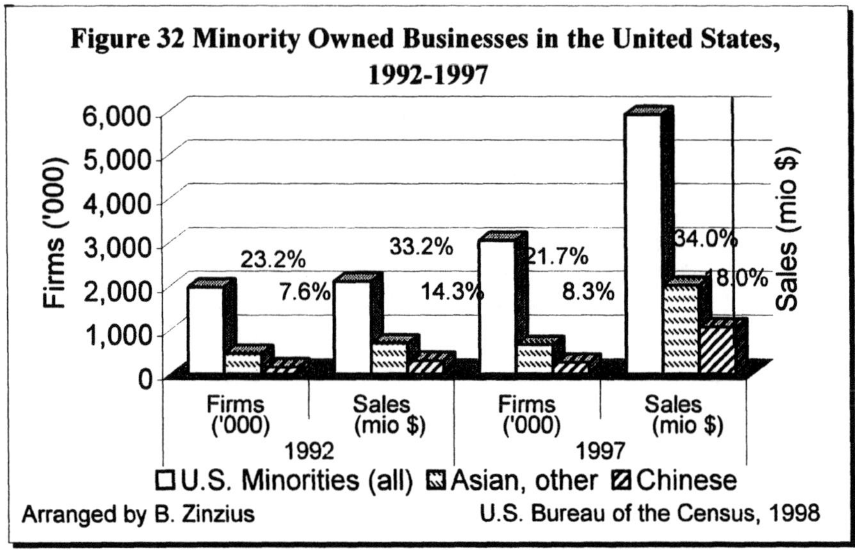

In a recent publication, *America's 100 Top Asian Entrepreneurs,* over 80,000 Asian entrepreneurs were considered, and the final top ten contained five Chinese and three Taiwanese, several of them billionaires.[49] First on the list is Charles Wang, who was born in 1944 in Shanghai. His company *Computer Associates International* had a market capitalization of $25 billion in 2002.

Second is Cyrus Tang, who produces furniture, scrap metal and pharmaceuticals. He was born in 1930 near Shanghai, and his annual revenues reach $1 billion. The Taiwan-born James Chu is fourth (*ViewSonic*-monitors), the China-born Bill Mow fifth (*Bugle Boy*-sportswear), the Taiwan-born Tai Fu Chen number sixth (*Sunrider International*-herbal foods), *Yahoo!*-founder Jerry Yang with over $1 billion in personal assets is in eighth position; he was born in 1968 in Taiwan. Tenth is Henry Yuen (*Gemstar*-VCR-software), who was born in 1951 in China.

An impressive list by many standards, showing the achievements of the Chinese in the American economy. The high number of 80,000 Asian entrepreneurs in the United States shows that the mentioned names are merely the tip of the iceberg. Chinese American success is especially visible in the heart of corporate entrepreneurship, Silicon Valley. A detailed study about immigrant entrepreneurs in Silicon Valley by AnnaLee Saxenian, Professor at the University of California, Berkeley, confirms that during the

---

[49] 2003 <http://www.goldsea.com/profiles/100/ 100.html> (March 14, 2003).

1980s and 1990s, Chinese Americans have developed an important position for the IT-industry.

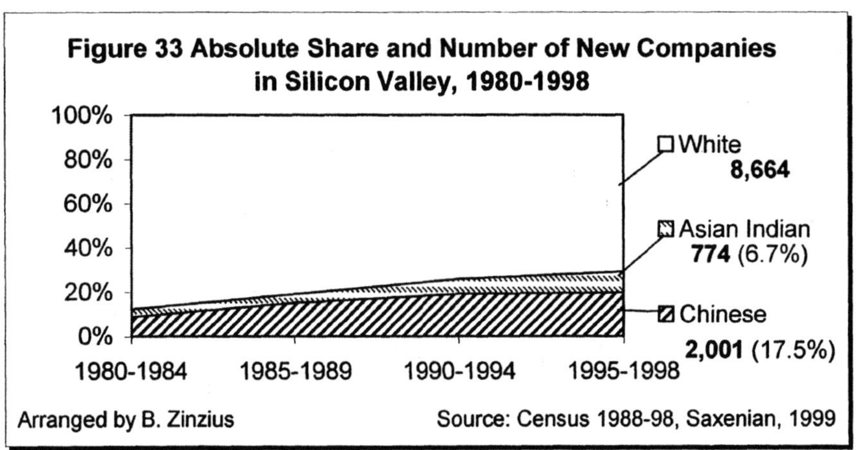

Chinese run more than 17% of all Silicon Valley companies founded since 1980, with a focus in computer and electronic hardware manufacturing and trade. In 1998, Chinese American companies in Silicon Valley generated over $13 billion revenue, and employed over 35,000 staff. 37 Chinese technology companies were publicly traded, and, with $317,555, Chinese entrepreneurs achieved the highest revenue per employee, compared to the industrial average of $242,105 (Saxenian, 1999, 24-25).

In 2002, total net sales grew to $19 billion, and over 71,000 staff worked for Chinese American companies (*Los Angeles Times*, November 19, 2002). This success is based on three main reasons. First, Chinese Americans have a sound education, and their number of Master and PhD-degrees in Silicon Valley is 40%, compared to 18% of the White population (Saxenian, 1999, 17).[50]

Second, many professional careers of Chinese Americans were stalled by the *glass ceiling*, a fact which frequently led them to start their own companies. Many examples support this claim, such as Alex Au, and David Lam, who both started their own companies after working over a decade in Silicon Valley. Au merged his startup company *Vitelic Semiconductor* in 1991 with the Taiwanese company *Mosel*; their combined net sales is over $150 million. Lam founded *Lam Research*, with net sales over $1 billion.

---

[50] See also Chapter 6 "Higher Degrees for Chinese Americans."

Becoming an entrepreneur is therefore often the only way to advance professionally and avoid the glass ceiling. Third, the Chinese have established a number of new immigrant networks—similar to the old *hui* organizations—which have built a strong professional and technical backbone.[51] These organizations focus on technical and economic support, rather than on political lobbying. Often Mandarin or Cantonese is their main language, excluding non-Chinese nationals from their networks.[52] Many organizations focus on specific technical, professional and economic support of Chinese Americans, including jobs, housing, and travel to China. The *Asian American Manufacturers Association* (*AAMA*) with over 700 individual members is an exception regarding political activities, as it promotes the growth of American technology enterprises throughout the Pacific Rim.[53] The increasing cooperation between mainlanders, Hong Kong Chinese and Taiwanese is also interesting to note; a development, which reflects the increasing economic and social relations across the Taiwanese Strait.[54]

These organizations are therefore an almost unique Chinese American institutions, which help them to build up economic strength. Two points are especially noticeable in the direct comparison to Japanese Americans, the early *model minority* among the Asian American ethnic groups: In 1980, both groups were almost equal in size. By 1990, however, the Japanese had fallen to half the size of the Chinese, and the downward tendency continues. The incomes of Chinese American companies exceed the national average. At 2%, the ratio of Chinese American ownership is equal to the ratio of Chinese American income in comparison to the national averages. Thus, anyone who still believes the Chinese to be the traditional *coolies* and the

---

[51] See Pan, 2000, 76–77; Chapter 1.2.2 "San Francisco Chinatown: A New Home".

[52]

Table 28 Selected Chinese Professional Associations in Silicon Valley, Founded	Members
Chinese Association for Science and Technology-USA (*CAST*), 1992	2,500
Chinese Institute of Engineers (*CIE*), 1979	1,000
Silicon Valley Chinese Wireless Technology Association (*SVCWireless*), 2000	3,000
Chinese Software Professionals Association (*CSPA*), 1988	1,400
Silicon Valley Chinese Engineers Association (*SCEA*), 1989	400
Chinese American Semiconductor Professionals Association (*CASPA*), 1991	1,600
North American Taiwanese Engineers Association (*NATEA*), 1991	400
Chinese Information and Networking Association (*CINA*), 1992	700
Chinese Internet Technology Association (*CITA*), 1996	600
North American Chinese Semiconductor Association (*NACSA*), 1996	600

Arranged by Birgit Zinzius   Individual organizations; Saxenian 1999.

[53] See also Chapter 8 "Economy: The New *Global Entrepreneurs*." For a detailed list of Chinese American organizations see Saxenian, 2000, 27–28.

[54] "Mainlanders Make Mark Among Chinese Émigrés." Pierson, *Los Angeles Times*, August 12, 2003. See also Chapter 3 "Taiwan: Democracy without Freedom."

Japanese the born businessmen is definitely mistaken. Chinese American owned companies not only beat the Black, Hispanic, and Japanese numerically, but also in total income generated. Hence, rich Chinese Americans must be richer and poor Chinese Americans poorer than the national average, even though there are relatively fewer elderly people and the family as an economic unit is more pronounced than in other groups. Also, in the middle class, women are more frequently employed, whereby the higher education only guarantees higher income if it was obtained in the United States, e.g. more often for native-borns.

These statements must be further examined in the analysis of family and education in Chapters 6 and 7. The old Chinatown is the nucleus of the Chinese American economy in the Bay Area, which supplies a more extensive picture than statistical data can. Furthermore the social contrasts within the group, which function as the measure of economic differences, can be well-established in these surroundings. Also, the initial question concerning an autonomous Chinese economy can also be answered as a result of the answer to the question on economic harmony.

Exceptional Characteristics of Chinese American Business World

In the following section the exceptional characteristics of the Chinese American business world are to be examined and evaluated. In traditional trades, which are usually not available to immigrants because they require local knowledge, Chinese are obviously not well represented. Precision jobs, traders, and repair companies do not accept many Chinese and thus, in 1980 there were less than 50% of the national average employed in these areas.

Ethnic business plays a correspondingly important role as an alternative to the general market. New immigration from Taiwan and Hong Kong has differentiated this classical model drastically: In administration and religious employment, the Chinese proportion is below average, whereas the Hong Kong Chinese proportion is above and the mainland Chinese below average (15.2% Chinese; 20.7% Hong Kong Chinese; 17.2% national average). The reasons for their strong representation is, on the one hand, their language skills and the western structure of Hong Kong's administration and, on the other, the emigration tendency of those religiously involved in connection with the takeover of Hong Kong by China. Hong Kong has many Christian institutions, e.g. the elite schools are confessionally bound. Only a few Chinese are employed in farming, forestry, or fishing (2.9% United States average, 0.5% Chinese Americans). There are a number of reasons, most of which stem from the low presence of Chinese in rural areas. In the 1870s, the Chinese drew back to the Chinatowns of the cities, e.g. San Francisco, due to pogroms. Until 1947, it was forbidden for Chinese to possess land. In the

1940s, the California Chinese began to move to the Chinatowns in the East. All new immigration, e.g. *brain drain*, is concentrated on the cities as shown in employment, income, and ethnic business statistics. Some careers, preferred by the old immigrants from mainland China are obviously not desired by the other groups. In these categories, the Chinese proportion may be equal to the national average, but only because mainland Chinese are over-proportionately represented (*machinists* and *mechanics* in 1990: 9.3% United States average; 9.9% Chinese; 15.2% mainland Chinese; 4.8% Taiwanese). Immigration barriers for certain careers create bottlenecks for mainland Chinese. In this case, the different distribution is based on the educational picture of the immigration groups, since Taiwanese are usually well-educated, whereas until the 1980s, mainland Chinese were usually "simple" people. The sector services and professionals (mainly older or second generation immigrants) are the new mainstays of the Chinese American business world. In both groups, the Chinese Americans are over-proportionately represented.

The ethnic Chinese can definitely be distinguished as a group with special characteristics when compared to the whole population. The exceptions are, however, no longer as predominant as they were historically. The spectrum of careers has grown immensely and resides mainly between lower services and middle management, a result of the new immigration from Hong Kong and Taiwan. Of the employment in specific fields, one can say that Chinese are relatively weakly represented in crises-endangered careers, e.g. seasonal or trendy careers. The rule that the vocational and social position in the originating country determines that in the recipient country, or the dream of a quick social promotion in the United States do not coincide with reality. The Chinese family union, however, increases the individual income, reduces the cost of living, and supports social promotion. Ethnic business, which affects a large number of low incomes and average incomes, is an important integration instrument and an economic factor of increasing value. Statements about individual occupations must be treated with caution, since it is not always clear which special tasks are connected to which levels of the categories devised by the Census Bureau. An example is management and executive positions in which Chinese are often represented, although, as shown, they have been unable to move into top positions. Some of the statistical groups overlap, whereas other figures differ significantly.[55] Statistical trends should be analyzed further with data from other sources.

Clearly identifiable is the fact that, Chinese American society has a strong middle class that is moving out of the ghetto situation into better districts and maintains its standard of living with a relatively high number of

---

[55] Regarding classification of occupations, see also footnote 14 in this chapter.

household members being employed. Career-wise, this middle-class has not arrived, nor has it fully secured its position. Rather, it is much more matter of the majority of self-employed, who are continuously dependant on an increase in ethnic business, or a matter of the more highly qualified who have not obtained a position equal to their education. This strong middle class has, in comparison to the historical two-class society, gained in predominance. In comparison to the White, however, traditional middle class, including public service, still lags behind. The difference between rich and poor is more pronounced among Chinese Americans than in White society. Finally, some future perspectives: After the nomination of Dr. Chang-lin Tien as the Chancellor at Berkeley in 1990, Takaki's statement that there were no Chinese in top positions at universities must be reevaluated.[56] Tien's belief in "diversity"[57] expresses what will soon be reality in business: Asians in executive positions will bring along further Asians in step with the proportion of Asians in the local environment, their capabilities, or personal relationships.

The nomination of Elaine Chao as Secretary of Labor, the first Chinese American woman to serve in a presidential cabinet, is a strong confirmation of Tien's perspective.[58] Capital cannot be overlooked as a key factor. Affluent Hong Kong Chinese have transferred companies or production subsidiaries to the United States and are taking over leadership position themselves. Mainland Chinese companies are following, like Lenovo, who purchased IBM's computer business in December 2004. A number of mainly younger Chinese, most with an education at America's elite universities, are climbing up the career ladder. They stem from families who have transferred some of their Pacific Rim trade activities (trading, investments) to the Bay Area. These upwardly mobile individuals will receive strong support, whereas the future of the group and the question whether Chinese Americans can be considered a *model minority* becomes the center of interest.

The worldwide recession at the end of the 1990s slowed the American economy significantly, increasing unemployment and inflation. In order to revitalize the economy, President George W. Bush implemented massive tax cuts in 2003, similar to the measures taken by President Reagan. In contrast to President Reagan's program, however, these tax cuts target also corporate income taxes and are less geared towards high-tech or minority businesses

---

[56] Dr. Chang-lin Tien served as the seventh Chancellor of UC Berkeley from 1990–1997. In 1998 he was considered by the Clinton Administration as a candidate the cabinet position as Secretary of Energy. Dr. Chang-lin Tien died on October 29, 2002.

[57] For details see Chapter 6 "Education."

[58] Elaine Chao, born in Taiwan in 1953, is the wife of Senator McConnell, and a Washington insider since the Reagan-Bush era. She was nominated as Secretary of Labor by President George W. Bush in January 2001. See also Chapter 8 "Chinese Breaking the Ceiling."

(*Businessweek*, January 28, 2003). The *National Minority Business Council* (*NMBC*) Minorities criticized also the opposition of the Bush-administration towards race-conscious university admission policies as divisive and unfair, fearing that an end of *affirmative action* will hinder minority employment and entrepreneurial opportunities. John F. Robinson, Chairman of commented: "The gains that have been made for minority and women entrepreneurs and others in minority community should not be put in jeopardy by a Supreme Court decision that could undo half a century of progress for minorities in this country."[59]

---

[59] "National Minority Business Council Opposes Bush Administration Stance in Affirmative Action Case." NMBC Press Release, January 17, 2003. <http://www.nmbc.org> February 14, 2003. See also the detailed discussion about affirmation action in Chapter 6 "The Long Road to Top Universities."

6. EDUCATION

Whiz Kids—Scholastic Attitude and Educational Success

By surveying education with attention to different school levels, we investigate in this chapter the effects and consequences of Chinese immigration on American schooling. This will be done in the broader context of educational reforms in the United States after 1965. Thus the presence of the Chinese, their success, and the reactions inside and outside of educational institutions will be taken into account. Tendencies will be presented regarding potential changes within the institutions, as well as the social development and integration behavior of the group, beginning with common stereotypes and their background.

The media-charged word *whiz kid* is etymologically derived from wizard, which means "a genius or prodigy" (Webster, 1993). During the 1980s, this became attached to the stereotype of successful Americans of Asian descent, with Chinese Americans often standing at the forefront. Asian youths and adults are better than the average American or other ethnic groups at tests intended to determine IQ, learning ability, and cognitive thinking abilities.

Asian Americans show stronger scholarly aptitude than White Americans. A 1980 survey by the Department of Education shows that Asian Americans receive the grade "A" more often than White Americans or any other ethnic minority. The survey also shows that the failure rate of Asian Americans in eight subjects—from English to Art—is lower than that of any other ethnic group, and in subjects requiring non-verbal skills the results were exceptional. In entrance examinations for universities—tests which examine the ability of research and analytical thinking—their group achieved the highest number of points scored. In math they achieved an average of 518 points, whereas Whites achieved 491.[1] In 1990, all five scholarships given by the renowned *Westinghouse Science Talent Search* were given to Asians. In 1991, 18 of 40 finalists for the same scholarships were Asian Americans.

In 1995, the University of California initiated a study about educational disadvantages, which confirmed that Asians have the highest test scores among all ethnic groups. 32.2% of all Asian high school graduates in California were eligible for the University of California, compared to 12.7% of the statewide average, 12.3% of the White, 5.1% of the Hispanic, and

---

[1] In 1987, a *Time Magazine* article, "The New *Whiz Kids*," discussed the success of Asian Americans at school and university. Brand, 1987, 42.

3.9% of the Black population (Outreach Task Force, University of California, 1997, 4). Asian Americans continue to receive awards far more often than other ethnic groups. In 2002–03, 50% of the finalists of the *Intel Science Talent Search*, and 50% of the *Siemens Westinghouse Competition* finalists were Asian Americans.[2] These results reflect the fact that approximately 37% of Asian Americans have a college degree, compared to only 24.6% of White Americans (U.S. Bureau of the Census, 2002).[3]

In studies intended to explain the superiority of Chinese, some parameters have been developed to highlight the differences in attitude and action: Attitude toward school, cognitive development, extracurricular activities, parental expectation, parent-child relationship, and sex.[4]

Extracurricular Environment—The Home

> "Our parents made us attend school. We did not like it. Every day after school, five days a week, we hated learning calligraphic letters and reading texts that we did not understand. We did not see any sense in learning a language that was only spoken at a few homes and, as in my case, was a different dialect than the official Cantonese we were taught. Worse was the fact that our teachers never dared to explain anything to us. I spent four years copying or repeating words without ever knowing their meaning." (Mary Lee, 1999).

The Chinese school, which many Chinese Americans attend in addition to compulsory school, supplies sufficient friction for the generation conflict. According to filial piety—subordination toward parents—Chinese American children must do everything to provide pride to their parents and the Chinese family (Fong, 1996, 71-83; Lin, 1993, 271-86). Thereby, the most is expected from the elder children who also receive the greatest support. Often, this is for the eldest son, and the needs for the rest of the family are reduced accordingly. Recent data about the use of Information Technology among Asian Americans, for example, confirm their parents' strong educational support: 65% of all Asians have a computer, and 56% have access to the Internet, compared to 51% and 41% of the national average. Internet access of Chinese American children between three and seventeen years is 71.9%, compared to the nationwide average of 65% (U.S. Census 2000, P23-207).

---

[2] In 1998, Intel assumed sponsorship of the *Westinghouse* award and renamed it *Intel Science Talent Search*. The new *Siemens Westinghouse Competition* was established in 1999.

[3] For decades, Asian Americans have had the highest rates of college graduation. In 1980, 32.9% of all Asian Americans had a bachelor's degree or higher, 36.6% in 1990. Figures for White Americans were 17.1% in 1980 and 21.5% in 1990, and for Hispanics they were only 7.6% and 9.2% (*Our Education*. U.S. Census, 1990 and 2000).

[4] For comparisons between various family characteristics of Chinese Americans, see Fong, 1996, 71–83; Lin, 1993, 271–86; Yao, 1985a and 1985b.

Parents make both material and ideological sacrifices in order to have more time with their children. Parents help with homework, have more belief in the teachers than Anglo-Americans, and respect their authority, a point which they underline with their children. The children often continue to live with the family after completing their studies. They are, however, expected to work hard at school and university, because competition and order are of high importance in Confucian work ethics. Chinese American parents try to give their children the best possible education, since most have themselves felt that even with academic degrees they did not find employment meeting their educational standards.

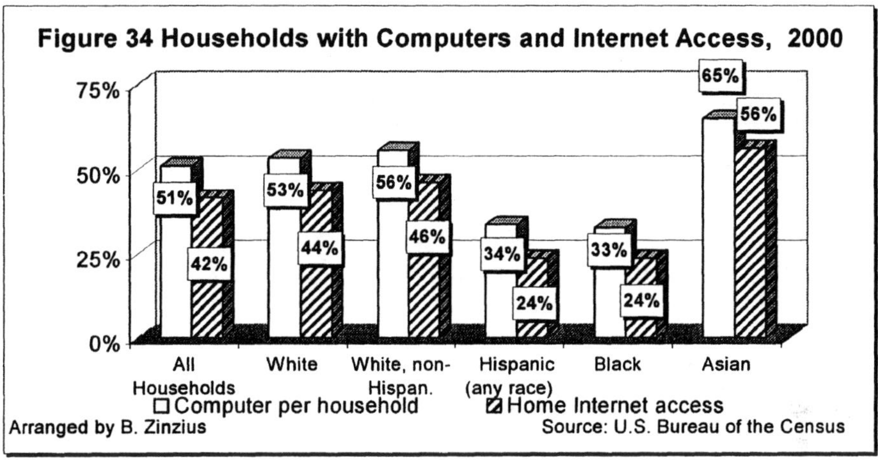

The basic theory that education is the best way to success leads to their believing in a close connection between social status and academic success. Thus, through education, they seek to maintain or improve their position in society. The goal of many parents is to have a PhD in the family. Sharon Lee remembers how, when she intended to switch from medicine to psychology, her parents were shocked, but then pushed her to complete her doctorate. To have a PhD in the family was in the end more important (Interview, 2001).

The breadth of social origin of Chinese parents is immense, ranging from parents of fifth or sixth generation in the United States, to the large wave of 650,000 Indo-Chinese immigration in 1978. The Chinese students that remained in the United States after the Tiananmen Square Massacre in 1989. Even with this diversity, the Chinese in the United States can be split into two classes relative to their income and education: Those who are educated and have a high income are integrating into American society. In 1990, 21.2% of all Chinese American men and 22.0% of all Chinese American women above 25 years old had a college degree, compared to 14.4% and 12.0% of the national average. Foreign-born immigrants—

excluding students—are less educated, have little income, and are strongly linked to tradition. Often Chinese American kids help their parents who remain through language and culture distant from American society. Nevertheless they decline to fulfill the high expectations of their parents and, thus, to lose the educational characteristics of the White Americans, sovereignty and individualism. This conflict often leads to loss of respect towards the parents. Typically, Chinese parents always want the best for their children, but are never satisfied with their achievements. "Your book is number four on the bestseller list?" asks Daisy Tan of her daughter Amy Tan, author of *The Joy Luck Club*. "Good. And who is number one?" (Interview, 1991). "If you obtain 80 points, they will ask why you did not achieve 85. And if you achieve 85, they ask you why not 90?" (Interview with Fred Wong, 2001). "When we went on memorial day to see the grandparents, uncle, auntie, and all relatives, my two-year old son wore his *Bob-the-Builder* tool belt. Grandfather mentioned: 'Oh, no good. This is hard work, you should learn holding pens and sit in the office.' The next week they bought him a doctor set." (Interview with Lee Kwang, 2003). The pressures of parents, school, and society to which Chinese American children are subjected are often not withstood. Asian American students show more psychic disturbances than other ethnic groups (Sue, 1985; Kitano, 1988, 173; Lorenzo, 2000). These problems often lead to drug abuse and suicide.[5] In the ecstatic descriptions of Chinese American successes in the media, the increasing number of suicides and suicide attempts of Chinese youths is often only mentioned as a side-line (McBee, 1984, 47). In 2001, the *Surgeon General* suggested collecting further information on suicide rates among Asian Americans due to a lack of detailed data (Satcher, 2003). These problems are not based on this balancing act between two cultures, because in China the students are also under pressure from their environment. To maintain face, a Chinese family must have successful children. Successful children are a family's pride.

Attitude Towards School

In the 1980s American and international researchers, lead by the psychologist H.W. Stevenson, studied the attitudes of Asian and American students toward schooling. They compared schoolchildren from Taipei in Taiwan, Sendai in Japan, Minneapolis (MN), and Chicago (IL).

---

[5] Suicide is also a topic in Chinese American literature. Ona, a central character in the novel *Bone*, commits suicide (Ng, Fae, 1993). See Chapter 8 "Cultural Awakening."

It was found that American children spend far less time on academic activities than Chinese and Japanese children, resulting in far lower scores. Chinese students are more resolute with their homework than their White counterparts.[6]

A different, comprehensive survey between 1985 and 1995 showed that in San Francisco Chinese high school students spend twelve hours a week on homework, whereas Whites only about eight, and the average American only four. The switch from leisure time to learning is easy for Chinese Americans. Anglo Americans prefer group activities, especially sports and religious activities, whereas Chinese are more homely and follow individual and cultural activities, e.g. music and languages. Confucianism values mind over body.[7] Confucianism teaches one to offer the teacher the same respect as the parent. The teacher cannot be countered; their word is ultimo ratio. Thus, students throw themselves with greatest discipline at school and studies. Chinese students are so respectful that they often dare not oppose unfairness or make the teacher aware of a mistake.

A teacher, Molly Kwong, gave a typical anecdote: A student received the wrong workbook from her teacher, but she did not complain. Out of fear of criticizing her teacher she tried for months to follow the course (Interview 1998). Even with their efficient work morale teachers often accuse Chinese Americans of monotony and thus a lack of problem solving thinking (Givens, 1984, 5). The impression given by Chinese American students transfer of being passive and subordinate is a stereotype that teachers sometimes indulge by not asking for opinions (Interview with Shirley Hune, Hunter College, 1991). For Ronald Takaki, Chinese American traditions are comparable to what is known in western culture as "the Protestant ethic." (1979, 150). High activity is a phenomenon of the first and second generations. The preparedness to work hard at school slows in the third, says Barbara Schneider, Professor at Northwestern University, who surveyed two primary schools in Chicago (Brand, 1987, 46).

---

[6] In the fifth grade, American children spend 19.6 hours, Japanese children 32.6 hours and Chinese children 40.4 hours per week for school. Even on weekends, Asians are more diligent: On average Saturdays, Chinese study 83 minutes, Japanese 37 minutes and American children 7 minutes. Further details can be found in: Stevenson, 1994).

[7] *Beyond the Classroom* summarizes an extensive, ten-year study about educational shortcomings in the United States. Steinberg, Brown, and Dornbusch indicate that the lack of *authoritative parenting* in mainstream American families, and ethnic attitudes towards learning, are major reason for the decline in American student achievement and the outstanding results of ethnic groups like Chinese Americans (Steinberg, 1996, 19–20).

Primary and High Schools in San Francisco

Statistical evidence support these impressions. About one-third of San Francisco's residents are of Asian origin, and more than half of all applicants at schools are Asian (Census 2000). The number of White students drastically declined from 41% in the period between 1967–68 to 9.6% in 2003–04. The number of Chinese students, which represent the majority of all Asian students, increased from 13.5% to 31.1% in the same period. The overall percentage of Chinese students is therefore far higher than their population share of 19%. This fact reflects the younger age of the Chinese group, compared to the aging White population. With 36.1%, the highest percentage of Chinese students is, however, found in high schools, compared to 32.1% in middle schools, and 28.6% in elementary schools (San Francisco Unified School District, 2004).

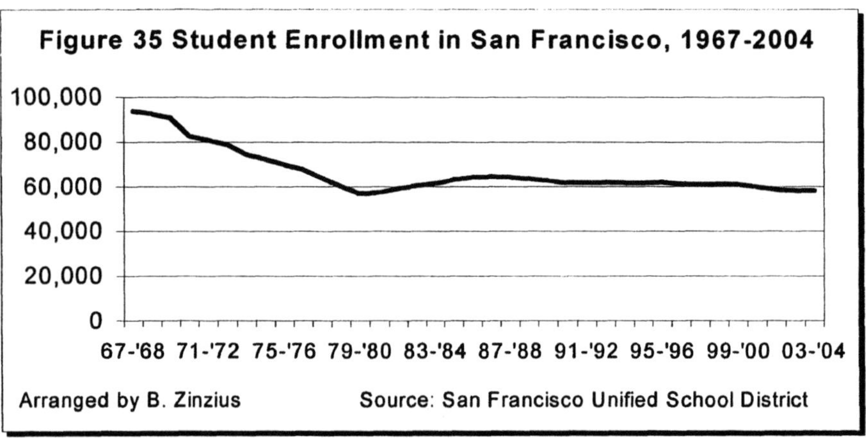

Busing, the balancing of school populations by transporting children to schools in other areas, which has been used to hinder the isolation of Blacks, is therefore becoming a greater reality for all ethnic groups, including Asians. In 1983, the *National Association for the Advancement of Colored People* (*NAACP*) sued the San Francisco Unified School District (SFUSD) on behalf of Black students because of racial discrimination. Subsequently, the San Francisco Unified School District set fixed ethnic quotas (*racial caps*), which were to be in place until 1999, for all public schools. Neighborhood schools were not allowed to enroll more than 45% of any given ethnic group, alternate schools faced a cap of 40%. Until 1994, the Chinese had reached these racial caps in many schools, and thus Chinese parents filed a Class Action Suit (*Ho vs. San Francisco Unified School District, 97-15926*) against the *racial cap* based on the same grounds as the *NAACP* in 1983, e.g. racial discrimination. A court settlement between the School District and the

Chinese plaintiffs in 1999 ended the quotas and adopted a *race-neutral* enrollment plan, called *diversity index* (*San Francisco Examiner*, June 14, 2002). In 2000, 75 of 118 schools had a White student population of less than 10%, and in only 4 of 118 schools the number was higher than one-third. Today, there is no school with a consistent majority of Whites in San Francisco. The percentage of Chinese Americans is further increasing in several schools in San Francisco, whereas other ethnic groups are decreasing. In 2003–04, Lowell High School had 55.4% Chinese students, compared to 16.7% White (San Francisco Unified School District, 2004).

Since the Chinese American families have low numbers of children, it can be presumed that the majority of these children originate from the large immigration wave of the 1970s and 1980s, which would show a low adaptation rate in the school population. In the 1970s the school population in San Francisco dropped dramatically from 93,000 in 1968 to 56,000 in 1980, due to a baby slump. By 1990, it had only recovered to 63,000, and since then has again receded to 57,805 in 2004. The major increase since the 1970s can be attributed to the Chinese, who used the new quota system from 1968. Thus, the increase occurred predominantly due to new immigrants.

This statement can be verified by checking the language capabilities. An example shows how lingual non-adaptation may be applied to our analysis. In 1990 in Cabrillo, there were 41.1% Chinese, 7.4% other Asian, 2% Hispanic, 26.8% White, 10.6% Black, and 11.6% other non-White students. Of these, 39.4% spoke little or no English. If one presumes, and probably legitimately, that the majority of Whites and Blacks speak English, then it must have been Chinese and other Asians—together approximately 50% of the school population—that spoke little or no English (Limited English Proficiency-LEP/No English Proficiency-NEP). The figures for 2002 mirror the continued flow of immigrants: While the number of Chinese students declined slightly to 40.1%, the LEP/NEP ratio grew to 48.1%.

Further examples underscore this hypothesis: The Chinese Education Center that only teaches Chinese had 98.6% Chinese students in 1990, of which 91% were considered LEP/NEP. The figures for 2002 are 98.7% Chinese students, and 96.6% are considered LEP/NEP. The main reason for lack of adaptation among Chinese must be new immigration, or short-term residence in the United States. Looking at the LEP/NEP figures in comparison to the configuration of the school population one must ask whether it is not more opportune to speak of adaptation or non-adaptation among the White, English speaking population who, in a short time, have had to come to terms with the fact that they have become a minority.[8]

---

[8] Carol Ness discusses this trend in "The Un-Whitening of California." *San Francisco Examiner*, April 14, 1991, A1, A10.

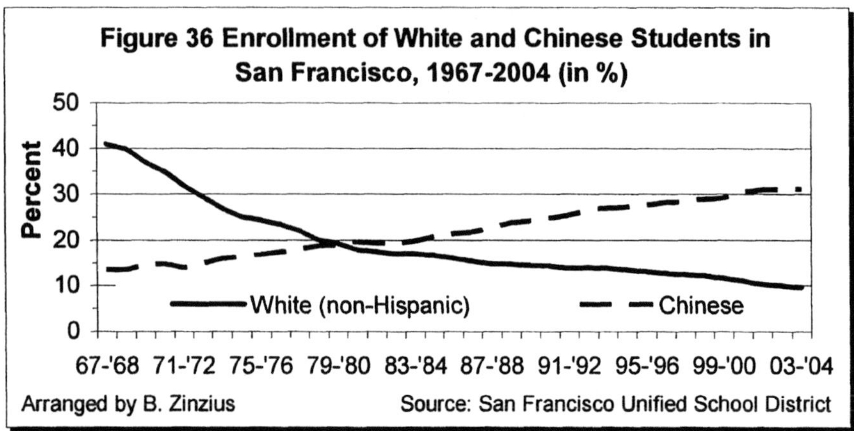

At Lowell High School White children wanted to start a "Whites Club" like their colored colleagues in order to represent their interests better. The school would not accept it out of fear that approval would be deemed as a racist step (Ness, 1991, A10).

In 2001-02, Lowell High School had 27 clubs, including five for ethnic groups, but none for the White students, which make up just 17%.[9] The numbers support the somewhat bold and strange assertion of a new minority: Cantonese and Spanish are two most spoken Non-English languages. In one-fifth of all households with kindergarten children and one-third of households with high school attendees Cantonese is spoken. In 2000, 29.2% of the school population in San Francisco was considered LEP/NEP, compared to 25.0% of California, and 9.6% of the national average.

Subsequent to a complaint brought by Chinese parents against the San Francisco School Board,[10] a law came into being that forces all school districts to pay special attention to and provide support for LEP/NEP children.

---

[9] The Lowell High School is supposedly a jumping-off place to Berkeley, Harvard and Yale. In the graduation class of 1987 were 18 Changs and 18 Fongs, 6 Lees as well as 49 Wongs (Frank Viviano, *Far Eastern Economic Review*, March 24, 1988).

[10] *Lau et al. vs. Nichols et al.* The Education Board was charged with violation of Article 14 of the Constitution as. In total 1,800 Chinese students were barred from a rightful education in San Francisco according to the indictment. If upheld, the Education Board would be barred from receiving governmental funds due to racial discrimination (*Civil Rights Act* from 1964, section 601).

Another office decreed that those schools with more than twenty LEP students had to provide school programs with *English as a Second Language* (*ESL program*).[11]

Table 29 San Francisco Unified School District—School Profiles, 2002-03[12]

2002-3	Chinese (in %)	API	SAT	GATE	LEP / NEP	Average attendance	Dropouts
SFUSD—average	31.0%	–	986	8.8%	29.2%	94.7%	2.5%
Alice Fong Yu ES	38.3%	789	–	12.8%	16.7%	97.4%	0.2%
Balboa HS	11.1%	440	773	1.3%	28.0%	89.3%	0.0%
Buena Vista ES	1.1%	682	–	2.5%	38.6%	94.4%	0.5%
Cabrillo ES	40.1%	798	–	6.5%	48.1%	95.7%	2.7%
Downtown HS	5.1%	–	737	0.4%	16.4%	–	–
Lowell HS	55.0%	933	1,227	47.5%	0.7%	97.6%	0.0%
Newcomer HS	53.0%	–	–	0.0%	91.6%	96.0%	7.4%
Treasure Island ES	21.8%	649	–	3.6%	46.4%	92.1%	2.3%

Arranged by B. Zinzius   Source: San Francisco Unified School District, 2002

The *Lau vs. Nichols-case* and certain other laws, especially the *Bilingual Education Act* of 1968, changed the American education system. It is no longer seen as part of the public interest to ignore the student's mother tongue as part of educational planning at Californian schools. This does not solve the problem. Among the LEP students in California in 1980, 37% were Asians and Pacific Islanders. Their number has thus more than doubled, mainly due to economic flight from Southeast Asia. Use of English as the sole communication method was an important and radical instrument for Americanization in the past, which often split the children of new immigrants from their parents. The Supreme Court gave no specific theory for implementation in its verdict against an LEP/NEP-opposed school, and federal funds were cut by the Reagan administration. Due to the *Bilingual Education Act*, California has created new programs, but their application is hindered by a lack of trained teachers. As a consequence, in 1991 the General Assembly passed the *English Fluency in Higher Education Act* to ensure language abilities of faculty members at bilingual schools.

---

[11] For further literature, see: Ling-chi Wang. "Lau vs. Nichols: The Right of Limited-English-speaking Students." *Amerasia Journal*, No. 2, 1974; Equal Educational Opportunity: Hearing before the Select Committee on Equal Educational Opportunity of the U.S. Senate, 92nd Congress, 1st Session, Part 9B, 4715–4754.

[12] *GATE: Gifted and Talented Education*. Official figures of the *SFUSD*-Report, 2003. *API: Academic Performance Index* in California (scale 200–1000). This index, which is still being refined, was newly introduced in 1999 and measures the performance of schools.

Among the LEP-students in 1996 in San Francisco, languages taught comprise: Spanish (35.8%), Cantonese (34%), Filipino (5.1%), Vietnamese (4.3%), Mandarin (2.1%), Khmer (1.6%), and Korean (1.2%), (San Francisco Unified School District, 1996). Over 30 years of bilingual education have produced a broad variety of programs, and opinions.

Part of American society sees bilingual education as an advantage in an increasingly globalized economy.[13] Dr. Laureen Chew, Professor of Asian American Studies at San Francisco State University, stated recently, "The ability to deal with diverse populations and proficiency in another language are our competitive one percent-ers. Multinational jobs equal success." (Gifford, 2000). Stevenson indicates that languages such as Chinese or Japanese stimulate memorization rather than association, enabling different learning abilities (Stevenson, 1994, 47). Others are much more skeptical of the programs, fearing an *Asianization* of society, or claim that native-language education prevents social integration and reduces language abilities (*San Francisco Chronicle*, July 18, 1997).

Ethnic minorities, however, are not necessarily connected with Limited English Proficiency. With less than 1% LEP/NEP students (0.7% in 2002–03), the elite school Lowell High School has the lowest percentage in the whole United States, in contrast to the average LEP/NEP rate of the seventeen San Francisco high schools of 18.8%, i.e. more than a third of all students are instructed in a non-English language. In 2002, 67% of all students at Lowell High School were Asians, 55% were Chinese; 47.5% of all students received the classification "*GATE*-Gifted and Talented Education." The ethnic composition of the staff, however, does not necessarily reflect the student situation. In 2000, 22% Asian, and 61% White teachers were facing 73% Asian students, and 18% White students.[14]

In 2002, the public Newcomer High School, which as its name implies is mainly attended by new immigrants, 91.6% LEP/NEP students were in attendance, of which 53.0% were Chinese. The staff comprised 52.9% Chinese teachers and 33% Chinese administrative personnel. There were, however, only 2.4% White students, but 11.7% White teachers and 11.1% White administrative personnel. At both extremes of adaptation and non-

---

[13] Governmental agencies offer numerous services in multiple languages. The California Drivers License Test can be taken in seven languages, including Cantonese, and the San Francisco Unified School District offers five different language versions of their website.

[14] In 1990, only 8.8% Chinese teachers and 21.7% administrative personnel, or 18% Asian teachers and 30.3% administrative personnel were available at Lowell High School, facing students of which almost half were Chinese. In contrast, 65.6% of all teachers, and 43.4% of all clerical staff were White. While Lowell High School complies with the race-neutral enrollment plan, it has initiated three outreach programs to attract underrepresented minorities, e.g. Blacks and Hispanics (Yee, Lauren, 2000).

adaptation, Newcomer and Lowell High Schools have not met the challenge posed by the increasing ethnic diversity in their students with a corresponding ethnic diversity in their school personnel. With the increasing reputation of the school, the percentage of non-White personnel declines. Even so, or maybe for this reason, pressure from Asian parents on the schools is very high.

Again, as between 1930 and 1950 with *Progressive Education*, the American school system has insufficient personnel to realize such an innovative theory on a wide basis. Only one-third of all *English Language Learner (ELL)* students are in programs that use bilingual approach. In the case of lacking bilingual education for Asians, one, however, cannot only name lack of support from White parents and missing federal funds as causes. On the Asian side, two phenomena are important: The high percentage of new immigrants, which is not countered by sufficiently well-versed Asian (especially Southeast Asian) teachers. In this specific case, it is a fact that many ABC (American-born Chinese) are, as a consequence of their America-oriented education, culturally and lingually too far from their origin country to be of assistance to the newly immigrated. Often, American-born of the second or third generation no longer speak Cantonese. Furthermore, most of the new immigrants are from Taiwan and North China and speak Mandarin. The strongly career and success oriented Chinese are also not interested in indulging in the unattractive career of teaching.

Despite the efforts of schools to comply with the *Bilingual Education Act*, its implementation is difficult in a society whose ethnic composition is constantly changing. Ken Lau, whose lawsuit (*Lau vs. Nichols*) was a trigger for many programs, did not benefit, as the act came too late for him. "Today, I can't read a Chinese newspaper, and I sort of wish I had studied more so I could work in a foreign country like Hong Kong," he mentioned in 2002.[15]

These constant problems of bilingual teachers are a great burden to bilingual education—37% of all K-12 students in California speak a language other than English as their native language, whereas only 8% of all teachers hold bilingual credentials. Furthermore, an increasing lack of political support and a growing resentment from a White-oriented lobby led to legal Propositions in California (1998) and Arizona (2000).[16]

---

[15] "Ambivalent in Any Language." *Boston Globe*, July 22, 2002, 1.

[16] Proposition 227 is the brainchild of Ron K. Unz, a software millionaire and former gubernatorial candidate (Morahan, 1998). Unz cited the small number of Asian patents in Information Technology as an example of their limited achievements. He did not mention, however, that Chinese-Americans are the most successful ethnic entrepreneurs in America, running 20% of Silicon Valleys high-tech companies. See Chapter 5 "Chinese American Entrepreneurs—Breaking the Ceiling."

In both cases, voters opted for a mandatory *English only* policy in schooling and business. In California, Proposition 227 had a broad support (61%), including 67% of non-Hispanic White, 57% of the Asian, 48% of the Black, and 37% of the Hispanic voters.[17] "Voters sent the message that all students should learn to master English as soon as possible. Fluency in English is essential in competing for jobs in a global economy," said Ron Low, spokesman for Governor Wilson. "Proposition 227 is an opportunity to replace a system that has failed minority students with something that gives them a fighting chance at the American Dream," indicates Frank Purcell, the spokesman for Randy Cunningham (R-CA), (Morahan, 1998). Proposition 227 is, however, sharply criticized by educators, who believe that a focus on *English only* will decrease cultural and linguistic knowledge, and reduce educational achievements. The legislation is seen as detrimental to the multicultural society, and even anti-immigrant: "How long will an aggressive, anti-immigrant electorate be permitted by the federal courts to vote away the rights of language minorities to self-determination and equal access to education through bilingual instruction?" asks Dr. Mora, Associated Professor at the San Diego State University (Mora, 2000).[18]

Chinese Americans, however, with their strong commitment and attitude towards learning, will be less affected by the *English only* policy than other minorities such as the Hispanics. Chinese success in higher education will be further supported by new legislation, such as a reduction of racial caps or benefits in favor of an open competition based on merits.[19]

In 2001 a sweeping reform was introduced on a nationwide level, the *No Child Left Behind Act (NCLB)*, which received strong bipartisan support. It replaces the *Elementary and Secondary Act* (*Bilingual Education Act*) of 1968, and changes the federal role from kindergarten through grade 12-education significantly. The act has four basic reform principles: stronger accountability for results, increased flexibility and local control, expanded options for parents, and emphasis on proven teaching methods.[20]

---

[17] 72% of California's voters are White, while only 52% of its residents are White. 28% of the electorate is comprised of members of minority groups, while 48% of the total population are minorities. Thus, the vote on Proposition 227 reflects the interests of White voters rather than the overall population.

[18] In 2002, Dr. Mora received the *Award for Excellence in Research and Scholarly Activity* from the *California Association for Bilingual Education.*

[19] See also Chapter 6 "*Affirmative Action* or Multicultural Society?"

[20] The accountability system of the *No Child Left Behind* involves several critical steps, including regular and detailed reports on achievement gaps from disadvantaged, racial and ethnic minority groups (U.S. Department of Education, 2003).

Asians, especially ELL-students, will be affected in several ways. The increased emphasis and regular monitoring of English abilities will shift focus from *bilingual education* to English, reflecting a new, monolingual approach.[21] Furthermore, the increased flexibility will allow states and local education agencies to change existing national programs, as the examples of California and Arizona already show.

It is interesting to note that these new policies like *English Only* are implemented at a time where Asian and Hispanic immigrants have reached all time highs, and *Bilingual Education* was gaining acceptance and showing its merits. "Ten years ago, Chinese language schools were almost empty—nobody bothered to learn Chinese. Now, the classes are packed." (Sharon Wang, 2003). Many Asians, and especially the Chinese, however, are already among the top achievers in American schools, reflecting their scholastic attitude and commitment. An analysis of their further progress in higher education will give insight about their future advances.

Higher Degrees for Chinese Americans

The Chinese are, as shown, entering into the best educational institutions, but we cannot comment whether the mass attendance of Chinese at San Francisco schools will also be followed with success. We begin by looking at the first decade since the fall of the immigration barriers.

Table 30 Percentage of High School Graduates by Age and Race, 1980

	White	Chinese
Men, 25-29	87%	90%
Men, 45-54	69%	69%
Women, 25-29	87%	87%
Women, 45-54	70%	58%
Prepared by B. Zinzius		U.S. Bureau of the Census

In 1980, ethnic Chinese of all ages showed 71.3% had received a high school diploma, a rate slightly lower than the average for all Pacific Islanders, but higher than the rate for total population, which was at 67%.[22]

---

[21] This change marks a complete reversal in language policy. Whereas the 1994 version of the *Bilingual Education Act* included to "develop the English skills ... and to the extent possible, the native language skills" as one goal of LEP students, the *English Language Acquisition Act* stresses skills in English only (Crawford, 2002).

[22] For young Chinese between 25 and 29 years, the percentage raises to 90.2% for men and 87.4% for women (White: 87% and 87.2%); however, it ranks behind other Asian groups such as Japanese (96%).

Compared with Japanese, Koreans, and Asian Indians, one can see that the younger Chinese generation has caught up dramatically, since the percentage of Chinese high school diploma holders from 45–54 years old was 68.7% (men) and 57.7% (women). In contrast, among Koreans 90.4% of men and 68.5% of women high school diplomas, among Japanese 88.1% of men and 82.5% of women held them. The 45- to 54-year-olds also lower the Chinese average.[23]

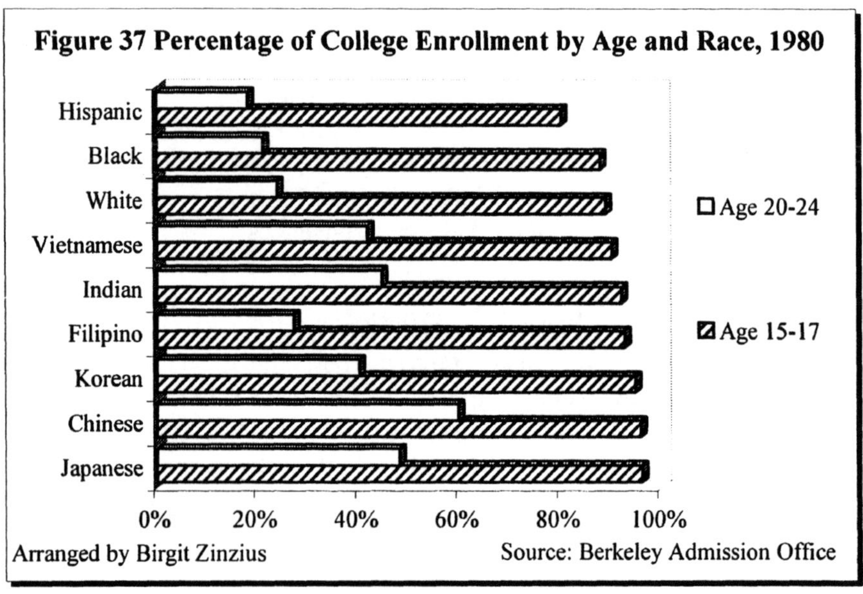

Comparison of the obvious sex-specific differences shows that the distance between *yin and yang* has dramatically decreased. Men from 45–54 years of age have a percentage of high school graduates 11% higher than that of women, whereas the difference between men and women of the ages 25–29 has shrunk to 2.8%. Other Asian groups have not followed this emancipatory movement to the same degree.[24]

---

[23] See Chapter 5 Chapter 5 "Law and Age Structure," and Fessler, 1983, 210, telling that the *"old-timer"* Chinese have a high percentage of illiterates.

[24] In 1980, within the Korean group, men had an advantage of 14.5%, within the Vietnamese 12.1% and Asian Indian 5.6%.

The table shows that the deficit was mainly due to elderly Chinese women. Looking at the active school population of the United States as a whole, one immediately notices the high percentage of Chinese: They seem to be the frequent users of the system. The higher and longer the education, the more Chinese are represented. In the age group from 15–17, the Chinese have caught up to the leading Japanese, and in the college ages of 20–24 they have clearly taken the lead. In comparison to the Chinese, not even half the number of Whites attended college in 1980.[25] Dividing immigrants according to their educational level (high school versus college) shows that the length of stay in the United States has a positive influence.[26]

While this is valid for all Chinese, generally speaking, the mainland Chinese have, in comparison to Taiwanese and Hong Kong Chinese of all age groups, the higher percentage of immigrants with lower educational levels.[27] In 1980, 20% of all men and 13% of all women had graduated from college, while the Chinese were achieved rates of 44% and 30%. Following this development into the more recent past, one can see that until 1988 the Chinese had the highest increase in graduates with 73.4%, in comparison to 7.9% for the total population.

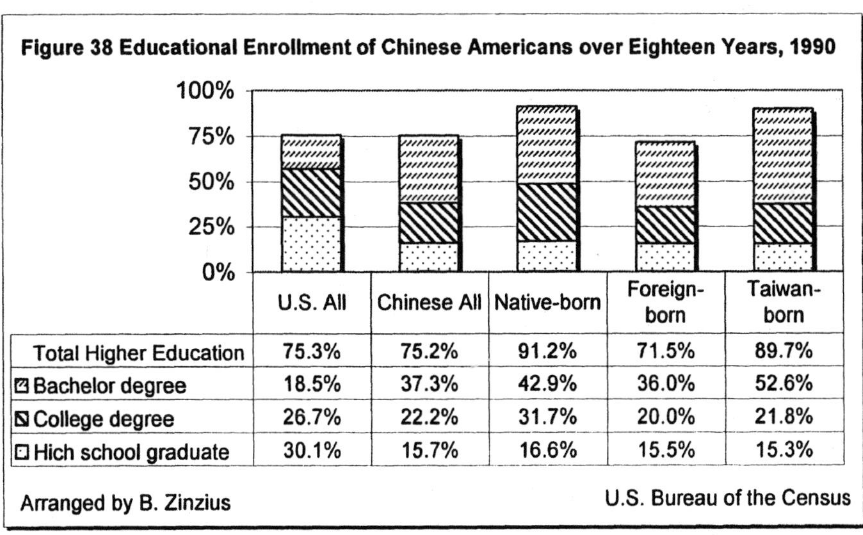

Figure 38 Educational Enrollment of Chinese Americans over Eighteen Years, 1990

	U.S. All	Chinese All	Native-born	Foreign-born	Taiwan-born
Total Higher Education	75.3%	75.2%	91.2%	71.5%	89.7%
▨ Bachelor degree	18.5%	37.3%	42.9%	36.0%	52.6%
▨ College degree	26.7%	22.2%	31.7%	20.0%	21.8%
▢ Hich school graduate	30.1%	15.7%	16.6%	15.5%	15.3%

Arranged by B. Zinzius   U.S. Bureau of the Census

---

[25] 59.8% of the Chinese, 48% of the Japanese, but only 23.9% of the White population.

[26] In 1980, the mainland Chinese immigrated between 1960 and 1964 had 54% high school graduates, those immigrated between 1975 and 1980 only 44.9%.

[27] In 1980, 15.7% of the mainland Chinese had less than five years of schooling education, whereas Taiwanese had the highest percentage of high school graduates—89.7%—and even 74.4% college graduates.

The Chinese are pushing into the renowned private institutions. The development of scholarly careers shows that American-born Chinese are ahead of all the other ethnic groups, meaning that they have a record of longer attendance at school and universities. The percentage of native-born Chinese that attend more than sixteen years of school is exceptionally high, namely 51.2%. Within this group low education has reduced dramatically and is about 2% for those over 25 years old. Generally, high increases in education, as shown by the Chinese, are indicators of strong and new immigration, which tries to compensate for lack in education and to increase its status with good graduation results.

The tendency to obtain higher education by the native-born Chinese is contrasted by the initially relatively low educational standards of the newly immigrated. A striking contrast to the decline of the educational achievements of American-born White, since new White typically bring with them high educational standards—a tendency contrary to that of the Chinese. In general, Asians seek economic and social success via education. In 1980, over half of all adult Asian Americans were college graduates (Gardner, 1985, 24), whereby the American-born Asians were the elite. The figures from 1990 support these data. 91.2% of all native-born Chinese hold a high-school diploma, 42.9% a university degree, and even 52.6% of the Taiwan-born Chinese hold a university degree. The national average for high school diplomas is 75.3%, and only 18.5% of all Americans hold a university degree.

Table 31 Average SAT Scores by Parental Income and Race/Ethnicity, 1995			
Income Below $20,000	$20-40,000	$40-60,000	Above $60,000
Black 666	737	778	810
Hispanic 711	781	853	904
White 899	933	949	955
Asian 818	925	972	1050
Prepared by B. Zinzius			Outreach Task Force, 1997

The differences in educational levels between American and foreign-borns require further explanation, as this cannot only be attributed to the exceptional perseverance of the Chinese Americans. A major factor is that the majority of all mainland Chinese emigrants in the age group 30 to 40 who came to the United States via family reunion were often hindered in their educational progress by the results of the Cultural Revolution. Often, they are poor relations of southern Chinese who could not afford lengthy education. The figures concerning the education of foreign-borns, i.e. 13.9% in 1980 with less than seven years of education, underline this fact. The data for 1990 show, however, that the educational level of foreign-born Chinese is increasing. This can be seen especially in the category of college graduates, which includes foreign students. 36% of all foreign-born Chinese completed college, compared to the national average of just 18.5%. These data show that the Asians, and in particular the Chinese, have higher rates of educational attainment and far higher numbers of college and university degrees.

Is this educational success only related to ethnic attitudes, such as learning times, or are other factors behind this success, such as economic advantages? In 1997, the Outreach Task Force of the University of California published its report on educational disadvantages, based on state and nationwide data. The report revealed crucial factors for educational success, measured as SAT results, and revealed that, "racial and ethnic disparities in college preparation and eligibility are not simply a reflection of economic disadvantage or low family income alone, but also reflect *educational disadvantage*" (Outreach Task Force, 1997).[28]

The Outreach Task Force initiated a four-point strategy "to assist students in overcoming educational disadvantages while also attracting to the University a student body broadly to represent the state." These programs are aimed African Americans, American Indians, and Hispanics, while Asians were clearly ahead of all groups. It can be assumed that Asians in the high-school system are predominantly American-born. After viewing their success, it is thus important to further analyze foreign-born Asians, in particular Chinese.

The Influx of Chinese Intellectuals—*Brain Drain*

The Chinese educational success comes less from recent attempts by the schools to adjust to Asians than from the Chinese's ability to become integrated into the American system. Generally speaking for higher education, the length of participation has a positive influence. Regarding university education it is evident that, similar to the case of primary schools, the recent immigration in the form of "lateral transfers" from the Chinese to the American educational system is having a direct influence.

This phenomenon becomes interesting since the weaknesses of the American system are more noticeable in schools, at least for those, which supply candidates for the universities. In the case of Asian students who attend universities directly after their arrival, this weakness is circumvented, which opens many interesting perspectives.

---

[28] The movie *Homeless to Harvard* was a huge success in 2003, depicting a homeless girl who achieved her dream of attending Harvard. The reality is different, and only 3% in the top 146 colleges come from the bottom quarter of the American population (*Jakarta Post*, April 17, 2003).

Is it really true, as the German politician Heiner Geissler describes in his controversial paper on the multicultural society, that Americans are hoping for an "intellectual push" from Asia?[29] Or are Asian immigrants more successful because of a failure of the American education system?[30] We must therefore turn our attention to the current and historical developments of *brain drain*, looking at both its quantitative and qualitative aspects. Chinese students studying abroad are not a new phenomenon. Since the middle of the nineteenth century, Chinese students have been sent by their government to leading universities in the United States.[31]

Chinese students chosen for their academic aptitude have continued to flow into America, Japan, and Europe. This educational emigration saw growth phases in the last decade of the Qing-Dynasty (1900–1911), from 1925 until the Nationalist period shortly after World War II, and especially since 1979. The early immigrants sent their sons back to China for education. Across the Pacific, there was no flight from political or educational systems.[32]

The most important reason to study overseas was the desire and requirement to modernize China. Patriotism motivated progressive intellectuals to study abroad, just as belief in good Chinese tradition had encouraged the emigrants to send their sons home. Already in the 1930s, a couple of hundred Chinese, sons of first generation immigrants, attended American colleges after graduating from high school. In 1946–47, a massive increase to 1,688 students occurred, and this number doubled to 3,916 in 1948–49.

Did these students find good positions in America? Until the first quota in 1943, there were no Chinese who stayed after completing their studies. The first official so-called "stranded students" were recorded in 1949, during the founding era of the People's Republic and the American support of Chiang Kai-shek. At this point, the United States became a refuge for fleeing intelligence, which was disliked in their home country, and obviously non-

---

[29] "The Americans allow tens of thousands of young Asians to enter their country, and all are eager to learn and work. The country expects an intellectual push." [translated from German] (*Geissler*, 1991, 75).

[30] Since the 1980s, reforms to improve educational standards in America have failed, including the Bill Clinton's 1994 *Goals 2000* program, which was blocked by the Senate. Only in 2001, President George W. Bush implemented the *No Child Left Behind* program, which started sweeping changes and annual performance tests for schools and students (Berlak, 2001; U.S. Department of Education, 2003).

[31] Yung Wing (1828–1912) was the first Chinese to graduate from Yale in 1854. Yung Wing's autobiography, *My Life in China and America*. New York, H. Holt 1909 and Y.C. Wang: *Chinese Intellectuals and the West*. Chapel Hill, University of North Carolina Press, 1966, imparts the impression of first scientific contacts between the East and the West.

[32] See further discussion in Zinzius, 1988, 65.

conformist. The United States had guaranteed to provide immigrant status to all intellectuals fleeing from China until 1952. In addition, education was financed if support from home ceased. Only a few American-born Chinese, a few of whom became doctors in Chinatown, attended American universities at that time (Lyman, 1974, 57).

The Korean crisis brought an initial decrease in educational immigration, but numbers began to rise again in 1959–60 to arrive at 19,266 (mostly Taiwanese) in 1969–70, just after the deletion of the quota regulation in 1965. In 1979–80, 28,508 Chinese students were attending American higher educational institutions, 17,560 from Taiwan, approximately 10,000 from Hong Kong, and 1,330 from the People's Republic.

The Tiananmen Square Massacre in 1989 increased the flow of Chinese intellectuals abroad to the point of an outright exodus, with many of them becoming stranded students. Support from the Chinese community comes not only from Taiwan, but also involves groups that were previously committed to China. The *Chinese Student Protection Act (1992)* by President Bush gave 53,000 mainland Chinese students an extension of their visas, which were subsequently changed into green cards.[33] Only a few of the 29,000 Taiwanese and 11,000 Hong Kong Chinese students, who were studying at the same time without immigrant status in the United States, returned to their homelands. This phenomenon is regarded by the governments in Beijing, Taipei, and Hong Kong as *rencai wailiu, chucai jinyong,* or in English *brain drain.*

The Chinese government in Beijing is sufficiently concerned about the massive loss of its higher educated and technically qualified citizens. The negative results of the Cultural Revolution are a definite warning. On the other hand, this is also seen as releasing pressure from the intellectuals on the regime. Thus, just as 40 years ago in Taiwan, no action is taken against *brain drain* and, according to Richard Baum, Professor and Director of the *Center for Chinese Studies* at the University of California, Los Angeles; the illusion exists that the right people might possibly return at the right time.[34]

As part of this phenomenon, high government officials also send their children to study in the United States, e.g. former Chairman Deng Xiaoping, sent his grandchildren. Since several years, the governments in Beijing, Taipei, Hong Kong, and Singapore are trying to tempt their greatest talents into returning by offering higher wages, finances for research, and greater personal freedom (Interview with Ling-chi Wang, 1992). Chinese

---

[33] See Chapter 3 "Quota and Non-Quota Immigrants."

[34] See Jay Mathews. "Chinese Are No. 1 Group Students Here. Rapid Influx Occurs Despite Restrictions." *Washington Post*, May 1, 1989. See also Chapter 6 "From *Brain Drain* to *Brain Gain*—Returning to the Homeland."

intellectuals, however, no longer trust the governments in Beijing and Taipei. Most have given up trying to play a leading role in China's modernization. The Chinese press characterizes the strong flow abroad of the educated elite as *chugouzhao, chuguole* and *chuguobing*, i.e. panicking and illness.

Contrary to the past, it is now possible to obtain a highly qualified university education in the United States and then begin a career in research and education, something that highly motivates students. The liberal immigration laws of 1965 have thus created new prospects. Either the whole family now emigrates to provide education for the children in the United States, or the students themselves bring in their families via family reunification (Chan, 1991, 180–1). Studying has thus become a substantial possibility of achieving non-quota immigration, which can then be turned into long-term residence (Fessler, 1983, 209, 273; Kwong, 1987, 36; Zweig, 1995) and set in motion the so-called chain migration, especially during the 1990s.[35]

The figures of the 1980s confirm the trends, namely that the Taiwanese have the highest level of education among all immigrants. These are mainly the children of those who fled from mainland China in 1949 and thus not members of the classical poor from Southern China, but rather those in the excellent school programs in Taiwan.

Whoever was able to reach the highest levels of the rigid and competition-oriented schools in Taiwan usually obtained a public post. Today, the goal is to begin graduate studies in the United States or Europe. Thus, the national education system and the difficult school career become the selection committees that provide the United States with the desired candidates: The test requires comprehension of the English language, military service must be completed, financial resources have to be sufficient, and the acceptance by an American university must be attained.

Teachers and bureaucrats press the best students into the areas math, physics, or engineering, even if their interests lie in other areas. The best are thus trained for their "export" to the United States: 70%–80% of the graduates from science faculties of Taiwan University go to the United States for their graduate studies. If they earn a Masters or PhD from a top American

---

[35] Asians amounted to the highest number of all "educational" immigrants in 1990. In 1979 just 97,000 Asian students studied at American Universities. In 1989, this number was already 232,000. By comparison, only 26,000 African students studied in the United States, 43,000 Europeans, and 45,000 Latin American (Statistical Yearbook, 1991, No. 269). This trend continued throughout the 1990s, and in 2002, Asian countries held the top five positions among all nationalities, totaling 302,058 students. Canada is ranked sixth, Mexico seventh, and Germany with 9,613 students is a distant ninth behind Indonesia and Thailand with 11,600 students each. See also Chapter 3 "Immigration between 1965 and 2000," under "Chain-Migration."

university, they can enter into their respective trade at the highest level. Taiwan's elite, especially those from mainland China, push their children to become permanent residents in the United States—"there is no higher bureaucrat who does not have a descendant in the United States."

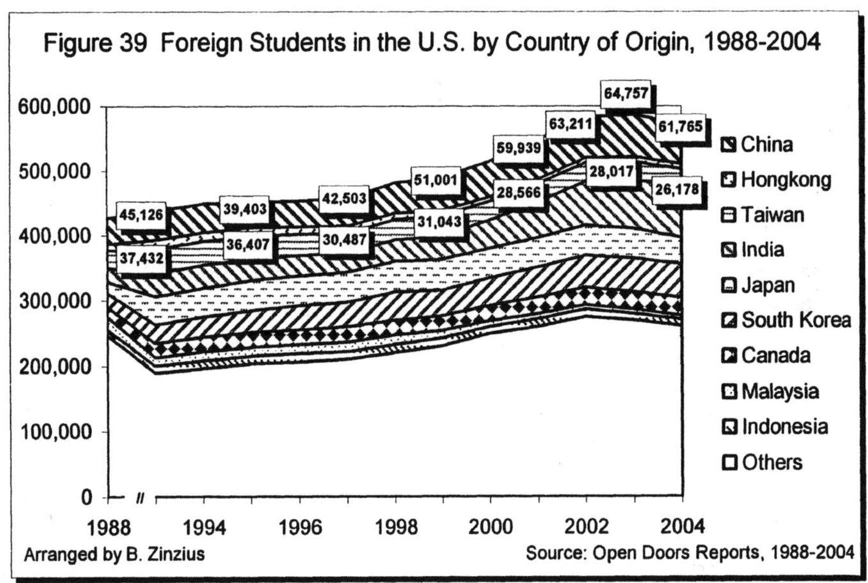

Between 1965 and 1985, 278,000 Taiwanese students went to the United States for their graduate studies and were the largest group of foreign students.[36] Together with the politically persecuted and the stranded students of the 1950s, they represent the basis of the Chinese upper class in San Francisco, known as *uptown-Chinese* in contrast to the poor Chinatown inhabitants, the *downtown-Chinese* (Kwong, 1987).

This group seems to be responsible for the drastic improvement in education, income, and business status of the Chinese recorded in the statistics.[37] In comparison the mainland Chinese are educationally less well prepared. In 1988, 40,000 mainland Chinese students studied in the United States, thus being the largest group, standing ahead of the 26,660 students from Taiwan and the 10,650 students from Hong Kong.[38]

---

[36] Since 1949, almost 800,000 Taiwanese studied in the United States. Taiwanese Ministry of Education, September 1999. <http://www.edu.tw/bicer/cb271.htm> (January 10, 2003).

[37] See also Chapter 5 "Business Structures and Income."

[38] See statistic: Foreign Students in America (1988 and 2000). Foreign (non-Immigrant) Students Enrollment in Institutions of Higher Education by Region of Origin, 1976 to 2000, and by Field of Study, 1980 and 2000.

As of 2000, the Chinese retained their position as the ethnicity with the highest number of students studying in the United States: 63,211 mainland Chinese, 28,930 Taiwanese and 7,757 Hong Kong Chinese students studied in the United States, combining for 99,898 Chinese students. The second-ranked Asian Indians totaled for 66,836 students.[39] The number of foreign students stagnated in 2001/2, since then it fell – partly due to rising tuition cost. In 2004, Chinese accounted for 16.6% (95,296) of all foreign students: 61,765 mainland Chinese, 26,178 Taiwanese, and 7,353 from Hong Kong. India had with 13.9% (79,736) the second largest contingent.[40]

This flow of Chinese intellectuals into the United States will continue in the future. The question now becomes how will these intellectuals develop outside of their cultural surroundings of their homeland, how long will they stay abroad, and what kind of Chinese identity will become most predominant there? A further, important question is of interest for future developments: Will Chinese intellectual networks develop in the United States that then will determine the future of the originating countries? If so, the United States would contain an Asian think tank that provides financial, intellectual and technical support for Asia, especially China. *Brain drain* would, thus, actually be *brain gain*, a topic that will be addressed later in this chapter.[41]

The Long Road to Top Universities

The University of California, Berkeley first counted its students according to ethnic characteristics in 1966. Chinese and Japanese mainly represented the Asian group, with 2.7% and 2.5% respectively. Asian immigrants, their children, and their grandchildren are now filling Americas top universities. In 2000, Asian represented only 3.6% of the American population and 10.9% of the Californian population; whereas 20% freshmen at Harvard, and 45.2% of freshman at the University of California, Berkeley are of Asian descent.

In 1977, 1,936 Asian Americans applied at Berkeley, and in 1987 the number already reached 6,698; by 2000, the number had climbed to 10,278. The Chinese are the largest group with 4,544 (20.2%), double their share in the population. The number of Asian-American freshmen grew at Harvard

---

[39] "Open Doors Report, 2002; Foreign Students in the U.S." *Institution of International Education Network*, November 2002.

[40] Gardner, Deborah and Witherell, S. "Open Doors 2004: International Students in the U.S." *Institution of International Education Network*, November 10, 2004.

[41] Ling-chi Wang elaborates on this problem in the publication "Just how this center will shape the identities of Chinese is impossible to predict." (Wang, 1991b, 206).

alone from 3.5% in 1976 to 12.8% in 1986, and 19% in 1999. In the same period, it grew at MIT from 5.3% in 1976 to 29% in 1999, at Stanford from 5.7% to 11.5%, and at Berkeley from 16.9% to 45.2%, a number equaled by the University of California, Los Angeles.

On campus, these high freshmen figures lead to anti-Asian tendencies and discriminatory phrases like "look out for the Asian invasion." The university abbreviations are being ironically reinterpreted, e.g. MIT to "Made in Taiwan," UCLA to "University of Caucasians living around Asians." This predominant anti-Asian feeling at universities is based on the general feeling of being overrun. It seems that a high social toll must be paid, in order that more than 90% of Chinese American youths of college age can study at higher educational institutions (Alba, 1985a, 89).

Between 1986 and 1996, more than 250 racist acts were recorded, from swastika paintings to death threats. Chinese are mainly hated as high achievers who push up the scores in sciences and thus increase the competition (*National Institute Against Prejudice and Violence*, Baltimore, MD). Anti-Asian graffiti covers Harvard library. In a paper handout, Berkeley's undergraduate library was shown as a pagoda (Givens, 1984, 9). According to Sanford Pagganucci, student conduct officer at Berkeley, until now there have been no signs of racist actions or race-based disturbances, at least not of a level that would require disciplinary action from the university. Animosity is shown in the day-to-day contact of students and their interaction (Eisenberg, 1990, 11). The strong support by the Chinese American student organization, where they help each other by learning together or organizing test papers, has a negative effect on their surroundings.

Paul Carey, a White American, feels discriminated and left out by his Chinese colleagues who are the majority in the engineering courses at Berkeley. Some unofficial exam information is not distributed outside of the ethnic group. Carey actually speaks of a secret organization. He even loses his interest in sports, since the Chinese Americans sits at desks when White Americans play football, baseball, or basketball (Interview, 1992). "*Affirmative Action* is nothing more than federally organized discrimination of Whites," said a student and one of the initiators of the subsequently banned "White Student Union" at Temple University in 1991. Everyone's results should count and nothing else.

Has the fear of Asians become institutionalized? Students of the so-called *Ivy League* universities were traditionally children of Whites, only who jostled the key positions in industry and politics among themselves via alumni and networking activities. Especially the Jews, who represent 11% of the students at *Ivy League* universities—all others groups represent only

3%—have been defensive towards any attempts to open the gates of these traditional institutions to other groups through *affirmative action*.[42]

Always the forerunners of the rights of the individual, which are understood as the best defense against racial discrimination, Jewish representatives see the changes in the matriculation regulations as a dangerous subversion by ethnically founded group criteria. In this defense based on the individual's right to education, the Asians see discrimination of groups with a strong immigration. The increase of matriculated Asian Americans is by no means comparable to the increase in applicants. The ratio of applicants to matriculated students is more unsatisfactory for Asians than for other groups and, according to Asian representatives, too great a discrepancy to be coincidence. A survey in 1983 identified that of 25 top universities this ratio among all ethnic groups, including Whites, was the worst for Asians. The Chinese scholars Ling-chi Wang and Sucheng Chan, have identified the defensive position of the *Ivy League*:[43]

> "Because they are only too aware of the 'pipeline' function of higher education, those responsible at the universities have tried to keep the number of Asian American students to a minimum. Too many Asian Americans receive the vocational training at American universities, which will catapult them into the middle class. Some will obtain positions of power. But then they would be in a position to remove the legal barriers, which have withheld the group as a whole from social promotion." (Interview with Wang, 1991).

As long as only a small Asian group is successful, this fits the paradigm of the American Dream, but should it become whole hordes, then the fear of the yellow peril arises. This danger touches not only Whites, but also other minorities, e.g. Blacks and Hispanics, who themselves feel discriminated against as a race by the Asians. In this case, the social component plays a

---

[42] *Ivy League* is the name generally applied to eight prestigious universities: Brown, Columbia, Cornell, Dartmouth, Harvard, Pennsylvania, Princeton, and Yale. In 2002, Asian students, with over 15%, and Jewish students, with 11%, have two- to three-fold higher enrollment rates at the *Ivy League* than their actual percentage of population.

[43] Professor Ling-chi Wang was born in Xiamen, Fujian, China, and studied at Princeton and University of California, Berkeley, where he is chair of the *Ethnic Studies Department,* as well as founder of the Commission for Admission Rights to Universities. Wang is well-known as a community activist, dedicated to a multiracial, democratic America. Wang, together with Sucheng Chan are both known as the founders of *Asian American Studies.* Sucheng Chan, Professor for History and head of the *Asian American Studies Program* of the University of California, Santa Barbara, graduated at the University of Hawaii (1965) and received her PhD at University of California, Berkeley in 1973. She is author of *This Bittersweet Soil: The Chinese in California Agriculture, 1860–1910* (1986) and *Asian Americans. An Interpretative History* (1991). See also Autobiography of Sucheng Chan "You're Short, Besides!" in: *Making Waves.* 1991, 265–273, where Ms. Chan is defending her rights as a disabled person and as a Chinese American.

major role. In contrast to the historical phenomenon, which drowned the country in a wave of cheap labor, now highly qualified scientists, technicians, and entrepreneurs are coming. There was, until recently, insufficient space at the top of the social pyramid for the Chinese climbers.

Chan's evaluation is clear: "The defensive reaction to the emergence of Asian Americans is racist because those who have hitherto monopolized power and privilege do not want to share their elite status with non-Whites."[44] The question that emerges is whether Asian representatives believe that the low rate of matriculation at higher education institutions represent a return of racist behavior.[45] Can the ever-increasing intensive competition among ethnic groups be measured by matriculation at universities?

Historically speaking, the *Civil Rights Act* of 1964 forbid any so-called gentlemen's agreements, especially those against entry of Jews, Hispanics, and Blacks into public places, ranging from restaurants to schools. At the same time this act was an important step toward the new immigration laws of 1965, which opened the floodgates of Asian immigration. The criticism of the representatives are largely based on the thesis that, since the 1980s, Asians have no longer reached rates of matriculation equal to the increasing number of applicants and their school achievements. A visionary intent, which also slows the aftermath of liberal immigration ruling, can be implied.

Regarding the ratio between applicants to matriculated students at some top universities, the following picture immerges: At Harvard, the ratio for all freshmen was 15.9% compared to 12.5% for Asian Americans, at Princeton 17% to 14% and at Yale 18% to 16.7% (Admission Offices Yale, Berkeley, Princeton and Harvard).[46]

The deviation from the average for Asians is clear, but from an isolated view not exceptional. At Berkeley, Brown, and Yale, the rates for Asian matriculation are equal to that of Whites for the period 1985 to 1987 (Brand, 1987, 8). In 1991, the freshmen at Berkeley could be split into 34% Whites, 31% Asians, 21% Hispanics, and 7% African Americans (Muchnik, 1991, 8), percentages that compare closely to their representation in society.

Between 1982 and 1985, the ratio of matriculation for Asian Americans at Stanford was only 66% to 70% of that of Whites, thus also representing a clear difference. These figures, which also contain the high quotas for

---

[44] Unpublished manuscript: "Racism and the Model Minority: Asian Americans in Higher Education." Chan, Sucheng, and Wang, Ling-chi, 1991.

[45] See Heritage Foundation, *Executive Foundation*: "Ending College Admission Quotas Against Asian Americans," June 30, 1989.

[46] In 1983, a statistical survey at high schools in the East revealed "The percentage of Asian Americans admitted lagged behind those of all other ethnic groups, including Whites."

Asians, allow the belief that the criticism concerning matriculation practice at universities need not be interpreted as bias against Asians.

It is probably rather the case that the decreasing position of White students should not be given up without a fight against the numerical superiority of the education-hungry Asians.[47] Other criticisms of university practice, however, are based on the introduction of special barriers for Asian students in the 1980s (Bunzel, 1987, 60).[48] With regard to the exemplary character of the described discussion concerning the social development of Chinese Americans, it is worthwhile to evaluate thematically the road to the top. A review of matriculation criteria should give us sufficient information concerning the problem. Within the relatively similar spectra of criteria, Harvard and Berkeley seemingly have different accentuations.

In 1989, of 13,000 applicants at Harvard 11,000 were considered "highly qualified," but only 2,000 or 15% were accepted. Of these 2,000 only 200–400 achieved their goal due to excellent test results. The majority, however, were offered admissions thanks to a combination of good results and non-academic abilities. The rest entered due to excellent achievements in extracurricular areas, e.g. sports or music. In cases of where students showed equal results, those with an alumni relation were preferred. According to the official statements of the universities, an equal distribution of various talents is important, whereby talent is not defined by good test results, but by special abilities.[49]

At Berkeley, the priorities are different, with more emphasis on the test results. In addition to the school grades (GPA) and the SAT test[50] used by most universities, there are three more achievements tests, namely English Composition, Mathematics I or II, and a choice of English literature, a foreign language, science or social sciences (American or European History).[51]

---

[47] See also an article of Au, Jeffrey K.D., "Philosophical Questions for the 1980s and Beyond." In: *Reflections on Shattered Windows*. Ed. by Gary Y. Okihiro, Shirley Hune, Arthur A. Hansen, John M. Kiu. Washington: Washington State University Press, 1988.

[48] Further information in Bunzel, John H. and Au, Jeffrey K.D., "Diversity or Discrimination? Asian Americans in College." *The Public Interest*, Vol. 87, 1987, 49–62.

[49] See Harvard and Radcliffe, *Official Register of Harvard University*, 1988–1989. The percentage of Asian Students increased from 12.5% in 1987 to approximately 20% in 1990. In 2001, 17% of all Harvard Students were Asians, and the same number is predicted for the following years (2005: 17.4%).

[50] Since a reform in 1993, two SAT tests exists, SAT I: Reasoning Test, formerly known as SAT—Scholastic Aptitude Test, and SAT II: Subject Tests, formerly known as Achievement Test. The SAT I comprises:
 1) Verbal test: Critical reading skills (200–800 points).
 2) Arithmetic test: pre-algebra, algebra and geometry (200–800 points).
 3) Equation test for comparability (no points). The combined score of SAT I is 400–1600.

Until 1997, 50% of the available places are distributed according to scores. Since 1998, admission officers thoroughly reviewed all of the applications it received, taking into account essays and personal information as well as academic records and test scores (Berkeley Admission Office, 1999). Whereas in 1989, 37% of all applicants were accepted, until 2001, this rate has fallen to 24.7% (8,953 admissions compared to 36,227 applicants). These numbers reflect the highly competitive situation at Berkeley.

To guarantee an equal representation of the social spectrum, especially minorities, a number of extra-curricular qualified applicants are accepted at Berkeley. These are usually from groups with weak representation at the university, e.g. Blacks, Hispanics, Native Americans, Filipinos, handicapped, rural school graduates, athletes, musicians, students of foreign universities and others. Obviously, the Chinese Americans do not belong to this group, since they already represented 30% of the students in 1990. Good grades are therefore no guarantee for matriculation. The test criteria employed by all universities stress lingual aptitude above mathematical understanding. Final evaluation is basically untouchable, due to the manifold criteria and their complex interconnections. Especially the non-academic ones seem to be based on a very broad scale of application and evaluation. In 1987 and 1988, the results of School Aptitude Tests at top universities were as follows: In mathematics the Asians achieved an average of 522 points and Whites only 490. In the verbal tests, however, the Whites were equally ahead with an average of 445 points to 408 of Asians (scale from 200–800).[52]

The differences in the verbal and mathematical tests seem to eliminate each other, but many Asians protest against what they regard as illegal reasoning in the use of tests where lingual aptitude is over-emphasized. With regard to the actual weighting of the test results and to legal views, this criticism does not seem misplaced.

Paragraph 6 of the *Civil Rights Act* forbids discrimination according to race or origin, especially at those institutions that are federally financed, which is the case for public and all the large private universities.[53]

All tests challenge problem-solving techniques, including the SAT II Test, which measures subject-specific topics (College Board, 2002). Admission offices may look at SAT scores, in combination with GPA, class rank, extra-curricular activities, College application, campus interviews, and admission essays.

[51] High School GPA equals 4,000 points, SAT, ACT test (3) are maximum 800 points each, totaling 4,000 points. In total, 8,000 points are achievable. 1989, 94% of all applicants had a GPA of 3.0 or higher, in 2001 the number was 98.5%.

[52] See *New York Times-Sunday*, September 9, 1989, "Asian Americans Press Fight for Wider Top-College Door." Julie Johnson, 1, 8.

[53] *Civil Rights Act of 1964*, Title VI, Section 601 (which refers to the 14th Amendment of the constitution); see also *Lau vs. Nichols Law*, 414 U.S. 563, 1974.

In this context, the statements from universities are meaningful. At Berkeley, it was stated that not only grades, but also other criteria, e.g. race, extracurricular activities, references, publications, and personality structure, play a role in the decision making process. Fred Hargadon, *Dean of Admissions* at Stanford, explained in a *New York Times* interview in 1986 that Chinese American students were probably turned down because they only had good grades.[54] Stanford's own examination board, however, already determined in 1984 that students of Asian descent with ratings equal to those of European descent had lower matriculation ratios.[55] The heads of universities argue that across the board Asians have relatively low results with regard to non-academic criteria. The question is whether this relates to the stereotyped "relentless bookworm" or the feared yellow peril. In any case, at least the criteria stems from a period when mostly Whites attended the top universities.

Both students and teachers claim that universities pursue "institutional racism," since, until now, they have done little to increase the number of employees from ethnic minorities, to expand curricula teaching about other cultures, and to demonstrate general interest in the special interests of ethnic minorities. The request for greater awareness with regard to this subject stems from the lifestyle of the generation that lived through the civil rights movements of the 1960s and 1970s and whose children are today's students.

The generation of the "freedom summer" and "Selma March," however, does not seem to have passed on much to their children. Many do not have any contact with people of foreign culture until they meet them on campus. There the confrontation reaches dimensions of a great social experiment and many are overwhelmed by it. In the last twenty years much has happened: More and more women, handicapped, members of the lower class, and people of different skin color are accepted at universities, which changes life on campus and creates fears among the more traditionally oriented. As described earlier, the Chinese, who already represented a consistent student group in the 1920s, usually returned to their homeland as higher bureaucrats or scientists (until 1949). If they stayed, they hardly expected to obtain a job equal to their educational level.

---

[54] See Au, 1988, 54. Stanford introduced an additional qualification for admission officers to restrain this phenomenon in the future, see *New York Times*, August 3, 1986, 40–47.

[55] See *Annual Report*, "1985–1986, Committee on Undergraduate Admissions and Financial Aids," Stanford University, 1986, 5.

A survey of 58,000 Asian and White students showed that neither in their club activities, nor in their student parliament activities were the Asians falling behind.[56] One criterion, however, that gives advantage to Whites is the continuous preference for children of university employees or alumni, along with other criteria, e.g. *affirmative action*, athletic achievements, geographic preference, etc. Due to the current history at top universities, Whites will theoretically continue to have this privilege (Au, 1988, 54). University staff is more predominantly White than those attending the schools. Asians can hardly use the alumni quota to achieve matriculation.

A correct analysis of the problem also requires discussion of the self-inflicted lockouts by the Asian students. At Brown it was identified that Asian students place an exceptionally high number of applications for biology and medicine courses. Brown University, however, believes in upholding ethnic equality within the individual faculties (Brown Admission Office). According to Paula Bagaseo, specialist for *affirmative action*, many Asians apply to universities close to home so they can work and still remain with the family. Rather than visiting a top university elsewhere, they prefer to attend lower esteemed institutions, e.g. if they do not matriculate at Berkeley or Stanford (*New York Times*, September 9, 1989). Often, they are on waiting lists so that they may switch to the local elite university at a later date.

Yat-Pang Au, an eighteen-year-old *whiz kid*, explained to me that he finished Gunderson High School in San Jose summa cum laude, the best in his class with the highest grade A and was member of the school Supreme Court. Berkeley turned down even this highly qualified applicant in 1988 because he had applied for a "highly competitive" major, namely engineering. Had he applied at a different university or had he applied for a different major, he would have immediately obtained a place. Yat-Pang is now studying electronics at De Anza College in San Jose so he can stay at home. Next year, he intends to reapply to Berkeley, to be admitted as a junior (Interview with Yat-Pang Au, 1989).

Are these lopsided applications and choice of location possibly further reasons for the relatively low number of matriculations compared with their number of applications? Defined as a hypothesis: The selection process for Asians could seem more stringent than for other groups since a large number of Asian applicants concentrate on a few universities and a few classes.[57]

---

[56] Peng, Samuel et al., "School Experiences and Performances of Asian American High School Students." Washington, DC: U.S. Department of Education, 1984.

[57] 1991: Asian Americans in freshmen classes: Harvard, 19%; University of California, Irvine: 51%; Stanford, 18%; MIT, 22%. In 2000: Harvard, 19%; University of California, Irvine: 42.6%; Stanford, 25%; MIT, 29%, Berkeley, 45.2%.

Evaluation of Recognizable Tendencies, Berkeley as an Example

California's higher education system is one of the public institutions which is noticing the new Asian immigration most dramatically. A strong growth is applicable to all three levels of education. Public colleges and universities have the highest number and the highest percentages of Asian students.

On the community college level, San Francisco's Community College has the largest quota of non-English mother language students of all San Francisco. In the area of the University of California, Berkeley and Los Angeles have the highest rate of Asians. This is comparable to the previously discussed Asian tendency to move to larger cities or urban areas where non-English speakers also find jobs.[58]

Berkeley and Stanford are elite universities and have the highest numbers of Chinese in all of California due to their Bay Area location. Berkeley is especially desirable, not only due to the good name and good education that supports the Asian route to success via education, but also because it is financially possible, contrary to private institutions. Berkeley with its high rate of Chinese students represents a major focus point for Chinese *brain drain* and local *whiz kids*. Thus, San Francisco, the focal point for the historical immigration of mostly poor and uneducated Chinese, continues to attract the educated of following generations, both for new immigrants as well as second or third generation descendents equally.

The majority of educational immigrants seem prepared to remain in California on a long-term basis. In 1980, only 5% of Asian students declared an Asian country as home, although many (11.6% Chinese and 34.5% Japanese) were holding F-1 non-immigrant visas (Chan, 1981, 15). Approximately 90% of all Asian students at Berkeley are from California, whereby 56.3% Japanese and 79.3% Filipinos are from the nine counties of the Bay Area. Already in 1980, 60% of all Asian students were of Chinese origin, with American and foreign-born equally represented.[59] In 2000, 45.2% of all freshmen at Berkeley were Asian, compared to 34.7% of White freshmen; in comparison, in 1966, the percentage of White freshmen was 60%.

---

[58] See Chapter 4 "Habitat," and 5 "Business Structures and Income," which demonstrate a dislike for Asian immigrants in rural areas of California. See also Chan, Sucheng. "Contemporary Asian Immigration. It's Impact on Undergraduate Education at the University of California, Berkeley." Centre for Studies in Higher Education, South Hall Annex University of California, Berkeley, 1981, unpublished paper.

[59] In 1980, 4,703 Asian students were matriculated at University of California, Berkeley, of which 2,798 were Chinese, almost 60%. Of these Chinese, 50.5% were American-born, 49.5% foreign-born.

Since 1991, the number of Chinese American freshmen rose from 2,000 to over 4,500.[60] Thus, Berkeley will become the Chinese American elite university of the future. Regarding California, the Asians represent a larger percentage of students than they represent of the total population (1990: 9.6% Asians, 31% Asian students at Berkeley; 2000: 10.9% Asians, 45% Asian students at Berkeley). Even only looking at the nine most populated counties, the percentage of Asian students is still very high.

The ethnic deviation between students and staff at university is even more extreme than in the case of schools. 89% of personnel is White, thereof 84% also male. In comparison, in 1984, when the Chinese students represented 25%, only 5% of staff were Chinese Americans (McBee, 1984, 42). Staff networking is, accordingly, still one-sided. The tendency of the White university establishment to hold on to its privileges created a valve in the middle of the 1980s with the attempt to break the Asian attack on Berkeley. Thus, in 1984, the university introduced three suggestions for change:

o   GPA should be increased from 3.75 to 3.9
o   Asian students in the *Educational Opportunity Program* (EOP)[61] should no longer be hindered from transferring to other universities
o   The required grade for the verbal part of the SAT should be raised[62]

The introduction was met by an outcry from the Asians. The third suggestion had to be dropped. It is hardly by chance that in 1990, Chinese born Dr. Chang-lin Tien[63] was named Chancellor in the hope of regaining peace with the Chinese American community in the Bay Area.

From the example it becomes clear that a general increase in GPA requirements cannot be described as racial discrimination. Furthermore, the non-academic criteria of the GPA, along with other remnants of White privileges, apparently hinder the strongly academic-oriented Chinese Americans. The introduction of official instructions that would singularly discriminate against Asians, such as increased requirements in verbal admission tests, however, is not possible due to the high dependence of Californian institutions upon the surrounding community, even in case these instructions are based on *affirmative action.*

---

[60] One of the reasons for the strong increase of Asian students was the death of affirmative action in 1999. See <http://goldsea.com/AAU/berkeley_2000.html> (December 14, 2003).

[61] *Educational Opportunity Program*: A specialized program for students with a disadvantage resulting from their social heritage. EOP supports students not achieving the required test points, but having the abilities for a career at the university.

[62] Minimum 400 points. See Chan, 1991, 180.

[63] See also Chapter 5 "Exceptional Characteristics of Chinese American Business World" on Chancellor Tiens accomplishments.

Chinese Staff and Ethnic Diversity

Will the predominantly White university administration maintain its complacent position or will it adjust to the changed situation of the students? From 1990–1997, the new reigning Chancellor at the University of California, Berkeley was Chang-lin Tien, a Chinese who was not even born in America. It is the first time that such a leading position at an elite university was given to a member of the Chinese American group, who incidentally achieved top grades at one of these universities.

Tien has an exemplary curriculum vita for the immigration of Chinese elite. He was born in Wuhan, where his father was a university professor and financial advisor to the Chiang Kai-shek regime. Like many *Kuomintang* public officials, he fled with his family during the Japanese occupation to Shanghai and then, in 1949, to Taiwan. Tien's wife is the daughter of a *Kuomintang* general. In the 1950s he went in the flow of Taiwanese *brain drain* to America where he studied engineering at the University of Louisville and subsequently obtained his PhD at Princeton. He became an American citizen in 1969. His three children are Berkeley graduates.

Above and beyond the academic role, the Chancellor position at Berkeley is of eminently political and economic importance. The fact that Tien was the choice of then-University of California President David Gardner, an advisor to the president of the United States, underlines the importance of Pacific Rim business to the American economy. Tien, himself, stemmed from a banker family and was a Member of the Board at Wells Fargo Bank. Due to his open personality, he was well liked in the community, a fact which Taiwanese bankers usually mistrust. He had also earned the esteem of the high tech companies in Silicon Valley and was perceived to be a man who approached Asian interests with a progressive view (Muchnik, 1991, 7–10). Chancellor Tien, for many years the captain of the flagship among University of California institutions, was very aware of the mainly political reasoning for his promotion: "Some say that I've become chancellor because I'm Asian. I'm very pragmatic, so I don't get too bothered by that perception." (Interview with Chang-lin Tien, 1991). In the 1990s over half of the professors at Berkeley retired, which opened up interesting opportunities for Tien to initiate a stronger ethnic orientation. According to Tien, International and Women's Studies were to receive more emphasis. Thus, members of minorities and women should preferentially fill positions. "Excellence through Diversity" was his guiding motive. Tien believed: "We have to uphold the excellence level. There are very highly qualified women, African Americans, Latinos, Asian Americans, and Native Americans. If we don't tap that talent, it would be a great waste." (Irving, 1991, 9).

In September 1991, the Professor for Asian American Studies, Elaine Kim, took over as Women's Representative in the highest administrative office at Berkeley.[64] She is a community activist and one of the initiators of *Asian Women United of California.* She became advisor to the Vice Chancellor for Hiring and Promotions at the University, a position that is becoming especially important due to retirements. "I will place a high priority on hiring women of color," she says. She recognizes her new position as a direct result of the nomination of the Chancellor.

Networking slightly differently, the nomination of bestseller author, Maxine Hong Kingston, as senior lecturer for American Literature also occurred at the beginning of Tien's administrative period. Already in 1991, newly hired ethnic minorities represented 25%, of which 26% were women and were thus, far better represented than the previous academic staff numbers, where they represented only 11%. Much criticism existed against Tien's concept of maintaining quality standards by ethnic differentiation of students and staff. Conservative faculty members opposed changes in the curricula; an anti-diversity movement started. Members of this movement, both liberals and conservatives, felt that forbidding anti-racist and sexist comments (hate speech codes) at universities were an infliction on freedom of speech, as protected by the First Amendment. Political correctness was not Tien's priority. He did not believe that ethnic diversity automatically meant a drop in the educational standard (Wong, B., April 12, 1991, 9). The necessity of excellence through diversity can be followed. Since 1991, every student at Berkeley must pass an Ethnic Studies course, whereby a minimum of three of the following ethnic groups must be discussed: African Americans, Native Americans, Asian Americans, Hispanics/Latinos, and Euro-Americans. The knowledge of the ethnic diversity in the American population is a prerequisite for the implementation of previously untapped resources. Consequently, this knowledge must be reflected in the educational plans.

Also the curricula of many colleges should follow this course: Even against much opposition, today, we no longer find only the cultural history and humanities of the western world. "Curricula have changed dramatically," says Ernest Boyer, president of the Carnegie Foundation. "Women and members of minorities demanded that. And seriously, that was good for the universities." With regard to the current events, Boyer's comment sounds farsighted. "If at universities people of different cultures cannot treat each

---

[64] Elaine Kim is the past President of the *Association for Asian American Studies;* member of the National Council of the *American Studies Association;* co-founder and member of Board of Directors of *Asian Women United of California;* and a member of the *President's Comission on Women in U.S. History,* 1998–2000.

other fairly and with respect, how do we expect this to happen in towns and cities?" (Gibbs, 1990, 40-43).

The concentration of Asian students at preferred institutions and its consequences can be seen in the example of the Chinese Americans at Berkeley. While this phenomenon might have a negative influence on the matriculation quota, it does provide some very interesting opportunities and initial steps for changes in institutional life at American elite universities. In the described case, a potent local lobby hindered the bias against Chinese students and promoted Chinese American elements within the university administration and staff.

Choice of Courses—Nerdy Math and Science Wizards

With greater clarity attained on the phenomenon of Chinese concentration at certain institutions, we may now turn to the tendencies in their choice of courses. Similar to the reduced choice of location, this problem shows a negative and a positive side, at least in the Chinese American view. The negative side is that the huge popularity of certain courses increases competition immensely, thus knocking out many applicants.

Data from Berkeley indicates that Chinese prefer engineering sciences, whereby the number of applicants is very high within groups who have recently come to the United States. Of those who have a student visa, 33% choose an engineering major; 43.2% of new immigrants do so, and 40.3% permanent residents do so. The longer the residence, the lower the interest in engineering, e.g. it is only 25.4% for the foreign-born American citizens and 18.5% for those born in the United States. The opposite can be said for Social Sciences, including Law: Among the American-born this course is relatively well represented with 15.6%, but only marginally among student visa holders with 5.8%. The next most demanded courses are biology, including medicine, and physics with 10.6% and 12.6% respectively. Unappealing to Chinese students are the humanities (1.9% to 3.1% for the whole group) and economics (6.8% to 8.7%). The tendency is clear: Engineering at the top of the scale, humanities at the bottom, where obviously, lingual aptitude is more important. The one-sided orientation is increased for new immigrants: In this group, physics is the most requested course after engineering (12.6% of F-1 visa holders; Chan, 1981, 27). Their one-sided orientation makes the relatively low matriculation quota more understandable, and reflects more than just the administration's desire to maintain ethnic diversity within the individual faculties.

A country's chance of continuously remaining a leading industrialized nation is often measured by its number of engineers. Whoever thinks that Asians, and especially Chinese, could represent the technical elite of the United States, does so definitely not without cause. One must ask whether the choice of Chinese students is due to personal interest or pertinent talent, or whether this route is perceived to offer the best success rate, even in the face of the existing barriers. In the 1960s, members of first generation Chinese immigrants attained exceptional success in science for the first time. Chen-Ning Yang and Tsung-Dao Lee received the Nobel Prize in Physics in 1957 and thus became leaders for the subsequent *brain drain*.[65]

Looking at the personal interests of Chinese students, one will identify that, in addition to questions of linguistic aptitude, cultural factors are initially important for the choice of courses. Chinese see students in (western) humanities as exotic bohemians and hardly the picture of success of western education. Mainly teachers and lawyers stem from the humanities, the first being undesirable due to the low-income and lack of social status, which most likely entails rejection back into their own group instead of projection into American society.

The second represents a rather unimportant social group according to Chinese tradition. A short step back to the topics of Chapters 1 and 2 clarifies this belief. In imperial China, law and justice as guarantors of human co-existence were deplored, which is a reason why today one encounters deaf ears when demanding the upholding of civil rights. Confucius was against this law.[66] His idea of Cosmo-social harmony was a form of formalized traditional law. Only first in 1912 were western style laws introduced and incorporated into Chinese lifestyle.

Even after Sun Yat-sen's promoted change from Confucianism toward western culture in 1919, Confucius's view that a law is a sign of an incomplete social order was widespread. A revival of Confucian ideology in 1930 increased this. Only since 1937, has China slowly developed a law-based system (Cohen, 1980). In the course of this development, law referral offices were opened in many cities and counties (Huang, Jy, 1979, 51). The "Orientation and Anti-Rights Movement" of 1957, however, brought with it the decline of lawyers, since taking a mandate was a "crime." Thus, lawyers were prosecuted and lost their jobs. Many were only freed from jail after Mao's death, since he perceived law to be administrative ruling.

Therefore, Chinese immigrants indoctrinated with Confucian teaching or Maoist law did not even think of taking up law or allowing their children to do so. Generally, the majority of Chinese Americans, with their roots in the immigrating generations of the 1930s to the 1970s, have this historical background and thus do not accept law as an occupation. Teachers had a high

---

[65] See Chapter 5 "Career and Legal Barriers," and 6 "From Brain Drain to Brain Gain-Returning to the Homeland."

[66] According to Confucius, the rites are an appropriate rule for society and cosmos. The untouchable basic principle, laid out in the Book of Morals, is that of society in harmony.

position in the Confucian era, but were hit heavily by the hate of intellectualism during the Cultural Revolution. A job, such as teaching, that does not have much promotion potential in American society is, therefore, hardly considered lucrative by success-oriented Chinese. Both jobs require long-term cultural identification processes, e.g. understanding of the schooling system and law, which go far beyond language aptitude. This supplies further reason for lack of Chinese teachers at American schools. Technical diplomas are different: Their market value is high and quickly transferable.

Another problem is the incapability of the university administration to prepare and coordinate Chinese students. The following statement during an interview with Chinese Americans best demonstrates this: "Now they think all we know is how to sit in front of a computer." (Interview with Simon Lee, 1998). Due to the difference between western and eastern cultures, many Chinese students believe the concept of "neutral science." Many choose sciences or math, because they expect an objective evaluation from the White professors. One interviewee explained: "I believe we choose the courses because they are secure and impersonal. One does not have to take a side or give clear personal views." (Interview with S. K. Brown, 1991).

Among new immigrants, the main problem during interviews is the language barrier. Foreign-born Chinese achieve poor results in language tests for university entrance applications: In 1981, nearly half (47.9% in contrast to 8.8% of American-borns) were in the lowest category (200–399) and only 7.2% in the highest. In mathematics it is the opposite: In the lowest category there were only 1.8% (0.9% for American-borns), in the middle category 35.8%, and 62.4% in the highest (59.7% for American-borns; Chan, 1981, 26). With regard to the poor knowledge of English among new immigrants and refugees, the selectors often make it easy for themselves and suggest science courses. An adaptation toward the situation of the student is not chosen, an improvement of their English aptitude is not intended.[67] A reason could be that until now only few Chinese Americans are employed in the science faculties. The students' uncertainty toward their position in the recipient society is transferred to the choice of study and trade.

It would be going too far; however, to insinuate that those Chinese students are pressured by American society into technical trades. New immigrant students, especially those from Taiwan and Hong Kong, have all attended excellent schools in their home country. Often they have excellent knowledge in math and computer sciences. Their cultural orientation thus matches nicely their educational orientation.

---

[67] "They put them into safe courses, such as science and math where they don't have to communicate." McBee, 1984, 42.

Learning techniques from their home countries are of great benefit to these students: They are trained to spend hours concentrating on homework. Chinese schooling involves much rote memorization. Thus, new immigrants have an advantage over American students, especially in areas that require concentration and constancy but not creativity and critical thought.[68]

In this context, a slightly different picture appears among "jump ship sailors" and refugees from Southeast Asia. They do not seem to possess the beginnings of regulated schooling nor aptitude in the English language. They await a totally new beginning in the United States, in which the younger ones are under pressure to succeed from their parents. The talented also seek out computer sciences and general sciences because here one can improve relatively quickly. This should not cover up the fact that especially those Chinese Americans have severe difficulties at universities and schools (McBee, 1984, 47). Whoever does not make the jump to the university is considered a failure by this group. The number of dropouts among Southeast Asians is very high.[69]

The home is a further component for single-sided orientation. Upper class Asians see themselves as *professionals* rather than in insecure businesses. Simple families prefer successful occupations for their children. In the end the result is the same: Doctor or Engineer. Nancy Chen, marketing specialist at IBM, says that she chose her career against the will of her parents. Business and existential risks were deplored by her parents' generation due to their own, often bitter, experiences (Interview, 1991).

Thus, the Confucian tradition and the desire for financial success create a combination of high efficiency and goal-oriented ambition. The other side of the coin is noticeable where the Chinese require eloquent representatives: "We are a community of technicians that desperately needs poets for its voice." (Interview with Cheryl Wong, 1991). A further motivation dictating the choice of studies could be that the community sees its greatest potential for success when it concentrates on a single point of attack. The matriculation difficulties for Asian students, also created by a one-sided orientation, is one of the major topics of Chinese American interest groups in San Francisco, which will be discussed.

---

[68] See also Chapter 6 "Education," under "*Whiz Kids*—Scholastic Attitude and Educational Success."

[69] In the Boston Schools, the dropout rate for Asians and Southeast Asians rose from 14.4% in 1982 to 26.5% in 1985. Brand, 1987, 45.

Affirmative Action or **Multicultural Society?**

Initially, *affirmative action* meant: Equal opportunity on education and jobs for minority groups and women, with special emphasis on removing historical barriers for those less prepared for social competition and on reparation for previously endured unfairness (Michaelson, 1996).

The concept of affirmative action, initiated by Presidents Kennedy and Johnson, targeted especially the Black population.[70] It is, therefore, useful to reflect on the societal notion of "race." Throughout history, the term "race" has been used as a justification for superiority and suppression. From the Nubian and Roman empires to the Japanese occupation of China, the German Holocaust, and the recent Balkan wars, nations used "race" as basis for their oppression of other people (Fredrickson, 2002). Until today, race has also been socially divisive in the United States—from the first enslavement of Blacks in 1619 to the civil riots in Los Angeles in 1992 (Takaki, 1994, Jacobson, 1999). The public definition, perception, and use of the term "race," and the attitude of the different racial and ethnic groups towards each other, is therefore paramount to a well-functioning society in multiracial and -ethnic United States.

"Race" can be defined by cultural, economic, ethnic, political, sociological, or scientific terms. During many centuries, however, predominantly biologic and genetic explanations have been used to define race, providing a scientific reasoning, while deflecting from social and political discrimination.[71] Only since the late twentieth century, scientific explanations of race have become more and more abandoned, driven by advances in human sciences, and general social changes. The fact that, during the twenty-first century, over half of the United States population will consist of Asian, Black, and Hispanic people leads inevitably to a change in the public perception of race.

---

[70] President Kennedy issued the *Executive Order 10,925* in 1961 to "take *affirmative steps* against discrimination." In 1965, President Johnson first used the expression *affirmative action* in *Executive Order 11,246*, creating the *Office of Federal Contract Compliance.*

[71] In 1758, the taxonomist Carl von Linné divided human beings in four racial groups: American, European, Asian and African. Already this first racial classification scheme mixed physical features and behavioral traits, using scientific terms, such as obstinate (American), gentle and governed by law (European), opinionated (Asian), and capricious (African) (Carl von Linné, *Systema Naturae*, 10th ed., 1758). See also *Webster's Third New International Dictionary* defines race as "a division of mankind possessing traits that are transmissible by descent and sufficient to characterize it as a distinct human type <Caucasian~> <Mongoloid~>." Springfield, MA: *Merriam–Webster*, 1993, p.1870. See also Chapter 1 "Regulation of the Chinese Question at Federal Level." The governmental report of the *Joint Special Committee* implied, that the Chinese were genetically predisposed to

The latest version of the *Encyclopedia Britannica* already reflects this development, confining race to a sociological concept.[72] This perception also finds increasing support by the government, and the U.S. Census Bureau defined race in 1997 as follows: "The racial and ethnic categories set forth in the standards should not be interpreted as being primarily biological or genetic in reference. Race and ethnicity may be thought in terms of social and cultural characteristics as well as ancestry." (*Office of Management and Budget–OMB*, 1997, p.58782). "Race is a social concept, and not a scientific one," says Greg Venter, head of *Celera*, the company that sequenced the human genome.[73] Like Venter, many scientists today reject racial classification of humans, as it is commonly accepted that less than 0.1 percent of the human genes are reflected in external appearance. Therefore, major ethnic groups, such as Whites, Blacks, or Asians, are far too heterogeneous to be categorized in a scientific way.[74] Medical groups, such as the *Human Genome Project*, the *National Institute of Health*, and advisers to the Surgeon General, call for a "Manhattan Project" to redefine the concept of race, and to change the term to "ethno-cultural group" (Koenig, 2001).

The American Anthropological Association, in a direct response to the new standards set forth by the *OMB* in 1997, proposed to eliminate the term "race" completely in the 2010 census, and suggested that "the combined term "race/ethnicity" serves as a bridge towards the elimination of the term race." (*American Anthropological Association*, 2001). In 2003, the *Racial Privacy Initiative (Proposition 54)* was started in California, a campaign to block state and government from classifying people by their race. The vote will be cast in March 2004, and, if favorable, it would eliminate the public use of race completely, making America "colorblind." Asian Americans are going to play a crucial role in this vote, which will affect many social aspects, including affirmative action.

---

perform "light labor," and thus, could not integrate into the American society (*Joint Special Committee*, 1877, 17).

[72] "Term once commonly used in physical anthropology to denote a division of humankind ... (e.g., Caucasoid, Mongoloid, Negroid). "Race" is today primarily a sociological designation." "Race" *Britannica Concise Encyclopedia,* Encyclopædia Britannica Premium Service, <http://www.britannica.com/ecb/article?eu=401660> March 10, 2003.

[73] *New York Times*, August 22, 2000.

[74] "In the scientific sense, the world is colorblind," indicates Prof. Templeton from Washington University, see "Human Races: A Genetic and Evolutionary Perspective" *American Anthropologist*, November, 1998.

Whereas affirmative action was embraced with wide solidarity by ethnic organizations during the Civil Rights Movement, it has been hotly disputed for many years.[75] During the 1960s, there was far less division over the terminology "race" and the acknowledgement of discrimination. The decision to use affirmative action derived from the Fourteenth Amendment of the Constitution, which guarantees equality.

At the turn of the twenty-first century, however, the discussions about affirmative action have become much more complex. Minorities in America have almost tripled, from 11.3% *non-White* in 1960, to 30.9% *non-White* in 2000, and are consequently gaining more influence. Minorities are also becoming much more diversified, and their places in the educational, financial, professional, and social spectrums much broader than that of the White majority. Racial lines have been blurred, forcing the government to add a *mixed race* category in the census of 2000.[76] Furthermore—at least in some states—former minorities are becoming majorities. These changes also require a revision of affirmative action in order to address the needs of the twenty-first century. In the general discussion, whether to continue affirmative action, or how to do so, has been largely reduced to the question of *quotas*, e.g. admission, employment or contraction quota. The issue, however, is too complex to be reduced to a simple yes or no, as in 1965.

For many years, California has been at the forefront of the affirmative action debate, as it was the case in *Bakke vs. University of California* in 1978. In July 1995, the *University of California Board of Regents* passed a resolution (SP-1), making it one of the first universities in the United States to, "…eliminate consideration of race, ethnicity, and gender in admissions. Recognizing the potential impact of SP-1 on diversity in future student enrollment, The Regents established the Outreach Task Force to identify ways in which outreach … could be employed to assure that the University remains accessible to students of diverse backgrounds." The strategy aims to initiate school-centered partnerships with *educationally disadvantaged schools*, and *academic development programs* for K-12 students (Outreach Task Force, 1997, 1).

---

[75] See Cahn, Steven M. *The Affirmative Action Debate.* (London: Routledge, 2002); Ibarra, Robert A. *Beyond Affirmative Action: Reframing the Context of Higher Education.* Madison, WI: The University of Wisconsin Press, 2000; Gertrude Ezorsky, *Racism and Justice: The Case for Affirmative Action.* (Ithaca Cornell University Press, 1992). Hyun, 1996, 69–77.

[76] More than 6.8 million Americans selected the new category *two or more races* in the census of 2000, e.g. 2.4% of the population. These are predominantly young people who will enter schools and employment over the next several decades. It has yet to be determined how this group will be affected and how it will influence the current developments in *affirmative action*, and the use of the term *race*. These hapas will be at the forefront of the debate about the future multicultural society of the United States.

This program was one of the first to establish and monitor alternatives to affirmative action. At the same time opposition for existing programs has come from different sides, especially from White who see racial preferences as a "reverse discrimination."[77] Many Asian, and especially Chinese Americans, feel that racial caps imposed by affirmative action hinder their educational progress, thus they support a race-neutral admission policy, favoring qualifications over quotas (*Washington Post*, June 20, 1998). There are, however, also many Asian Americans who support affirmative action, viewing it as a way to a multicultural, democratic America, and thus reflecting the diversity within one ethnicity.[78]

Jewish groups, who see their strong position within medical and law faculties at elite universities under fire, have recently backed away from earlier positions against affirmative action. Whereas Jewish organizations supported *Bakke* in 1978, they now believe that, "admission criteria designed to boost minority enrollment does not threaten their own foothold in elite colleges." (*Washington Post*, December 22, 2002). African, Hispanic, and Native Americans, however, are united in their support of affirmative action.

Already in the beginning of the 1990s, Congressman Dana Rohrabacher (R-CA)[79] introduced a bill (H. Con. Res. 147) to eliminate racial or ethnic criteria in college matriculation.[80] According to him, the sole problem was that Asians and other ethnic minorities were measured against separate criteria instead of being treated as Americans. Thus, Rohrabacher was one of the early politicians to call for elimination of racial quotas for university admission. His activities were not well regarded among Asian representatives, since, according to Henry Der,[81] former president of *Chinese for Affirmative Action*, they could be aimed at taking the wind out of the sails of his and similar organizations.

---

[77] The lawsuits *Gratz vs. Bollinger* and *Grutter vs. Bollinger* were decided by the Supreme Court in June 2003. Both are essential cases regarding *affirmative action.* In them, the Supreme Court further clarified its ruling from 1978. It allowed the narrowly tailored use of race as a selection criteria, but denied to grant minority preferences (Drehle, 2003).

[78] "APAs Speak Out Against Bush's Anti-Affirmative Action Stance." *Asian Week*, January 31, 2003. For detailed discussions see: "Beyond Self-Interest: Asian Pacific Americans toward a Community of Justice," (Chin, Gabriel, 1996) and "Being Used and Being Marginalized in the Affirmative Action Debate: Re-envisioning Multiracial American from an Asian American Perspective." (Wang, 1996a, 49–58).

[79] Dana Rohrabacher, a Republican Congressman since 1989 with less than 6% Asians in his District, was a writer for more than seven years for Ronald Reagan, and was politically active in Reagan's campaigns from the time he was nineteen years old in 1966.

[80] See *Heritage Foundation*, "Executive Memorandum," June 30, 1989.

[81] Henry Der was appointed as Executive Director of *CAA* in 1974. Under his efforts, *CAA* expanded as a watchdog for Chinese and other Asian American rights. Der left the *CAA* in 1996 to become Assistant Superintendent of Schools at the California State Department.

Paul M. Igasaki,[82] former lobbyist of the *Japanese American Citizens League*, comments on the intentions of the Republican Representative, as follows: "He [Rohrabacher] is trying to tear us away from the rest of the Civil Rights Community."[83] Senator Paul Simon, Democrat from Illinois, likewise did not support Rohrabacher. According to him the matriculation problem should not be abused to reduce affirmative action.

The majority of Asians did not support Rohrabacher, as Simon well knows.[84] Together with Senator Tom Daschle, South Dakota, he is one of the the most active supporter of Asian interests in Washington (Interviews with Paul Simon and Tom Daschle, 1990). Can there be a multicultural society of ethnic equality as long as affirmative action is used as a weapon? Rohrabacher's ideas, however, are gaining broader support, especially from the White population, but also from minorities.

A new chapter of affirmative action was opened in 1996, when a constitutional amendment, the *California Civil Rights Initiative*—also known as *Proposition 209*—passed by a margin of 54% to 46%. The Supreme Court rejected subsequent lawsuits against *Proposition 209*, now a part of the Californian Constitution, thus basically ending affirmative action in California. 76% of all Hispanic Americans, 74% of all African Americans, and 61% of all Asian Americans rejected *Proposition 209*, whereas 63% of the White population voted in favor of it.[85]

The *Initiative 200 (I-200)*, a similar legislation in Washington, captured 58% of the vote and was subsequently implemented as state law.[86] Critics see this development as a move towards elitism, and strongly disadvantageous for discriminated minorities, thus contrary to President Kennedy's and Johnson's affirmative action program.

Furthermore, the end of affirmative action in California and Washington can be a double-edged sword for Asian Americans, as they are the major

---

[82] Paul Igasaki was the executive director of the *Asian Law Caucus* in San Francisco, when President Clinton appointed him as the vice-chair of the *Equal Employment Opportunity Commission*, which he served from 1994 until 2002.

[83] Interviews with Henry Der, 1989, 1990, and 1991; see Scott Jaschick. "Conservative Lawmakers Attracts Interest and Ire with Crusade for *Asian American Students*." *Chronicle of Higher Education*, November 15, 1989, 21, 32–33.

[84] John D. Trasvina (Assistant of Paul Simon) "Most Asian American Students do not want to use this issue to attack affirmative action." Interview in 1990.

[85] "Demographic Profiles from the California and National Exit Polls." *Los Angeles Times*, November 7, 1996. Although other statistics suggest slightly lower levels of Asian support, they nevertheless confirm the trend: according to several resources cited by Hu, between 22% and 45% of all Asian Americans support *affirmative action* (Hu, 2003). Further details on *affirmative action* can be found under: "AAD Project-Affirmative Action and Diversity: A Web Page for Research." (Gutierrez-Jones, 2002).

[86] "The Battle for Color-Blind Public Policy." Zelnick, Robert. *Hoover Digest*, 2001

beneficiaries. A first impact can already be seen today, as admission figures of Californian universities from 1997 to 2000 show declining numbers for all ethnic groups, except Asians. African American admissions fell as much as 54% (U.C. Berkeley, Admission Office, 2001). Recent figures, however, are rebounding to levels prior to *Proposition 209* (*New York Times*, April 4, 2000).

These close margins show the American split over affirmative action, a divide that is found throughout all ethnical, political and social groups. Whereas President Clinton supports affirmative action while in office and continues to do so, President Bush voiced his opposition to racial admission criteria by using the same argument like President Johnson in 1965 to oppose affirmative action: "Our Constitution makes it clear that all people of all races must be treated equally under the law."[87] (*CNN*, January 16, 2003). National Security Advisor Condoleezza Rice, who benefited from affirmative action during her career at Stanford University, rejects "racial quotas."[88]

Secretary of State, Colin Powell, supports affirmative action, and criticized the administration's position as a form of "reverse discrimination" (*Jakarta Post*, January 17, 2003). And it was a Black businessman, Ward Connerly, who, through his *American Civil Rights Institute*, organized the major support for Proposition 209 and Initiative 200 (*Washington Post*, October 24, 1998, A1). The Asian American community is similarly divided. Taiwanese-born Secretary of Labor, Elaine Chao, is a strong opponent of affirmative action. Many Asian Americans, therefore, criticize her conservative position as being against minorities and the lower class. Prof. Ling-chi Wang sees her as a privileged immigrant, representing only part of the American Dream.[89]

As a strong supporter of affirmative action, Wang said, "I'm concerned that a lot of Asian-Americans don't understand or don't really appreciate the contributions of African Americans to protect the civil rights of Asian-Americans." (Mangaliman, 2002).

---

[87] On January 15, 2003, the Bush administration filed an *amicus curiae* brief in *Gratz vs. Bollinger* to argue against the existing race-conscious admission program of the University of Michigan, and thus hoped to stop *affirmative action* (*Asian Week*, January 31, 2003). Over one hundred petitions have been filed, many in favor of the University of Michigan. 88 Universities, 68 Fortune 500 companies (ChevronTexaco, DuPont, IBM, Pfizer, and Xerox), 24 U.S. states, military leaders, and labor unions support the arguments of the University of Michigan regarding racial quotas (Miller, Tom, 2003).

[88] CBS News. "Powell Defends Affirmative Action." January 20, 2003, <http/www.cbsnews.com/ stories/2003/01/21/politics/printable537363.shtml> (March 3, 2003).

[89] "Elaine Chao: Conservative, But How Compassionate Will She Be?" *Asian Week*, January 19, 2001. For further details about the discussion on Asian Americans and affirmative action see Wang, Ling-chi, 1996a.

Angela Oh, member of President Clinton's *Advisory Board on Race,* warned: "I think we [the Asian Americans] are going to pay a huge price for … *Proposition 209.* Even Whites lost out on Prop. 209. …This is going to come back and haunt us in many ways."

Michael Chang, former mayor of Cupertino, maintains that it is wrong to support affirmative action if only it benefits Asian Americans. University of California, Berkeley chancellor Berdahl vows, "I will personally phone as many of these [underrepresented minority] students as I can." (*Asian Week,* April 9, 1998). About 60% of all Asian American speak out in favor of affirmative action (*Asian Week,* January 31, 2002). The divide over affirmative action has also been reflected in the decisions of the Supreme Court. The last major ruling on the issue was in 1978 (*Bakke vs. University of California*), where the court issued a four-one-four split decision which allowed the narrow use of race as admission criteria for universities.

Since then, justices have been careful to avoid deciding on the constitutionality of racial admission criteria for a quarter century, and several cases were pending.[90] The debate heated up when two law students legally challenged the affirmative action program of the University of Michigan, which promotes ethnic diversity and uses race as a selection criterion. In June 2003, the Supreme Court ruled five-four that race could be used as a narrow selection criterion, so long as it was not the defining feature. At the same time, the Supreme Court struck down a broad system that assigns points for minority status in a six-three ruling.[91] The rulings try to keep diversity in the higher education system, confirming affirmative action for minorities. Chinese Americans will not receive special treatment because of their over-representation. Other Asian minorities, such as Pacific Islanders and Southeast Asian, are therefore already pressing for a separate treatment, especially preferential admission.[92]

How can equal treatment of all groups be assured to meet the outlines of the 14th amendment? The Outreach Task Force of the University of California exemplifies one approach. Another example is the "Ten Percent Approach" of Texas, which started in 1997 and may offer a good alternative.[93]

---

[90] "Affirmative Action or Reverse Discrimination: Trick or Treat?" Baker, Thomas E. *Jurist,* October 31, 2001. <http://jurist.law.pitt.edu/forum/forumnew35.htm> (March 9, 2003).

[91] For further details see "Court mirrors public opinion." Drehle, David von. *Washington Post,* June 24, 2003. "Affirmative Action Gets U.S. Court's Reprieve." *Asian Wall Street Journal,* June 24, 2003, A1, A12.

[92] Golden, Daniel, and Forelle, Charles. "How Far Does Diversity Go?" *Asian Wall Street Journal,* June 26, 2003, A5.

[93] "Texas's 10 Percent Experiment." *Washington Post,* October 28, 2002.

University officials see this approach as a way to achieve the goals of diversity, without adopting the means (*Washington Post*, November 4, 2002, A1). "The United States has been a racially and ethnically diverse society from its beginnings. But the conventional wisdom these days is that something radically new is happening now—that demographic changes are fundamentally transforming our society in unprecedented ways." (Thernstrom, 2002, 13). It will be seen over the next decade, how *affirmative action* and the term *race* will shape America's political and social landscape in the twenty-first century.

From *Brain Drain* to *Brain Gain*—Returning to the Homeland

Brain drain is a serious problem for many countries, especially for developing economies such as China's. The United States is by far the most attractive place to study, and the flow of foreign students into the United States reached almost 600,000 in 2002, with 100,000 coming from China alone.[94] A variety of factors contribute to this development, including, scientific, economic, cultural, and political (U.S. Embassy Beijing, 1997).

The majority of Chinese students in the United States, e.g. 70%, desire to return to their homeland. Political instability and lack of job opportunities, however, are major obstacles for their return (Saxenian, 2002, 51-52). The political situation in China has significantly changed during the 1990s, driven by the explosive growth of the economy.

With a strong need for academic and management professionals, numerous organizations, initiatives, and regular conferences have been formed in China, such as the *China Development Institute*, or the *Transfer of Knowledge Through Expatriate Nationals* (*TOKTEN*), which are trying to attract overseas Chinese students and motivate them to return to China. Many Chinese cities labeled skyscrapers in Chinese: "Returning Student Entrepreneurial Building," and the Chinese government is aggressively vying to win some of the country's brainpower back. In October 2002, a job fair in San Jose titled "China meets Silicon Valley," which was sponsored by the Chinese Consular General, attracted more than 4,000 Chinese-born engineers.[95]

---

[94] In 2001–02, 582,996 foreign students studied in the United States. This foreign *brain drain* contributed nearly $12 billion to the American economy, making it the fifth largest service sector (*Boston Globe*, November 27, 2002). Furthermore, foreign students are often highly skilled and knowledgeable, increasing the cultural spectrum at Universities.

[95] "Aggressive push by China to reverse brain drain," *The Straits Times*, November 27, 2002.

These efforts are supported by Chinese American networks in the United States, which promote cooperation and exchange with China.[96] With strong political and organizational support, and with vacant jobs created by the expanding economy in China, there will be no problem for returning students to find attractive positions in their homeland. The question is whether income and living standards will be attractive enough to motivate overseas students to return home. The situations in Taiwan, Hong Kong, and Korea indicate that they will: The economic growth of these countries during the 1980s and 1990s was accompanied by an increasing number of returnees. In 2000, only 30% of the Taiwanese students returned.[97] The majority of those who stay are the highly skilled scientists, often holding a PhD degree (Johnson, 2002, 127).

Table 32 GDP Growth and Returning Students in Asia, 1980–2000

	1980		1990		2000	
	GDP[98] per capita (US$)	Returning Students[99]	GDP per capita (US$)	Returning Students	GDP per capita (US$)	Returning Students
China	290	10%	370	12%	812	>30%
Hong Kong	8,719	31%	14,849	45%	24,187	>50%
Taiwan	4,459	36%	8,063	54%	12,704	72%
United States	12,303	–	23,263	–	35,884	–

Arranged by B. Zinzius

These data clearly show that *reverse brain drain*, e.g. brain drain in the originating countries, is strongly correlated with the financial situation in the receiving country.[100]

---

[96] See also Chapter 8 "Economy: The New *Global Entrepreneurs*."

[97] Korea's development correlates well with that of Hong Kong and Taiwan. In 2000, the GDP per capita in Korea averages US$13,420, and 89% of Korean students returned from the United States. In 1980, 41% of all Korean students had returned from abroad (GDP/capita: US$3,093), in 1990 65% (GDP/capita: US$8,712). United Nations, 2002; Synovate 2003.

[98] Real GDP per capita, in 1995 US$. IMF/IFS statistics; Synovate 2003; country statistics.

[99] Cervantes and Guellec, OECD, 2002; Johnson, Jean, 2002; *People's Daily Online*, 2001.

[100] Saxenian calls this reverse flow of students *brain circulation*, an expression which seems less suitable to the situation. Circulation means an equal flow, whereas in this case, the scientific flow is largely one-sided, based on the balance of Chinese migration. The 110,696 students from the People's Republic of China, Hong Kong Special Administrative Region, and Taiwan, which studied in 2002–03 in the United States, were contrasted with 3,911 American students which studied in China (*Open Doors 2003*, 2004). Whereas American students in China study mainly humanities, Chinese students in the United States study engineering and high-tech related topics, which they use as a basis to start businesses and ultimately set up companies in their native homeland. 73% of all Chinese American entrepreneurs and high-tech workers consider starting business in their country of birth (Saxenian, 2002, 2, 51).

Although the average GDP per capita in China is still below $1,000, the income disparity between hinterland and coastal regions is at least threefold. Therefore, income levels in prosperous areas, such as Shanghai, have already surpassed $3,000, a level that triggered the return of expatriates in Korea and Taiwan. Guo estimates that a per-capita GDP of $4,000 will lead to a significant increase of students returning to China.[101]

Already today, Chinese banks are offering multimillion-dollar startup capitals, and companies are willing to pay multiples of local salaries and fringe benefits for returning overseas Chinese. Headlines in Chinese newspapers confirm the return of oversea Chinese to the mainland.[102]

In the beginning of the 1990s, the Tiananmen Square Massacre not only increased the number of refugee students from China, but the *Chinese Student Protection Act* reduced the number of returning students after the incident as well.[103] The economic slump and the terrorist attack on September 11, 2001 practically reversed the situation. Increased security measures hinder visa applications, and growing racial tensions motivate the return of students after the completion of their studies. Thus, the percentage of Chinese students returning to mainland China is rising consistently. A Chinese proverb describes the situation: *San si nian he dong san si nian he xi*, which literally means: "Someone who lived thirty years on the east bank of the river, should then live thirty years on the west bank to provide balance." (*Los Angeles Times*, November 25, 2002).

Since the end of the 1990s, the number of Chinese students returning to China has drastically increased, and in 2001 the figure was already 30%. More and more high-profile cases have become visible. Chinese American managers and executives are leaving good positions in the United States to start in information or biotechnology companies in China, where the sprawling business opportunities are often compared to Silicon Valley in the 1980s.[104]

This development may create a new type of migrant, the *retro-sojourner*. Many of the Chinese students have brought their families to America, often including their parents and siblings. The return to China often leaves the

---

[101] "Overseas Study Will Inevitably Lead to Integrating Chinese Scientists and Engineers into the International Community of Science." Guo, Y., CIES Meeting, Washington, DC. March 13, 2001.

[102] "Many Chinese Students return Home after Studying Abroad." *Peoples Daily Online*, August 13, 2002; and "China's Job Market Sees a Reversal of Brain Drain." *China Daily*, April 4, 2002.

[103] See Chapter 3 "Definitions," under "Changes in the Situation in the Countries of Origin."

[104] "China's Brightest Minds Return From Abroad For Better Opportunity." *Asian Wall Street Journal*. March 6, 2003, A1, M8.

family behind in the United States, forcing the returnee to live, for a second time, as an uprooted (*retro-*) *sojourner,* this time in his native homeland.

The analysis of this chapter can be summarized as follows:

1. Asians represent a three times higher proportion of students than their proportion of society.[105] Californian elite universities have up to 45% Asian students of which approximately 50% is Chinese.

2. For many years, Chinese represent the highest number of students ever registered in the United States. Additionally, there are the students of Chinese ethnic origin from India, Indonesia, Japan, Korea, Malaysia, Singapore, and Vietnam.[106]

3. Whereas, until World War II, Asian students returned to their homeland or, if they stayed, took a position unequal to their qualifications, the situation has fundamentally changed. Previously, the universities were the assembly line of the White elite and today they are the pipelines for Asians aiming at leading academic, entrepreneurial and management positions. The students are the main reason for the so-called *chain migration.* Since the 1990s, an increasing number of students have been returning to their homeland, resulting in a strong know-how transfer and new phenomena such as *retro-sojourners.*

4. Chinese American interest groups claim that the matriculation barriers are their main targets. The *Lau vs. Nichols* (1974) and the *Ho vs. San Francisco Unified School District cases* (1999), with the subsequent changes in Californian school regulations forbid discrimination against language inability, which paves the way for the removal of verbal tests from entrance examinations, still considered one of the major barriers for a massive increase in Asian students at elite universities. The latest Supreme Court decisions, *Gratz/Grutter vs. Bollinger,* smoothes the way for the Chinese Americans even further.[107]

---

[105] Nationwide, Asians represent 3.7% (Asian and Pacific Islanders) and Chinese 0.9% of the total population. In San Francisco however, 30.8% are Asians and 20.6% are Chinese; see also Chapter 4 "Habitat." U.S. Bureau of the Census, 2002.

[106] In 2001, almost 100,000 ethnic Chinese students in total, of which 63,211 came from mainland China, 28,930 from Taiwan, and 7,757 from Hong Kong. In addition, 4,141 came from Singapore, 7,395 from Malaysia, 11,614 from Indonesia, and 2,531 from Vietnam (*Open Doors,* 2002).

[107] See also "Affirmative Action Gets U.S. Court's Reprieve." *Asian Wall Street Journal,* June 24, 2003, A1, A12; Drehle, 2003.

5. Although the high work ethic of Asian students declines among third and fourth generation Asian Americans, it is strongly maintained not only by cultural factors, e.g. family, but also by the continuous massive flow of new immigrants.

From the strong socioeconomic change within the Chinese American group described in Chapters 3 to 5, a major difference within today's family situation and that of the historical immigration can be deduced. The important function that education has for the creation of the integration chain and for the horizon of the emigrants leads to the conclusion that school and studies are also important for the creation and development of relationships. Until now, the family has only been seen as the means and support for promotion in society for Chinese Americans. Now, it must be applied as a mirror to identify multi-faceted changes of lifestyles.

7. FAMILY STRUCTURES

From a Bachelor Society to a Family Society—Historical Models

The family in American society is changing rapidly. The traditional family, in which both parents live with their children, is becoming more infrequent. The number of single households is increasing along with the number of single parents. During the period 1960–2000, the number single households grew from 14% to 25.5%. The number of children in single-parent families grew in the same period from 9% to 31.9%, and even more within the group of African Americans. In 2000, 53.3% of all Black children lived with either only the mother or the father. By contrast, among Asian Americans over 80% of all children lived with two parents, the highest rate of all ethnic groups. The social consequences of this development cannot yet be identified. The question is whether it is a crisis that will lead us to something substantially new or one that will eventually return us to traditional family bonds. In looking for answers, the Asian family model stands out, with the Chinese often being described as the *model minority*. The Chinese American family is said to be more stable, has lower divorce rates, makes only minor use of social security, and creates less crime.[1]

Is the Asian family model then a successful model to be emulated by society as a whole? To answer this, one needs first to identify whether the typical Chinese American developed from historical models or whether it evidences simply an incomplete transition to the recipient country. Furthermore, one must identify in the highly diversified immigrant group of the last decades whether there exists a predominant type with marked characteristics. The traditional family in China was, politically speaking, the nucleus of society, representing an economic and social base unit. It especially represented the sole security within the hierarchy of Chinese society. Only within the family clan could men be promoted or achieve higher social status. Marriage was one of the most important factors in the achievement of a clan's economic interests and political power. In the merger of families, it was understood that they be of equal social level. A marriage thus underlined the social status of the family. Marriage was, in effect, a business deal agreed upon by the family heads. An indication that this was pure business can be seen in the use of intermediates. The personal

---

[1] Further studies may be found in: Huang, Lucy Jen. "The Chinese American Family." In: *Ethnic Families in America. Patterns and Variations.* Mindel, Charles H. (Ed.). New York, NY: Elsevier, 1976, 124–147; Fong, R. "Socialization Issues for Chinese American Children and Families." *Journal of Social Work in Education*, No. 18, 1996, 71–83.

relationship between the bride and groom were of minor importance within this system, since they often first met on their wedding day. The classical Chinese marriage may be characterized by patriarchy and exogamy, with the single focus on the continuation of the male line. The written contract, including the regulation of the dowry, must be seen as its lawful basis. The family, and not the individual, was important in the choice of partner, the closing of the contract, and the definition of the goals of the merger.

The Chinese marriage thus had to be seen namely as an institutionalized joining of two individuals and not the social expression of their wishes. The partners did not meet as two individuals with special feelings, but as representatives of their sex, representatives of *yin* and *yang*.[2] In Confucianism the woman is a second-class person. Subordination, especially that of women toward their men and the children toward their parents even after reaching adulthood, was the most important principle of society. Contrary to Taoism, which postulates the equality of *yin* and *yang*, the hierarchical world of the Confucians was intended to support the state, which allowed total control of all social activities. The Chinese family bloomed within this model. The unusual situation of the split of the emigrating family is usually described as the separated family. Only the sociologist Lyman begins his work on Chinese families with the intact emigrant family and believes the separation to be a minor criterion (Lyman, 1974). Other scholars have defined this as an abnormal situation for a Chinese family. Thus, they are not useful to describe the Chinese family, since this characteristic is valid for all other emigrating societies.[3]

Due to its centuries-old, stable position, the Chinese emigrant family can be described as the separated Confucian family, whereby the "Confucian family"[4] is the extended family. This family type was predominant in the rural emigrant regions of southern China well into the twentieth century. This point of view is based on a specific aptitude of the Chinese family to overcome the migration situation. The marital situation of the early emigrants underlines this thesis.[5]

---

[2] The Confucian interpretation of the world is based on the existence of a dualism, where everything pairs with a counterpart as *yin* and *yang*. In a commentary of I Ching, *yin* is explained as the dark and *yang* as the bright. They are symbolized by the absorbing (*yin*), water, and feminine, as opposed to the penetrating (*yang*), fire, and masculine. Huang, A., The Complete I Ching, 1998.

[3] See *Glenn*, 1983, 44.

[4] For derivation *see* Zinzius, 1988, 98 et seq.

[5] See Chapter 1 "Chinese Emigration to California from 1848 until 1965," under "Family Relationships during Emigration."

Considering the large anomaly in the ratio of the sexes favoring the men, it is surprising that a large percentage of those living in California in the nineteenth century were married (26% to 50%, depending on the source; Coolidge, 1909, 502). According to Chapters 1 to 3 on the female Chinese population in America, it is clear that most of these marriages could not have been between emigrant partners.[6]

Many men shunned the costs and risks of having their wives join them, since they intended to eventually return to their home. Furthermore, at that time, as it is still the case today, a Chinese marriage was a very expensive undertaking. This financial aspect consequently raised the average age of marriage. Still, there must have been other reasons for the continuation of separation. The high return rate of earlier immigrants (up to 70%) suggests that there was sufficient money available to allow the passage of the wife (Nee, 1972, 45; Tsai, 1986, 34).

Passage from China to the United States bloomed until the exclusion in 1882 and even after that many businessmen were accompanied by their wives or women thus declared—often prostitutes. This practice occurred even though Chinese law did not allow legal emigration and in fact explicitly forbid it for extended travel of husband and wife (Zo, 1978, 101). The list of reasons not to have their wives join is long in the general literature, but does not sufficiently determine the reason for existence of the separated family. The separated family clearly identifies itself as fully functioning, even though the partners are split, e.g. supporting of the village society of the emigrant, creation of male heirs who often joined the father with the guarantee to return to the heart of the family after their working life. The minor role played by emotional relationships among couples, along with the definition of the woman as recipient of orders, manager in the house of the in-laws, and nanny, supports the functionality of the separated family. Emigration of the wife would have interfered, if not destroyed this system. Within this constellation, one finds a major reason for the creation of this bachelor society.

Husband and wife had clearly defined tasks on both sides of the Pacific. Classical role-splitting required that the woman—independent of her emotions—obey her husband and be economic with the finances, which he regulated as the breadwinner, but only within the guidelines of his responsibility toward the family. The most important role of the woman was to produce male heirs and thus guarantee the continuation of the patriarchal line. For the emigrant society, this role was immensely important. More often

---

[6] See article about Canada: Peter Li. "Immigration Laws and Family Patterns: Some Demographic Changes among Chinese Families in Canada." *Canadian Ethnic Studies*, XII:1, 1980, 59–74.

than not, the men would let their almost adult sons follow rather than their wives, even if they were financially capable of paying her passage. This choice was influenced by the Confucian dictates requiring that a father be responsible for his son's education. It guaranteed the continuation of the family tradition in a foreign area, while maintaining the family within China through the tasks fulfilled by the wife.

The Confucian family was structured to overcome the strongest of burdens, which was the case for the separated families of the Chinese American type.[7] Although the special functionality of the separated Confucian family is not described in the literature, there have been attempts to put the Chinese immigrant family into certain orders. They speak of the *split family* from 1850–1920, of the *small producer family* in which all family members live and work together in the period up to 1965, and from then until the present of a *dual-wage-type* in which both partners work outside of the family clan with a loose relationship to the children. In this three-phase model, the separated family is a structure often found in various cultures throughout the world, such as foreign workers in Europe. The dual-wage family is closer to the crisis-type, which exists in America today.

In the following section, we will evaluate whether the structure proposed by Glenn, which postulates the deletion of two historical models and the majority of the low-income dual-wage families, is valid for today's Chinese American society, even though it is based on an inexact definition of the immigrant family. The examination of the historical part has already shown that a family society existed earlier than believed by research. How has the Chinese American family actually developed in the recent past?

The Change in the Ratio of the Sexes

Well into the 1960s the unequal ratio of the sexes was probably the largest social problem for the Chinese in America. Subsequently, Chinese ghettos were believed to be places where male society lived out its vices, from opium consumption to gambling to prostitution.[8]

Even in 1960, 61.5% of all Chinese immigrants were men, but at that time the situation was changing rapidly. From 1966 until 1975, 52% of all Chinese immigrants were women. In 1980, an almost equal ratio of men to women (102.2:100) was reached for the first time, and in 1990 the ratio

---

[7] Especially during the Cultural Revolution, the husband and wife often worked in separate locations and had only rare occasions to meet. Thus, it might happen easily that the man lived far from the family and traveled back home only sporadically. See also Lin, 1993.

[8] Detailed explanation see Zinzius, 1988, 49–62.

tipped in the favor of women (99.3:100). These changes can be related to the overall higher number of female immigrants, especially from Taiwan, along with the higher number of female births in the United States. At least, the Taiwanese are the only Chinese group whose numbers show an unequal ration in favor of men. The 1980 census showed for the first time that the sex ratio of all foreign-born Chinese Americans above 15 years was equal. This occurred after a far stronger immigration of Chinese women in the 1970s.[9] The previously unfulfilled requirements of the bachelor society had been satisfied.

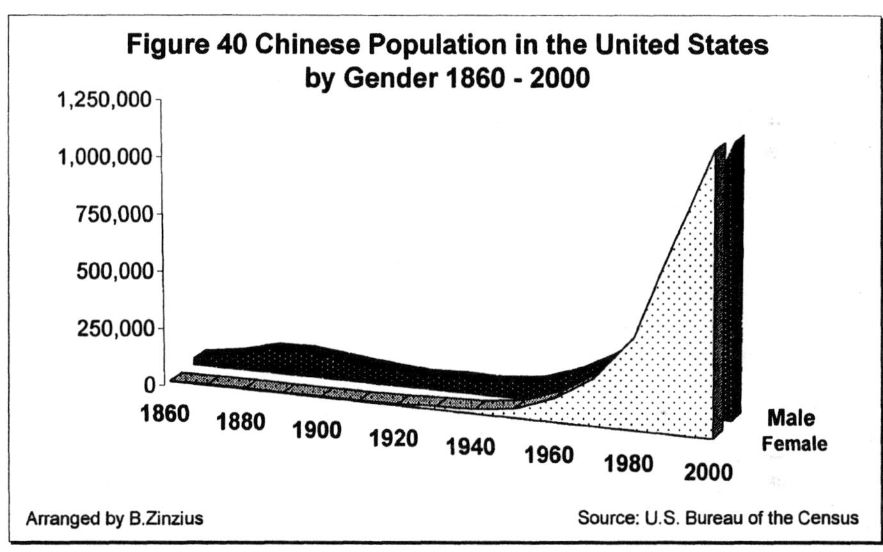

And still, upon closer examination, some of the traditional structures are still visible. In 1980 only 8.5% of all foreign- and American-born Chinese women were single, compared to 13.9% of all women in the United States. The number of single Chinese males, however, was higher than the average for all men (4.7%:3.4%). At the moment, no assumptions can be made about the family status of the Chinese population, in which foreign-born members are again in the majority.[10] On the contrary, the differences between all three groups are striking. The number of married mainland and Taiwan Chinese is relatively large in comparison to American society. Mainland Chinese men are clearly more often married than their female counterparts.

---

[9] See Chapter 7 "The Change in the Ration of Sexes."

[10] In 1970, the foreign-born Chinese represented 46.9%, in 1980 63% of the total Chinese population in the United States (Nee, 1972, 87). This percentage grew to 69.4% in 1990, and receded to 62.4% in 2000 (U.S. Census 1990, and 2000, PCT19).

This ratio is quite different for the Taiwanese, and even more predominant among emigrants from Hong Kong. Here, two-third of men and one-half of women are single. Equally clear is the fact that even with the high rate of marriages among Taiwanese, there are still more single men and women than the general American average. The varied marriage rate, however, is met by a low divorce rate for all three groups. The closeness of the mainland Chinese ratios to that of the whole population seems to be proven by the fact that it alone shows similar divorce statistics to the whole population, something especially true for widows.

To evaluate these tendencies, we must compare the quantitative analysis to some alternatives: Even with all the differences among the Chinese, the numbers show a relatively low conflict potential and few social problems, which would typically arise from family separation and widowhood. The figures seem to show that the more Western the group becomes the more the intent to marry decreases. Whereas in 1980, 70%–80% of mainland Chinese were married, only 60%–70% of Taiwanese and 40% of Hong Kong Chinese were married. Noticeable is the high percentage of married couples among mainland Chinese. In contrast to the other groups, this could reflect a stronger bond to the Confucian family ideal.[11] In comparison to the Hong Kong Chinese, the mainland Chinese group is old. 50% are over 45 years old, only 48% are between 14 and 44 years old.[12] The high percentage of widows in this group can be related to the stability of this older age group, since women in general have a longer life expectancy than men.

Table 33 Family Status of Chinese Americans above Fifteen Years, 1980 (in %)

1980	U.S.-all male	female	Mainland male	female	Taiwanese male	female	Hong Kong male	female
Single	29.7%	22.8%	17.1%	10.4%	36.2%	26.3%	63.6%	47.3%
Married	60.6%	55.2%	76.9%	71.9%	62.1%	68.1%	34.5%	47.9%
Separated	1.9%	2.6%	1.2%	1.3%	0.4%	0.9%	0.5%	0.6%
Widow	2.5%	13.3%	2.7%	13.7%	0.4%	2.6%	0.4%	2.4%
Divorced	5.3%	7.1%	2.1%	2.6%	0.9%	2.1%	1.0%	1.8%

Arranged by B. Zinzius   Source: U.S. Bureau of the Census

Furthermore, there is a tendency among mainland Chinese to marry younger women from China who probably outlive their husbands. With regard to the higher percentage of elders, one can believe that the mainland Chinese more conservative and family-oriented lives than the Taiwanese or Hong Kong Chinese. Stability within the family seems to be desired more by

---

[11] See Chapter 7 "From a Bachelors Society to a Family Society—Historical Models."

[12] See Chapter 5 "Business Structures and Income," under "Active Population," and "Legislation and Age Structures."

men than by women, who seem to want to break with their traditional role. The Taiwanese contingent is very young, with 90% under 44 years of age. The high percentage of married couples suggests that they are more family-oriented than their native-born counterparts.

With the Hong Kong Chinese one must also take into account that they emigrate at a younger age. In fact, the statistics show that the majority ranges from 15 to 25 years old, a group which tends to be less family-oriented but more career driven and places a higher priority on education, thus explaining the lower percentage of married couples. A cross-check shows that the number of marriage-willing mainland Chinese lies far behind due to the elder age group. This fact is, however, insufficient to explain the tendencies among the Taiwanese, who are also younger. More Hong Kong Chinese women marry than men, a fact that could be interpreted as a desire to cling to the traditional family role, while the men have made the transition from the traditional structures. Other interpretations cannot be excluded at the moment.

Table 34 Family Status of Chinese Americans above Fifteen Years, 1990

	U.S. (all)		Chinese (all)		Native-born		Foreign-born	
	male	female	male	female	male	female	male	female
Single	25.8%	19.4%	35.7%	28.0%	51.6%	48.4%	30.7%	23.2%
Married	64.3%	59.2%	59.8%	59.9%	40.4%	40.9%	64.9%	64.4%
Separated	2.1%	2.5%	0.9%	1.2%	0.9%	1.0%	0.9%	1.2%
Widowed	2.7%	11.1%	1.4%	7.6%	2.9%	4.8%	1.4%	8.2%
Divorced	7.2%	10.3%	2.3%	3.3%	4.2%	4.9%	2.0%	2.9%

Arranged by B. Zinzius — Source: U.S. Bureau of the Census

During the 1980s, the marital situation of Chinese Americans changed considerably. Increasing numbers of immigrant students and of native-born students caused the young generation of education-oriented Chinese Americans to grow, leading to fewer marriages, especially among those below 35 years old. Marriage rates of foreign-born are still above the national average, whereas those of the native-born with 40.7% (men: 40.4%, women: 40.9%) are considerably below the national level of 61.8% (men: 64.3%, women: 59.2%). The low percentage of married women—54% of those below 34 years old—confirms the focus on education rather than on family (see Chapter 6). The above-average rate of married foreign-born Chinese women, in combination with their high household income and low number of workers per family, shows that this group consists of large high-income families.[13]

---

[13] See Chapter 5 "Median Incomes, Occupations, and Working Women."

Table 35 Women's Marriage Rate, 1990

Age	U.S. (all)	Chinese (all)	Native-born	Foreign-born	Taiwan-born
15–24	21.0%	7.9%	3.9%	10.0%	4.8%
25–34	75.7%	69.6%	54.0%	73.0%	73.5%
35–44	90.2%	90.8%	82.0%	92.4%	96.3%
15–44	63.7%	60.5%	39.2%	66.4%	60.3%
25–44	82.4%	79.8%	66.4%	82.5%	86.3%

Prepared by B. Zinzius   Source: U.S. Bureau of the Census

The family status of Chinese Americans strongly indicates that Confucian family values still have a strong influence on their social norms. The low divorce rate of 2.8%, compared to 8.8% of the national average, is just one example for their family-oriented values, in contrast to more individualistic norms of mainstream America. The Chinese American family—in many ways—resembles the American Dream of high family values, hard work and economic success. Is it a *model minority* for America? A detailed analysis of the age distribution of Chinese Americans will further indicate the current and future development of Chinese Americans.

Household, Family Size, and Age Structure

Interpreting the family as a solidarity union supports the previously created picture, since, in comparison to the overall population, more Chinese live in one family and in one household than the national average.

Interestingly enough, family size does not coincide with the number of children.[14] Chinese households often include more relations beyond the first degree than average. This fact is especially relevant for those who immigrated between 1970 and 1980. Reuniting families is thus not only a question posed by migration theory, but a day-to-day reality among Chinese. With regard to the low number of children per family,[15] one could suppose that the regulation of one child per family in mainland China is also respected in the United States.

---

[14] The average number of family members per household in the United States is 3.27, whereas the Chinese family averages 3.65 (Gardner, 1985). By 1990, the numbers had dropped to 3.16 for the national average and 3.6 for the Chinese (U.S. Census, 1990).

[15] Table 36 Birthrates of United States and Asian-American Women, 25 and 34 Years, 1980

	U.S.	Asian	Japanese	Chinese	Filipino	Korean	Indian	Vietnamese
Total	1,476	1,201	908	939	1,270	1,244	1,336	1,773
Native-born		951	768	669	1,520	996	1,343	1,468
Foreign-born		1,268	1,104	1,024	1,227	1,252	1,336	1,777

Arranged by B. Zinzius   Source: U.S. Bureau of the Census, 1980

Most childless households are, as can be expected, among the Taiwanese. On the other hand, mainland Chinese, who have the highest marriage rate, do not have more children per household than the Taiwanese. Although, they usually have more children than the Taiwanese, who seem to hold the model family of one to two children. Were one to create a social ordering according to the number of children, the Taiwanese would stand in the middle class between the rich Hong Kong Chinese and poor mainland Chinese. The total Chinese contingent would fall just behind the Japanese, but far ahead of the White population with respect to the low number of children.

Table 37 Family Characteristics of Chinese Americans, 1990

	US (all)	Chinese (all)	Chinese Native-born	Chinese Foreign-born	Taiwanese
Median age	33.0	32.3	16.3	36.7	31.0
Person per household	2.6	3.1	2.5	3.3	3.5
Three or more workers	13.4%	19.0%	14.4%	19.9%	14.2%
Person per family	3.27	3.65	–	–	–

Arranged by B. Zinzius   Source: 1990 Census; Chinese American Data Center 2002

These statements have to be analyzed further, taking into account the different migrant flows in addition to the primary family characteristics. In 1990, 69.4% of all Chinese Americans were foreign-born, reaching 62.4% in 2000. Until native-born Chinese dominate their ethnic group, immigrants will be the major factor influencing age and family composition in the coming decades. Three major immigrant groups of Chinese Americans have been indicated earlier: workers and skilled professionals, students, and family members of earlier immigrants under the reunification process (see also Chapter 3). The latter two groups make up the largest part of the middle-aged Chinese. In 1990, the median age of Chinese Americans was 32.3 years old, compared to the national average of 33.0 years old. Their age distribution, however, is completely different, with a peak between 25 and 35 years old, and fewer young and old people.

In 2000, the age distribution of the United States' population remained similar, while the median age increased from 33.0 to 35.3 years as a result of the aging population. The median age of the Asian American population grew less, rising from 30.1 years in 1990 to just 31.1 years in 2000.[16] The higher percentage of 25 to 35 year-old Chinese Americans does not necessarily lead to an above-average age of Chinese over the next decades.

---

[16] Based on the census of 1990 data, and the average age of Chinese immigrants (32.4 years in 2000; INS, 2001), the median age of Chinese Americans will still be below the nationwide average, probably increasing the gap.

In addition to looking at long and short-term historical developments, one also has to take actual migration trends into account. With the booming Chinese and Taiwanese economies, an increasing number of immigrants are returning to their native homeland, meaning that the over-representation of 25-35 year-olds will continue in the future.[17]

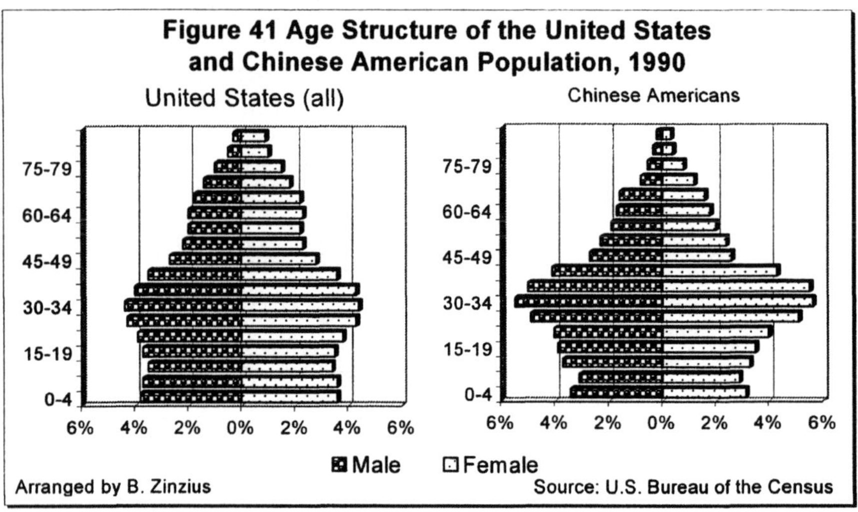

The new phenomenon of adoption must also be addressed with respect to its influence on the number of Chinese Americans. Since the easing of adoption regulation by the Chinese authorities in 1992, over 30,000 Chinese children have been adopted by United States citizens. Over the past decade, China has therefore replaced South Korea as the number one foreign adoption country (Evans, 2000).

Analysis of Current Results: Attitude of Married Couples

The following hypothesis should be considered: Why is the number of children so low among the Chinese? Clarification of this interesting question will supply specific information concerning the incorporation of this group. What explains the low divorce rate? Why are so many men still single, although the ratio of the sexes has distinctively changed? Why are so few Hong Kong and Taiwan-Chinese married?

---

[17] Up to 2000, a third of all Chinese students returned to China, a number growing by 13% every year (*People's Daily Online*, 2001).

Fertility, Children, Birth Rate

The low birthrate for the Hong Kong Chinese as a whole contrasts with the Chinese population pyramid, which shows many at a fertile age. The strong immigration of this age group has been indicated as a major reason for this phenomenon. It is, however, noticeable that in 1980 the American-born group between 25 to 34 gave 40% fewer births than the foreign-born group.[18]

In comparison to the whole population, Chinese women of all categories have a lower number of children, sometimes up to 30%–40% fewer. There must, therefore, be other reasons behind the native-born choosing to remain childless. Remarkable also is the low number of children among higher educated Chinese women, which is equal only to Japanese women. In 1980, the number of Chinese women with four years of college education was approximately double that of Whites at about 30%. The average number of children among native-born Chinese is comparable to that of women who have received between thirteen and sixteen years of education.

In fact, the number of children declines continuously with the increasing length of education. This tendency cannot always be generalized, since, for example, Japanese women of average education tend to have more children than those with less education. A further indicator is the fact that in comparison to the whole population Chinese Americans bear their children relatively late. This piece of the puzzle also fits into the ripening belief that family planning is dependent on the length of education. Career plays a major role on the family attitude of Chinese American women.[19]

Table 38 Chinese Americans in the United States-Fertility Rates, 1990				
Age	U.S. (all)	Chinese (all)	Native-born	Foreign-born	Taiwan-born
15–24	305	51	40	57	29
25–34	1,330	690	493	733	734
35–44	1,960	1,703	1,379	1,761	1,941
15–44	1,223	875	518	973	970

Prepared by B. Zinzius   Source: Chinese American Data Center, 2002

---

[18] For Filipinos and American Indians, the birthrates are lower for the *foreign-* than for *native-borns*.

[19] In mainland China today, education is strongly promoted. Throughout the country one can see advertisements calling for a late marriage—27 years for women, 29 years for men. In 1990, the legal age for marriage was 20 years for women and 22 years for men (Chinese Marriage Law, issued in 1981). The effects of the law can be seen in the average marriage age, which climbed from 20.2 years in 1970 to 24.5 years in 1999.

The fact that native Chinese American women have fewer children than foreign-born clearly supports this fact, together with their lower marriage rates between 15 and 34 years.[20] The relatively high number of persons per household has nothing to do with large numbers of children. In 1980, over 50% of Chinese American families were childless, and grew to 53.5% in 1990.[21]

As we shall see more closely in the following section, when one takes the low divorce rate into account it becomes evident that, even considering the differences within the group as a whole, family and career are not two independent or diverging lines. On the average, children have little influence on career and financial development. This fact, however, does not necessarily mean that Chinese families represent success-oriented model units.

Divorce Rate

In the United States today, for every second marriage there is one divorce; however, over 80% of divorcees remarry.[22] More than half of the children born today will live through their parents' divorce before they are eighteen. In 1990, the divorce rate for the Chinese Americans as a whole was 2.3% for men and 3.3% for women. For foreign-born, it was 2.0% for men and 2.9% for women, compared to 7.2% of the national average for men, and 10.3% for women. For all three Chinese populations, the divorce rate is lower than that of the total population. How can one explain this low divorce rate?

The Chinese strongly value the opinion of others. Stanley Sue, Professor of Psychology and Asian American Studies at the University of California, Davis, and Director of the *National Research Center for Asian American Mental Health*, believes that "family pressure and that of the immediate surroundings is so high that a divorce would result in strong belief of fault, especially for women." Divorce brings a lot of stress, since the Chinese associate a broken marriage with loss of face. The nineteen-year-old Linda describes her mother's reaction to divorce as follows: "My mother was so ashamed. She told her brother only much later, even though he had already been divorced himself. It hurt her pride and she felt she had left herself open to criticism." (Interview, 1990).

---

[20] See Chapters 5 "Business Structures and Income," and 6 "Education."

[21] Chinese American families with children under 18 years: All–53.5%; Native-born–44.7%; Foreign-born–55.2%; Taiwanese–65.3% (Chinese American Data Center, 2002).

[22] Figures for divorce statistics depend strongly on the perspective. Looking at the married population over a period of time, the number of divorces is rather high and includes people who marry and divorce repeatedly. In contrast, looking at the total population at a specific time, the number of divorcees will be much lower.

Harry Kitano, Professor of Sociology at UCLA, believed that there is still a double value system concerning divorcees.[23] A Chinese woman is marked. She has more difficulties than a Chinese man to find a new partner (*Asian Week*, April 1, 1991). For the Chinese woman, a divorce is inconceivable within the values of the traditional Confucian family. Lai Ann Tong (1984, 211) writes about the Chinese American evaluation of divorce: "The intact family is often more important than personal freedom. A divorce, the destruction of all familiar structures and relationships, is no way to solve problems." Divorce means loss of face for the family, as well as for the divorcees.

Many Chinese still see marriage as a contract. One does not marry for love, but from the belief that one must be married to have children. Sue shows that within the family-oriented society it is difficult to overcome the barriers preventing discussion of internal family problems and thus bring the conflicts to the surface.[24] Only slowly are Chinese pairs realizing that divorce can provide a solution to marital problems. Since the traditional marriage was the joining of the sexes with economic goals, the emotional problems were hidden behind a seemingly functional facade.[25] Exactly this point of view could explain the surprisingly high number of divorces among mainland Chinese, who nevertheless remain more traditionally oriented than the other two groups. Until recently, love marriages were obviously few and far between. Some Chinese say that they only know romantic relationships from foreign films and the words of Western pop music and now want to experience it, and not just dream of it. Therefore, many are going through with the divorce, especially those who married in the 1970s, when they married for security and status instead of love.

Until 1950, divorce was not considered a possibility in mainland China. Thereafter, 70% of the claims came from women, and, since the new divorce laws of 1981, the divorce rate–as percent of marriage–has increased continuously from 5.5% in 1985 to 14.4% in 2000. The United States, for comparison, has one of the world's highest divorce rates with 52%.[26]

In 2000, now that divorce is increasing in mainland China, many Chinese pairs explain their divorces due to the fact that they no longer love each other and have fallen for someone else. Also, alcoholism and its consequences for the partnership are used as reasoning. Estelle Chun, lawyer

---

[23] Professor Emeritus Harry H.L. Kitano, one of the world's leading authorities on race and ethnic relations, passed away in Los Angeles on October 19, 2002 at the age of 76.

[24] Professor Stanley Sue was awarded the 2001 *Academic Senate Distinguished Public Service Award* for his accomplishments in Asian American psychology.

[25] See Libby Wong "U.S. Chinese Encounter Divorce, The "D" Word." *Asian Week*, January 4, 1991, 10.

[26] "Non-US Divoce rates." <http://www.divorcereform.org/gul.html> (March 03, 2003).

of the *Asian Pacific American Legal Center*, sees male gambling and maltreatment of wives as a major reason for divorce.

For the men, the seemingly quicker integration of Asian women into American society is a problem.[27] Especially, the success of Asian women in their careers makes the men insecure[28] (*Asian Women's Shelter.* Interview with Elaine Sit, 1991 and *Gum Moon's Women's Residence*, Gloria Tan, 1991). Women contribute highly to the well-being of the family and are often well-educated, but they also discontinue their careers if the future of the family is secure or if the couple desires children. A reason for this could also be seen in the fact that it is more difficult for women than men to enter into top corporate positions.

Intermarriage—Interracial Dating

Mixed Marriages

According to Gordon's assimilation phases,[29] assimilation by marriage is a core component of minority integration, independent of sociological or ethnological factors. Among all forms of social contact, according to Dinnerstein, mixed marriages have the greatest effect on assimilation (1975, 146). Strongly supporting this thesis, Betty Lee Sung sees intermarriage as an indicator of acceptance of a group by the whole population (Kantrowitz, 1986, 80). Intermarriage is, thus, a central part of cultural amalgamation.[30] In 1960, only 0.4% of all American marriages were mixed race pairings. This number grew from 0.7% in 1970 to 1.9% in 1980, and 2.6% in 2000, and continues to increase rapidly.

In 2000, 74.5% of Asians married among their pier group, 91.2% of Blacks sought to marry Blacks, whereas among Native Americans the rate was only 46.2% (U.S. Census Bureau 2000, table P20-537). Mixed marriages can be considered as an attempt to escape "ghettoization" and as a determinant of success. In the first place, however, the historical barriers must be evaluated. Asian women returning with GI's from American bases in the Pacific placed American law under strong scrutiny. Until 1948, California was one of 39 states that forbid marriages between Whites and

---

[27] See Sheryl WuDunn. "Divorce Rate Soars as Chinese Decide Love is Part of Marriage." *New York Times*, 7, August 16, 1991. Caroline Chung. "Asian Women's Shelter offers 'refuge from the storm." *The Richmond Review*, 3, May 4, 1992;

[28] See Chapter 5 "Business Structures and Income," under "Middle Family Income, Middle Class and Working Woman," and "Ethnic Business and Racial Labor in Chinatown."

[29] Gordon, Milton M., *Assimilation in American Life*, New York, 1964.

[30] See Marriage assimilation—amalgamation by Zinger, Milton J. "Ethnicity." In: *Annual Review of Sociology*, 11, 1985. 151–180.

non-Whites (Chinese, Filipinos, Japanese, Koreans and Southeast Asians; *Asian Women United of California,* 1989, 11). Only on June 12, 1967, did the United States Supreme Court declare all state laws prohibiting miscegenation as unlawful. Since the mid-1970s, one can see a high degree of interracial marriages among Asian Americans, which leads us to believe that the historical barriers within the recipient country have been overcome. Kitano and Daniels see the new trend in connection with a combination of historical determinants, demographic variables, destruction of discriminatory laws, relaxing of family control, better opportunity for education and career, reduction in racial barriers in the housing market, and stronger individual preference for partner choice (Kitano, 1988, 178). This description contains environmental, group-specific determinants, as described in previous chapters. An expansion of these determinants is therefore deemed unnecessary in the following comparison of the special relationship between Chinese partners. Traditionally, Chinese have preferred not to marry into another ethnic group. Since the 1960s, however, this tendency has been changing continuously. Between 1970 and 1980, the number of Asian Americans who married non-Asians doubled from 118,114 to 235,707 (Kantrowitz, 1986, 80). New studies reveal that over half of all Japanese Americans, 40% of Chinese Americans,[31] and 30% of Korean Americans have interracial relationships (Sung, 1987, 5).

Table 39 Interracial/-ethnic Marriages in the United States, 1960-2000[32]

	1960	1970	1980	1990	2000
White	0.4%	0.7%	2.0%	1.9%	2.6%
Black	1.6%	1.9%	3.4%	7.2%	8.8%
Asian	24.0%	29.4%	31.2%	30.0%	25.5%
American Indian	31.5%	51.5%	67.3%	73.6%	53.8%
Hispanic	–	–	–	2.9%	26.9%

Arranged by B. Zinzius   Source: U.S. Bureau of the Census

Recent figures from the census of 2000 show that 81.5% of all Chinese American men, and 77.9% of all Chinese American women are married to

---

[31] In 1990, the *San Francisco Chronicle* even claimed that 70–80% of American-born Chinese women marry outside their ethnic group (February 12, 1990).

[32] The absolute number of interracial married couples in the United States was in 1960: 149,000; 1970:310,000; 1980:953,000; 1990:1,461,000; and 2000:2,090,000.

Since 2000, new combinations of the racial status are possible, e.g. indicating *two or more races*. To be consistent, the arranged table does not include people of mixed race (*two or more races*), which represent 16% of the total Asian population. See Chapter 4 "Habitat," for further details. U.S. Census 1960–1990, tables *Race of Wife by Race of Husband*, and U.S. Census 2000, PHC-T-19 and P20–537. Furthermore, since the Census 1980, Hispanics are classified as *ethnic group* and not as *race*. U.S. Census 1960–1990, tables *Race of Wife by Race of Husband*, and U.S. Census 2000, PHC-T-19 and P20–537.

Chinese Americans, 8.3% of the men and 5.6% of the women are married to other Asians, whereas 8.9% of the men and 15.3% of the women are married to White and Hispanic partners, only 0.3% of Chinese men and 0.5% of Chinese women are married to Blacks (Le, 2003a).

Thus, it can also be maintained is that more women than men marry outside of the ethnic group. Since the number of American-born Chinese is always increasing, the number of mixed marriages will also increase in the next decades. This phenomenon is especially noticeable among second or third generation Asian Americans. Mostly, they have a higher level of education and higher incomes than their parents or grandparents who often had to battle with difficulties in the New World. In 2000, almost every second American-born Chinese married outside his or her ethnic group.[33]

Betty Lee Sung, Professor Emerita for Asian Studies at City College of New York, CUNY, and author of a book on mixed marriages by Chinese Americans, believes that the high number of mixed marriages is a sign of fast growing acceptance within society.[34] Marriage to non-Asians, according to Sung, indicates the total assimilation in the United States. Only a generation ago, such mixed marriages seldom occurred due to cultural incompatibilities. Today, the basic beliefs of American-born Chinese have changed, and recent studies confirm the increasing assimilation of immigrants (Alba, 1997, 826).

An example is the married musician couple, Gary Glazer and Jeanny Look: Jeanny was born in America and sees herself as American. Therefore, their marriage is no longer a mixed marriage in the regular sense. Furthermore, Gary believes that in a concert hall nobody cares what one looks like but how one plays (Interview, 1990). Other opinions differ. Frequently, interviewed couples brought up the family complaints against mixed marriages. Many Chinese American parents, especially foreign-born, are concerned about the decline of family bonds due to the mixed marriage. "… it's the worst thing that could happen. The parents disown their children. They are terribly, terribly hurt", says Ms. Young Yu. Asian parents worry that culture and tradition will be lost if their children choose a partner of non-Asian origin. For many Chinese families, such a loss is devastating. Sometimes, parents no longer want to have anything to do with their

---

[33] 45% of all American-born Chinese husbands marry non-Chinese, 26.5% marry non-Asians. 45.4% of all American-born Chinese wives marry non-Chinese, 31% marry non-Asians. These are the second highest percentages of exogamy among all Asian ethnicities. Only American-born Filipino have a higher percentage: 53% of the husbands and 68.5% of the wives marry outside of their ethnic group (Le, 2003b).

[34] In 2001, the City University of New York established the Asian American / Asian Research Institute (AAARI), and Prof. Sung took the responsibility as the Chair of the Board of Directors. On May 10, 2002, the AAARI held the Asian American Leadership Conference on rebuilding and Healing New York after the September 11, 2001 tragedy.

children. Connie Young Yu is worried about being rejected (Interview, 1992). In other cases, families reunite once children are born. Paul Chan, a 26-year-old gas station owner, married his blonde, blue-eyed first love, 25-year-old Laura against his parents' wishes. Since the birth of their twin sons, says Chan, his family loves his wife, too. "But only because they are boys," laughs Laura, "if they had been girls, they would no longer have looked at me." Chan admits that they would then at least have held against it that he did not marry a Chinese woman (Interview, 1989).

A further change in young Chinese families in America is that the families no longer prearrange the marriage. Parents are still asked for their approval, which remains very important, but daughter and son alone make the final decision. In this respect, Chinese Americans and highly educated mainland Chinese are very close. Generally speaking, the Chinese in mainland China have fewer opportunities to meet foreigners, but, wherever possible, the chance of marriage to a foreigner is used as an escape. Sometimes, it is not the desire for the foreign, but more the desire to leave one's own group, which causes this reaction (Interview with Jeanny Look, 1990).

The inadequacies of the Chinese and their "failure" are always measured against the "autonomy" and "success" of the White. A typical refrain heard in interviews is: Chinese American boys are childish at parties, and make their partners shy with their immature and unmanly actions. By contrast, Chinese men complain strongly about the women's over-assimilation toward America.[35] In my series of interviews, I asked a mainland Chinese why he prefers dating foreign-born to American-born Chinese. He answered that American Chinese-born girls were not "Chinese" enough. With the word Chinese, he compounded language, culture, and interests. "Chinese American girls have different interests. They try to be like White Americans. We have nothing in common." (Interview with Fred Wong, 1991). The recent success of Chinese American men, however, may well change their attitude towards Chinese American women and interracial relationships, as they also adapt towards the West.

Interracial Relationships

Friction between older and younger generations and the claims of Asian men are obviously not hindering the continuation of a trend. Furthermore, the social changes in the 1960s increased the acceptance of cohabitation in the population, and, combined with the increasing marriage age, led to increasing numbers of unmarried couples. In 2000, 6.5% of all couples in the United

---

[35] See also Chapter 7 "Marriage in the Homeland—*Gum San Haak*."

States were not married (U.S. Census 2000, P20-537, table 8). This phenomenon can be seen especially among the Asians, and since the 1990s, the combination of an Asian woman with a White man has become a main theme of the multicultural Bay Area society.

Due to such relationships, Asian women are continuously leaving behind frustrated Asian men and White women. Examples of career women, so-called "high profile women," of Asian origin are plentiful: The authors Amy Tan, Maxine Hong Kingston,[36] and newscaster Connie Chang all have relationships with non-Asian men. For this new phenomenon new slang has been developed. One speaks of White men with "Asian-Women-Syndrome;" they are "Asian-Women-Aholics" or "rice queens," a phrase from the gay scene where White-Asian relationships are also considered "hot." A statistical survey of marriage records in San Francisco County shows that the number of Asian women who later marry Whites is four times that of those who marry Asian men (*San Francisco Examiner*, February 12, 1990). Nationwide, the percentage of interracial marriages between Asians and Whites lies between 25% and 30%. The percentage for women is about three times as high as for men, and the overall percentage among the ethnicities varies between 4% for Korean men to 33% for Filipino women. American-born Asians are much more likely to marry Whites, ranging from 8.3% for Korean men to 51.8% for Filipino women (Le, 2003a).

A look at the heading "relationships" in the *Bay Guardian*, known for its competence in all questions of "what's on" and meetings, clearly shows that an increasing number of White men favor Asian women.[37] This seemingly new trend has old roots in America. Fantasies about Asian women have controlled the American male psyche for generations, a secondary effect of United States military bases in the Pacific and various pacific wars. Since 1940, more than 200,000 Asian women have married GI's. The erotic-exotic appeal of Asian women also found its way into the cinema with films like *The World of Suzie Wong, Full Metal Jacket*, and *Heaven and Earth*.

They all reflect a female stereotype, which most Asian women believe to be oppressive. Exotic femininity stands in strong opposition to a very family-oriented relationship between the sexes, at a time when men and women study, work, and raise children together. Bicultural relationships usually add a dose of romance in an otherwise drab situation. Different stereotypes still exist in the thoughts about Asian women: "Cherry blossom girls" who are passive, nice, exotic-looking girls who are subordinate and serve their man

---

[36] See discussion about Amy Tan and Maxine Hong Kingston in the literature part of Chapter 8 "Cultural Awakening."

[37] It has, nevertheless, to be mentioned that the majority of White American men favors intra-ethnic, rather than inter-ethnic relationships.

represent the one side. On the other side stand the successful image of a new Asian reality in which Asian women symbolize energy, intelligence, and the economic vitality of Pacific Rim business, which makes them a status symbol. The main character of *Double Happiness* is a 20 year old Chinese American women, torn between the love of her family and her desire for independence, which also leads her into an interracial relationships with a White graduate student.

On the Berkeley campus, where the number of Asian students has drastically risen since the last third of the twentieth century, the most obvious combination of multicultural relationships within the Bay Area produces and reproduces itself. Asian female students explain that White males join in Asian language classes or become members of the *Asian Business Association* to meet Asian women. Therefore, they are called "eggs," white on the outside, yellow inside. Asian women who associate with White males are called "twinkies" or "bananas," outside yellow, inside white (*Washington Post*, July 4, 1999, B3). The Asian female students explain that before they came to Berkeley they did not feel exceptionally pretty, but today on campus they feel very desirable (Interviews with May Lee, Molly Kwong and Elaine Chen, 1991). Researchers of the University of California, Berkeley Diversity Project found corresponding resentment among White women, who felt put down by these "Asians who are the fantasy objects of desire."

White culture has labeled Asian men as unmanly. In films like Karate Kid or Rambo, they are reduced to brutal muscle packages. Fred Wong, a Chinese who has argued against these preconceptions says: "Asian men live in celibacy, are sexless, or considered rapists. A White has to come along and protect the woman from the Asian. One thing is sure: The Asian doesn't mess around." (Interview with Fred Wong, 1991).

Some Asian American students would not consider mixed relationships questionable if the women dated Blacks or Hispanics as well, but they seem to stick to Whites. Their co-students believe this is because they live in a society dominated by Whites. Are racism, sexism, and social climbing motivation for love and relationships? The high percentage of interethnic marriages of Chinese Americans allows the following concept: On the one hand, the fact that White men participate in mixed marriages is a sign of assimilation, reflecting the social position gained by their Asian partners. On the other hand, this is also a sign of the continuation of preconceptions and stereotyping of Asian American women. Thus, among all the possible combinations of interethnic relationships available to Asians, this one—Asian woman with white man—is strongly predominant. A recent study about exogamy and cohabitation in the United States confirms this fact. Asian women have the highest percentage among the major ethnic groups in the United States—White, Black, Hispanic, and Asian—to have a partnership outside their ethnicity. 32.3% of all Asian wives and 57.1% of all cohabiting Asian women have non-Asian partners. Asian men exhibit similar statistics: 21% of all Asian husbands and 47.7% of all cohabiting Asian men have non-Asian partners (Harris, 2001, Figure 2b).

The growing number of mixed Chinese American couples is one example of the increasing ethnic groups in the United States, a fact that is also reflected also in the multiracial children of these couples. Nationwide, over 6.8 million Americans, 2.4% of the population, identified themselves as belonging to *two or more races. White and Hispanic and another race* represent 1.9% of the American population—the largest mixed-racial group in the United States.

These are, however, just over 2% of their ethnic group. In comparison, 6.4% of the Black population, and 13.6% of the Asian population is of mixed race or ethnicity.[38] Asian Americans are, therefore, 5.8 times more likely to have children from interracial relations than the White population, and almost twice as frequently as the Black population. The smaller ethnicities, such as American Indians and Pacific Islanders, have even higher tendencies towards mixed marriages—due to their higher exposure to the larger ethnic groups. Another factor is habitat, e.g. Hawaii for Pacific Islanders, a state with the highest percentage of multicultural population (24.1%), and thus a high social acceptance for intercultural relations. In 2000, Asian Americans of mixed heritage totaled over 2.1 million, making it the second-largest Asian sub-group. These so-called *hapas*[39] are expected to surpass all other Asian Pacific groups by the next census in 2010. Of the 2.7 million Chinese Americans, less than 15% have a mixed heritage, and about 10% are of mixed race.[40] The number of mixed-race Asians will undoubtedly grow, and it is already today a strong sign of the adaptation and integration of Asians into American society.

---

[38] Mixed race is defined as having one parent of Asian or Pacific Islander descent, and another of some other race, such as White, African American, or American Indian. Mixed ethnicity is defined as having parents of more than one Asian or Pacific Islander group, but not some other race.

[39] "*Hapa* is a Native Hawaiian word, originally meaning simply "part" or "mixed," with no racial or ethnic meaning. The Japanese Hawaiian population adopted the term *hapa* to refer to people of mixed Japanese and European heritage. Today the word *hapa* includes AfroAsians, EurAsians, Latin Asians, Native Asians, and mixed APAs." (Dariotis, 2002).

[40] Estimates about the growth-rate of mixed-race Asian Pacific Islanders are difficult as the census of 2000 was the first count for people of mixed heritage.

Their integration will certainly challenge traditional definitions of community, language, culture, tradition, or food. The limits of this community are, however, hard to define. Members include Tiger Woods, who describes himself as "Cablinasian,"[41] or Keanu Reeves, who has a mixed-ethnic father of Chinese Hawaiian descent. Future research has to establish the importance of this development, which is certainly a part of increasing globalization and will also influence American society.

As we have seen, Asian women have better chances than men to participate in mixed marriages. The mostly poor and uneducated mainland Chinese have little chance of finding a non-Chinese wife.[42] Mixed marriages of Chinese Americans cannot be seen as an indicator for successful assimilation and complete acceptance, since predominantly only the women are marrying outside their ethnic group, and, as we shall see shortly, the contrary tradition of purification of marriage in the ethno-cultural sense is continuing. The factual results of such a mixing process seen in recent studies cannot, however, be overlooked. The one-sidedness of this "female mixed marriage" is partly based on the quick emancipation of American-born Chinese women and possibly on lack of interest of American women in Asian men. These constellations may well provoke a reopening of traditional connections to the homeland, similar to those of the *split family*.[43]

Marriage in the Homeland—Gum San Haak

In addition to these new developments, which can be described as the westernization of Chinese American society, definite tendencies of return towards traditional forms is also occurring. The open policy of United States towards mainland China since 1979 has made many Chinese Americans aware of their Chinese origins. Since then, there has been a continuous flow of Chinese American visitors to mainland China. In the same way that the number of visitors grew, so did the number of Chinese Americans returning in search of a wife (Xingci, 1988, 21). Even before the founding of the People's Republic of China, it was an old tradition for foreign Chinese from Taishan to *Gum San Haak*, return to China in search of a wife.[44]

---

[41] "It does [bother me to be called African American]," said Tiger Woods on *Oprah*. "Growing up, I came up with this name: I'm a 'Cablinasian.'" (Kamiya, 1997).

[42] See Chapter 7 "Marriage in the Homeland—*Gum San Haak.*"

[43] Hiegamy: A person's attempt to raise his or her social status via marriage, as well as the possibility of integration into a society which is defined by races and social classes. See also Chapter 7 "From a Bachelor Society to a Family Society—Historical Models."

[44] *Gum San Haak*: Travelers to the *Golden Mountain* of America, overseas Chinese returning from the United States.

An old ballad from Taishan describes the desire to marry an overseas Chinese from the perspective of the mainlanders: "Don't let your daughter marry a peasant, whose feet are full of dirt. Wish your daughter a happy bride of *Gum San Haak*, whose hands are full of gold."

In the near past, projects have been developed at the Zhongshan University in Guangdong. In 1983, one of these questioned single overseas Chinese in China about their business and legal situation and their education. The most predominant characteristic was that over 90% of these Chinese Americans named their origins from Taishan county in Guangdong.[45] Approximately 30% emigrated in the 1980s and have permanent residence status. Most Chinese that travel to Taishan are new emigrants who are not familiar with American culture, do not speak the language, and do not know the people. Usually, they have low-income jobs and long working hours, thus making social contacts difficult.[46] It was mostly men from larger cities like New York City, San Francisco, Los Angeles, Chicago or Boston who were questioned. Only 16% of interviewees were female. On average their age was 31 and that of their choice partner 27.

Three dominant factors in the choice of partner combine to make a Chinese partner most desirable: First, one may thus fulfill the parents' wish to marry someone from the home province; second, the widespread number of relatives in China, and Taishanese in the United States, can easily arrange a marriage; and third, even low-income Chinese Americans can afford a traditional wedding, as many have saved a long time for this special occasion. Exceptional is that half of these American Chinese already know their future partner. An intermediary is sent to the United States to plan the joint future. Clanships and districtships play a major role in the marriage arrangements. A marriage to a member of the same clan is also popular in the United States. Many Chinese are very proud of their cultural heritage and try to maintain their ethnic identity by marrying an "unspoiled" Chinese-born. For the Chinese woman, a marriage to an overseas Chinese man means the opportunity to leave her country and lead a better life elsewhere.

Even if by American standards the individual income of poor Chinese Americans seems relatively low, it is an enormous value to mainland Chinese. Within the Chinese group one sees here, as so often elsewhere, the distinction between *FOB*, fresh-off-the-boat, and *ABC*, American-born Chinese. Usually, there is little contact between *ABC* and *FOB*. Different culture and upbringing has left its marks. *FOBs* usually have very little chance of finding a partner in the United States, therefore they travel to

---

[45] See Chapter 1 "Chinese Emigration to California from 1848 until 1924."

[46] Over 90% are *blue-collar workers*. Men work in restaurants, women mostly in sweatshops. See also Chapter 5 "Business Structures and Income."

China to seek a bride. But there are also the slightly better placed, lower management employees who do not seek an autonomous, Americanized woman, but a "proper" Chinese woman who still possess traditional beliefs about marriage and family. *Gum San Haak* has become more attractive since Chinese and American relations have become closer.

Traditionally, under Chairman Mao Zedong, marriages with foreign Chinese were disregarded and considered as an uncritical acceptance of western civilization. This attitude has changed since the National Congress of 1979 and attaining permission to marry a foreigner has been simplified significantly in 2003.[47] Additionally, American immigration has become looser, allowing wives and children of American nationals and permanent residence holders to immigrate to the United States. This law allowed many a meeting in the United States. In the 1980s many Chinese were able to visit their homeland for the first time.

In my own circle of friends, I was able to see how foreign and American-born men have difficulties finding a partner, since American women of Chinese origin have set high standards, or, as the Chinese say, have been "fouled" by the western world and are "no longer Chinese." Income, position, and looks have an exceptionally high influence on the chances of Chinese. The responses of Chinese men concerning Chinese women from China are exceptionally diverse. They describe them as hardworking, subordinate, clean, proud, and of good personality. It is questionable whether Chinese American men have expectations concerning Chinese women similar to those of Whites when talking of the so-called "catalogue women" from Southeast Asia. Presumably, for some available men the wish for a Chinese wife is very close to an unusual assimilation, namely, a refreshing of Chinese tradition according to American stereotypes. At least, this interpretation shows that many Chinese Americans live in the past and have not been influenced by male and female emancipation. The wife should be pretty and well-dressed, so she is presentable for her husband. Furthermore, she should bear children and look after her parents-in-law. Already, some Chinese men do not want to look after their parents. They prefer autonomy without any interference from their parents, which is common in China (Interview with John Wong, 1991).

An important aspect of *Gum San Haak* is that the spouse speaks Chinese, can cook Chinese food well, and lives according to Chinese

---

[47] The marriage with a foreigner or emigrant became simple during the recent years. Until 2003, a physical checkup and the consent of the *danwei* (workers unit) was needed to prove one's single status in order to get married. Since October 2003, a new regulation bars any organization from "having a say" in an individual's decision to get married ("New Rules Delink State Knot from the Marriage Process." *People's Daily*, August 15, 2003).

tradition. This fact can be based on cultural ideology. For many Chinese, marriage to an American of any ethnic origin would be equal to being a traitor to Chinese culture and tradition. Marriage to a Chinese partner, however, maintains not only traditions, but also the cultural imperative of obedience toward the parents. The argument thus comes full circle: Whoever cannot flee from parental pressures is a candidate for *Gum San Haak*, and those who seek emancipation from the family will see an opportunity in intermarriage.

Final Discussion of the Family Model

Glenn's historical distinction of Chinese American family types is based on two determinants, the situation in the recipient country and immigration laws. The argument that purely cultural determination of the Chinese family would cause further continuation of the family models has its purpose in supporting this interpretation (Glenn, 1983).

These family models cannot, however, be as clearly differentiated over time as Glenn has proposed.[48] The *split family* existed until the 1960s when it was succeeded by family reunification and intermarriage. The *small producer family* did not die out in 1965, but still exists today, especially in Chinatown. Low income or certain trades do not singularly determine the *dual-wage family*, but its varieties need to be seen in terms of different countries of origin, differences in education, and social backgrounds. These modern immigration families not only represent the *core family* consisting of parents and unmarried children. Rather, these households with multiple children seldom occur, whereas those with relatives of second or higher degrees are growing.[49]

Glenn's characterization of the three family types leaves neither room for socially differentiated analysis of the complexity of Chinese American society, nor is it sufficient to explain the mechanisms of social mobility. The *dual-wage family* is only one form in Chinese American society in which rich and poor are more extreme than in the total population. As a result, the breadth of Chinese American family forms is large, and the continuous development of special traditional forms is noticeable. Based on the findings in Chapters 4 to 6, four general family types can be distinguished:

---

[48] See Chapter 7 "From a Bachelors Society to the Family Society—Historical Models."

[49] See Chapter 7 "Family Structures," under "The Change in the Ratio of Sexes," and Chapter 5 "Business Structures and Income."

1. *Multi-generation families* with traditional Chinese values. The high number of family members and family-reunification immigrants demonstrate the continued importance of this type.
2. A broad spectrum of *dual wage families*. Low-wage workers in ethnic enclaves and new FOB-immigrant entrepreneurs in high-class areas are the basis for this type.
3. European-style *core families* are common among assimilated immigrants and American-born Chinese. This group includes multiracial hapas, as well as Chinese expatriate managers dispatched to American subsidiaries.
4. Bachelor society-like *split families* are frequent among Chinese workers and students. A new type of *split-family* also emerges: Chinese Americans increasingly return to China as *retro-sojourners* to take up new challenges, often against the will of their family, which stays behind in America.

In all these family categories we are dealing with extremely career and success oriented families with few children, and based on solidarity among adults rooted in the Asian forms of the *extended (multigenerational) family*. Size and structure of the family is highly dependent on the education of the married couple. Ethnic business supports the traditional form of the small business family and excels as a solution to integration. New, *global entrepreneurs* overcome the glass ceiling by starting their own businesses and establish themselves as successful businessmen in the American society.

The Chinese mentality hardly allows assimilation in the form of passive adaptation to the recipient society, and with its success rate, there is no reason why it should assimilate in this way. Along with the *dual-wage family*, common family models are being dug up to show the predominant White family as the modern standard which is only garnered with some exotic emigrant types. We must, however, question how the average White family in the United States intends to compete with the successful and future oriented Chinese American family and its ethnic and global network of support. Today's social and group structures of Chinese Americans are an answer to a special situation in the recipient country, but not in the sense of a total assimilation to a functional and sensibly geared immigration law. Rather, the law has always interpreted Chinese immigration incorrectly and reacted either too late, or without taking into account the specific Chinese culture, family values and networking abilities, which differ significantly from the West.

Since the single sociological components of the autonomous Chinese success have been shown, we can compare these with a *model minority*, as planned. So as to not engage in an unequal comparison, e.g. myths and statistical facts, it will be based on situations from the community in San Francisco. These pictures should be incorporated into a tight web of Chinese American identity.

8. CHINESE BREAKING THE CEILING

A Model Minority?

The terminology *model minority* was invented in the 1980s initially to describe the Japanese, and later the Chinese, as the best among Asian immigrants. More recently, the term has been increasingly transferred to Asians a whole. In view of the foregoing discussion of the Chinese in pioneer society, the contrasts could hardly be greater. Previously considered un-integratable outsiders, today they represent the American Dream. What criteria have been adopted lately to allow this change in attitude towards the Chinese for the better?

Again, the question must be raised whether the Chinese can be regarded as a homogenous group to whom one confers the uniform status of *model minority*. Analysis of origin, social status, occupation, and values has shown a widespread spectrum, often with worlds of difference lying between subsequent generations. Does possibly only one elite, one certain country of origin, one particular generation belong to this special clique, or is, in fact, the groups as a whole and its functionality meant? Secondly, one must ask from what point of view is the term *model minority* to be appraised. Do the Chinese offer a valuable contribution to a multicultural society, or do they only relive the ideals of American society better than other minorities?

Finally, this terminology of *model minority*, stemming from the description of Japanese Americans in the 1960s, found its way into the Asian American vocabulary via the slow acceptance of an ethnic identity. It is, however, specifically used as a comparative category. Other minorities are expected to follow Asians in their thoughts and action, because they are believed to be willing to learn, disciplined and modest, hard working, and undemanding (Kim, 1986, 411). According to Kim, this represents the way of thinking of an American *majority society* and is, therefore, more convincing.[1]

According to Chinese American activists, the praised modesty of Asians is nothing more than inactivity of a *silent minority*, caused by racism, ostracism, and fear. In both of these opposing interpretations of Chinese virtues, no differentiation is made within the group, but it is clear that the one refers to the Chinese who gained success from hard work whereas the other refers to those who became victims of discrimination. The ideal in this majority picture of Chinese (undemanding, willing to learn, etc.) seems to

---

[1] The Chinese American press itself highlights contributions of successful Chinese as indicators for the progress of American society.

underline the fact that they have come to terms with the situation they found upon arrival. They have not functioned to change society or give it new direction. Mirrored in the economic crisis at the beginning of the 1990s, this means the majority is seeking someone to represent the achievements of its ideal, as well as those lacking qualities. The Chinese group obviously fulfils this requirement.

The education system, which has recently come under close scrutiny, seems to be the "passing lane" for Chinese on their way to success. From the ghettos of the cities, which seem to present a failure in obtaining a fair society before the eyes of all Americans, Chinese immigrants step out into the middle class and the best neighborhoods. Until the 1990s, the Chinese have not made themselves noticeable through strong representation of their interests, e.g. potent lobbyists or influential personalities. Clever, friendly smiling, successful businessmen of Chinese origin symbolize an America of deregulation in the process of becoming, or returning to, the business paradise of self-made-men.

The songs of praise from former Presidents during Chinese New Year festivities are not without cause. In 1984, President Reagan took in the hope of all Chinese, and all other immigrant minorities, for the American Dream:

"Asian and Pacific Americans have helped preserve that [American] dream by living up to the bedrock values that make us a good and a worthy people. I'm talking about principles that begin with the sacred worth of human life, religious faith, community spirit, and the responsibility of parents and schools to be teachers of tolerance, hard work, fiscal responsibility, cooperation, and love." (Reagan, February 23, 1984a).

Similar, President George H.W. Bush said in 1991:

"America owes a debt of gratitude to the many ethnic groups that have helped to shape the character of our Nation. Sharing a rich and diverse heritage, Americans of Chinese descent have long been recognized for their many contributions to America's social, cultural, and economic development." (Bush, George H.W., February 11, 1991).

President Clinton greeted the Lunar New Year in 2000 as follows:

"Asian Americans play a key role in all segments of our society, from scientists who have helped to build our national defense and to power our unmatched technological progress, to the artists whose talents grace our literature, stage and screen. America is strengthened by these contributions, and we must work to ensure that Asian Americans are afforded every opportunity to be active and equal participants in our national life." (Clinton, February 3, 2000).

The factor of cultural heritage[2] mentioned by President Bush Sr. is a substitutable parameter in the success story of the Asian group, as Reagan's speech also shows. Hidden behind Chinese culture one finds common values, e.g. family and hard work, which finally are all used to maintain the American Dream, White American style.[3]

Even if this vision has currently become mainstream, it is not valid in comparison to the category *model minority*. The latter in fact creates a competitive situation among minorities, instead of engendering a comparison of a minority with the majority. The frequently used comparison of Chinese, or Asians, with African Americans, the so-called *failed minority*, exemplifies this view of American society. The educational system in California has not changed yet with regard to its enrollment system at universities, despite the majority of Asian students found in some schools.[4] This discloses the inflexibility of the White Americans in accepting the decline of their majority status, and thus the increasing globalization of the American society.

Majority suggests a position at the helm of society, whereas minority means having no dominant cultural characteristics. Are the Chinese classified as *model minority* because they have kept silent until now? The supporters of the model minority concept, whilst they explicitly talk of good and bad culture, bring the consequences of this comparison between African Americans and Chinese Americans to our attention.[5]

The African Americans are without strong family ties, without ties to the homeland, and without cultural roots abroad. Thus they are more American than most other groups and their desire for equality has not succeeded, despite their political militancy in the 1960s. Should, therefore, social capital and *ethnic solidarity* of the Chinese group not be seen the foundation of their success, even though they were previously criticized for having exactly these qualities?

---

[2] To celebrate Asian and Pacific Islanders culture in the United States, the *Asian-Pacific American Heritage Week* was introduced by President Carter in 1978. President George H.W. Bush expanded the holiday in 1990 to the month of May, as the first Japanese immigrant to the United States arrived in May 1843.

[3] In 2003, President George W. Bush's Lunar New Year message did not address Asian or Chinese American achievements: "The Lunar New Year has traditionally celebrated the rejuvenation of the earth and the start of the new farm season. Today, for many Asian Americans it represents a period of new beginnings and renewed hope. During this time, individuals around the world reaffirm the value of friendship, celebrate family, and look forward to a hopeful future." (Bush, George W., January 22, 2003).

[4] See Chapter 6 "Education."

[5] See Osajima, 1988, 167.

To be a *model minority* is not a question of figures, neither of population nor income levels. This is clearly shown with the example of the Chinese. They mostly settle in urban and suburban areas, the majority being in California—they usually represent the majority of the population and their average incomes are so high because the areas they live in have high income levels. On the other hand, the number of Chinese living under the poverty level, especially among foreign-born is higher than in other minority groups. The Chinatown inhabitants of today, therefore, do not fit the term *model minority*, rather they reflect the problems of other ethnic groups such as the Black and Hispanic.[6]

The enigma behind the term Chinese[7] as a sociological category cannot be unveiled by the functional, but vague concept of the *model minority* terminology, as thus far presented. Future opportunities of the Chinese also cannot be identified. Tomorrow, the acceptance by a perceived "majority" could be transferred to another minority group, which is thus seen to represent the realization of the American Dream. The *model minority* terminology in its current function of maintaining the American Dream, or negatively speaking, of warning of Asian success, is incorrect in describing the actual situation of Chinese Americans. It does, however, show the necessity to reestablish the previous analysis of political reticence, family solidarity, business success, and intra-social togetherness, in light of recent tendencies.

Politics: From Opium Hall to City Hall

Until recently, Chinese interests have only been weakly represented in Washington, as the history of immigration legislation has shown. The conclusion that behind this phenomenon generally lies a marginal political organization and representation of interests might not be far fetched, but it is not certain.

Political participation within the Chinese group was, however, historically directed toward the homeland. The isolation of the immigrants by the recipient society and the retreat into Chinatowns created an organizational form that reflected homeland structures, in general, but ones adapted to the new surroundings. The political and social withdraw into the Chinatown society was a protection against the hostile surroundings. For a long time, there was little opportunity to penetrate American structures. The

---

[6] See Chapter 5 "Business Structures and Income."

[7] See Chapter 3 "Immigration Legislation" under "Definitions" about the indifferent linguistic use of this expression, even on an official level.

Chinese could not obtain any civil rights until 1943, when President Roosevelt abolished the discriminating category of *ineligible for citizenship* during the Sino-American honeymoon. How strong their inner support was for politics can be seen in the support of the Chinese Republic against Japan in the 1930s, as well as in the split of the Chinatown residents into supporters of Chairman Mao Zedong and the *Kuomintang*, which ended with the lengthy superiority of the Chiang Kai-shek supporters. The splitting of China into separate entities, along with single-sided American support of an undemocratic Taiwan until President Nixon's historic visit to China in 1972, paralyzed any political discussion among Chinatown inhabitants.[8]

When the first outwardly cooperative Chinese groups were created during the Civil Rights Movement, they initially had to overcome the old political orientations and structures. Fighting the Establishment seemed the most important task. Its influence did not simply disappear with the dissolution of the battle lines within American foreign policy and the second-generation movement out of the ghettos, but, in fact, received increased support from the economic and war refugees of the 1970s from Indochina and Hong Kong.[9] The *community* was reinforced by the common language, Cantonese, social and educational institutions, e.g. from the Chinese School to vocational courses. Thanks to their extensive real estate ownership in the Bay Area, the *Six Companies* maintained their clientele from the housing requirements of new arrivals, elderly and socially weak, as well as the rental of business locations to the ever-increasing number of small businesses. The *Chinese Chamber of Commerce* was not only responsible for the demands of the small commercial businesses and merchants of ethnic background, but also for the organization of community festivals, e.g. the Chinese New Year Festival.

It was difficult for organizations, such as *Chinese for Affirmative Action*, *Chinese American Democratic Club*, and *Organization of Chinese Americans* to compete.[10] Not only was the development slowed by the competition of the old organizations in Chinatown, but they had to recruit their clientele, an educated and wise middle and upper class with attitudes varying from ethnocentric to exceptionally acclimatized, from heterogeneous surroundings.

---

[8] The expression *China Factor* is used in this context. Organizations guided from *Kuomintang* have the support of the American government, as well as of the merchant class. This class not only has an ideological dominance, but also supplies cheap labor, thus exploiting the descendants of the *sojourners*. For the development of the Chinese American relation see Chapter 3.

[9] For details see Pan, 2000, p. 68, 86, and 267 et seq.

[10] This ideological direction had various influential factors: the American pacifism and the Civil Rights Movement of the 1960s, as well as the development of an ethnic consciousness in the context of the Chinese Cultural Revolution.

While the *Chinese Chamber of Commerce* brought the business interests of their clientele to the forefront through the former Mayor, Art Agnos,[11] the new organizations lost some of their influence when the Civil Rights Movement slowed. Today, a new balance of power is in the making. The power of the influential groups is diminishing as a whole. None of the organizations or their coalitions is dominating the community ideologically. Supporters of the People's Republic of China need no longer hide and many intellectual Chinese Americans have developed their own values. The traditional organizations are still important for the elderly and the new immigrants. Young Chinese Americans, however, have turned their backs on the old kind of organizations. Not only the old clichés of being identifiable by Chinese traditions turns them off, but also political representation of the Chinese race within the American society seems less attractive than a career in business or science. Business-oriented associations are replacing the old organizations and provide a professional, *hui*-like support for the Chinese community. They especially enable new immigrants to set up businesses and develop networks in the Pacific Rim area (Saxenian, 1999, 29-30).

A major characteristic of political activity among Chinese Americans remains, however, their concentration on the local community. On the one hand, this is caused by the traditions and isolation of the old organizations within Chinatown and, on the other, by concentrated Chinese expansion in specific geographic or urban areas, which represents an intensive networking based on family emporiums.[12]

Continuous trench warfare with changing coalitions and sympathies keeps Chinese American politics alive. *Chinese for Affirmative Action* (*CAA*) and *Six Companies* were bound by a fine oppositional thread against the then-governing Mayor Agnos during elections. Thus, the fractions within the community not only run between the old and new organizations. The *Chinese Chamber of Commerce* and *Six Companies* are opposed, but not only due to their differences of opinion over Mayor Agnos. The latter have recently responded to attempts at rapprochement by intellectual activists surrounding Henry Der, Ling-chi Wang, and Germaine Wong, of the *CAA* by participating in a joint Fundraising Dinner of the *CAA*, in 1990, thus showing signs of solidarity.[13]

---

[11] Art Agnos served as Mayor of San Francisco from 1988 to 1992.

[12] See Chapter 4 "Habitat," under "Countrywide Characteristics of Asian Communities."

[13] This "historical dinner," as it was judged in community circles, brought "old-fashioned-hardliners" and young activists together at one table, allowing them to achieve results. The *Six Companies* not only support the Eastern Medicine in Chinatown hospitals, but also social projects of new organizations.

The *CAA*, founded in 1969, is the only long-term successful organization to have grown out of the Civil Rights Movement. Initially, it worked against general discrimination of Chinese in American society. It later became a professional law and service office serving specific interests of the Chinese in the Bay Area. Social involvement and the identification with specific Chinese interests are areas where *CAA* and *Six Companies* repeatedly meet, although their clientele are not always the same, since the *CAA* represents the acceptance of Chinese interests within society as a whole, whereas the Chinatown organization seeks the maintenance of the community as a social and cultural unit. An external occasion of solidarity, which superficially unified many old and new organizations, was the protest against the suppression of the Chinese democracy movement at Tiananmen Square in 1989. Nevertheless the political situation in the Chinese states still has an effect on the interests of the community.

Recently, Chinatown has regained economic importance after the automation of the 1960s seemed to doom small businesses.[14] Not only unskilled labor, small entrepreneurs, and the refugee generation of the 1970s survive from Chinese ethnic business, but also businessmen from Taiwan and Hong Kong, who earn their money through import and export, financial services, or ethnically oriented media.[15] This makes Chinatown attractive for new political ambitions. Originally, the *Chinese Chamber of Commerce* did not have the importance in San Francisco that it did in United States partner countries in Southeast Asia. It's founding in 1970, however, was the first sign of the economic strength of overseas Chinese, an orientation point for a generation of higher educated businessmen and women with entrepreneurial skills. Early alumni networks had their origins in Hong Kong's renowned schools, such as La Salle, Wah Yan, and St. Paul's.

Rose Pak, adviser at the *Chinese Chamber of Commerce* and Chinatown activist, was able to maintain good relationships to the mayoral office during Agnos's tenure, from 1988 until 1992, and able to place twenty Chinese Americans in important positions. The most important nomination was that of James Ho to Assistant Mayor and Head of the Economics Department. Ho's foreign policy activities allowed many millions of dollars in investments to flow into the Bay Area from Hong Kong. The respective business interests will have to be analyzed in detail. Pak, however, stumbled over her alliance with Mayor Agnos in 1989, and opposed the reconstruction of the Embarcadero exit to Chinatown which many inhabitants were in favor of, even if only for tourism.

---

[14] See Chapter 1 "Chinese Emigration to California from 1848 until 1924."
[15] See Chapter 5 "Business Structures and Income."

Supportive of the former Republican Mayor, Frank Jordan (1992–1996), is Pak's opponent, Florence Fang, wife of the business magnate John Fang. Restaurant owner Fang (*Grand Palace*), however, claims that there will be no large-scale representation of Chinese community interests in the Fang era, as was the case during Agnos's time. She claims not to be interested in public debate of other people's interests, but wants to maintain her business interests (*San Francisco Chronicle*, December 13, 1991). The obvious discrepancy between Fang's openly demonstrated political disinterest and massive support of the mayor in the function of the community gatekeeper can be clarified by looking at the family history.

John Fang who died in April 1992 at the age of 66 was the president of the *Pan Asia Venture Capital Corporation*, a financing company for Fang's media ventures. He began his career as a translator, reporter, and journalist in Taiwan (*New Life Daily*) after completing his studies in Nanking, China. After arriving in the United States in 1952, he studied journalism at University of California, Berkeley and subsequently began building his empire. Initially, he co-published the *Chinese Daily Post* in San Francisco and then printed *Chinatown Guides*. Some of his creations are particularly minority papers, like the *Chinese TV Guide* and a Hispanic weekly, *Mission Life*, but also include *Asian Week*, a weekly magazine published for more than two decades. After his death, his youngest son, Ted, took over the position as publisher of *The San Francisco Independent*, which is distributed free of charge thanks to many advertisers, and *Asian Week* (Interview with John Fang, 1990). In 2000, the Fang-family purchased the *San Francisco Examiner* from the Hearst Corporation, which had to sell the newspaper after the acquisition of the *San Francisco Chronicle*. Ted Fang indicated that, "as a native San Franciscan and Asian American, he would bring a completely new perspective to the *Examiner*." (*Asian Week*, August 4, 2000).

John Fang was an active Republican. In April 1992, Senator Nancy Pelosi (D-CA) who maintained good relations with Fang, especially after the Tiananmen Square Massacre, read a commemorative speech for Fang, whom she wanted remembered as a pioneer of Asian American journalism and a supporter of the Chinese group: "...having fled communism, John provided inspiration and support to China democracy activists."

In the new Jordan administration, Fang's son John is responsible for Trade and Business, as well as the regional transport system BART. He founded the *Asian American Voter Project* to fight against previous election abstinence of Asians. The second son, Ted, however, is a member of the *Chinese American Democratic Club* (*CADC*, founded 1970). Slightly aside of mainstream democrats, the *CADC* has practically the same history as the *CAA*. The Fang-Dynasty sees the community as a medium in which to pursue its business interests and makes it part of their private ownership, wherever it can. I was able to experience this personally during my internship at the pro mainland China community paper, *East West*, which folded in 1989. It succumbed to the battle for advertisers against the Taiwan-oriented *Asian Week*.

The competitor's founder and owner, John Fang, had previously stepped into the political controversy within publishing during his time as the publisher of the pro *Kuomintang* paper *Young China*.[16] Fang founded *Asian Week* at the end of the 1970s, after giving up on *Young China*. This most influential weekly for Chinese Americans became popular outside of the community when Fang had it handed out to delegates of both parties on the steps of the Capitol during the 1984 convention. During the promotion of the Fang-Dynasty, Henry Der of the *CAA* warned about the danger of City Hall falling under the influence of a small segment of community interests (*San Francisco Chronicle*) and Harvey Wong, previously president of the *Six Companies*, mentioned that while the success of the Fangs brought publicity for the Chinese American cause, these special interests also tended towards overestimation of the subject. An earlier high functionary in City Hall commented, "Family success comes before any ideology." (Interview with Wong, 1990).

Investigating the recipes for Chinese family success in politics that reach beyond the common high value of the family in society reveals some very interesting things come to light. The simplicity with which members of upwardly mobile Chinese families move within circles, strengthened by ethnic organizations, but politically flexible between Republican and Democrat, is obviously supportive of their political careers. This ease of movement was already noticeable of the political connections of the Fangs with the somewhat varied orientation of individual family members.[17]

---

[16] "*Asian Week* was determined to beat *East West*, and it did" said Serena Chen. "They went after every advertiser we had, making sure anyone who advertised in *East West* was offered a reduced rate in *Asian Week*. They put a lot of pressure on the people." Interview with Serena Chen, ex-managing director *East West*, 1989. The competition was very tough. When *East West* preliminarily closed and we had to move, with our equipment, to smaller premises, the Editor Gordon Lew advised to take the software home in order to prevent sabotage, as often happens.

[17] Until the 1980s, there was no uniform Chinese en-block voting, as for example the Mexicans, who have many similarities with the Chinese. See Chapter 3 "Immigration," under "*Immigration Act* of 1990." It is estimated that about one third of the Chinese voted Republican, one third Democratic, and the remainder was undecided. Asian voting patterns changed, however, during the 1990s. In the 1992 elections, Democrats were trailing Republicans by 31:55, in 1996 the ratio was 43:48, and in 2000 the Democrats were leading by 54:41. A study sponsored by the *Chinese American Voter Education Committee* found an 82 percent preference for Democrats and an only 16 percent preference for Republicans ("Asian Americans and President Bush." *Asian Week*, January 19, 2001).

One must also add the ability to take up the interests of other minority groups, thus instigating new interethnic social coalitions. A candidate need not necessarily be a candidate from one's own race. During the era of Madame Chiang Kai-shek's America visits, the Taiwan-friendly fraction especially gained experience in the financing and public support of politicians amicable to their cause.[18] In the 1991 battle for City Hall, the architect Thomas Hsieh, one of eleven members of the *Board of Supervisors* in San Francisco, lost to the Democrat and White American, Frank Jordan, supported by the Fangs.[19] Hsieh is mainland Chinese and a Board Member of the *Chinese Chamber of Commerce* (something that possibly stood between him and the Fangs). His stiff and conservative style found no general support, even though his candidacy doubled the number of the registered Chinese electorate (*San Francisco Chronicle*, May 10, 1992). Even the electorate is not fixed on an ethnic candidate. "Asian American voters often support White mainstream politicians, perhaps in the belief that they have more clout than Asian Americans." (Interview with Him Marc Lai, president of the *Chinese Historical Society*, San Francisco, 1992).

Mike Woo, born in 1952, is the grandson of a laundry owner and son of the ex-president of the *Chinese American Citizen Alliance*—a pro-Republican organization with lobbyists in Washington. In 1993, Woo was a candidate for the Mayor's Office in Los Angeles, where he received 46% of the citywide vote, e.g. second among 24 candidates. He had the strong support of the Asian American community, like Thomas Hsieh, and was also supported by President Clinton.[20]

In contrast to Hsieh, he showed greater political elasticity. Although only few Asian voters were in his district, he was elected to the City Council as the only Asian by a coalition of real estate owners, homosexuals, renters, and pensioners. His decisive speech against the police beating of Rodney King in March, 1991, which set off civil war-like racial unrest in Los Angeles, his support of refugees from Latin America, and the legalization of street hawking, obtained the recognition from many Hispanics and Blacks. It is important to note that these are not exceptional individual or community exceptional careers. The time in which the superior educated second generation believed that the Chinese chances of success lay in their emancipation from their ethnic surrounding and ambivalence to their greater surrounding is over, at least politically.

---

[18] See Chapter 2 "Between 1924 and 1965."

[19] The directly elected *Board of Supervisors* has far-reaching competencies, especially regarding economic policies for the city and county.

[20] „I endorse Michael Woo because I believe he is the best person to reinvigorate the economy and ensure safety." President Clinton, *White House Press Office*, May 15, 1993.

The necessary cultural support of national pride—proud to be Chinese—needs to be analyzed.[21] Some current responses of politically active and successful Chinese read like a definition of the positioning of the Chinese group. During his candidacy, Thomas Hsieh said: "I really feel like Asians are waking up, there are more and more Asian candidates for state, local and national offices." (Interview with Thomas Hsieh, 1990). During a fundraising dinner for Woo, in October, 1992, Lawrence Low, lawyer in San Francisco, proclaimed: "We've arrived economically, we've arrived educationally. The third thing is to arrive politically ... and it's time." (Speech on October 2, 1992, in Lawrence's house in Presidio Heights). The statements of local politicians are similar to those of mobile Chinese who are entering the virgin territory of national politics, only the route to success seems different.

Claudine Cheng, former president of the *Organization of Chinese Americans (OCA)*, operating in Washington and successfully cooperating with the *Chinese American Citizen Alliance (CACA)*[22] during the creation of the *Immigration Acts* of 1990 (*IA 1990*), was quoted by *Asia Week* in August 1992, as follows:[23]

> "We are considered the *model minority*, people who have kids that do well academically, people that are doing well financially, but that's not everyone. I feel we have a long way to go politically in this country, to get our people elected, to get our people appointed to offices, because we need to have our own representatives to make sure our voices are heard in the political process." (*Asia Week*, August 1992).

The decisiveness of the activists should, however, not cover the fact that the basis for Chinese American politics is still relatively small. In 1990, the Asian group represented only 5% of the registered electorate for the mayoral election in San Francisco, although the percentage of Asian populous is almost 30%. Chris Cheung, who worked in various voter-registration campaigns, sees political abstinence stemming from the repressive domestic policies in the countries of origin, which have taken away all motivation for political activity (*Los Angeles Times*, March 9, 1992). Ling-chi Wang of the *CAA* also identifies cultural roots for the aversion. Still many Chinese,

---

[21] See Chapter 8 "Cultural Awakening."

[22] In 1895, a group of *American-born* Chinese in California founded the organization *The Native Sons of the Golden State*. They were reacting to a White movement, trying to achieve a political supremacy of the White over the Chinese. The Name was later changed in *Chinese American Citizen Alliance*. In 1935, the organization started issuing *The Chinese Digest*, the first English journal of the group. When Mao Zedong came to power in the 1950s, a power shift occurred within the organization: Republicans were supported. This change was triggered by the opinion that the group had to express their anti-Communistic status. As a counter-reaction, the *Chinese American Democratic Club* was founded.

[23] See Chapter 3 "Between 1965 and 2000," under "*Immigration Act* of 1990."

representing the majority of new immigrants, concentrate on political activities in their homelands. The rough surroundings of American politics have until recently probably deterred Chinese voters, since family welfare is traditionally more important than a political career. Although the immigration level is high among Chinese, parents often do not vote and educate their children not to take political responsibility in society (Interview, 1992).

The family can be a haven from "dirty" politics, and this opportunity is surely taken by many immigrants due to the variety of economic opportunities in the United States. It can, as shown, represent the power base for the career-interested Chinese who combine economic success with political activism. In between stand a large number of rich and educated who massively support their candidate financially without directly wanting to involve themselves in political activity. Daphne Kwok, Executive Director of the *OCA*, told me: "It is perhaps ironic that, although Chinese don't yet participate in politics in a big way, they do give a lot of money." (Interview, 1992).

During the presidential campaigns in 1988, Asian Americans donated more than $1,000,000 for both candidates, Bush and Dukakis, a figure that was only surpassed by the traditionally strong Jewish lobbyists. In the financing of their candidates, the organizations have created a generous network within the Chinese communities, which are spread, island-like, across the nation. Thomas Hsieh sees his election failure in San Francisco only as a small, short-term halt in his career. Fundraising within the whole country brought him $650,000 for his campaign.

During President Bill Clinton's 1996 re-election campaign, the financial support by the Chinese American community reached unprecedented heights. At the same time, these donations were severely tarnished by illegal campaign contributions, often from foreign citizens or corporations, who are considered illegal contributors (Timberlake, 1998). The *Democratic National Committee* had to return over $2.25 million, including $300,000 from fund-raiser Johnny Chung, which he allegedly received from the head of the Chinese military intelligence, General Ji Shengde.[24] Chung later pleaded guilty to illegal fund-raising. This scandal, dubbed *Chinagate*, involved many overseas Chinese, such as the Indonesian Riyadi-family, and many witnesses left the country to avoid prosecution.[25]

Long prior to these donations, national political activities of Chinese Americans had started as early as in the 1950s. In 1959, Hiram Leong Fong,

---

[24] CNN, <http://www.cnn.com/allpolitics/stories/1999/05/12/chung> (September 12, 2002).

[25] Prof. Ling-chi Wang indicates that the increasing political activities of Asian Americans pushed aside original Asian American interests in favor of moneyed politics. (1996b).

the son of Chinese immigrants born in Hawaii, was the first Asian American to be elected to the United States Senate, where he served until 1976. Dr. March Fong Eu was elected Secretary of State in California in 1974 as the first Asian (Chinese) American woman to be elected to any state government office in America. She served five consecutive terms until 1994, and lost a new bid for candidacy in 2002.

Since the middle of the 1990s, three factors contributed strongly to the political awakening of Chinese Americans. First, Chinese Americans have been treated with suspicion since the cold war, often leading to overcritical accusations and unequal treatment.[26] One of the most publicized events was the government's case against Dr. Wen Ho Lee, a scientist at Los Alamos National Laboratory, who was accused of leaking state secrets to China.[27] After several month of detention, the government was forced to release Lee, making the authorities look foolish and reckless.[28]

Second, a strong support for Chinese Americans by influential politicians began in the late 1980s. In 1989, President George H. W. Bush appointed Elaine Chao as Deputy Secretary of Transportation (Chao, 1998). During President Clinton's tenure, Chinese Americans gained far greater political influence than ever before through increased representations in appointed federal and civil service positions.

Clinton and Gore appointed the most diverse administration in American history, including the strong consideration of Chang-lin Tien as Secretary of Energy.[29] In 1998, David Wu (D-OR) became the third Chinese American and the first Taiwanese-born to be elected to the House of Representatives. In 2000, the Senate confirmed the appointment of Norman Mineta (D-CA) as Secretary of Commerce, the first Asian American member of a president's cabinet (Underwood, 2000).

In January 2001, despite—or because—of a tremendous loss of voters from the Asian American Community, President George W. Bush appointed Elaine Chao as the first Chinese American woman in a cabinet. Republican senatorial candidate Matt Fong commented, "President-elect Bush deserves our gratitude for not only selecting a highly qualified individual, but one who also breaks historic ethnic barriers." (*Asian Week*, January 19, 2001). Within

---

[26] "Chinese Americans Fear Affirmative Action." *Asian Week*, September 16, 1999.

[27] Prof. Ling-chi Wang sent an open letter to President Clinton on October 6, 2000, urging him to issue an apology on behalf of the executive branch of the government (Wang, 2000).

[28] The controversy became a major impetus for the community to organize as a political force. "Profiles in Outrage," *Time Asia*, September 25, 2000; "Lee Case Proved to Be an Awakening," *Los Angeles Times*, September 25, 2000; "Wake Up Time," *Asia Week*, November 19, 1999. For a detailed article on Asian American political candidates see Tsai, L., 2000.

[29] See also Chapter 5 "Education."

the first two years of his Presidency, Bush appointed 77 Asian Pacific Americans to government jobs, making it one of the most ethnically diverse administrations and cabinet (*Asian Week*, July 26, 2002).

Third, Chinese Americans are mobilizing themselves and gaining political momentum on the national, state, and regional levels. In 1999, fourteen Asian American candidates were running for the Board of Supervisors in San Francisco, and since Thomas Hsieh in 1988, there have always been Asian Americans on the city's board. And the next generation of Asian Americans is already preparing: Tom Hsieh, the son of Thomas Hsieh, plans to run for the Board of Supervisors (*San Jose Mercury News*, June 26, 2000). A new chapter is just beginning in Chinese Americans integration into and influence on American society. Their political voice is not only supported by mainstream America, it is also strongly nurtured within their own community. Early political organizations, such as the *Asian American Voters Project*, and the *Chinese American Voter Education Committee* (*CAVEC*) support the Chinese political activism. The *80–20 Initiative*, founded in 1998 by the former Lieutenant Governor Woo (D-DE), claims over 600,000 supporters including many prominent Asian Americans. The initiative aims to persuade 80% of all Asians to vote cohesively for a specific candidate in elections, thus increasing their political power significantly. During the 2000 election, the initiative showed a strong potential to represent Asian Americans as a political force (Watanabe, 2002).

Since the late 1980s, a various organizations have been established, thrusting Chinese Americans from the political backstage into the limelight. The *Chinese American Political Association* (*CAPA*) promotes the active participation of Chinese Americans in politics. Similarly, *Chinese Americans United for Self-Empowerment* (*CAUSE-Vision 21*) encourages political empowerment; and the recent initiative *model minority* wants to "provide scrutiny in every possible way, so as to educate, inform, provoke, and inspire movements by individuals and groups toward Asian American empowerment."[30] The *Conference on Asian American Pacific Leadership* (*CAPAL*) encourages and helps students and young leaders to become active in public services and politics.

---

[30] See details under: *Model Minority—A Guide to Asian American Empowerment.* <http://www.modelminority.com> (December 14, 2002).

Other organizations, such as the *Asian American Government Executives Network* (*AAGEN*), the *Organization of Chinese Americans* (*OCA*), and the *Leadership Education for Asian Pacifics* (*LEAP*), strongly support Chinese American political activism.[31]

These efforts are further strengthened by famous Chinese Americans. In 1989, the *Committee of 100* (*C-100*) was co-founded by the world-renown architect I.M. Pei and other distinguished Chinese Americans, such as Yo-Yo Ma.[32] The *Committee of 100* lobbies economical and political leaders of the world, and "fosters a better understanding between United States and China and Chinese Americans with the American people."[33] This statement shows a major focus of Chinese Americans: Cooperation among the Chinese themselves, and with the American mainstream, a cooperation which is inevitably is designed as the basis for economic cooperation and expansion.

Economy: The New *Global Entrepreneurs*

The political achievements of Chinese Americans are based on their strongly growing population, the increased adaptation towards the American political system, and their economic success. Chinese Americans have long left behind the stereotyped jobs of the early immigration, although these low-wage jobs in Chinese restaurants, sweatshops and laundries still provide support for new immigrants and long-term Chinatown inhabitants.

Today, despite the glass ceiling, Chinese Americans occupy leading positions in several business segments of the American economy, especially technology, biotechnology, fashion, finance and real estate. An increasing number of companies is owned and managed by Chinese Americans, some of them are among the youngest and wealthiest people in the world. Their success has been built on several factors, among them the determination and desire of immigrant students, especially during the Information Technology

---

[31] The Asian American net "Homepage," <http://www.asianamerican.net> and *OCA*, 2003, "Homepage," <http://www.oca.com> provide many links to political and economic websites designated for Chinese Americans.

[32] Ieoh Ming Pei is one of the most important architects of the twentieth century, and a leading figure in the *C-100*. He was born in 1917 in Canton, and lived in Shanghai and Hong Kong before coming to the United States in 1934, where he graduated from Harvard. Among his most famous buildings is the East Wing of the National Gallery in Washington, the Bank of China in Hong Kong, and the entrance of the Louvré in Paris. With the money received from the *Pulitzer Prize*, Pei established a fund for Chinese Students in the United States. For further information on Yo Yo Ma, see Chapter 8 "Cultural Awakening."

[33] For details see *Committee of 100*, "Homepage," <http://www.committee100.org>.

boom in the 1990s, a strong ethnic network of the Chinese Americans in the United States, and the financial support of wealthy overseas Chinese in Asia.

The expanding economic strength of Chinese Americans will be detailed by studying a small group of influential Chinese Americans in the Bay Area in the 1990s, with emphasis on their personal backgrounds, their business interests, and their political and social connections. In a second part, an overview about successful Chinese American entrepreneurs in the United States in 2000 will be given in order to highlight recent advances and achievements. Subsequently, the new economic power that is represented by these top entrepreneurs will be analyzed in this context.

The top stars among the Chinese climbers are identifiable by a number of common characteristics. They are from rich family dynasties, often from Hong Kong, have received a good education within the United States and are internationally active. Usually, they do not belong to those whom the glass ceiling phenomenon hinders from rising to the top. They are already at the top when they arrive in the United States. This elite holds capital reserves, which makes many projects accessible. Businesses are secured through connections to politicians and intensive networking within families and alumni. $250,000 were collected from Hong Kong businessmen alone for Mayor Agnos's campaign in 1988. Via the Assistant Mayor, James Ho, and the *Chinese Chamber of Commerce*, the Chinese yuppies have direct access to the best business locations in Chinatown where they have pushed out small traders and business. They are sure to be able to handle their Western business partners, while having reservations about the Whites' ability to evaluate the Asian offensive correctly.

Caleb Chan is one of five children of the president of Crocodile Garments Ltd. in Hong Kong, Shun Chan, who controls a significant portion of Lacosté businesses and is among richest men in Hong Kong. Caleb Chan is mainly involved in hotel businesses in San Francisco, buying one of the best hotels at Parc Street. His other objects are in California, Pine, and Market Streets. Chan has residencies in Vancouver and Hillsborough, one of the most exclusive quarters in the Bay Area. He also has a University of California, Berkeley diploma.

Victor and Richard Li, sons of Li Ka-shing, one of the wealthiest men in the world, studied both at Stanford during the 1980s. Richard worked later as a fund manager at a bank in Toronto, while Victor managed real estate business in Vancouver. Both have returned in the early 1990s to manage their father's conglomerate in Hong Kong, while at the same time they made large investments in American companies, including a $10 million investment in *Critical Path*, a San Francisco-based communication technology company founded in 1997, and a similar investment in *VLINX* in 2000, an e-commerce portal. The Li Ka-shing family was valued at over US$26 billion in 2002, and their Bay Area investments at an excess of $100 million.[34]

Vincent Tai is an architect in San Francisco. His company *Tai Associates* built a housing complex with golf course in 1990, among numerous other large projects in the Bay Area, including historical buildings in the Financial District of San Francisco. From a 1979 partnership with the Li Ka-shing's *Cheung Kong Holding Ltd.* in Hong Kong, resulted the purchase of the China Basin Building, which was sold after its renovation, only three years later. Tai is an ex-student of Berkeley and an alumni of the Diocesan Boys School in Hong Kong.

Anthony Chan stems from a rich family with most of its property in Shanghai. With his partners, he created a twelve-floor office building in Sutter Street, and various shopping malls mainly in the South Bay Area. He is a member of the investment group *Hong Kong Association* and lives in Hillsborough. After attending St. Stephen's College in Hong Kong, Chan attended Berkeley.

Leslie Tang Schilling is the daughter of the Hong Kong textile magnate, Jack C. Tang. Schillings's headquarters for her real estate business Union Square Investments is the building which she owns at Market Street, San Francisco's main shopping street. She purchased a number of buildings in Downtown and Lafayette, including a building at Union Square she obtained from Ferdinand Marcos. In 2000, her businesses held capital investments, valued at a minimum of $150 million. She graduated from Berkeley, lives in San Francisco, and is a Board member of the Massachusetts Institute of Technology–MIT, the University of California, *San Francisco Foundation*, and *KQED*–a TV and radio station, among many others. Her grandfather, father, and brother studied at MIT, and the family has donated millions of dollars to the University for numerous buildings.

James C. Ng, 58, was the former president and executive director of the *United Savings Bank* (*USB*) in San Francisco.[35] A company with its headquarters in Hong Kong, it purchased the bank in 1986 and subsequently invested millions. The *USB* acquired a new headquarters in Van Ness Avenue with 32 branch offices, mostly in northern California, as well as $1 billion in deposits. Half of the customers are Asian. Mr. Ng, alumni of the Diocesan Boys School in Hong Kong, studied at Golden Gate and San Jose Universities and lives in Hillsborough.

William Chang, 49, previously a port commissioner in San Francisco, is the eldest son of a Chinese father and Japanese mother. The family has its

---

[34] See also Chapter 8 "*Guanxi* and *Xinyong*–Chinese Business Networking."

[35] James Ng joined the *First Pacific Bank* in 1999, where he served as an executive director until 2001.

property mainly in Shanghai and San Francisco, among which is the building at Montgomery Street, in the best business. Chang buys business properties in Oakland and San Francisco and then renovates them. Chang grew up in Hong Kong, attended the renowned Millfield Institute in Somerset, England. He graduated in economics at Harvard. He founded the *Asian Business League* and served Mayor Agnos' quick action group for a sports arena (*China Basin Ballpark*) for the San Francisco Giants. Chang lives in San Francisco.

This list can be continued ad infinitum. Shanghai and Hong Kong are the main original sources of these entrepreneurs and their business activity. In the People's Republic of China, where the majority of emigrants in the historic phases came from Guangdong province, today the Western-oriented port city of Shanghai seems to be the point of departure for elite emigration. This includes Nobel Price Laureate Tsung-Dao Lee, the computer technician and entrepreneur An Wang, and the Lieutenant Governor of Delaware, I.M. Woo, who all come from Shanghai. Hong Kong has become a springboard, either for education and/or for the business interests of Chinese Americans. The Diocesan Boys School has over 150 active alumni in the Bay Area, such as Daniel C. Tsui, Nobel Laureate in Physics in 1998, the San Francisco Assistant Mayor, James Ho, Hotel owner Lawrence Lui, the architect Vincent Tai, the banker James Ng, and Professor Ling-chi Wang—a mainland Chinese who also completed his higher education in Hong Kong. Today, Wang is the Director of Asian American Studies at Berkeley, where a number of prominent Chinese have studied. This is the right point in time to take a short and indiscreet peek behind the scenes of Chinese networking, just imagine the following dinner setting.

At the Fook Yuen Restaurant in the luxury city of Millbrae in the summer of 1990, twelve of the richest Hong Kong Chinese in San Francisco met in a reserved room for lobster, pork skin, and shark fin soup. Toasts were given with forty-year-old Hennessy. Next to these entrepreneurs sat the members of the Planning, Parks, and Port Commissions of the City, including Assistant Mayor, himself a successful businessman. The discussion revolved around family, friends, and the future, altering between English and Cantonese. The participants discussed about a Chinese investor, whom someone had declared to be the best dressed businessman in the city, that he was expanding his business empire over the whole world and in the most expensive cities, while his wife ate a sparing daily lunch at the VIP lounge in Chinatown, only to hasten home at five o'clock to cook for the family. Banker William Chung declared that his wife was the senior financial officer in the family, due to the dowry brought into the marriage, and thus drove the family Jaguar while he had to drive a Honda. Christopher Lin who had studied violin at the Diocesan Boys School was to be heard that he had just bought his daughter an original Stradivarius.

On the mobile phone, the then-Mayor, who is of European descent, wanted to know whether he should join the group. He liked to present himself to the Hong Kong yuppies as "one of the boys" who understood friends and family, just like themselves. Senator Simon, for whom the Chinese diaspora had collected donations during a one-evening visit to San Francisco, said of the mayor: "Nobody is doing a better job of getting the Chinese behind him than this guy." The discussion finally turned to this unusual American Way, with its mixture of business and politics in a humorous undertone. The Banker inquired about the agitated rumors in which the San Francisco Giants were to leave the City and asked what the value of the team was. Someone believed it to be about $40–50 million. "Why not just buy them then? Let's just buy them," was his answer.

In a far larger and more serious context the same summer, heads of state and presidents of multinational companies joined to hold the first Pacific Rim Forum. Assistant Mayor, James Ho, announced the following interesting data: Of the overseas direct investment in the United States, 50% came from Japan, of which 76% was concentrated in California. In 1989, 13,000 jobs in the Bay Area were dependent on the trade within the Pacific Rim, the trading volume had reached $5.7 billion. Pacific Rim companies had invested $2.6 billion in real estate to hold 106 headquarters and offices. The subsidiaries within the Pacific Rim had increased by 48% from 1984 to 1989. Until 2001, these figures grew significantly. Total value of California exports in 2001 was $68.2 billion, 60% thereof in high technology, mostly originating from Silicon Valley. The Pacific Rim trading volume has quadrupled to $23.1 billion, and exports to China alone have surpassed $1 billion. Despite the economic crisis, only exports to China had a significant growth (32%), and China is now the seventh largest export destination for the Bay Area. This volume is expected to double by 2005, and to triple by 2020 (Bay Area Economic Forum, 2001).

At second look, the Pacific Rim is not only an international trading market. Ho spoke of family trade: 34% of all high school graduates spoke Chinese. Chinese own 37% of all minority businesses in San Francisco and employ over 50% of all related employees. Over 25% of the Chinese businessmen acknowledge close and regular ties to mainland China, 73% indicated that they would consider to start business in their native country in the future (Saxenian, 2002, 21).

The local economy profits in a multitude of ways from the Pacific Rim. The same can be said of the high value products and services from the Bay Area, which are designed for the trading partners due to the relationships between the people and their requirements. From the designer business to the clothing industry, which is serviced by the small cutting shops in Chinatown,[36] from the computer industry in Silicon Valley to the large service industries, like banks, insurance companies, legal aid agencies, or hotels, a whole region has concentrated on the Asian trade.

During the 1980s and 90s, Chinese Americans have been particularly active to develop the economic, financial and scientific cooperation between the United States and China. Numerous organizations have been established on both sides of the Pacific Rim to enhance cooperation between the two countries, one factor that helps establish businesses in the United States, increasing the Pacific trade, and thus contributes to Chinese *brain gain.*[37]

The *Association of Chinese Professionals (ACP)* "Promotes cultural, economic, and technological cooperation and exchange between the US and China ... by using the members expertise in science, technology, management culture, education and other areas, and their natural connections with China."[38] Organizations such as the *China Association for International Exchange of Personnel (CAIEP)*, *Chinese Information & Networking Association (CINA)*, *China Oversea Talent Network (COTN)*, and the *Silicon Valley Chinese Oversea Business Association (SCOBA)*, have similar goals. These are just a few of the many organizations that advertise and communicate bilingual in Chinese and English, especially on the Internet, thus truly connecting the American side with China.

The increased flow of Chinese students since 1980 received a further boost by the *Chinese Student Protection Act* in 1992, which enabled many Chinese to find work or establish business in the Unites States. Especially the technology boom of the 1990s was a fertile ground for start-up companies, and many Chinese Americans have and are successfully establishing businesses in the United States in technology, fashion, biotech, finance and real estate. In 1997, Chinese Americans owned 18% of all minority-owned businesses in the United States and represent a major economic force, especially for the Pacific Rim business.[39]

With the determination of new Chinese immigrants and American-born Chinese, their economic advances will certainly not stop here. They will be a link between the United States and Asia, as an essential part of the Pacific Rim business. At the same time, many of the successful entrepreneurs were born in China and retain, at least, part of their Chinese roots. They are

---

[36] See Chapter 5 "Business Structures and Income," under "Ethnic Business and Racial Labor in Chinatown."

[37] See also Chapter 6 "Education," under "From *Brain Drain* to *Brain Gain*—Returning to the Homeland."

[38] Detailed information can be found at <http://www.acp-atlanta.org>, including an extensive list of links to other Chinese American organizations.

[39] See also Chapter 5 "Chinese American Entrepreneurs."

therefore prone to look back, establishing not only direct business links with the booming Chinese economy, but investing in China—thus transferring technology and know how—or even returning to their homeland.

Guanxi *and* Xinyong—*Chinese Business Networking*

One Chinese expression, which ranks among the most-widely used in the West, is *guanxi*. Basically, *guanxi* means "relations," and it stands for connections defined by reciprocity and mutual obligations, a network of family, friends and acquaintances who can provide material or immaterial support of any means, based on personal favors.[40]

These personal relations are very important in China and an essential part of everyday life, especially in business.[41] For the Chinese, these relations are based on a strong personal trust, called *xinyong*.[42] The Sinologist Yen Ching-hwang describes it as follows: "The importance of the concept of *xinyong* in Ethnic Chinese business is beyond doubt. One can probably postulate that Ethnic Chinese business cannot operate without it. Firstly, it functions as a lubricant for Ethnic Chinese business; secondly, it functions as a sanction against any improper business behavior, and thirdly, it short-cuts financial transactions." (2002, 37–42).

These personal relations within the ethnic Chinese community are also a major force behind the relations between Chinese Americans and China, especially since the economic opening in the early 1980s. Foreign Direct Investments (FDI) into China have profoundly transformed the country in the past twenty years and developed it into one of the largest economies in the world. In 2002, FDI in China exceeded $52 billion, making it the largest receiver of foreign capital worldwide, and in 2003 it grew again 3% to $53.5 billion. By contrast, Japan received only $19.5 billion in foreign investments in 2001 and 2002 respectively.

Where does this enormous investment come from? At a first glance, almost 80% comes from Asian countries, America and Europe account only for about 10% each. However, further examination presents a different picture. There are various reasons why the source country may not accurately reflect the origin. Most overseas Chinese investments are made via Hong Kong subsidiaries, not only because of taxes but also to conceal the scale and

---

[40] *Guanxi* is not a personal concept rather it indicates a personal relationship loaded with affection and mutual obligations (King, 1994).

[41] See Zinzius, 2000 and 2004.

[42] The concept of personal trust and connections can be found throughout Asia, but the level of personal relation is much higher among the Chinese community than, for example, in the Korean *chaebol* or the Japanese *keiretsu*, where business relations are regulated more by political or corporate governance and policy, rather than by personal relations.

origin of investments into mainland China (Studwell, 2002, 72-3). Recent studies have further proven that FDI in China is positively related to the population share of ethnic Chinese in the source country, showing the significant role of ethnic Chinese networks in FDI in China (Gao, 2000 and 2002; Tong, 2001).

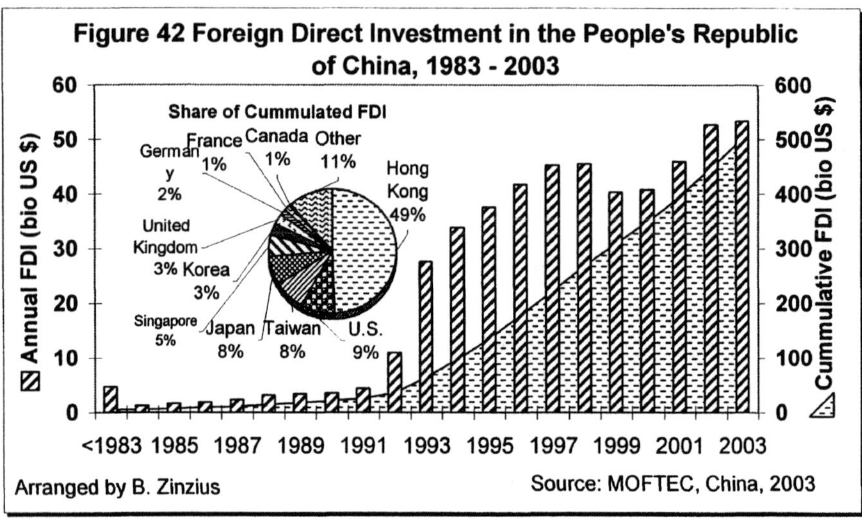

Ethnic Chinese, especially from Southeast Asia, are among the main investors in China. Families and investors, such as Chearavanont from Thailand (their poultry-firm *CP Group* is the largest single investor in China), Riyadi and Liong from Indonesia, Li Ka-shing[43] and Peter Woo from Hong Kong, and Robert Kuok from Malaysia, just to name a few, have all invested billions of dollars in China. These investments are made via international banks, often via a network of banks, which the overseas Chinese community has established themselves. The *Oversea-Chinese Banking Corporation (OCBC), United Overseas Bank Group, Overseas Union Bank,* and *First Pacific* all rank among the hundred largest financial institutions in Asia, and serve specifically ethnic Chinese overseas investors to expand into Southeast Asia, and especially to reinvest in China. The importance of the overseas Chinese investors has long been recognized by the government, including Deng Xiaoping and Zhu Rongji, who mentioned "We sincerely hope that all the overseas Chinese entrepreneurs will continue to participate in China's modernization drive." (Zhu Rongji, 2001).

Their headquarters is often in Singapore or Hong Kong. The banks have subsidiaries throughout the Pacific Rim region, but also numerous branches

---

[43] See also Chapter 8 "Economy: The New *Global Entrepreneurs.*"

in the United States, especially in states with high percentages of ethnic Chinese, such as California and New York. Thus, they are able to channel Chinese American funds into China, as well as from China into America, often via Hong Kong. China is today already the second largest holder of United States Treasury securities with $90.4 billion, only surpassed by Japan with $359.2 billion (*Asian Wall Street Journal*, January 20, 2003, A1, A4).

Table 40 Accumulated Foreign Direct Investment in China by Source Countries[44]

Country or Region	Ethnic Chinese Population		Inward FDI to China (US$ 83–02)	% of total FDI	FDI per Chinese (in US$)	Outward FDI from China (US$, 79-02)
Hong Kong	6.4 mio	94.9%	215.5 bio	45.2%	33,672	4.07 bio
Indonesia	7.3 mio	3.5%	0.9 bio	0.1%	123	0.07 bio
Japan	0.2 mio	0.1%	42.4 bio	7.8%	212,000	0.08 bio
Malaysia	7.6 mio	26.0%	3.1 bio	0.6%	408	-
Philippines	1.2 mio	1.5%	1.3 bio	0.2%	1,083	-
Singapore	3.3 mio	76.8%	27.7 bio	4.7%	8,394	0.07 bio
South Korea	0.1 mio	0.1%	19.2 bio	2.4%	192,000	0.11 bio
Taiwan	22.5 mio	100.0%	41.7 bio	7.1%	1,853	-
Thailand	6.1 mio	10.0%	7.5 bio	0.5%	1,230	0.21 bio
Vietnam	1.9 mio	2.3%	0.5 bio	0.1%	241	0.09 bio
Asia (excl. HK, Taiwan)	**30.3 mio**	**1.7%**	**84.4 bio**	**16.8%**	**278**	4.93 bio
Australia	0.5 mio	2.9%	2.4 bio	0.5%	4,854	0.43 bio
Europe	**0.9 mio**	**0.2%**	**51.0 bio**	**6.3%**	**56,667**	0.26 bio
Canada	0.9 mio	2.8%	1.9 bio	0.4%	2,111	0.84 bio
USA	2.7 mio	0.9%	37.9 bio	8.8%	14,037	0.43 bio
Latin America	**0.6 mio**	**0.1%**	**31.4 bio**	**5.8%**	**52,333**	**0.29 bio**
Total (excl. HK, Taiwan)	**36.1 mio**	**0.9%**	**501.7 bio**	**100%**	**7,694**	9.34 bio

Arranged by B. Zinzius   Source: MOFCOM, China, 2003; governmental sources

[44] Ethnic Chinese Population data derive from individual government Census data, and from Nationmaster, 2004. These figures contain, nevertheless, various sources for incorrect counts. First, ethnic population data are not regularly accounted for in Asia, including mixed-ethnic data. Many of the Chinese that are living since generations in Asian countries have often married outside of their ethnicity, so it is uncertain as to which ethnic group they are attributed. Furthermore, for decades Chinese were persecuted in several Asian countries, especially in Indonesia and the Philippines. To conceal their ethnic origin, Asian overseas Chinese are therefore often hiding their ethnic origin, many even changed their names. Percentages for Indonesian ethnic Chinese range therefore from 1.5% to 6%, depending on the source. Inward FDI data derive from the World Bank and from MOFCOM sources. Taiwanese FDI figures are probably understated as many Taiwanese investors are channeling their funds through third-country subsidiaries, such as Virgin Islands. Economists estimate that Taiwanese investments in China exceeded US$100 billion already in 2000 (Asian Week, July 6, 2001). Outward FDI data are from Savant, 2003; *see also* Gao, 2002. These outbound FDI data show an increasing and new trend of Chinese companies to invest abroad. Many Western countries are experiencing this phenomenon.

With no foreign debt and foreign reserves of over $350 billion, China is the second largest financial power. China is already a major investor in the United States with estimated investments of $30 billion (*Jakarta Post*, December 17, 2002, 17). Strongly increased marketing campaigns for Chinese products are increasingly visible in the United States[45] and Europe, and the Chinese are even investing in Japan (Sauvant, 2003; *Asian Wall Street Journal*, February 7, 2003, A1, A8).

In 2000, Chinese Americans in the United States were estimated to hold investable assets of up to $150 billion. Many brokerage houses have hired bilingual staff that speaks Chinese, and during the peak of the Internet-bubble, Chinese-language websites offering Internet trading received more than five million hits in 1998 (*Businessweek*, September 25, 2000). Chinese Americans are an important part of American industry, and businesses run by Chinese and South Asian entrepreneurs in Silicon Valley account for $19.5 billion in annual sales, and 72,000 jobs.

Examples of Chinese American investors show their increasing interest in China over the past several years, especially in sectors such as Telecommunication, Information Technology and Biotechnology. The Taiwanese-born American Jim Sha, Vice President at *Netscape*, invested in *Sina*, a Chinese Internet Portal that had done one of the most successful IPOs in China. Wu-Fu Chen, also a Taiwanese-born American, was named the *Business Man of the Year* in 2000 by *Red Herring*. He has co-founded fourteen IT-related companies, several have been sold successfully. Jerry Yang, the multimillionaire and founder of *Yahoo!* has several investments in China, including the local website of *Yahoo!*. David Chu, co-founder of *Nautica*, and Jen-Hsun Huang, president of *Nvidia*, have considerably invested in China. Another example is Hao Hong, the president of *Asymchem*. Born in Beijing, Hong has lived in the United States for twenty years and founded *Asymchem* in 1995. In November 2002, he announced a $10 million investment in a high-quality chemical plant in Tianjin. The Hong Kong-born John Chen is one of the latest examples. Educated at Brown University he managed the turnover of Sybase to become one of the largest independent software companies in the world. Sybase has considerable investment in China where it runs 45% of the Telecommunication database market. In 2004, Chen became also a Board Member of the Walt Disney Company, among many other functions. Similar cases of medium-scale

---

[45] Yao Ming is the latest Chinese American sports superstar to arrive in the United States. The seven-foot-five-inch basketball player has earned immediate celebrity status with the Houston Rockets, including a place in the All-Star team in his rookie year. He has multi-million dollar contracts with *Nike*, and Chinese companies, such as *Yanjing Beer*, have started sponsorships in the NBA and are marketing their products in America.

investments are widespread, but have much less visibility than the large investment of multinational companies. However, their number will continue to increase, and the influence of Chinese Americans in these Sino-American economic relations will further expand.

Guanxi and *xinyong* will be major drivers of business relations within the ethnic Chinese community, giving ethnic Chinese a clear advantage compared to the West in this Pacific Rim axis. A new Asian confidence can not only be seen in the economy and politics, but also in culture. The cultural scene of the Chinese American society is moving on to take on a leading role.

Cultural Awakening

Although the Chinese were closely connected to the civil rights movements of the 1970s, their new ethnic identity was not reflected in American culture. The prerequisites for an artistic self-expression of the Chinese in America have long been disadvantageous. Confucian tradition dictated: face had to be kept, strong feelings could not be publicly displayed, and were therefore unsuitable for Western art forms, such as literature, theater, or movies. Problems were not to be discussed openly, neither in the family, nor in the Chinese community, and especially not in front of the broader American public.

The special history of immigration had nevertheless determined the fates of many families, who had overcome many hardships either individually or collectively. In the middle of the 1970s, a public movement to search for a Chinese immigrant identity started slowly among Chinese Americans, something that would have previously been deemed impossible. Such a movement could only start within a new generation, being closer to the American way of life than to the traditions of their parents. Also, this generation had to be old enough to articulate themselves.

Meissenburg indicates that only fully assimilated members of a minority would be able to conquer the problems they had to overcome in the process of acculturation. On the contrary, Chinese American literature cannot be brought so easily into such a scheme. One fraction tries to confirm their contribution to the American society, the other in contrast is quite militant; assimilation versus ethnic pride and identity. In Meissenburg's analysis, the social problematic of the artists is undervalued, and the importance of the assimilation process overrated.

Thus, it is necessary to evaluate critically whether *cultural awakening* is a part of acculturation, rather than just a result of it. Chinese American art as a whole participates in this process, independent of diverging opinions regarding the relevance and importance of the content of the art.[46]

Lacking social recognition for certain professions—especially within a society counting on fast success—posed a problem for writers and performers both among the White and Chinese Americans. This situation changed with the Chinese's increasing commercial success and their recognition by the public. At the front of literary developments came Maxine Hong Kingston and Frank Chin, both born in 1940, followed by a younger generation of writers born in the 1950s and 60s, who have been increasingly successful since the end of the 1980s.

Amy Tan's *The Joy Luck Club*[47] (1989) became the most successful bestseller of a Chinese American woman surpassing Kingston's *Woman Warrior*. Young women are interested in the past of their mothers, thus discovering China and learning about themselves.[48] The novel *The Joy Luck Club* begins with an introduction that deliberately contains a parable of occidental Christian culture:

> "The old woman remembered a swan she had bought many years ago in Shanghai for a foolish sum. The bird, boasted the market vendor, was once a duck that stretched its neck in hopes of becoming a goose, and now look!—it is too beautiful to eat."

This parable clearly reflects the story of the ugly duckling becoming a swan. Symbols and metaphors of various kinds are the basis of the metamorphosis of the useful but ugly duckling into the pretty but useless swan. This parable represents the dream of a different, better, and fulfilled life, of the wishes and hopes of her mother, who immigrated to the United States hoping to live a better life. It is also a metaphor of the dreams of her mother, now projected onto her daughter, overlooking that she is no swan but a small duckling. For example Suynan Woo, a Chinese mother, who strongly believed that America is the land of endless possibilities where everything is possible. She thus tried to make a *Wunderkind* out of her daughter Jing-mei. She wanted nothing more than that her daughter to become a second Shirley

---

[46] For the definition and development of the Chinese American literature see Meissenburg, Karin. *Writings on the Wall*, 1987, 11–27.

[47] *The Joy Luck Club* sold over 4,000,000 copies and received the *National Book Award* and the *New York Times Book Award* in 1989. The book was translated into 25 languages—including Chinese. In 1990, Tan received the *Bay Area Book Reviewers Award for Fiction* (*Fred Cody Award*) and the *Commonwealth Club Gold Award*.

[48] Amy Tan was born in 1952, 2–½ years after her parents had emigrated from China to the United States. Her father, an electronic engineer, and her brother died within a few months of each other of brain cancer when she was fifteen. According to her mother, Amy should have been a doctor and hobby pianist. Instead she studied linguistics and actively worked with disabled. Today she lives with her husband in San Francisco and New York.

Temple, or at least a concert pianist. The daughters in Tan's book are proud of their mothers and admire their strength and sharp senses. They are full of softness when listening to the tragic and beautiful stories from their mother's homeland, and they love them unconditionally. They nevertheless suffer under immoderate demands, which the mothers connect to their deep love. Quite often they react bitterly at their mothers' involvement in their private lives. Sometimes they are also ashamed of their mothers, keeping to their antique, superstitious beliefs. Ideas that do not fit their lives. What then happened to the woman from Shanghai and her swan? During the immigration to America, custom officers confiscated the swan. All she had was a feather and the memories of her beautiful, adorable swan. She wants to tell this story to her daughter, but she still waits—even being already quite old—until she can tell this story in "perfect English." The swan becomes a symbol of her life in China, an experience she wants to share with her daughter but is unable to do because her dream has become true for her daughter: "Over there nobody will look down on her because I will make her speak only perfect American English." Therefore, the mother, not being able to express herself in perfect English, is unable to tell this story, the symbol of her own life. Alone in a strange country, whose language she could not master, the American Dream that has come true for her daughter estranges her more and more. Whereas the mother is still close to Chinese culture and tradition, the daughter tries to integrate her into the American mentality as much as possible. This disruption, the impossibility of combining two worlds, is expressed in the words of the mother Lindo Jong from *The Joy Luck Club*: "I wanted my children to have the best combination: American circumstances and Chinese character. How could I know these two things do not mix?"[49] Amy Tan's mother Daisy, a daughter of a wealthy Shanghai family, had to leave three daughters from her first marriage behind. In *The Kitchen God's Wife* (1991), her second bestseller, Amy Tan tells the story of her mother's life. As in *The Joy Luck Club*, Amy Tan talks about Chinese mothers and their American daughters, about secrets of the old and the lures of the New World. Winnie Louie sees herself forced to tell her daughter the whole truth about her life. Thus she tells her daughter about the magic and the terror of her youth, the gruesome disappointment of her first love, and about the fire and kitchen god and his wife.

In 1995, Tan published the bestseller *The Hundred Secret Senses*, a magic realistic novel about a cross-cultural relationship between two half-sisters. The story centers on the Taiping Rebellion of the 1850s and 60s. After several years working on her latest book, she realized after the death of her mother that she did not know much about her. *The Bonesetter's Daughter*

---

[49] *The Joy Luck Club*. Amy Tan, 1989, 289.

(2001), her fourth novel, focuses again on cross-generational relationships. Tan creates a tale of old China and contemporary California, a mixture of grief and memory, beauty and excavation, woven through the intricate world of mothers and daughters. In the acknowledgements of *The Bonesetter's Daughter* she writes, "The heart of this story belongs to my grandmother, the voice to my mother." Another Chinese American artist addressing generational conflict is Wayne Wang, who has made a movie based on Amy Tan's book *The Joy Luck Club* (1993).[50] Here, he continued a theme used in his earlier films, such as *Chan is Missing* (1981), *Dim Sum* (1985) and *Eat a Bowl of Tea* (1989).

Wang turned to a non-Asian theme in his project *Smoke* (1995), a relaxed and talky character study, which was followed by the feature adaptation of Mona Simpson's *Anywhere But Here* (1999). His most recent project is *The Center of the World* (2001), a dark look at sexual mores. In *Dim Sum*, he playfully yet poignantly examines the conflict between a widowed Chinese mother and her Chinese American daughter. Geraldine's mother, in expectation of her own death, is pressing her for marriage. The sense of duty towards her mother prevents Geraldine from moving into her own household, since she knows that her mother will not marry again. A second marriage is unthinkable for the Confucian-raised mother. These conflicts between Chinese traditions and American values are the center stage of many Chinese American writings, movies and theater plays. The importance of this generational conflict and its variations runs much deeper than a mere literary motif and deserves more attention. A main motif for the Chinese American art scene is the problem to define one's location. The individual is largely identified through society and history, and he or she has special obligations towards his or her family. A separation process from the parents, as occurs in the Western society, is not practiced in the Confucian system, as we have seen in the earlier family-sociological chapters in this study.

In addition to Amy Tan, Maxine Hong Kingston is the best known Chinese American author since World War II.[51] She is married to an American of Russian-Jewish and Irish-Portuguese descent that was born in Stockton, California.

---

[50] In the making of *The Joy Luck Club*, a highly publicized adaptation of Tan's novel, Wang moved decisively towards mainstream. Produced for Disney's Hollywood Pictures, the critically acclaimed film opened with excellent box office receipts in major urban centers and became a solid success.

[51] President Clinton honored Kingston's accomplishments in thought and culture with the *National Humanities Medal* in 1997.

Her father emigrated in the 1920s from a village in the four districts of Guangdong—the classical emigration area of southern China. His wife followed in 1939, one year later Maxine was born. Her parents lived in poor conditions and earned their living in the laundry business. Although they had lived for many years in America, they still only spoke "Sze Yap," the dialect of the four districts.[52] The strongly autobiographical character of her works is typical of Chinese American art.

The autobiographical character is, however, less a result of adaptation than of the necessity to digest the differences between the cultures of their country of origin and their present homeland. Contrasts between these poles can be so extreme that the search for a stable personality is quite difficult, if not totally impossible. Finding one's place is an unstable, continuous, and flowing process, and still is a major objective for many authors. Because autobiography is a trait coming from Occidental-Christian culture and remains a strange concept for Chinese, it often becomes a stumbling block for them. Kingston's books are exotic Western novels for those—especially Frank Chin—who deem traditional Chinese elements as worthy of development and try to build a bridge across both cultures based on these elements. It is a serious and not yet settled conflict among Chinese American writers and artists.

Kingston's first novel, *The Woman Warrior: Memoirs of a Girlhood among Ghosts* (1979) tells five different stories of women in which the mother-daughter relationship plays a central role. The literary "I" position of the author melts with a figure of the Chinese mythology—the sword fighter—and escapes her own childhood. The differentiation between fiction and reality is Western. Kingston places the Chinese form on the side of the fiction. The autobiographic and, for us, the real side corresponds to patterns of perception of the White America.

In Kingston's novel, the Chinese fighter—now the mother of Maxine—becomes a slave and wife in an American sphere between fiction and reality. She escapes her sad existence by telling wonderful tales. Like her mother, Maxine feels expelled. Out of protest, the daughter remains silent for years in her new environment. The liberation in a loud, direct, and American way gives Maxine the possibility to voice her story, which would not have been possible by using traditional Chinese styles—and especially as a woman. Having overcome her speechlessness, the author now has the possibility to use the English language as an expression of her shock, to write about herself

---

[52] Maxine Hong Kingston teaches as a senior lecturer at the University of California, Berkeley's Department of English. In 1990, she received the call from the Chancellor Dr. Chang-lin Tien. Prior to that, she had taught in Californian high schools, as well as at the Business College in Honolulu, Hawaii.

and the traditions of her family. The flowing boundaries between mythology and the sparse details of reality—which have no linear line—make it difficult to find a niche for *Woman Warrior*.

The concept and the different literary techniques, such as the flashbacks and visions of the future and the use of the Chinese mythology and poems, speak against the novel's classification as autobiography in the classical sense.[53] The subjectivity seems to be deliberately set in contrast to the militant parts. The individual is largely dominated by the symbols of existence, such as "wife" and "Chinese American."

The novel *China Men* (1980), which Kingston wrote parallel to *Woman Warrior,* was conceptualized as a male counterpart to the silent fighter.[54] Descriptions about the departure of her ancestors for the Holy Land America are a mixture between fiction and reality. The story of the "Golden Mountain" is based on a true historical story. Again, there are several stories, spanning three generations. The father, having been educated as a teacher in China, vents his frustrations towards the family because the laundry business in America does not bring the expected success. He sanctions his family by silence.

The grandfather works for the Central Pacific Railroad and loses his job after completion of the transnational railroad line to California. As an American citizen, he vegetates without family and is plagued with homesickness, until the family brings him back to China. The daughter does not understand him. The great-grandfather, having landed as a sojourner in Hawaii, had become union leader of sugar cane workers at a shout party. Language becomes his weapon. Thus, although generation-wise very distant, he is the closest ally of the daughter. Language and speechlessness again become main topics. The generational conflict turns into a field of tension between speechlessness and discovery of a new language. In Chapter Four, several of the author's relatives appear. They represent different positions towards the old and new homeland within one family. The cousin, fighting in World War II on the American side, resists the call of the mother to go back to the old homeland. When she dies, however, he is haunted by guilt, which he can only overcome by visiting her grave in China. Another relative sees California as his new homeland, despite the fact that his wife lives in China and in contrast to his Communist uncle. This uncle only eats bran out of fear that the Capitalists might poison him. All three figures in *China Men* express that a breach with the old homeland is impossible. The necessary respect towards parents, obligations for the wife, political positions, and the existence in America are all based on connections to the Chinese homeland.

---

[53] Maxine Hong Kingston. "Cultural Mis-Readings by American Reviewers." 1982, 55–56.
[54] *China Men* won the 1981 *American Book Award* and was runner-up for the *Pulitzer Prize*.

The stressful relationship to China, the generational conflict, and the language are the main topics of Chinese American art and can be found consequently in a broad spectrum of works. A major sign of differentiation is found in variation of the main characters' views towards China: A fusion of different cultures, a rediscovery of old cultural roots that determine the future even in a strange environment, or a coexistence of both cultures side-by-side.

Frank Chin's anthologies of Chinese American writers *"Aiiieeeee!"* and *"The Big Aiiieeeee!"*–already the titles suggest a scream coming out of speechlessness—present the fates of different immigrants in forms based on Chinese tales.[55] Both, Kingston and Chin studied at Berkeley. Whereas Chin remained directly part of the Chinese American art community in California, Kingston moved for seventeen years to Hawaii, where she turned to scholarly work and became a visiting Professor at the University of Hawaii, Honolulu. She returned to the Bay Area in 1984, and—since 1990—teaches at the University of California, Berkeley.[56] Chin reproaches Kingston—as well as other writers such as David Henry Hwang and Amy Tan—for superimposing Christian-White preconceptions onto the Chinese legends and for building facile stereotypes of Chinese Americans on them, although they know those legends only from storytelling. Chin claims that Kingston reinvented the hero of a well-know children's song with her sword-fighting hero. This hero has the character of a Western White woman who is a victim of the Chinese culture (*The Big Aiiieeeee!*, 1991, 5). Maxine Hong Kingston, on the other side regards Chin as a macho, who does not stand for a particular identity and is unable to accept a female literary success.

Kingston's novel, *Tripmaster Monkey. His Fake Book* (1989),[57] tells the story of a crazy Chinese American writer living an easy life in San Francisco in the 1960s. The character fits Kingston's literary counterpart, Frank Chin. Thus, this story is part of the dispute between Chin and Kingston. The stereotypes that Chin points out, and that have nothing to do with the real feelings and fate of the immigrants, can be easily seen in David Hwang's play, *M. Butterfly* (1988).[58]

---

[55] See *Amerasia*, 1991, 162–164; 81–103.

[56] See Chapter 6 "Education," under "Chinese Staff and Ethnic Diversity."

[57] *Tripmaster Monkey: His Fake Book* earned the 1989 PEN West award.

[58] The author David Hwang, his father, a Shanghai banker, and his mother, a professor of piano, received the *Tony Award* for the best American play for his *"M. Butterfly."* David Hwang was born in 1957 and studied at the University of Southern California. His play *M. Butterfly*, a large success in the US and now also on stage in England, is based on a true story. The diplomat Rene Gallimard remembers in his cell the beautiful Chinese Diva, who enchanted him with her love. He completely falls in love with this fragile, adorable lady. She looks to him like a butterfly: fragile and untouchable. Why should he assume that this beautiful lady is a spy working for the Chinese government? How should he know that this

In this play, based on a true story, a French diplomat falls in love with a Chinese opera singer, playing a women's role and only at the end revealing his true identity. Critics see a concession toward White American taste in the figure of the leading actor, emphasizing the exotic and feminine features of Asian men. Positive voices see it as an ideal vehicle of criticism of imperialism, racism, homophobia, and sexism. Hwang's latest musical, *Flower Drum Song*, opened in 2002. It strives to create an authentic atmosphere of the Asian American club scene of the 1950s, while at the same time, aiming to show the complexity and richness of Asian American people.[59]

Frank Chin is also connected to the theater. He founded the *Asian American Theater Company* in San Francisco and received honors for his plays *Chickencoop Chinamen* and *Year of the Dragon. Chickencoop Chinamen* was the first Chinese American play to be well-received in New York. Chin's comment towards David Hwang's play, *M. Butterfly*, which can be read in the introduction of *The Big Aiiieeeee!*, was quite severe: "The good Chinese man, at his best, is fulfillment of the white male homosexual fantasy, literally kissing white ass. Now Hwang and the stereotype are inextricably one." (Chan, Jeffrey, 1991, xiii). Hwang said in an interview that Chinese Americans have to go through different phases in order to find themselves. The first one would be quite easy—to please the White American environment. Chin's comments, however, emphasize that within the Chinese American art community, there can be little tolerance for differences in tone.

Chin continues his crusade against standardized pictures of Chinese Americans in his novel with the fitting title *Donald Duck* (1991). *Donald Duck* is a twelve-year-old boy who considers his family unworthy of him. He does not want to be Chinese and hates living in Chinatown. He would prefer to be Fred Astair than the son of a Chinese restaurant owner. *Donald Duck's* attitude changes however when he starts to receive nightly visits from mythological figures and his forefathers, who worked in the railroad

---

person even was a man? Was his love a phantom, or have his senses been captured by a vision? *M. Butterfly* is the story of a man falling to a vision, a man creating a lover out of his passion, a man as a casualty of his own imagination. In 1998, Hwang earned three *Tony Award* nominations for his recent Broadway production *Golden Child.* In his most personal and emotional work to date, he draws on true stories of his great-grandfather's break with Confucian tradition and the impact of these decisions on succeeding generations.

[59] *Flower Drum Song* is originally a novel by C.Y. Lee (1957), which was the basis for the homonymous 1960s musical and film by Rodgers and Hammerstein, the first musical and movie about and starring Asian Americans, to reach an international audience. Labeled "inauthentic" because it was created by non-Asians, it centers around Asian American stereotypes of the 1950s and 60s, and the so-called *Chop Suey Circuit*, Cotton Club-like night spots featuring Asian revues. Hwang, October 13, 2002. <http://senrs.com/a_new_musical_by_rodgers_and_hwang.htm> (November 12, 2002).

construction business. He learns to see himself and the culture and identity of his forefathers in a new light. Chin's hints towards the American stereotypes of Chinese heroes are very clear. In his novel *Gunga Din Highway* (1994)

Chin continues his assault against Chinese stereotypes.[60] The novel is a furious tour of American cliché and movie making. Longman Kwan is a film and TV actor who specializes in "The Chinamen Who Dies" and Charlie Chan's son number four. His son Ulysses, however, wants nothing to do with authentic Chinese culture: A Chinese American father-son struggle, pointing out stereotypes. Chin's most recent book, *Bulletproof Buddhist*, continues his ironic style, making him one of the most visible voices in Chinese American writing today.

How close even the title of Frank Chin's *Donald Duck* comes to reality documents the name of the movie director Wayne Wang. Wang's parents fled from Shanghai to Hong Kong in 1949. His mother gave him the name of the Hollywood idol John Wayne, whom she first saw in the movie *"Red River"* shortly before in Shanghai. Arthur Dong takes up those stereotypes again in his 1989 documentary movie, *The Forbidden City*. The movie tells about the first Chinese American nightclub in San Francisco in the glamorous 1930s and 40s. Here, the viewer sees the Chinese Americans not from the known family perspective but as an ensemble of actors who try to gain their role in the society by imitating famous American movie stars, thus building a bridge between the societies. Interviews, archive material, and pictures reconstruct the elite and international atmosphere of the appearance of the "Chinese Frank Sinatra" or "Chinese Fred Astair."

Fae Myenne Ng belongs to a new generation of Chinese American writers. She worked over ten years on her first novel *Bone* (1993), a story of a family of three daughters from San Francisco's Chinatown.[61] She received many awards for *Bone*, including the selection as one of the "best of young American novelists" by the highly regarded publication *Granta*, but some Chinese Americans also criticized the novel because "it is not their story."

One of the most recent Chinese American writers to win high accolades is Ha Jin, a former member of the People's Liberation Army, who was born in Liaoning Province in northern China and emigrated in 1985 to the United States. His novel *Waiting* (1999) received the *National Book Award* for fiction in 1999, as well as the *PEN/Faulkner Award*.

---

[60] *Gunga Din* (1939) is a controversial movie starring Cary Grant about racial tensions in the British-occupied India. The hero is the Indian water-carrier Gunga Din, who, despite being ridiculed by all, sacrifices his life to become a British soldier.

[61] Ng received the *Lila Wallace–Reader's Digest Literary Fellowship*, the *Pushcart Prize*, a *National Endowment for the Arts Award*, and a *Fellowship in Literature from the American Academy of Arts and Letters* for *Bone*.

Ha Jin lives with his wife and their son outside of Atlanta, where he is Young J. Allen Professor of English and Creative Writing at Emory University.[62]

Generation conflicts and intra- and inter-cultural struggles of Chinese Americans are not only a major theme in mainstream American literature, but in an increasing number of children's books.[63] Laurence Yep, a native Chinese American, is the leading author of Chinese American children literature.[64] His highly acclaimed *Golden Mountain Chronicles* series, a sequel to his book *Child of the Owl* (1977), comprises seven books until to date. The series deals with Chinese American history from a child's perspective, bringing topics such as immigration and cross-cultural issues to American children and young adults. Since his fist success, *Dragonwings*, the need for cultural tolerance is a prevalent topic in Yep's work.

Professor Russell Young, a second-generation Chinese American, who teaches education at the San Diego State University, has published five children's books. His latest work *Dragonsong: A fable for the New Millennium* (2000) was the recipient of the *National Association of Multicultural Education Children's Book Award* in 2000. Huy Voun Lee's title *At the Beach* tells the story of Xiao Ming, who learns to write Mandarin in the sand (1994). The book was recommended by the *American Booksellers Association*. Mainstream Chinese American authors also write for children, including Amy Tan. Her books *The Moon Lady* (1992) and *The Chinese Siamese Cat* (1994) are being developed into a children's television series. Recently, children's books cover increasingly diverse topics, such the growing number of adoptions of Chinese children. *Our Baby from China: An Adoption Story* is a pictorial about White Americans picking up their newly adopted daughter in China (D'Antonio, 1997).[65] The fast-growing list of children's books reflects the number of native-born and *hapa* Chinese Americans.

---

[62] Jin earned his doctorate in 1993 from Brandeis University. He published two collections of poetry, *Between Silences* (1990), and *Facing Shadows* (1996), and two collections of short fiction, *Ocean of Words* (1996), which received the *PEN/Hemingway Award*, and *Under the Red Flag* (1997), which won the *Flannery O'Connor Award*.

[63] Smith gives a detailed overview of Chinese American children literature (Smith, 2002).

[64] Yep was born in 1948 in San Francisco and attended parochial school in Chinatown, where he felt like an outsider because he spoke no Chinese. Since the 1970s, Yep has published over 60 children's books on Chinese and Asian American topics. He won numerous awards, among them the *Boston Globe-Horn Book Award* in 1977 (for *Child of the Owl*) and in 1989 (for *The Rainbow People*), the *America's Children's Book of the Year Award* in 1986 (for *Dragon Steel*), and the *Focal Award* in 1992.

[65] China is the largest source for foreign adoptees in the United States. See Chapter 3 "Chain Migration."

Several themes in Chinese American art combine literary contrasts, but literature, movies, and theater. Awakening from silence is followed by a fight with different identities—the Chinese, the American, and the Chinese American—and exactly in this order. Thus, the literary fiction often sees a triad of places, China, Chinatown, and the attempt to escape, e.g. towards the white suburb. An example is Wyman Wong's comedy *Whiskey Chicken*,[66] which is set in Chinatown in the 1950s. A family tries to escape the ghetto by moving to the suburb. Everybody is united behind the idea except for the patriarch of the family, who does not want to leave Chinatown. The actor playing the stubborn family head, Dennis Dun, talks about a new role for Chinese American actors: A monster who drinks, behaves beastly, and is sarcastic. Dun is used to playing different roles, and by doing this one he believes he can learn about different aspects of his own personality.

TV-movies and advertisements do not interest him but nevertheless give him the opportunity to be accepted as an American. As a representative of a foreign culture, Dun also played successful roles in movies such as Bertolucci's *The last Emperor* as well as Michael Cimion's *The Year of the Dragon*. But his passion is geared towards plays such as *Whiskey Chicken*, where he feels he can develop his own Chinese American identity (*San Francisco Examiner*, February 1, 1990).

In the play, Dun experiences in three different working areas what the novel is telling in separate living situations. In everyday business, all three identities are often mixed. Nelly Wong, who belongs to a militant-communistic tradition in the Chinese American reality,[67] describes this in her poem "Where Is My Country?". She reflects on language skills:

Channeled in the white businessman
Who discovers that I do not sound Chinese?
Garbled in a white woman
Who tells me I speak perfect English?
Webbed in another
Who tells me I speak with any accent?
Where is my country?
Where does it lie?

---

[66] Wyman Wong grew up in the Bay Area and worked at the *Examiner*, after which he became editor for the *New York Daily News*, being responsible for "Entertainment."

[67] Nelly Wong is an activist in the *Freedom Socialist Party* and a member of the women's group *Radical Women*. Her poems have been published in many anthologies and journals, and in books such as *Dreams in Harrison's Railroad Park* (1977) and *The Death of Long Steam Lady* (1986). She is a member of *Affirmative Action* at the University of California, San Francisco.

In *China Boy* (1991), Gus Lee describes his own fate. The seven-year-old Kai Ting grows up in San Francisco in the 1950s. His father is a former *Kuomintang* officer from Shanghai. After immigrating to the United States and after the death of his mother, he marries a white woman. His stepmother becomes a missionary figure in their life. She tries to deprive the immigrants of all cultural ballast. "No Chinese food, no songs or books, and no Chinese spoken here. The family must learn to eat liver and sauerkraut without chopsticks." (*Asian Week*, July 26, 1991, 15). The antipathy against his stepmother and his Confucian education are handicaps. Gus alias Kai grows up in a Black neighborhood in San Francisco, where he is stamped an outsider by the Hispanics and Blacks.

The experiences of violence bring the small Kai to learn boxing at the YMCA. In addition to the painful experiences, the book offers many insights into minority relations that are unusual for Asian American literature. Lee constructs an alternate image of the Chinese American: Kai overcomes being an outsider by learning that fighting and physical power belong to Western society. Simultaneously, Lee revives a martial-heroic tradition of the Chinese classic, as in *The Three Kingdoms*.[68]

Gus Lee wants to take up the challenges of his American environment. The path of Kai and Gus splits at the end of the novel, but the further path of the author's life shows the connection to his fictive character. At the age of 17, Gus left his parent's home and went to West Point, where he hardened at least his body at the military academy. Norman Schwarzkopf encouraged the weak mathematics student to change to the University of California, Davis, where he studied political sciences and law (Interview with Gus Lee). A rare career for a Chinese American.

In 1994, Lee published the novel *Honor and Duty*, the sequel to *China Boy*. Kai Ting, Lee's alias, adapts with ease to the life at West Point. To his surprise, he finds that it is a Chinese institution in Western dress, committed to the ancient saying: "Subdue the self and honor the rituals." Asked about the possibility of another sequel with Kai, Lee indicated: "Yes, I still owe him a capstone for the trilogy. But I haven't formalized yet."[69]

In 2003, Lee published *Chasing Hepburn: A Memoir of Shanghai, Hollywood, and a Chinese Family's Fight for Freedom*. The book is a lively

---

[68] Lo Kuan-chung wrote *The Three Kingdoms*, a collection of legends from the fourteenth century. The deeds of the men and women in *The Three Kingdoms* are based on a certain moral codex. Charity, brotherly love, and equality were the ideal living rules. Those, not obeying these rules were ousted from society, even in case of important military or governmental figures. Leong, Russel. "Frank Chin: An Authentic One." *Amerasia Journal*, vol 14, No. 2, 1988, 164.

[69] After Gus Lee received his law degree in 1976, he entered the Army as prosecutor and judge. His experience in Korea was the basis for the novel *Tiger's Tail* (1996).

memoir that centers around his family during the Civil War in China in the early 1930s.

One genre of Chinese Americans writers is less visible in the United States, those that write in their native Chinese language. Bai Xian Yong, who is openly gay, wrote his novel *Niezy* (Crystal Boys) about a group of homosexuals in Taiwan. Nie Hualing wrote *Sangqing yu Taohong*, a work about an illegal immigrant with a split personality, after she had left Taiwan to live in the United States. These Chinese-language works are published in Taiwan, Hong Kong, and increasingly in China, yet few have been successfully translated into English.[70]

Actor, writer, and director Peter Wang is proud to be a Chinese American. "Even in my wildest dreams I did not imagine that I would ever play Shakespeare" said Wang. "His plays are wonderful, but what do I have to do with them? I do not look like Hamlet at all. I would prefer to play a hero out of Chinese Mythology, an Emperor or a general of the Qing-Dynasty. But nevertheless, it is time to raise our voices and cry out loud what we have to say, so everybody can see that we also have an identity." Chinese American actors and directors try more and more to contribute a piece of their identity into the American culture. Some were able to draw authentic portraits of Chinese Americans. Peter Wang was a Professor of engineering sciences before he worked in the American movie industry. Wang, too, talks about cultural identity, as shown by the visit of a Chinese American in the land of his forefathers. His movie *A Great Wall* is a realistic portrait of a Chinese American family, and Wang plays the leading role as patriarch Leong Fang himself, a father who emigrated from Beijing to the United States. He learns about the difficulties of the Chinese Americans to achieve top positions in the professional world. A less qualified coworker gets the job as general manager because he is White. Leo Fang has a modern family, his wife is American-born, and his son has a White girlfriend. In the fitness studio, his wife is regarded as a White with Asian features, and she gets her Chinese recipes from cookbooks, just as her White friends do. During a visit to Beijing after 30 years—his relatives have never seen her homeland before—especially the son is a cause for embarrassment, continually putting his foot in it by not having any knowledge of Chinese culture. His sloppy appearance is seen as a sign of poverty, his embracing as overly expressive. He loses a table tennis match against a Chinese model pupil at the moment he loses his temper and touches the table. From the son, the daughter of the host family learns the meaning of privacy: to receive the letters from the mother unopened. However, because of the contact with the son Paul, the daughter neglects her studies. For this she has to pay a high price by failing

---

[70] See also Cayley, John, *Contemporary Émigré Writers*. In: Pan, Lynn, (Ed.), 2000, 134–5.

an exam and losing the possibility to go to the University. Several theater companies promote Asian American culture. Among the oldest are the *Los Angeles East West Players* (founded 1965), *New York's Basement Workshop* (1971), *San Francisco's Kearny Street Workshop* (1972), and the *Asian American Theater Company* (1975).[71]

The emergence of new media can also be noted among young Chinese American artists. In 2001, the Tenement Museum in New York has recreated an installation about the life of contemporary Chinese American immigrants in New York in 1997, displaying the "reconstructed" apartment of the Lee family. This exhibition can now be seen in the Internet under the self-ironic title *Banana: A Chinese American Experience.*[72] Video and Internet art has become a new communication tool for Chinese American artists.

Chinese Americans have the need for their own culture as a result of the connection between their historical experience and the living environment. Asian tradition, fight for survival as one of America's color minorities, and their participation in chosen areas of the White Americans civilization reveal a not yet completed fusion process.[73]

It is disputable how far these elements should be merged in order to have something new. Can the fighter from the Chinese mythology be an American housewife? The positions of Frank Chin and Maxine Hong Kingston, leaders of different fractions differ significantly. The proverb that silence is golden and speaking is silver is no longer true in life of Chinese Americans. Chinese American artists have learned to raise their voices. The profession of artist or actor for Chinese Americans, which was rejected by their parents, is now becoming accepted within the community due to growing success.

Existing stereotypes of Asians are changing, and the—until today—limited presence of Asian Americans in contemporary television seems to increase. Early Chinese American movie and television characters depict only Chinese stereotypes, such as Bruce Lee as martial arts specialist, or the Chinese cook Hop Sing in *Bonanza*, played by Victor Sen Yung between 1959 and 1973. One of the earliest Chinese Americans starring in movies was Anna May Wong.[74] Her numerous roles were confined to stereotypes, and glass ceiling prevented her to get a leading role during long career.

---

[71] See also Him Mark Lai, in: Pan, Lynn (Ed.), 2000, 261–273.

[72] See details at: <http://www.tenement.org/banana/lee_home.swf> Further information about Chinese American performing arts, activities, video programs and exhibitions can be obtained through the NYJPW Chinese-American Arts & Culture Association, established by John and Penny Cheng-Hua Wang in New York: <http://www.nyjpw.org>.

[73] Detailed reviews and articles can be found at: <http://www.chinese-art.com>.

[74] Anna May Wong was born as Wong Liu Tsong in 1905 in Los Angeles as daughter of Chinese American immigrants. She played in numerous Hollywood movies between 1922 and 1960, and the stereotypical characters she played had often names like Lotus Blossom.

Until recently, many shows, such as *L.A. Law*, *Chicago Hope*, or *Murphy Brown*, have not included a single regular Asian American character, despite the high percentage of Asians in cities like Los Angeles, New York, or San Francisco. Lucy Liu is a prominent example of how this situation is changing. Born in 1967 as daughter of Chinese immigrants, Liu was raised in the Italian neighborhood of Queens and graduated from Stuyvesant High School and the University of Michigan at Ann Arbor. Fluent in Mandarin and martial arts, she had her break on Fox's *Ally McBeal* in the Episode *They Eat Horses Don't They*. She took the icy role of Ling Woo, suing a radio station for sexual harassment, and was a full-time member between 1998 and 2001. Liu had many more notable screen appearances, including in the *X-files*, *Beverley Hills*, *Nash Bridges*, and *ER*. Recent movies include also two parts of *Charlie's Angels* in 2000 and 2003, together with Drew Barrymore and Cameron Diaz. Her celebrity status has put Chinese Americans in the today's mainstream entertainment. Lisa Lu, Joan Chen, B.D. Wong, and Martin Yan, the PBS cooking show host of *Yan Can Cook*, are further examples.

The anchorwoman Connie Chung has been working as a frontline television journalist for *ABC* for years. Furthermore, actors with full or partial roots in the Chinese American community should also be mentioned, including the highly decorated Keanu Reeves, who has a Chinese Hawaiian father and an English mother. Among directors and producers, Chinese Americans are also becoming increasingly visible and successful. Janet Yang teamed up with Oliver Stone in the movie adaptation of Amy Tan's *The Joy Luck Club*. Amy Chen, an award-winning radio journalist, finished her debut work as filmmaker with *The Chinatown Files* (2001), a video documentary exploring the roots and legacy of the Cold War Chinese American community during the McCarthyism of 1950s and 1960s. The Film, which took ten years to produce, features prominent Chinese Americans, such as Henry Chin, Him Mark Lai, Ling-chi Wang, and Kathy and Rolland Lowe.

Another well-known Chinese American producer is Felicia Lowe, who produced *China: Land of my Father* in 1980.[75] Lowe has taught film production and advanced script writing at Stanford University and San Francisco State University. In 1996, Lowe produced a one-hour documentary of San Francisco's Chinatown. The film *Chinatown* received the *CINE Golden Eagle Award* in 1996, and the *Silver Apple* in 1997 for its outstanding portrait of the neighborhood over 150 years.

She left the United States in the 1930 and found greater artistic freedom in Europe. In the 1940 she returned to Santa Monica, where she died in 1961 of a heart attack.

[75] *China: Land of my Father* received an *Emmy* nomination, a *CINE Golden Eagle* and an *American Film Festival Red Ribbon Award*. Her film *Carved in Silence*, with its historical material about Chinese immigrants on Angel Island, received also several awards. Currently,

The most prominent among the Chinese American producers is Ang Lee. Born in 1954 in Taipei, in 1975 Ang Lee went to the United States, where he studied theater directing at the University of Illinois and film production at New York University. He currently lives in New York. His first internationally acclaimed movie was *The Wedding Banquet* (1993), which earned several awards. With his international reputation growing, Lee directed *Eat Drink Man Woman* in 1994, a film focusing on generation conflicts. After producing several English-language features, such as *Sense and Sensibility* and *Ride with the Devil*, in 2000 he produced *Crouching Tiger, Hidden Dragon*, a Chinese-language Kung Fu movie set in the early nineteenth-century Qing dynasty. The film received fourteen Oscar nominations and sixteen British Academy Award Nominations, finally earning four British Academy Awards and four Oscars, including Best Director and Best Foreign Language Film. With its Chinese theme and phenomenal international success, *Crouching Tiger, Hidden Dragon* opened a new chapter in Chinese American art and its recognition in the United States. In addition to Chinese American filmmakers, some Chinese artists immigrate to America for few years, to return later to their homeland, such as Chen Kaige. Only after his return to China, he could start his career with movies like *Yellow Earth* and *Farewell My Concubine*.

Chinese American musicians have also broken the cultural silence, as in literature and filmmaking. Fred Ho is a successful Jazz musician and composer, combining classical Chinese music with American Jazz. He created a very special, bilingual opera, *A Chinaman's Chance* (1987). The contemporary opera tells about a coolie rebellion on the ship from China to the United States. Music and libretto express fear and anger.

Ho is deeply influenced by the African American musical context of the twentieth century, including Charles Mingus, Duke Ellington, and John Coltrane. The result is an elaborate and soulful music, embracing a new century of American multiculturalism. Ho has composed various other works, including the martial arts ballet and music theater epic *One Upon a Time in America* and a feminist fantasy action opera called *Warrior Sisters: The New Adventures of African and Asian Womyn Warriors*.[76]

Lowe is developing a dramatic, feature-length film based on a novel by Laurence Yep, "Child of the Owl." <http://www.pbs.org/kqed/chinatown/ctbios.thml>

[76] Ho has received several prestigious awards, including *National Endowment for the Arts* and *Arts Music Composition Fellowships*, and a *Distinguished Artist Lifetime Achievement Award* in 1988. His co-edited book *Sounding Off! Music as Subversion / Resistance / Revolution* was the 1996 winner of the *American Book Awards*.

Like Ho, Jon Jang has been a leading Jazz musician and composer in the San Francisco Bay Area. His Album *Self Defense!* deals with anti-Asian violence in the United States. His album *Tiananmen!* is his most influential piece, a song about the riot and slaying that happened in 1989.[77] Ho and Jang are both outstanding artists and are activists in the Chinese American cultural community (Zhang, Wei-hua, 1994). The most influential Chinese American musician is probably the cellist Yo-Yo Ma. Born in 1955 to Chinese parents in Paris, at the age of four his family came to New York. He graduated in 1976 from Harvard, and since then has published over 50 albums, including 14 *Grammy Award* winners.

Yo-Yo Ma established the *Silk Road Project* to promote the study of the cultural, artistic and intellectual traditions along the ancient Silk Road. In addition, he is one of the co-founders of the *Committee of 100*.[78] The formerly silent minority has been swept by a scream of *Aiiieeeee!*, that denies and almost accuses the older, silent immigrant generations. Loudness and force are no longer only a means of suppression for the White society, but a way to freedom for the Chinese Americans.

In the fashion world, award-winning designer Anna Sui has been able to establish a world-renown brand during the 1980 and 1990. She has opened many outlets worldwide, including in Japan. Vivienne Tam, who was born in Guangzhou, China, is also currently one of the most successful designers, and her clothing design try to marry the East with the West, with many inspirations from her homeland China.

One of the highest regarded designers today is Vera Wang. Born in 1949 to Chinese immigrants, she began her design career in 1990, when she presented a highly regarded wedding dress line. Since then, many international celebrities, including Sharon Stone, Meg Ryan, Jane Fonda, and Halle Berry, wear her dresses.[79]

The Chinese American art community is another form of cultural awakening that needs to be mentioned. Hundreds of artists, traditional painters, sculptors, or contemporary performance artists, have immigrated from mainland China or Taiwan, and, together with second or third

---

[77] Jang has also collaborated with esteemed writers and poets, such as Maxine Hong Kingston and Genny Lim. He has also written music for theater, including a dramatic adaptation of Maxine Hong Kingston's *Woman Warrior*. He has received awards from the *National Endowment for the Arts, Cal Performances-UC Berkeley* and the internationally acclaimed *Kronos Quartet.*

[78] See also Chapter 8 "Politics: From Opium Hall to City Hall."

[79] Chinese Americans are also present in other cultural areas, such as sports. Michael Chang, Amy Chow, and Michelle Kwan are high-profile representatives for the Chinese American community.

generation-artists from the United States, are an important part of Chinese American Culture.

Early emigrant painters, such as C.C. Wang found their way to America as students or teachers, whereas later generations often left China to escape political oppression, including Hung Liu, and Gu Wenda. Other internationally renown Chinese American painters include Ai Weiwei, Cai Guaquiang, Chen Yifei, Ting Shao Kuang, and Yeho Yueon-Goyh.[80] Associations such as the *Chinese American Arts & Culture Association,* established in 1997, broaden the support and exposures of Chinese American artists.

For Chinese Americans, cultural awakening means going back to their own roots, but not in the sense of an internal reflection. It is not Chinese literature in Chinese for a Chinese community that brings the success for Chinese American writers, but the digestion of their own history in English, making it available for both cultures. The artistic expression of Chinese immigrants to the United States still has deep, unused potential. Ling-chi Wang indicates that in the cultural area, the Chinese American community has the highest potential for further development. James Ho pointed out the commercial potential of Chinese American arts. He wrote in *Publishers Weekly* that there has not been a more successful ethnic literature since the discovery of the Jewish writers in the 1950s. Chinese American culture and artwork will accompany the Chinese success in the United States critically. Reasons for the success lie, in the increasing population, high level of education, and the economic importance of the Pacific Rim.

Confucianism and bourgeois-enlightened thinking share an attitude of not tolerating contradiction. Both are gender-oriented, define clear and rigid gender roles, and are shaped by their roles of the male and female spheres within their societies. Nevertheless, they mutually exclude themselves. While playing with both systems, the authors slip through the rigidity of both systems. They question the exclusivity of both, for example the strict male and female roles. Situated between cultures, between Eastern mythology and Western history, traditional Chinese collectivism and Western enlightened individualism, they also stand in between both socio-cultural models of reality. The artists soon could achieve what Chinese Americans could not achieve in the professional world: Breaking through the glass ceiling into the elite. This mobility can be shown using a classification scheme that records cultural diversity. The first group is composed of uprooted sojourners, who are culturally bound to China. For them, Chinatown offers a haven from a hostile environment. The second group has been educated—or even born—in

---

[80] For detailed information see *Always Bright: Paintings by American-Chinese Artists.* Xue Jianxin et al. (eds.), Dumont, NJ; Homa & Sekey Books, 1999 (*Vol. I*) and 2001 (*Vol. II*).

the United States and therefore has incorporated many ideas of the American society. Members of the second generation are often totally assimilated, including many of the multiethnic and multiracial *hapas*, who add their cultural identity to the mainstream American population.[81]

Another group loves the homeland but cannot return, perhaps for political reasons. The communistic uncle in Kingston's *Chinamen* is one of these who has accommodated himself, without wanting to be American. The last group, impressed by the civil rights movement, consists of teachers, scientists, and artists, sometimes all in one. They learned that it is well worth preserving *ethnic pride* but require that it be shown on the outside rather than inside. The education of this group does not necessarily lead to negligence of their ethnic identity, as for the totally assimilated, but is used as a vehicle of their affirmation.

---

[81] See also Chapter 4 "Habitat," and Chapter 7 "Interracial Relationships."

9. CONCLUSION

This analysis shows that Chinese Americans are the fastest-growing and most successful minority in the United States. However, delving beneath this general statement, this report reveals that there are no unique Chinese Americans, but that their ethnicity has many diverse facets. Trying to lump them together with stereotypes such as *model minority* focuses on selected, generalizing aspects, while such generalizations do not show the broad spectrum of this ethnic group, such as descent, social and economic layers, values, or their level of assimilation and integration in the United States.

There is a definite cultural identity and solidarity among Chinese Americans, but with many distinct types and different orientations – even within one family. Old Chinese and Taiwanese refugees and emigrants resemble sojourners and adapted Chinese, the earliest immigrants. They contrast with American born Chinese, including those of mixed ethnicity, which have been brought up in the United States, and thus are more a part of its culture. More recently, new immigrant types can be seen: students, professionals and retirees. The students and professionals strive for the American Dream, which the retirees, often affluent Chinese that accompanied their children or relatives, enjoy. This diverse spectrum of cultural roots has nonetheless common grounds. Ethnic Chinese are often proud of their heritage and closely connected among their cultural peers.

The variety of professional success attained by the Chinese and the distribution of the incomes among them are as broad as their differences in their sociocultural orientation. One could say this is typical for all immigrants in the United States. The Chinese, however, are unique in several crucial respects: Many Chinese seem to have a long-term strategy for life, which is rooted in Confucianism, the Chinese system of values and standards.

The community of the family becomes apparent in the reunification of the traditionally separated immigrant families. Until today, family-based immigration is the strongest category for Chinese immigration; even second and third degree relatives were integrated to such an extent that they produced distinct chain migration. At the same time, this large family forms a social net, and so they are rarely dependent on governmental aid. Social success is identified with education. Therefore, a Chinese family often sacrifices greatly to ensure the best education for their children. This pressure leads to extraordinary results in high schools, colleges and universities, often creating *whiz kids*. The top American universities are the main aims of this pursuit of education, and the Chinese intelligentsia does not settle for the mediocre schools in the educational system.

Ethnic infrastructure, including low-wage jobs, exist especially in California's Bay Area and New York City, which still makes these regions the center of attraction for Chinese immigrants. Today, only inexperienced tourists find New York's and San Francisco's Chinatown a romantic must, and their days as an old Chinese ghetto are long past. An ethnically driven economic system offers a wealth of opportunities to Chinese immigrants. The rise of an established merchant middle class and a high rate of employment can be credited to ethnic businesses, which have also undergone a dramatic shift. While apparel manufacturers and sweatshops still exist, many of these low-cost businesses have moved to other countries, such as Mexico or, ironically, mainland China. Ethnic businesses have moved up the value chain and include trade, services and high-tech manufacturing. First-generation immigrants that were supported by an ethnic network of organizations and connections have founded many companies. At the turn of the millennium, Chinese American companies generated already more than 100 billion dollar, especially in high-tech areas like Silicon Valley. Their networking comprises an increasing professional and economic cooperation among the worldwide Chinese diaspora. The Chinese Americans are thus a part of the increasingly important and global network of overseas Chinese, who contribute significantly to the foreign direct investment and economic development in China. Based on their diversity and professional success, the term global or cross-cultural entrepreneur seems therefore more appropriate for the Chinese Americans than the expression model minority. This is especially true for the new immigrants that are realizing the American Dream.

In 2005, more than 2.7 million Chinese Americans were living in the United States, the only major immigrant group, except Asian Indians, which continued to grow significantly during the 1990s, in contrast to European, Hispanics and other Asian ethnicities. Since the 1980s, Chinese Americans have therefore also been recognized as an important consumer group with more than 100 Billion dollar spending power, creating an ethnically oriented market specifically for wealthy Asian and Chinese consumers.

The high concentration of Chinese generates a will to represent their political interests, especially among these born in America. A growing network of large families with political connections is replacing Chinatown and civil rights organizations, and their networking is beginning to embrace local economic and political spheres. The development of the Chinese Americans is continuous and soft-spoken, without drumbeats or violence, following the typical patterns of the ethics of Confucianism and thus going unnoticed by many. This development and the rapid dynamism over the last few years, however, signal the increasing influence of the Chinese in the United States.

Projections indicate that, by 2100, the Chinese American population will grow at least tenfold to 25 million, representing over three percent of the American population. This growth will be caused by the further opening of China and by the equilibrium between immigrants and returnees, a factor that will be strongly influenced by the economic and political developments in China. The continued increase of Chinese immigrants also signals a general shift in the ethnic composition of the American society, which is changing from a eurocenteric to a global, multicultural society. Chinese Americans are gaining the same status that European immigrants have held since the seventeenth century, and they are establishing themselves as an influential, rejuvenating and integral part of the United States.

China's economic growth has already succeeded in partially reversing the brain drain of the 1970s and 1980s, and it is a trend that may well develop into a brain gain. The extraordinary familial links and the ethnic networks help overcome the barriers erected by the White Americans on the way to reaching top management positions and entrepreneurial success. Moreover, the Chinese are moving into key positions in education, politics and American society. By utilizing a strong and influential lobby, their dedicated ethnic loyalty and international networking abilities, the Chinese could acquire a firm grip on American and international economy and politics.

China's development toward the world's largest economy will place the Chinese Americans in a key economic and political position. Their influence and power in the United States will be a crucial element for the development of economic, political and social relations between the two largest economies of the twenty-first century.

APPENDIX

Figure 43 Asian and Pacific Islander Alone Population in the United States, 2000

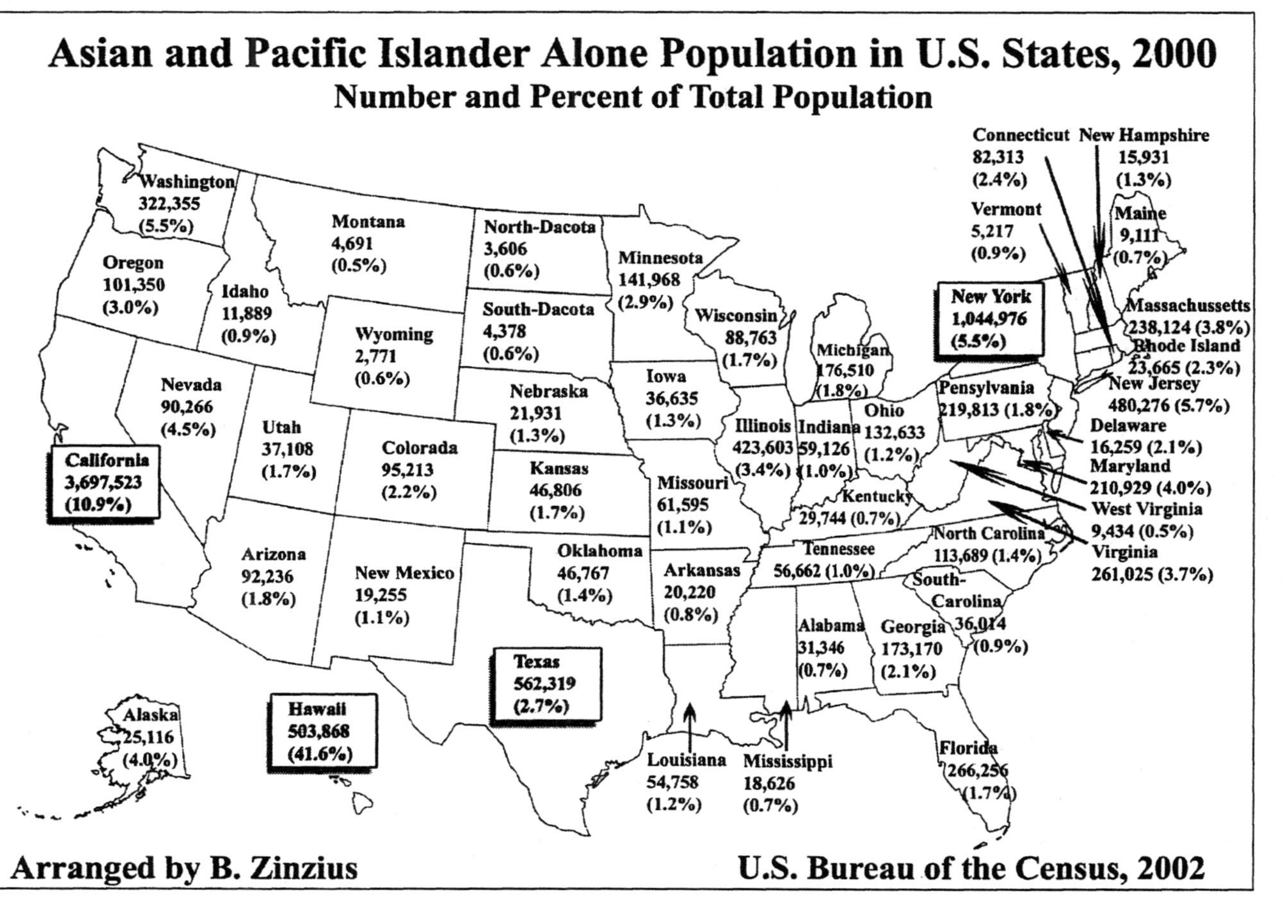

Figure 44 Chinese Alone Population in the United States, 2000

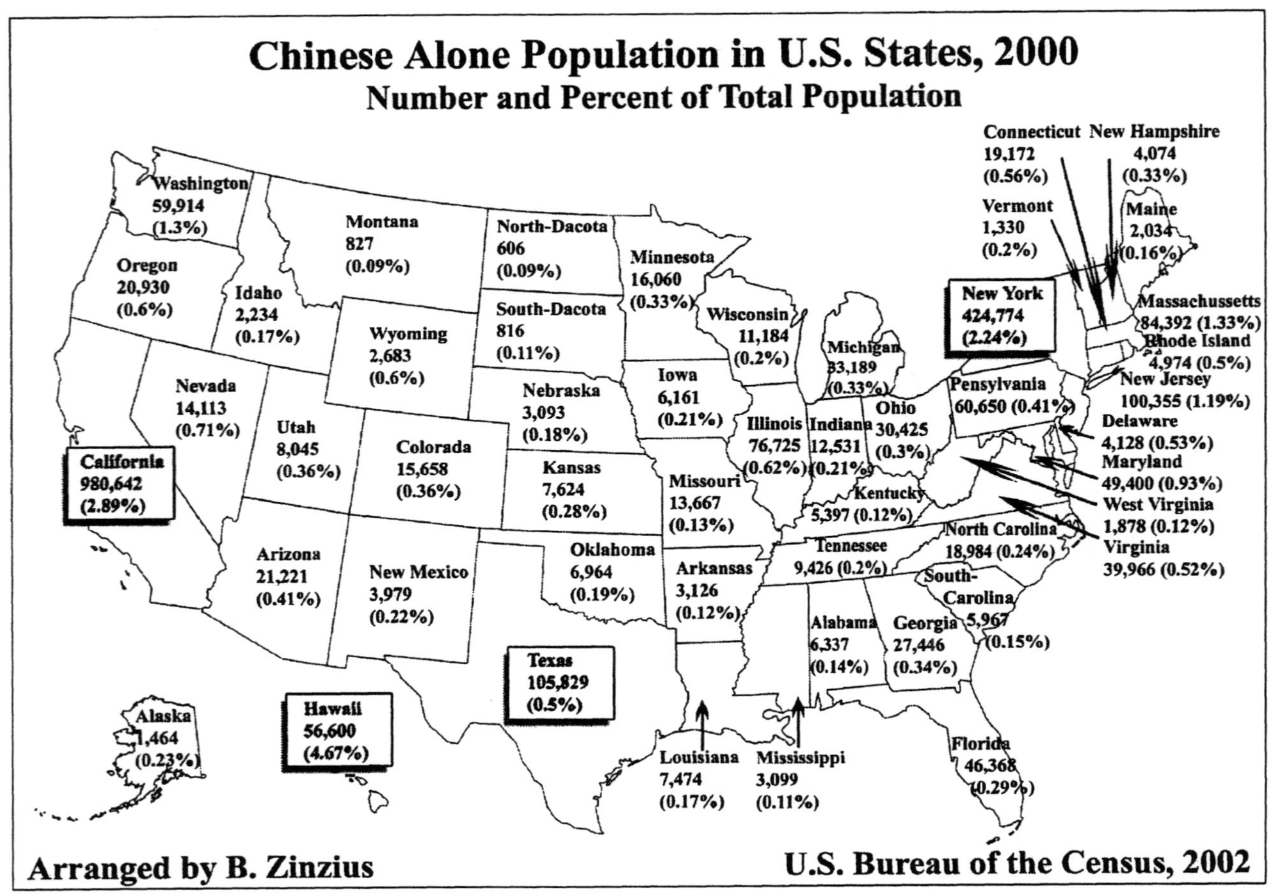

Table 41 Chinese in the United States, by State of Residence 1870-1930						
	1870	1880	1890	1900	1910	1920	1930
Alabama	-	4	48	58	62	59	52
Alaska	-	-	-	-	-	-	-
Arizona	20	1,630	1,170	1,419	1,305	1,137	1,110
Arkansas	98	133	92	62	62	113	251
California	49,277	75,132	72,472	45,753	36,248	28,812	37,361
Colorado	7	612	1,398	599	373	291	233
Columbia (Distr.)	3	13	91	455	378	461	398
Connecticut	2	123	272	599	462	566	391
Delaware	-	1	37	51	30	43	38
Florida	-	18	108	120	191	181	200
Georgia	1	17	108	204	233	211	253
Hawaii	-	-	-	-	-	-	-
Idaho	4,274	3,379	2,007	1,467	859	585	335
Illinois	1	209	740	1,503	2,103	2,776	3,192
Indiana	-	29	92	207	276	283	279
Iowa	3	33	64	104	97	235	153
Kansas	-	19	93	39	16	68	60
Kentucky	1	10	28	57	52	62	60
Louisiana	71	489	333	599	507	387	422
Maine	1	8	73	119	108	161	115
Maryland	2	5	189	544	378	371	492
Massachusetts	87	229	984	2,968	2,582	2,544	2,973
Michigan	1	27	120	240	241	792	1,081
Minnesota	-	24	94	524	508	275	217
Mississippi	16	51	147	237	257	364	561
Missouri	3	91	409	449	535	412	634
Montana	1,949	1,765	2,532	1,739	1,285	872	486
Nebraska	-	18	214	180	112	189	194
Nevada	3,152	5,416	2,833	1,352	927	689	483
New Hampshire	-	14	58	112	67	95	84
New Jersey	5	170	608	1,393	1,139	1,190	1,785
New Mexico	-	57	361	599	248	171	133
New York	29	909	2,935	7,170	5,266	5,793	9,685
North Carolina	-	-	32	80	51	88	68
North Dakota	-	8	28	32	39	124	103
Ohio	1	109	183	371	569	941	1,425
Oklahoma	-	-	38	58	139	261	206
Oregon	3,330	9,510	9,540	10,397	7,363	3,090	2,075
Pennsylvania	13	148	1,146	1,927	1,784	1,829	2,557
Rhode Island	-	27	69	366	272	225	197
South Carolina	1	9	34	67	57	93	41
South Dakota	-	230	195	165	121	184	70
Tennessee	-	25	51	75	43	57	70
Texas	25	136	710	836	595	773	703
Utah	445	501	806	572	371	342	342
Vermont	-	-	32	39	8	11	34
Virginia	4	6	55	243	154	278	293
Washington	234	3,186	3,260	3,629	2,709	2,363	2,195
West Virginia	-	5	15	56	90	98	86
Wisconsin	-	16	119	212	226	251	363
Wyoming	143	914	465	461	246	252	130
United States	**63,199**	**105,465**	**107,488**	**89,863**	**71,531**	**61,639**	**74,954**
Arranged by B. Zinzius				U.S. Bureau of the Census, 1990, Table C1-C11			

Table 42 Chinese in United States, by State of Residence, 1940-2000						
	1940	1950	1960	1970	1980	1990	2000
Alabama	41	187	288	626	1,505	3,929	6,337
Alaska	-	-	137	228	522	1,342	1,464
Arizona	1,449	1,951	2,936	3,878	6,820	14,136	21,221
Arkansas	432	592	676	743	1,275	1,726	3,126
California	39,556	58,324	95,600	170,131	322,309	704,850	980,642
Colorado	216	458	724	1,489	3,897	8,695	15,658
Connecticut	292	450	865	2,209	4,691	11,082	19,172
Delaware	39	85	191	559	998	2,301	4,128
Dist. of Columbia	656	1,825	2,632	2,582	2,476	3,144	3,734
Florida	214	429	1,023	3,133	13,422	30,737	46,368
Georgia	326	511	686	1,584	4,324	12,657	27,446
Hawaii	-	-	38,197	52,039	56,285	68,804	56,600
Idaho	208	244	311	498	905	1,420	2,224
Illinois	2,465	4,207	7,047	14,474	28,597	49,936	76,725
Indiana	208	496	952	2,115	3,986	7,371	12,531
Iowa	81	310	423	993	2,110	4,442	6,161
Kansas	133	315	537	1,233	2,425	5,330	7,624
Kentucky	100	335	288	558	1,318	2,736	5,397
Louisiana	360	526	731	1,340	3,298	5,430	7,474
Maine	92	77	123	206	484	1,262	2,034
Maryland	437	795	2,188	6,520	14,485	30,868	49,400
Massachusetts	2,513	3,627	6,745	14,012	25,015	53,792	84,392
Michigan	924	1,619	3,234	6,407	11,009	19,145	33,189
Minnesota	551	720	1,270	2,422	4,835	8,980	16,060
Mississippi	743	1,011	1,244	1,441	1,835	2,518	3,099
Missouri	334	519	954	2,815	4,280	8,614	13,667
Montana	258	209	240	289	346	655	827
Nebraska	102	202	290	551	1,106	1,775	3,039
Nevada	286	281	137	228	522	1,342	14,113
New Hampshire	63	93	152	420	790	2,314	4,047
New Jersey	1,200	1,818	3,813	9,233	23,369	59,084	100,355
New Mexico	106	166	362	563	1,442	2,607	3,979
New York	13,731	20,171	37,573	81,378	148,105	284,144	424,774
North Carolina	57	345	404	1,255	3,176	8,859	18,948
North Dakota	56	82	100	165	305	557	606
Ohio	921	1,542	2,507	5,305	9,917	19,447	30,425
Oklahoma	112	397	398	999	2,461	5,193	6,964
Oregon	2,086	2,102	2,995	4,841	8,036	13,652	20,930
Pennsylvania	1,477	2,258	3,741	5,461	13,294	29,562	50,650
Rhode Island	257	403	574	1,093	1,718	3,170	4,974
South Carolina	27	101	158	521	1,404	3,039	5,967
South Dakota	36	44	89	163	271	385	816
Tennessee	60	230	487	1,610	2,909	5,653	9,426
Texas	1,031	2,435	4,172	7,635	25,461	63,232	105,829
Utah	1,206	1,175	629	1,281	2,730	5,322	8,045
Vermont	21	34	68	17	271	679	1,330
Virginia	208	565	1,135	2,805	9,360	21,238	36,966
Washington	2,345	3,408	5,491	9,201	18,114	33,962	59,914
West Virginia	57	99	138	373	881	1,170	1,878
Wisconsin	290	590	1,010	2,700	4,097	7,354	11,184
Wyoming	102	106	192	292	392	554	609
United States	77,504	117,629	237,292	435,062	806,040	1,645,472	2,432,858
Arranged by B. Zinzius				U.S. Bureau of the Census Table C1-C11			

BIBLIOGRAPHY

Agnos, Art. *Interview by Birgit Zinzius*, March 6, 1990.

Alba, Richard D., and Nee, Victor. "Rethinking Assimilation Theory for a New Era of Immigration." *International Migration Review*, Vol. 31, 1997, 826-874.

"America's Asians: The Glass Ceiling." *The Economist*, June 3, 1989, 23–26.

American Anthropological Association. "Response to OMB Directive 15: Race and Ethnic Standards for Federal Statistics and Administrative Reporting." 2001, <http://www.aaanet.org/gvt/ombdraft.htm> (March 7, 2003).

Amoroso, Alfonso. "Regional Housing Needs Determination for the San Francisco Bay Area. 2001-2006 Housing Cycle Element." Association of Bay Area Governments. Oakland, CA: Alfonso, June 2001, <http://www.abag.ca.gov/planning/housingneeds> (February 14, 2003).

Anderson, Kay. "Asian Tsunami: The Consumer Counts. The Asian Market." *Home Accents Today*, September 2002, <http://www.homeaccentstoday.com> (March 21, 2003).

Annual Reports 1985–89 Stanford: Committee on Undergraduate Admission and Financial Aids, Stanford University, 1989.

Archdeacon, Thomas J. *Becoming American: An Ethnic History*. New York, NY: The Free Press, 1983.

Asian Women United of California (Ed.). *Making Waves. An Anthology of Writings by and about Asian American Women*. Boston, MA: Beacon Press, 1989.

Association of Bay Area Governments (ABAG). "Bay Area Census. Census 2000 Data." September 13, 2002, <http://www.abag.ca.gov/index.html> (February 12, 2003).

Au, Jeffey K. D. "Philosophical Questions for the 1980's and Beyond". In: Reflections on Shattered Windows. Okihiro, Gary Y., Hune, Shirley, Hansen, Arthur A. and Liu, John M. (Eds.). Pullman, Washington, DC: Washington University Press, 1988.

Au, Yat-Pang. *Interviews by Birgit Zinzius*. 1989.

Auerbach, Frank L. *Immigration Laws of the United States*. Indianapolis: The Bobbs-Merrill Company, Inc., 1955.

Barringer, Herbert R., Gardner, Robert W., Levin, Michael J., and Levin, Michael D. "Asian and Pacific Islanders in the United States." New York, NY: Russell Sage Foundation, 1993.

Barth, Gunther. *Bitter Strength. A History of the Chinese in the United States, 1850-1870*. Cambridge, MA: Center for the Study of the History of Liberty in America, Harvard University, 1964.

Bass, Michael. Das "goldene Tor": die Entwicklung des Einwanderungsrechts der United States. Berlin: Dunker & Humblet, 1990.

"Bay Area Asian Consumers' \$\$: New Study Portrays Asians as Marketers' Dream." *Asian Week*, March 16, 1990, 15-18.

Bay Area Economic Forum. *International Trade And The Bay Area*. "Publications," September, 2001, <http://www.bayeconfor.org/baefpubl3.cfm> (January 20. 2003).

Beaudry, James A. "Some Observations on Chinese Intermarriage in the United States." *International Journal of Sociology of the Ethnicity*, May, 1971, 58-61.

Beck, Louis. *New York's Chinatown. An Historical Presentation of Its People and Places*. New York, NY: Bohemia, 1898.

Bell, David A. "An American Success Story. The Triumph of Asian Americans." *Current*, 277, 1985, 33-39.

Bennet, William. "An Education Success Story: Making Something on Oneself." *Insight*, November 18, 1985, 74-77.

Berk, Bernard B. and Hirata, Lucy Cheng. "Mental Illness among the Chinese: Myth or Reality?" *Journal of Social Issues*, 29:2, 1973, 149-166.

Berling, Judith. "Confucianism." *Focus on Asian Studies*, Asia Society, AskAsia. Vol II, No. 1, 1982, 5-7.

Berlack, Harold. "The Bush Education Agenda; Tested for Failure." Education Policy Project CERAI-01-18, University of Wisconsin-Milwaukee, May 10, 2001.

Between Worlds. Contemporary Asian American Plays. Berson, Misha (Ed.). 1990.

Bevans, Charles I. *Treaties and Other International Agreements of the United States of America, 1776-1949*. Washington, DC, 1971.

Board of Supervisors, City and County of San Francisco. *Narrative Description*. San Francisco, CA: City and County of San Francisco, 1992.

Bouvier, Leon F. "The Fastest Growing Minority." *American Demographics*, May 7, 1981, 31-33, 46.

Bouvier, Leon F. and Agresta, Anthony J. "The future Asian population of the United States." In: Fawcett, James T. and Carino, Benjamin V. (Eds.), *Pacific Bridges*. Staten Island, NY: Center for Migration Studies, 1987.

Bowring, Philip and Lau, Emily. "Turning up the heat. Tougher Chinese line damages colony's prospects." *Far Eastern Economic Review*, February 14, 1991, 23-24.

Brand, David. "The New Whiz Kids." *Time Magazine*, August 31, 1987, 41-47.

Briggs, Vernon M. Jr. Employment Trends and Contemporary Immigration Policy. in: *Clamor at the Gates: The New American Immigration*. Glazer, Nathan (Ed.). San Francisco, CA: 1985, 135-160.

Brown, Fred. *Interviews by Birgit Zinzius*. 1989-1998.

Brown, S. K. *Interviews by Birgit Zinzius*. 1989-1992.

Brownback, Sam, Sen. Backing Hong Kong's Dreamers. *Asian Wall Street Journal*, March 8, 2004, A11.

Bunzel, John H. and Au, Jeffrey K. D. "Diversity or Discrimination? - Asian Americans in College." *The Public Interest*, 87, 1987, 49-62.

Bush, George H.W. "Gung Hay Fat Choy." *Asian Week*, March 1, 1991, 25.

Bush, George H.W. "Message on the Observance of the Lunar New Year, 4689." February 11, 1991, <http://bushlibrary.tamu.edu/papers/1991/91021101> (March 2, 2003).

Bush, George W. "President Bush's Lunar New Year Greetings." February 3, 2003, <http://www.politicalcircus.com/archive/printer_1076.shtml> (March 2, 2003).

Butterfield, Fox. "Are Asian Kids Really Smarter?" *New York Times*, August 3, 1986, 87-91.

Cabezas, Amado, Shinagawa, Larry Hajime and Kawaguchi, Gary "New Inquiries into the Socioeconomic Status of Philipino Americans in California." *Amerasia Journal*, 13:1, 1987, 1-21.

———— and Kawaguchi, Gary. Empirical Evidence for Continuing Asian American Income Inequality: The Human Capital Model and Labor Market Segmentation. In: *Reflections on Shattered Windows. Promises and Prospects for Asian American Studies*. Okihiro, Gary Y., Hune, Shirley, Hansen, Arthur A. and Liu, John M. (Eds.). Pullman, WA: Washington State University Press, 1988, 144-164.

————, Tam, Tse Ming, Lowe, Brenda M., Wong, Anna S. and Turner, Kathy. Empirical Studies of Barriers to Upward Mobility for Asian Americans in the San Francisco Bay Area. In: *Frontiers of Asian American Studies. Writing, Research, and Commentary*. Nomura, Gail M., Endo, Russel, Sumida, Stephen H. and Leong, Russel C. (Eds.). Pullman, WA: Washington State University Press, 1989, 85-97.

————. *Interview by Birgit Zinzius*, February 28, 1990.

Cahn, Steven M. *The Affirmative Action Debate*. London: Routledge, 2002.

California Advisory Committee. *Asian Americans and Pacific Peoples: A Case of Mistaken Identity*. Washington, DC: U.S. Government Printing Office, 1975.

California State Senate. *Chinese Immigration. The Social, Moral and Political Effect of Chinese Immigration. Policy and Means of Exclusion*. Sacramento, CA: 1877.

California Statutes. Sacramento, CA: 1855-1882.

Career Resources Development Center. *Bringing People and Jobs Together*. San Francisco: Career Resources Development Center, 1991.

Carey, Paul. *Interviews by Birgit Zinzius*, 1992.

Cervantes, Mario and Guellec, Dominique. "The brain drain: Old myth, new realities." Organisation for Economic Co-operation and Development, *OECD Observer*, May 7, 2002, <http://www.oecdobserver.org> (September 12, 2002).

Chan, Jeffey P., Chin, Frank, Inada, Lawson F. and Wong, Shawn (Eds.). *The Big Aiiieeeee! An Anthology of Chinese American and Japanese American Literature*. New York, NY: Penguin Books United States Inc., 1991.

Chan, Kenyon S. and Tsang, Sau-Lim. Overview of the Educational Progress of Chinese Americans. In: *The Education of Asian and Pacific Americans: Historical Perspectives and Prescriptions for the Future*. Phoenix, Arizona: Oryx Press, 1983, 39-49.

Chan, Majorie K.M. and Tai, James H.Y. "A Critical Review of Norman's *Chinese*." *Journal of the Chinese Language Teachers Association*, 1989, XXIV.1:43-61.

Chan, Sucheng. *Contemporary Asian Immigration and Its Impact On Undergraduate Education At The University of California, Berkeley*. 1981 (Unpublished).

———. *This Bittersweet Soil. The Chinese in California Agriculture, 1860-1910*. Berkeley, CA: University of California Press, 1986.

———. *Asian Americans*. Boston, MA: Twayne Publishers, 1991.

Chang, Chin-tsen. "Li and Law." *Chinese Culture*, 2:4, 1960, 1-17.

Chang, Iris. *The Chinese in America*. New York, NY: Viking Press, 2003.

Chang, Jeffrey. *Interview by Birgit Zinzius*, January 26, 1990.

Chapple, Karen. "Economic Development For A Bipolar Industry. The Case of Apparel Manufacturing in San Francisco." Berkeley, CA: Berkeley Planning Journal, 12, 1998, 72-102.

Char, Tin-Yuke (Ed.). *The Sandalwood Mountains: Readings and Stories of the Early Chinese Immigrants in Hawaii*. Honolulu, HI: University Press of Hawaii, 1975.

Chen, Allen T. "The United States of China." *Asian Week*, July 6, 2001.

Chen, Elaine. *Interview by Birgit Zinzius*, September 12, 1989.

Chen, Jack. *The Chinese of America*. New York, NY: Harper & Row, Publishers, 1980.

Chen, Jay. *Interview by Birgit Zinzius*, December 29, 1989.

Chen, Julia I. H. *The Chinese Community in New York: A Study in Their Cultural Adjustment, 1920-1940*. San Francisco: R and E Research Associates, 1974.

Chen, Nancy. *Interviews by Birgit Zinzius*, 1991.

Chen, Serena and Look, Jeannie. "US Civil Rights Commissioners Get An Earful From Asians." *East West News*, August 3, 1989, 1, 3.

———. *Interview by Birgit Zinzius*, 1989.

Chen, Shehong. *Being Chinese, Becoming Chinese American (Asian American Experience)*. Champaign, IL: University of Illinois Press, 2002.

Chen, Stanford. "So You Think You've Got it Made - Now What?" *East West News*, August 31, 1989, 2.

Cheng, David Te Chao. *Acculturation of the Chinese in the United States: A Philadelphia Study*. China: Fukien University Press, 1948.

Cherlin, Andrew J. (Ed.). *The Changing American Family and Public Policy*. Washington, DC: Urban Institute Press, 1988.

Chiang, Liu. "Chinese versus American Ideas Concerning the Family." *Journal of Applied Sociology*, Shanghai, 1992, 243-248.

———. "Contrasts Between Chinese and American Social Codes." *Journal of Applied Sociology*, Foo-Chow, 1992, 41-45.

Chin, Frank, Chan, Jeffey P., Inada, Lawson F. and Wong, Shawn (Eds.). *Aiiieeeee! An Anthology of Asian American Writers*. Washington, DC: Howard University Press, 1974.

Chin, Frank. *Chickencoop Chinaman. The Year of the Dragon. Two Plays*. Seattle, WA: Washington University Press, 1981.

———. *Chinaman Pacific & Frisco R.R.CO. Eight Short Stories by Frank Chin*. Minneapolis, MN: Coffee House Press, 1988.

———. *Interview by Birgit Zinzius*, October 27, 1989.

———. *Donald Duck. A Novel by Frank Chin*. Minneapolis, MN: Coffee House Press, 1991.

———. *Gunga Din Highway: A Novel*. Minneapolis, MN: Coffee House Press, 1994.

———. *Bulletproof Buddhists and Other Essays*. Honolulu, HI: University Press of Hawaii, 1998.

Chin, Gabriel, Cho, Sumi, Kang, Jerry, and Wu, Frank. "Beyond Self-Interest: Asian Pacific Americans toward a Community of Justice." *Asian Pacific American Law Journal*, 129, 1996. October 21, 1996, <http://www.sscnet.ucla.edu/aasc/policy/index.html> (November 6, 2002).

Chin, Tung P., and Chin Winifred C. *Paper Son: One Man's Story*. Philadelphia, PA: Temple University Press, 2000.

China Institute in America (Ed.). *A Survey of Chinese Student in American Universities and Colleges in the Past One Hundred Years*. New York, NY: 1954, 17-19.

Chinatown Economic Development Group (CEDG). "Homepage," 2000 <http://www.sfchinatown.com/about1.html> (March 10, 2003).

Chinese American Data Center. "Labor Force participation by Chinese-American, 1980-1990." March 2002, <http://members.aol.com/chineseusa/00lab.htm> (December 12, 2002).

Chinese for Affirmative Action. Bulletin 1991. San Francisco, CA: 1991.

Chinn, Thomas W. *A History of the Chinese in California: A Syllabus*. San Francisco, CA: Chinese Historical Society, 1969.

————. et al. (Ed.). *Chinese Historical Society of America. Tenth Anniversary, 1963-1973. Bulletin*. San Francisco, CA: Chinese Historical Society, 1973.

————. *Bridging the Pacific: San Francisco Chinatown and its People*. San Francisco, CA: Chinese Historical Society of America, 1989.

————. *Interviews by Birgit Zinzius*, 1990/1991.

Chiu, Ping. *Chinese Labor in California, 1850-1880: An Economic Study*. Madison, WI: Department of History, University of Wisconsin Press, 1960 (Unpublished).

Chong, Linda. "Trapping the 'yappies'." *San Jose Mercury News*, June 27, 1988, 1C, 8C.

Chow, Phillip and Him Mark Lai. *Outlines: History of the Chinese in America*. San Francisco, CA: Chinese American Studies Planning Group, 1971.

Chow, Willard. *The Reemergence of an Inner City: The Pivot of Chinese Settlement of the East Bay Area*. San Francisco: R&E Research, 1977.

Choy, Phillip P. *Interview by Birgit Zinzius*, March 6, 1990.

Chu, Judy. Asian Pacific American Women in Mainstream Politics. In: *Making Waves. An Anthology of Writings by and about Asian American Women*. Asian Women United of California (Ed.). Boston, MA: Beacon Press, 1989, 405-423.

Chun, Kevin M. (Ed.), Organista, Pamela B (Ed.), Marin, Gerardo (Ed.), and Sue, Stanley. *Acculturation: Advances in Theory, Measurement, and Applied Research*. Washington, DC: American Psychological Association, 2002.

Chung, Wing Ng. *Interviews by Birgit Zinzius*, 1991.

Chung, Wing Ng. The Chinese in Vancouver, 1945-80: The Pursuit of Identity and Power. Vancouver, Canada: University of British Columbia Press, 1999.

Clausen, Edwin and Bermingham, Jack. "Post - 1965 Chinese Immigration and the Professional and Intellectual Class: A Profile." In: *Chinese and African Professionals in California. A Case Study of Equality and Opportunity in the United States*. Washington, DC: University Press of America, 1982, 65-88.

Cleland, Robert G. *From Wilderness to Empire*. New York, NY: 1944.

Clinton, William J. "White House Greetings for the Year of the Dragon." The White House, February 3, 2000, <http://www.usa.or.th/news/press/2000/nrot015.htm> (March 02, 2003).

Close Up Foundation. *U.S. Immigration Policy*. July, 1998, <http://www.closeup.org/immigrat.htm> (December 22, 2002).

Cohen, Jerome A., Edwards, Randle R., and Chen, Fu-mei (Eds.). *Essays on China's Legal Tradition*. Princeton, NJ: Princeton University Press, 1980.

Code, William. The Family as an Element in the Social Structure. In: *The Family*. Code, William (Ed.). Englewood Cliffs, NJ: Prentice Hall, 1964.

College Board. "The New SAT. History of the SAT." The College Board, 2003, <http://www.collegeboard.com/about/newsat/history.html> (March 21, 2003).

Committee of 100. "Landmark National Survey on American Attitudes towards Chinese Americans and Asian Americans." April 25, 2001. <http://www.committee100.org/Published/articles/042501.html> (April 19, 2003).

Confucius. *The Analects (Lun Yü)*. Translated by D. C. Lau. New York, NY: Penguin Books United States Inc., 1998.

Congressional Research Service *Immigration Law and Policy 1952-1986, 100. Cong., 1st Session*. 1987.

Coolidge, Mary R. *Chinese Immigration*. New York, NY: Henry Holt and Co., 1909.

Cose, Ellis *A Nation Of Strangers. Prejudice, Politics And The Population Of America*. New York, NY: William Morrow and Company, Inc., 1992.

"County Makes Moves To Aid Asian Mentally Ill." *The Rafu Shii, Los Angeles Japanese Daily News*, February 11, 1987.

Crawford, James. "Obituary: The Bilingual Ed Act, 1968 – 2002." *Rethinking Schools online*, 16:4, Summer 2002, <http://www.rethinkingschools.org/archive/16_04/Bil164.shtml> (March 7, 2003).

Culin, Stewart. *China in America: Social Role of the Chinese Eastern Cities of the United States*. New York, NY: Philadelphia Press, 1887.

D'Antonio, Nancy. *Our Baby from China: An Adoption Story*. Morton Grove, IL: Albert Whitman & Company, 1997.

Daley, William, and Stotsky, Sandra. *The Chinese Americans (The Immigrant Experience)*. Broomall, PA: Chelsea House Publishers, 1995.

Daniels, Roger. *Asian American. Chinese and Japanese in the United States since 1850*. Seattle, WA: University of Washington Press, 1988.

———. *Coming To America. A History Of Immigration And Ethnicity In American Life*. New York, NY: Harper Perennial, 1991.

Dariotis, Wei Ming. "The Emerging Hapa Community." *Asian Week*, November 1, 2002.

Daschle, Thomas A. (D-SD), Senator. *Interviews by Birgit Zinzius*, 1990.

Davis, Floyd J. *Who Is Black?: One Nation's Definition*. University Park, PA: The Pennsylvania State University Press, 1991, 1-16.

Deane, Glenn and Hyoung-jin Shin, *Technical Report: Comparability of the 2000 and 1990 Occupation Codes*. New York, NY: University at Albany, Lewis Mumford Center for Comparative Urban and Regional Research, November 19, 2002.

Der, Henry. *Interviews by Birgit Zinzius*, 1989-1991.

Devine, George. *Interviews by Birgit Zinzius*, 1992.

Dicker, Laverne Mau. *The Chinese in San Francisco: A Pictorial History*. New York, NY: Dover Publications, Inc., 1979.

Dickson, Bruce and Harding, Harry (Eds.) *Economic Relations in the Asian-Pacific Region*. Washington, DC: The Brookings Institution, 1987.

Dillon, Richard H. *The Hatchet Men: The Story of the Tong Wars in San Francisco's Chinatown*. New York, NY: Howard McCann, 1962.

Dinnerstein, Leonard and Reimers, David M. Ethnic Americans: A History of Immigration and Assimilation. New York, NY: Harper and Row, 1975.

Domes, Jürgen. Die Ära Mao Tse-tung. Innenpolitik in der Volksrepublik China. Stuttgart: Kohlhammer, 1972.

Donaldson, Evan B. *International Adoption Facts*. "Adoption Institute, Facts About Adoption" 2002, <http://www.adoptioninstitute.org/FactOverview/international.html> (March 29, 2003).

Drehle, David Von. „Court mirrors public opinion." *Washington Post*, June 24, 2003, A1.

Dunne, Geoffrey. "Atop the Golden Mountain." *Good Times, Santa Cruz*, September 19, 1986, 11-14.

"Eat a Bowl of Tea." *Press conference*, September 19, 1989.

Eaton, Michael. *Chinatown. B.F.I. Film Classics*. London: British Film Institute, 1998.

Eaves, Lucile. *A History of California Labor Legislation*. Berkeley, CA: University of California Press, 1910.

Eberhard, Wolfgang. *A History of China*. London: Routledge & Kegan Paul LTD, 1948.

Eckrich, Teresa, Lew, Catherine, and Treisman, Joel. *A Pilot Assessment of Voter Registration in San Francisco's Chinese Community*. San Francisco, CA: Coro Foundation, 1986.

Eisenberg, Ira. "Fighting Words. Race and Free Speech at the University of California." *This World*, September 9, 1990, 9-12.

Eisenhower, Dwight D. "Public Papers of the Presidents: The Domino Theory, 1954." In: Woolley, John and Peters, Gerhard. *The American Presidency Project*. August 27, 2002, <http://www.presidency.ucsb.edu/index.html> (December 11, 2002).

"Ending College Admission Quotas Against Asian Americans." *Heritage Foundation, Executive Memorandum*. June 30, 1989.

Endo, Russel, Sue, Stanley and Wagner, Nathaniel N. *Asian Americans: Social and Psychological Perspectives. Vol. II*. n.p.: Science and Behavior Books, 1980.

Eng, Pat. "Death of a Chinese Immigrant Woman." *Asian Week*, September 15, 1989.

"Enhancing English skills for college students for whom English is a second language." *East West News*, August 10, 1989.

Equal Educational Opportunity: Hearing before the Select Committee on Equal Educational Opportunity of the U.S. Senate. 92nd Congress, 1st Session.

Evans, Karin, and Min, Anchee. *The Lost Daughters of China: Abandoned Girls, Their Journey to America, and the Search for a Missing Past*. New York, NY: J.P. Tarcher, 2000.

Ezorsky, Gertrude. *Racism and Justice: the Case for Affirmative Action*. Ithaca: Cornell University Press, 1992.

Fang, John. *Interviews by Birgit Zinzius*, 1990.

Fairbank, John King. *The United States and China*. Cambridge, MA: The Harvard University Press, 1983.

Fairbank, John King. *The Great Chinese Revolution: 1800-1985*. New York, NY: HarperCollins, 1987.

Fairbank, John King and Goldman, Merle. *China. A New History*. Cambridge, MA: The Harvard University Press, 1998.

Fallows, James. "Immigration-How It's Affecting Us." *The Atlantic Monthly*, November, 1983, 45-61.

Fawcett, James, Carino, Benjamin V. and Arnold, Fred. *Asian-Pacific Immigration to the United States-A Conference Report*. Honolulu, HI: East/West Population Institute, 1985.

Federal Emergency Relief Administration. *Unemployment Relief Census*. Washington, DC: U.S. Government Printing Office, Report No. 1: United States Summary, 1943.

Fei, John C. H. and Liu, Ts'ui-jung. "The Growth and Decline of Chinese Family Clans." *Journal of Interdisciplinary History*, XII:3, 1981, 375-408.

Feng, Pin-Chai, Morrison, Toni, and Kingston, Maxine Hong. *The Female Bildungsroman by Toni Morrison and Maxine Hong Kingston: A Postmodern Reading*. New York, NY: Peter Lang Publishing, reprint edition, 2001.

Fessler, Loren W. (Ed.). *Chinese in America. Stereotyped Past, Changing Present*. New York, NY: Vantage Press, Inc., 1983.

Feulner, Edwin J., Jr. *The Heritage Lectures 29. U.S. Foreign Policy in Asia and the Pacific*. Washington, DC: The Heritage Foundation, 1984.

Fong, Pauline L. *Education, Work and Family Aspirations of Contemporary Asian American Girls and Women. Summary Report of the Asian American Women's Education and Job Choice Project*. San Francisco: Asian American Women's Education and Job Choice Project, 1981.

Fong, R., and Wu, D.Y. "Socialization Issues for Chinese American Children and Families." *Journal of Social Work in Education*, No. 18, 1996, 71-83.

Franke, Wolfgang. *China und das Abendland*. Göttingen: Vandenhoeck & Rupprecht, 1962.

Franklin, John H., Chavez-Thompson, Linda, Cook, Suzan D. J., Kean, Thomas H., Oh, Angela, Thomas, Robert, and Winter, William F. *One America in the 21st Century. The Advisory Board's Report to the President*. September 1998 <http://clinton2.nara.gov/OneAmerica/cevent.html> (June 20, 2002).

Fredrickson, George M. *Racism: A Short History*. Princeton, NJ: Princeton University Press, 2002.

Gao, Ting. "Ethnic Chinese Networks and International Investment Evidence from Inward FDI in China." University of Missouri, MO: Working Paper, September 2000.

Gao, Ting. "Foreign Direct Investment in China. How Big are the Roles of Culture and Geography?" University of Missouri, MO: Working Paper, August 2002.

Gardner, Robert W., Robey, Bryant and Smith, Peter C. "Asian Americans: Growth, Change, and Diversity." *Population Bulletin*, 40:4 (October), 1985, 1-43.

Getting Together. *Chinese American Workers: Past and Present. An Anthology of Getting Together.* San Francisco: An Anthology of Getting Together, 1972.

Gibbs, Nancy. "Bigots in the Ivory Tower. An alarming rise in hatred roils U.S. campuses." *Time Magazine*, May 7, 1990, 40-43.

Gifford, Donna. "English Only? Preparing Kids for Multi-National Jobs is Key to Their Future Success." *Golden Gate [X]press*, SFSU. April 24, 2000, <http://xpress.sfsu.edu> (February 28, 2003).

Gilles, Laura. *Interview by Birgit Zinzius*, January 17, 1990.

Givens, Ron et al. "The Drive to Excel." *Newsweek on Campus*, April, 1984, 4-11.

Glazer, Nathan, and Moynihan, Daniel P. *Beyond the Melting Pot*. Cambridge, Mass.: M.I.T. Press, 1963.

———. "Beyond the Melting Pot: Twenty Years After." *Journal of American Ethnic History*, 1, 1981.

———. *A Changing American Population: With What Effect?* Washington, DC: Congressional Research Service, 1990.

Glazer, Gary. *Interviews by Birgit Zinzius*, 1990.

Glenn, Evelyn N. "Split Household, Small Producers and Dual Wage Earner: An Analysis of Chinese American Family Strategies." *Journal of Marriage and the Family*, February, 1983, 35-46.

Glick, Clarence. *Sojourners and Settlers. Chinese Immigrants in Hawaii*. Honolulu, HI: The University Press of Hawaii, 1980.

Gordon, C. and Gordon, E. G. *Immigration and Nationality Law*. New York, NY: Matthew Bender & Company, Inc., 1988.

Gordon, Milton M. *Assimilation in American Life: The Role of Race, Religion, and National Origins*. New York, NY: Oxford University Press, 1964.

Granet, Marcel. *Chinese Civilization*. London, Kegan Paul, Trench, Trubner & Co., Ltd. New York: Alfred A. Knopf, 1930.

Grubb, Joe. "San Francisco Housing Databook." Bay Area Economics Study, commissioned by the San Francisco Board of Supervisors. "Publications," 2002 <http://www.bayareaeconomics.com/publications.htm> (February 11, 2003).

Gu, Wei. "U.S. educated Chinese see more jobs at home." *Yahoo!Financial Service*, Reuters, April 16, 2003, <http://biz.yahoo.com/rc/030416/bizfeature_china_jobs_1.html> (May4, 2003).

Gulick, Sidney Lewis. *American Democracy And Asiatic Citizenship*. New York, NY: Arno Press, 1978 (1918).

Gum Moon Women's Residence. *A New Home. A Caring Family. An Open Invitation*. San Francisco, CA: Gum Moon Women's Residence, 1991.

Gutierrez-Jones, Carl. "The Affirmative Action and Diversity Project: A Web Page for Research." University of California, Santa Barbara. July 21, 2002, <http://aad.english.ucsb.edu/aa.html> (March 3, 2003).

Gyory, Andrew. *Closing the Gate: Race, Politics, and the Chinese Exclusion Act*. Chapel Hill, NC: University of North Carolina Press, 1998.

Habenstein, Robert, and Mindel, Charles H. The American Ethnic Family: Protean and Adaptive. In: *Ethnic Families in America. Patterns and Variations*. New York, NY: Elsevier, 1976, 413-429.

Hahn, Albert S. "Counting Multiracials in the 2000 Census: Implications for Asian Americans." Cambridge, MA: Asian American Policy Review, Volume IX, 56-75, 2000.

Harding, Harry *A Fragile Relationship. The United States And China Since 1972*. Washington, DC: The Brookings Institution, 1992.

Hareven, Tamara K. Continuity and Change in the American Family. In: *Making America. The Society and Culture of the United States*. Luedtke, Luther S. (Ed.). Washington, DC: Unites States Information Agency, 1987.

Harris, David R., and Ono, Hiromi. "Cohabitation, Marriage and Markets: A New Look at Intimate Interracial Relationships." University of Michigan, Working Paper, May 2001, <http://mywebpages.comcast.net/drharris/paa2000.pdf> (January 18, 2003).

Hayner, Norman S., and Reynolds, Charles. "Chinese Family Life in America." *American Sociological Review*, 2, 1937, 614-630.

Henning, Daniel, and Mangun, William. *Managing the Environmental Crises. Incorporating Competing Values in Natural Resource Management*. Durham, NC: North Carolina University Press, 1989.

Heritage Foundation, Executive Memorandum. "Ending College Admission Quotas Against Asian Americans." The Heritage Foundation, June 30, 1989.

Hirata, Lucy Cheng, and Bonacich, Edna. *Labor Immigration under Capitalism. Asian Workers in the United States before World War II*. Berkeley, CA: University of California Press, 1984.

————. Youth, Parents, and Teachers in Chinatown: A Triadic Framework of Minority Socialization. In: *Understanding and Counseling Ethnic Minorities*. Henderson, George (Ed.). Springfield, Ill.: Charles C. Thomas Publishers, 1979, 376-391.

Ho, James. "East Meets West at S.F. Forum." *San Francisco Chronicle*, October 9, 1990, C 9.

Ho, Christine. "The Model Minority Awakened. The Murder of Vincent Chin." USAsians.net, <http://www.us_asians.tripod.com/articles-vincentchin.html> (March 20, 2003).

Hong, Lawrence K. "Recent Immigrants in the Chinese American Community: Issues of Adaptions and Impacts." *International Migration Review*, 36, 1976, 509-514.

"Hong Kong: Labor Imports. *Far Eastern Economic Review*. 55:6, February 13, 1992, 21.

Hong Kong Government Trade Department (Ed.). "China and Hong Kong, Some Import Facts." Hong Kong, May 1992.

Hong Kong Government (Ed.). *Government Structure*. Hong Kong, August 18, 2002, <http://www.info.gov.hk/info/structure-e.htm> (December 11, 2002).

Horton, John. *The Politics of Diversity. Immigration, Resistance, and Change in Monterey Park, California*. Philadelphia, PA: Temple University Press, 1995, 20-21.

House of Executive Documents. Washington, DC: 47th Congress, 1st Session, vol. 1.

House of Executive Documents. Washington, DC: 49th Congress, 1st Session, vol. 1.

House of Executive Documents. Washington, DC: 53rd Congress, 2nd Session, vol. 1.

House of Executive Documents 333. Washington, DC: 78th Congress, 1st Session, 1943, Serial 10793, vol. 1-2.

House of Executive Documents. Washington, DC: 78th Congress, 1st Session, 1943, vol LXXXIX, 8583 and 8595.

How, Marlon K. *Songs of Gold Mountain: Cantonese Rhymes from San Francisco's Chinatown. Reprint.* 1987.

Hsia, Jayjia. *Asian Americans in Higher Education and at Work*. Hillsdale, NJ: Lawrence Erlbaum Associates, 1988.

Hsieh, Thomas. *Interview by Birgit Zinzius*, January, 1990.

Hsu, Francis L. K. *The Challenge of the American Dream: The Chinese in the United States*. Belmont, CA: Wadsworth Publishing, 1971.

Hu, Arthur. "Asian Americans: Arthur Hu's Index of Diversity" Hu, Arthur, 2002, <http://www.arthurhu.com/index.html> (February 9, 2003).

Huang, Alfred. *The Complete I Ching: The Definite Translation by the Taoist Master Alfred Huang*. Rochester, VT: Inner Traditions Intl., 1998.

Huang, Joe. *Chinese Americans: Realities and Myths Anthology*. Huang, Joe and Wong, Sharon Quan (Eds.). San Francisco, CA: The Association of Chinese Teachers, 1977.

Huang, Jy et al. "Recht in China - Aufsätze aus der VR China zu Grundsatzfragen des Rechts." *Mitteilungen des Instituts für Asienkunde*, 104, 1979, 51-52.

Huang, Ken and Pilisuk, Marc. At the Threshold of the Golden Gate: Special Problems of Neglected Minority. In: *Understanding and Counseling Ethnic Minorities*. Henderson, George (Ed.). Springfield, IL: Charles C. Thomas, 1979, 357-376.

Huang, Lucy Jen. The Chinese American Family. In: *Ethnic Families in America. Patterns and Variations*. Mindel, Charles H. and Habenstein, Robert W. (Eds.). New York, NY: Elsevier, 1976, 124-147.

Hune, Shirley. *Interviews by Birgit Zinzius*, 1991.

Hunt, Rockwell D. *A Short History of California*. New York, NY: Thomas Y. Crowell Co., 1929.

Hwang, David H. *M. Butterfly*. New York, NY: Plume Books, 1989.

Hwang, David H. *FOB And Other Plays*. New York, NY: New American Library, 1990.

Hyun, Helen H. "Invisibility and Overrepresentation: Affirmative Action and the Asian American Paradox." Cambridge, MA: *Asian American Policy Review*, Volume VI, 1996.

Ibarra, Robert A. *Beyond Affirmative Action: Reframing the Context of Higher Education*. Madison, WI: The University of Wisconsin Press, 2000.

"Illegal Immigrants: The U.S. May Gain More Than It Loses." *Business Week*, May 14, 1984, 126-129.

Irick, Robert L. *Ch'ing Policy Toward the Coolie Trade, 1847-1878*. San Francisco, CA: San Francisco Materials Center, 1982.

Irving, Carl. "UC chief has to be tough. New Chancellor Tien faces tests on admissions, hiring." *San Francisco Examiner*, February 16, 1991, 8-9.

Isaac, Harold (Ed.). *Images of Asia: American Views of China and India*. New York, NY: Harper & Row, 1972.

Jacobson, Matthew F. *Whiteness of a Different Color: European Immigrants and the Alchemy of Race*. Cambridge, MA: Harvard University Press, Reprint edition, 1999

Jashik, Scott. "Conservative Lawmakers Attracts Interest and Ire with Crusade for Asian American Students." *Chronicle of Higher Education*, November 15, 1989.

Jen, Gish. *Typical American*. Boston, MA: Houghton Mifflin/Seymour Lawrence, 1991.

Jiang Zemin. "Jiang Zemin's Speech at the Meeting Celebrating the 80th Anniversary of the Communist Party of China." China Internet Information Center, July 1, 2001, <http://www.china.org.cn/e-speech/a.htm> (December 11, 2002).

Johnson, Jean M. "Human Resource Contributions to U.S. Science and Engineering from China." *National Science Foundation*. Issue Brief, January 12, 2001.

———. "The Reverse Brain Drain and the Global Diffusion of Knowledge." *Science&Technology*, Summer/Fall 2002, 125-131.

Johnson, Julie. "Asian Americans Press Fight For Wider Top-College Door." *The New York Times*, September 9, 1989, 1, 8.

Joint Special Committee to Investigate Chinese Immigration. 44th Congress, 2d Session. Report No 689. Washington, DC: Government Printing Office, 1877.

Joppke, Christian. "The Resilience of Nondiscriminatory Immigrant Policies: Evidence from the United States and Australia." New York, NY: Russel Sage Foundation, working paper #205, April, 2003.

Jue, Linda. "Fear. Taiwan's Deadly Export." *San Francisco Focus*, April, 1985, 70, 72-79.

Kamiya, Gary. "Cablinasian Like Me. Tiger Woods' Rejection Of Orthodox Racial Classifications Points The Way to a Future Where Race Will No Longer Define Us." April 30, 1997, *Salon* <http://www.Salon.com/april97/tiger970430.html> (December 17, 2002).

Kantrowitz, Barbara et al. "The Ultimate Assimilation. Asian intermarriage, once taboo, is on the rise." *Newsweek*, November 24, 1986, 80.

Kennedy, John F. *A Nation of Immigrants*. New York, NY: Harper and Row, 1964.

Kenney, Charles. *Riding the Runaway Horse: The Rise and Decline of Wang Laboratories*. Boston, MA: Little Brown & Co., 1992.

Kibria, Nazli. *Becoming Asian American: Second-Generation Chinese and Korean American Identities*. Baltimore, MD: John Hopkins University Press, 2002.

Kim, Bok-Lim C. *The Asian Americans: Changing Patterns, Changing Needs*. Montclair, NJ: Association of Korean Christian Scholars in North America, Inc., 1978.

Kim, Elaine. *Interview by Birgit Zinzius*, March 6, 1990.

Kim, Hyung-Chan (Ed.). *Dictionary of Asian American History*. New York, Westport, Connecticut, London: Greenwood Press, 1986.

————. (Ed.). *Asian American Studies: An Annotated Bibliography and Research Guide*. New York, Westport, Connecticut, London: Greenwood Press, 1989.

King, Ambrose Yeo-chi. "Kuan-hsi and Network Building: A Sociological Interpretation." In: Tu Wei-min (Ed.) *The Living Tree: The Changing Meaning of Being Chinese Today*. Stanford, CA: Stanford University Press, 1994, 109-26.

Kingston, Maxine Hong. *The Woman Warrior. Memoirs of a Girlhood Among Ghosts*. New York, NY: Random House, 1977.

————. *China Men*. New York, NY: Alfred A. Knopf, 1980.

————. "Cultural Mis-Readings by American Reviewers" in Amithanayagam, Guy (Ed.) *Asian and Western Writers in Dialogue: New Cultural Identities*. New York, NY: MacMillan. 1982, 55-57.

————. *Tripmaster Monkey. His Fake Book*. New York, NY: Alfred A. Knopf, 1989.

————. *The Fifth Book of Peace*. New York, NY: Knopf, 2003.

Kitano, Harry H. L. *Interview by Birgit Zinzius*, March 6, 1990.

Klosson, Michael. *One Country, Two Systems, Five Years: U.S. Perspectives on Hong Kong*. June 6, 2002, <http://www.usconsulate.org.hk/cg/2002/060601.htm> (December 22, 2002).

Koehn, Peter H., Yin, Xiao-Huang, and Lai, Him Mark. *The Expanding Roles of Chinese Americans in U.S.-China Relations: Transnational Networks and Trans-Pacific Interactions*. Armonk, NY: M.E. Sharpe, 2002.

Kolankiewicz, Leon. *Immigration, Population, and the New Census Bureau Projections*. June 2000, <http://www.cis.org./articles/2000/back600.html> (January 22, 2003).

Konvitz, Milton R. *The Alien and the Asiatic in American Law*. Ithaca, NY: Cornell University Press, 1946.

Kuan-chung, Lo. *The Romance of the Three Kingdoms*. New York, NY: Longitude Books, 1990.

Kung, Shien Woo. *Chinese in American Life: Some Aspects of their History, Status, Problems and Contributions*. New York, NY: Greenwood Press, 1962.

Kwok, Daphne. *Interviews by Birgit Zinzius*, 1992.

Kwang, Lee. *Interview by Birgit Zinzius*, 2003.

Kwong, Peter. *Interviews by Birgit Zinzius*, 1991.

————. *Chinatown, New York: Labor and Politics, 1930-1950*. New York: Monthly Review Press, 1979.

————. *New Chinatown*. New York, NY: The Noonday Press, 1987.

————. *The New Chinatown*. New York, NY: Hill & Wang Publishers, revised edition, 1996.

Kwong, Molly. *Interviews by Birgit Zinzius*, 1991, 1998.

Lai, Him Mark. "A Historical Survey of the Chinese Left in America." In: *Counterpoint: Perspectives on Asian America*. Gee, Emma et al. (Ed.). Los Angeles, CA: Asian American Studies Center, Resource Development and Publications, University of California, Los Angeles, 1976, 63-77.

————. *The Chinese of America, 1785-1980*. San Francisco, CA: Chinese Cultural Foundation, 1979.

Lai, Him Mark, Yip, Jean P. (Ed.), and Leong, Russel (Ed.). *A History Reclaimed: An Annotated Bibliography of Chinese Language Materials on the Chinese of America*. Los Angeles, CA: UCLA Asian American Studies Centre Press, 1986.

————, Woo, Emma and Wong, Henry. *Interview by Birgit Zinzius*, October 28, 1989.

————. *Interviews by Birgit Zinzius*, 1989-1992.

————, Hom, Marlon K., and McCunn, Ruthann Lum. *Chinese America: History and Perspectives*. San Francisco, CA: Chinese Historical Society of San Francisco, 1996.

————, Lim, Genny, and Yung, Judy. *Island: Poetry and History of Chinese Immigrants on Angel Island, 1910-1940*. Seattle, WA: University of Washington Press, reprint edition, 1999.

————. "Geographical and Historical Notes on the Wuyi Region." Kehrer, Jon, 2002, Taishan Geneology. <http://www.apex.net.au/~jgk/taishan/notes.html> (April 7, 2002)

Lan, Dean. Chinatown Sweatshops. In: *Counterpoint: Perspectives on Asian America*. Gee, Emma et al. (Ed.). Los Angeles, CA: Asian American Studies Center, Resource Development and Publications, University, 1976, 347-358.

Le, C.N. "Interracial Dating & Marriage. Asian-Nation: The Landscape of Asian America." 2003, <http://www.asian-nation.org/issues3.html> (March 03, 2003a).

Le, C.N. "Interracial Dating & Marriage. U.S.-Raised Asian Americans." 2003, <http://www.asian-nation.org/issues3a.html> (March 03, 2003b).

Lee, C. Y., and Hwang, David. *The Flower Drum Song.* New York, NY: Penguin, 2002.

Lee, Evelyn. *Ten Principles on Raising Chinese American Teens.* San Francisco, CA: Chinatown Youth Center, 1988.

Lee, Gary. *Interviews by Birgit Zinzius,* 1991.

Lee, Gus. *Interviews by Birgit Zinzius,* 1991.

———. *China Boy.* New York, NY: Penguin Books United States Inc., 1991.

———. *Honor and Duty.* New York, NY: Knopf, 1994.

———. *Tiger's Tail.* New York, NY: Knopf, 1996.

———. *Chasing Hepburn: A Memoir of Shanghai, Hollywood, and a Chinese Family's Fight for Freedom.* New York, NY: Harmony Books, 2003.

Lee, Huy Voun. *At the Beach.* New York, NY: Henry Holt, 1994.

Lee, Jane L. "Investors in Chinese Brewers May Find Patience Pays Off." *Asian Wall Street Journal,* August 8-10, 2003, M1.

Lee, May. *Interviews by Birgit Zinzius,* 1991-2003.

Lee, Mary. *Interview by Birgit Zinzius,* 1999.

Lee, Robert. *Guide to Chinese American Philanthropy and Charitable Giving Patterns.* Brisbane: Pathway Press, 1990.

Lee, Rose Hum. *The Chinese in the United States of America.* London: Oxford University Press, 1960.

Lee, Sandra Soo-Jin, Mountain, Joanna, and Koenig, Barbara A. "The Meanings of "Race" in the New Genomics: Implications for Health Disparities Research." *Yale Journal of Health Policy, Law, and Ethics,* Volume I, Spring 2001, 33-75.

Lee, Sharon. *Interview by Birgit Zinzius,* 2001.

Lee, Simon. *Interview by Birgit Zinzius,* 1992, 1998.

Lee, Taeku. "The Backdoor and the Backlash: Campaign Finance and Politicization of Chinese Americans." Cambridge, MA: Asian American Policy Review, Volume IX, 2000, 30-55.

Lee, Virginia. *The House That Tai Ming Built.* New York, NY: Macmillan, 1963.

Lee, Yvonne. *Interview by Birgit Zinzius,* March 6, 1990.

Leong, Harding. "On Lok." *Interview by Birgit Zinzius,* February 5, 1990.

Leong, Russel. "Frank Chin: An Authentic One." *Amerasia Journal,* 14:2, 1988, 164.

Levy, Marion Joseph. *The Family Revolution in Modern China.* New York, NY: Octagon Books, 1963.

Li, Peter S. *Occupational Mobility and Kinship Assistance: A Study of Chinese Immigrants in Chicago.* San Francisco, CA: R and E Research Associates, 1978.

———. "Immigration Laws and Family Patterns: Some Demographic Changes among Chinese Families in Canada." *Canadian Ethnic Studies,* XII:1, 1980, 59-74.

Li Li, Nishio, Akihiro, Brereton-Miller, Patricia, and Rui Ma. "Country Brief 2001: People's Republic of China." The Worldbank Group, December 2001, <http://www.worldbank.org> (December 18, 2002).

Light, Evan E. and Wong, Charles C. "Protest or Work: Dilemmas of the Tourist Industry in American Chinatowns." *American Journal of Sociology,* 80:6, 1975, 1342-1368.

Light, Evan E. *Ethnic Enterprise in California. Business and Welfare among Chinese, Japanese and Blacks.* Berkeley, CA: University of California Press, 1972.

Lim, Genny, Lai, Him Mark, Chu, Daniel, and Wong, Ted (Eds.). *The Chinese American Experience.* San Francisco, CA: Chinese Culture Foundation of San Francisco, 1980.

Lin, C. and Liu, W. T. "Intergenerational Relationships Among Chinese Immigrant Families from Taiwan." In: McAdoo, H.C. (Ed.) *Family Ethnicity: Strength in Diversity.* New York, NY: Russell Sage Publications, 1993, 271-286.

Lo, Lucia and Wang, Shuguang. "Settlement Patterns of Toronto's Chinese Immigrants: Convergence or Divergence?" *Canadian Journal of Regional Science,* XX:12, Spring-Summer 1997, 49-72.

Loo, Chalsa and Mar, Don. "Desired Residential Mobility an a Low Income Ethnic Community: A Case Study of Chinatown." *Journal of Social Issues*, 38:3, 1982a, 95-106.

Loo, Chalsa and Ong, Paul. "Slaying Demons with a Sewing Needle: Feminist Issues for Chinatown's Women." *Berkeley Journal of Sociology*, 27, 1982b, 77-88.

Look, Jeanny. *Interviews by Birgit Zinzius*, 1989-1991.

Lopez, Alejandra. "Asians in California: 1990 to 2000." Stanford, CA: Center for Comparative Studies in Race and Ethnicity CCSRE, Stanford University, Report No. 8, April 2002.

Lorenzo, M.K., Frost, A.K., and Reinherz, H.Z. "Social and Emotional Functioning of older Asian American adolescents." *Child & Adolescent Social Work Journal*, 17 (4), August 2000, 289-304.

Low, Victor. *The Unimpressable Race. A Century of Educational Struggle by the Chinese in San Francisco*. San Francisco, CA: East/West Publishing Company, Inc., 1982.

Lowe, Dr. Rolland and Lowe, Kathy. *Interviews by Birgit Zinzius*, 1989-1991.

Lowell, Waverly B. (Ed). *Chinese Immigration and Chinese in the United States*. Washington, DC: National Archives and Records Administration, 1996.

Luo, Yadong. *Guangxi and Business*. Singapore: World Scientific Pub. Co., 2000

Luu, Amy. "The Chinese American Experience in San Gabriel Valley." Los Angeles, CA: Museum of Chinese American History, Summer 1999.

Lyman, Stanford M. "Red Guard on Grant Avenue." *Trans-Action*, April, 1970, 21-34. Chinese Americans. New York: Random House, 1974.

———. *The Asians in North America*. Santa Barbara, CA: Clio Press, 1977.

———. *Chinatown and Little Tokyo: Power, Conflict, and Community Among Chinese and Japanese Immigrants in America*. Millwood, NY: Associated Faculty Press, Inc., 1986.

Lyons, Judith A. "Republic Berman Due In San Francisco Chinatown For Immigration." *Asian Week*, 22 September, 1989.

Mack, Connie. *President Reagan's Economic Legacy: The Great Expansion*. Joint Economic Committee Staff Report. Washington, DC: Government Printing Office, October 2000.

Mangaliman, Jessie. "Asian-American post biggest gains; high tech drives immigration." Mercury News, March 7, 2002.

Mangiafico, Luciano. *Contemporary American Immigrants. Patterns of Filipino, Korean, and Chinese Settlement in the United States*. New York, NY: Praeger, 1988.

Mar, Don. "Chinese Immigrant Women and the Ethnic Labor Market." *Critical Perspectives of Third World American*, 2:1 (Fall), 1984, 62-74.

Mark, Diane Mei Lin and Chih, Ginger. *A Place Called Chinese America*. Dubuque, IA: Kendall/Hunt, 1982.

Mathews, Jay. "Chinese are No. 1 Group Students Here. Rapid Influx Occurs Despite Restrictions." *The Washington Post*, May 2, 1989, A3.

Mau, Ella. *Interview by Birgit Zinzius*, November 11, 1990.

McBee, Susanna, White, George, Galloway, Joseph L., Peterson, Sarah, Lynch, Pat and Bosc, Michael. "Asian Americans. Are they making the Grade ?" *US News and World Report*, April 2, 1984, 41-43, 47.

McGrath, Ellie. "Confucian Work Ethic. Asian-born students head for the head of the class." *Time Magazine*, March 28, 1983, 36-52.

Meißenburg, Karin. *The Writings on the Wall. Socio-Historical Aspects of Chinese American Literature, 1900-1980*. Frankfurt: Verlag für Interkulturelle Kommunikation, 1987.

Melendy, H. Brett. *Asians in America: Filipinos, Korean's, and East Indians*. Boston, MA: Twayne Publishers, 1977.

Michaelson, Martin. "Affirmative Action: Few Easy Answers." Washington, DC: Association of Governing Boards of Universities and Colleges. *Priorities, 7*, Summer 1996.

Miller, Stuart C. *The Unwelcome Immigrant: The American Image of the Chinese, 1875-1882*. Berkeley, CA: University of California Press, 1969.

Miller, Tom. "States Unite to Defend University of Michigan Affirmative Action Policy." February 20, 2003 <http://www.state.ia.us/government/ag/latests_news/releases/feb_2003/Michigan.html> March 29, 2003.

Minnick, Sylvia Sun. *Samfow: The San Joaquin Chinese Legacy.* Fresno, CA: Panorama West, 1988.

Min, Pyong Gap. "Asians' Immigration and Settlement in the New York-New Jersey Area." *World on the Move: Newsletter of the Section on International Migration.* New York, NY: Queens College, 1998.

Mithum, Jaqueline S. The Role of the Family in Acculturation and Assimilation in America: A Psychocultural Dimension. In: *Culture, Ethnicity and Identity.* McCready, William C. (Ed.). New York, NY: Academia Press, 1983, 201-263.

Miyagawa, Taiji. "The Politics of Interracial Dating." *East Wind,* 2:2 (Fall/Winter), 1983, 47-49.

Mora, Jill Kerper. „Proposition 227's Second Anniversary: Triumph or Travesty?" July 26, 2002, <http://coe.sdsu.edu/people/jmora/Propo227/227YearTwo.htm> (March 7, 2003)

Morahan, Lawrence. "California Begins English-Only Classes." Conservative News Service, August 5, 1998, <http://www.cnsnews.com/InDepth/archive/199808/IND19980805b.html> (March 12, 2003).

Morrison, Thomas K. "The Relationship of U. S. Aid, Trade and Investment to Migration Pressures in Major Sending Countries." *International Migration Review,* 16, 1982.

Muchnik, Irvin. "The Chancellor's Big Test." *San Francisco Chronicle. This World,* May 5, 1991, 7-10.

Nationmaster.com. "Map & Graph: People: Chinese Population." 2003-2004. <http://www.nationmaster.com/graph-T/peo_chi-pop> February 24, 2004.

Nee, Victor G. and De Brett, Bary. *Longtime Californ': A Documentary Study of an American Chinatown.* New York, NY: Random House, 1972.

Ness, Carol. "The Un-Whitening Of California. Majority turning into a minority. Shift may force Caucasians to come to grips with their identity." *San Francisco Examiner,* April 14, 1991, A1, A10.

Ng, Elaine. *Interview by Birgit Zinzius,* February 27, 1990.

Ng, Fae Myenne. *Bone.* New York, NY: Hyperion Books, 1993.

Ng, Johnny. "Houses passes the Bill." *Asian Week,* October 5, 1990, 27.

Ng, Louis. *Interviews by Birgit Zinzius,* 1992.

Ng, Ping. *Interview by Birgit Zinzius,* February 20, 1990.

Nichols, Michael P. *The Power Of The Family. Mastering the Hidden Dance of Family Relationships.* New York, NY: Simon & Schuster Inc., 1988.

Noen, David and Der, Henry. *Interview by Birgit Zinzius,* January 19, 1990.

Office of Management and Budget (OMB). "Race and Ethnic Standards for Federal Statistics and Administrative Reporting." Federal Register Notice, Directive No. 15, May 12, 1977.

Office of Management and Budget (OMB). "Recommendations for the Interagency Committee for the Review of the Racial and Ethnic Standards to the Office of Management and Budget Concerning Changes to the Standards for the Classification of Federal Data on Race and Ethnicity." Washington, DC: U.S. Government Printing Office, Federal Register, July 9, Part II., 36873-36946, 1997a.

Office of Management and Budget (OMB). "Revisions to the Standards for the Classification of Federal Data on Race and Ethnicity." Federal Register Notice, Vol. 62, No. 210, 58781-58790, October 30, 1997b.

Ong, Paul. "Chinatown Unemployment and the Ethnic Labor Market." *Amerasia Journal,* 11:1, 1984, 35-54.

Ong, Paul, and Miller, Doug. "Economic Needs of Asian American and Pacific Islanders in Distress Areas," and "Technical Supplement." The Ralph and Goldy Lewis Center for Regional Policy Studies at UCLA. Working paper #38, #39. Los Angeles, CA: University of California, July 2002a.

Ong, Paul, and Houston, Doug. "The 2000 Census Undercount in Los Angeles County." The Ralph and Goldy Lewis Center for Regional Policy Studies at UCLA. Working paper #42. Los Angeles, CA: University of California, December 2002b.

Ong, Paul (Ed). *The State of Asian Pacific America – Transforming Race Relations: A Public Policy Report*. Los Angeles, CA: Leadership Education for Asian Pacifics, Inc. (LEAP), 2002c.

Open Doors 2002. *The Annual Report on International Education Exchange*. 2001-2002. New York, NY: Institute of International Education, November 18, 2002, <http://www.opendoors.org> (December 3, 2002).

Open Doors 2003. *The Annual Report on International Education Exchange*. 2002-2003. New York, NY: Institute of International Education, November, 2003, <http://www.opendoors.org> (February 10, 2004).

Open Doors 2004. *The Annual Report on International Education Exchange*. 2003-2004. New York, NY: Institute of International Education, November 11, 2004, <http://www.opendoors.org> (December 6, 2004).

Orr, John B. The American System of Education. in: Luedtke, Luther S. (Ed.) *Making America*. United States Information Agency. Washington, DC 1987, 282-297.

Outreach Task Force. "New Directions For Outreach. A Report for the Board of Regents of the University of California." July 1997, <http://www.ucop.edu/acadaff/otf/otfrpt.htm> (October 10, 2002).

Pan, Lynn (Ed.). *The Encyclopedia of the Chinese Overseas*. Singapore: Archipelago Press, reprint, 2000.

Peffer, George A., and Daniels, Roger. *If They Don't Bring Their Women Here: Chinese Female Immigration Before Exclusion*. Chicago, IL: University of Illinois Press, 1999.

Pelosi, Nancy (D-CA). *Interviews by Birgit Zinzius*, 1990.

Peng, Samuel et al. *School Experiences and Performances of Asian High School Students*. Washington, DC: U.S. Department of Education, 1984.

People's Daily Online. "Brain Drain Fears Arise over Foreign Student Allure." February 26, 2001, "Homepage" <http://english.peopledaily.com.cn/200102/26/20010226_63381.html> (June 7, 2002).

Perrin, Linda. *Coming to America: Immigrants from the Far East*. New York, NY: Delacorte Press, 1980.

Perkins, Dorothy. *Encyclopedia of China. The Essential Reference to China, Its History and Culture*. New York, NY: Roundtable Press, 1999.

Pike, Otis. "Open U.S. Doors to fleeing Chinese." *Chicago Sun-Times*, June 13, 1989.

Plath, J. H. *Über die häuslichen Verhältnisse der alten Chinesen, nach chinesischen Quellen, aus den Sitzungsberichten der königlich bayerischen Akademie der Wissenschaften*. München: 1862.

Pomfret, John. "Chinese Find Freedoms Muffled." *Asian Wall Street Journal*. August, 28, 2003, A8.

Poon, Wei Chi und Poon, Boon Pui. *Interview by Birgit Zinzius*, January 23, 1992.

Poston, Dudley L., Jr. "Chinese, Overseas." In: Demeny, P.G., and McNicoll, G. (Eds.). Encyclopedia of Population. MacMillan Library Reference, 2nd Ed., 2003. Manuscript published in 2002. <http://sociweb.tamu.edu/Faculty/POSTON/Postonweb/Pubarticle/pubarticle.html> May 3, 2003.

Pottinger, Matt. "How Pro-Beijing Politician Made Hong-Kong Retreat." *Asian Wall Street Journal*, September 8, 2003, A1, A5.

Pu Yi, Aisin-Gioro. *From Emperor to Citizen: The Autobiography of Aisin-Gioro Pu Yi*. Translated by W.F.F. Jenner. New York, NY: Oxford University Press, 1988.

Ramirez, Anthony. "America's Super Minority." *Fortune*, November 24, 1986, 148-161.

Reagan, Ronald. "Annual Report to the Congress on the State of Small Business." March 1, 1982, <http://www.reagan.utexas.edu/resource/speeches/1982/30182b.htm> (January 20, 2003).

———. "The President's News Conference." October 19, 1983, <http://www.reagan.utexas.edu/resource/speeches/1983/101983e.htm> (October 17, 2002).

———. "Remarks at a Meeting With Asian and Pacific-American Leaders." February 23, 1984a, <http://www.reagan.utexas.edu/resource/speeches/1984/22384a.htm> (March 2, 2003).

Reimers, David M. *Still the Golden Door. The Third World Comes to America*. New York, NY: Columbia University Press, 1985.

Reports of the Visa Office. Bureau of Security and Consular Affairs, Department of State, 1968, 65.

Richardson, Allen E. *Strangers in their Land: Pluralism and the Response to Diversity in the United States*. New York, NY: Pilgrim Press, 1988.

Riggs, Frederick W. *Pressures on Congress. A Study of the Repeal of Chinese Exclusion*. King's Crown, New York, NY: 1950.

Rodino, Peter W. "New immigration law in retrospect." *International Migration Review*, 2:1, 1968, 56-64.

Rowley, Anthony. "Unwilling winners." *A World Affairs Journal*, September 20, 1990, 66-72.

Sakamoto, Arthur, and Furuichi, Satomi. "The Wages of Native-born Asian Americans at the End of the Twentieth Century." Cambridge, MA: Asian American Policy Review, Volume X, 17-30, 2002.

Sandmeyer, Elmer C. *The Anti-Chinese Movement in California*. Chicago, IL: University of Illinois Press, 1973.

San Francisco Unified School District (SFUSD). *Information About Schools*. 2003 <http://orb.sfusd.k12.ca.us/schdata/schdata.htm> (February 28, 2003).

Satcher, David. *Report of the Surgeon General, 2001. Mental Health: Culture, Race, and Ethnicity, A Supplement to Mental Health: A Report of the Surgeon General*. February 12, 2003, <http://www.surgeongeneral.gov/library/reports.htm> (March 15, 2003).

Sauvant, Karl P. "China: an emerging FDI outward investor. Research Note." UNCTAD, December 4, 2003.   <http://r0.unctad.org.7en7subsites/dite/fdistats_files/pdfs/China_Researchnote.pdf> December 29, 2003.

Saxenian, AnnaLee, and Edulbehram, Jumbi. "Immigrant Entrepreneurs in Silicon Valley." Berkeley, CA: Berkeley Planning Journal, 12, 1998, 32-49.

Saxenian, AnnaLee. *Silicon Valley's New Immigrant Entrepreneurs*. San Francisco, CA: Public Policy Institute of California, 1999.

———. "Silicon Valley's New Immigrant Entrepreneurs." La Jolla, CA: University of California, San Diego, Working Paper No. 15, 2000.

———. "Local and Global Networks of Immigrant Professionals in Silicon Valley." San Francisco, CA: Public Policy Institute of California, 2002.

Saxton, Alexander. *The Indispensable Enemy: Labor And The Anti-Chinese Movement In California*. Berkeley, CA: University of California Press, 1971.

Schaller, Michael. *The United States and China. Into the Twenty-First Century*. New York, NY: Oxford University Press, Third Edition, 2002.

Schwarzer, Mitchell. "San Francisco by Numbers: Planning After the 2000 Census." *San Francisco Planning and Urban Research Association*. Report 397, July 2001, 1-9.

Schwartz, Wendy. "The Asian and Pacific Islander Population in the U.S." Eric Clearinghouse on Urban Education, Boston, NY. *ERIC Digest*, 181, December 2002.

Scott, Franklin D. *The Peopling of America: Perspectives on Immigration*. Washington, DC: AHA Pamphlets No. 241, 1972.

Segal, Philip, Dean, Jason, Richardson, Karen, and Wonacott, Peter. "Asian Economy Survey. The Rise of the Asian Consumer." *Asian Wall Street Journal*. October 28, 2002, R1-R12.

Seagrave, Sterling. *The Soong-Dynasty*. New York, NY: Harper & Row, 1985.

Sheng, Mia Jin. *Interview by Birgit Zinzius*, November 12, 1989.

Shinagawa, Larry Hajime and Pang, Gin Yong. "Intraethnic, and Interracial Marriages among Asian Americans in California, 1980." *Berkeley Journal of Sociology*, 1988, 95-114.

Shinagawa, Larry Hajime and Pang, Gin Yong. "Asian American Panethnicity and Intermarriage." In: *Asian Americans: Experiences and Perspectives*. Fong and Shinagawa (Eds.). Upper Saddle River, NJ: Prentice Hall, 2000, 300-348.

Shinde, B.E. *Mao Zedong and the Communist Policies. 1927-1978*. Columbia, MO: South Asia Books, 1991.

Siao, Grace Wai-Tse. "Asians Lobbying Hard For Morrison Immigration Bill." *Asian Week*, September 7, 1990, 1, 4.

Sienkiewicz, Henry K. "The Chinese in California." *California Historical Society Quarterly*, 34, 1955, 301-316.

Sim, Shao-Chee, Parrott, James, Peng, Carol, Clark, Meghan, and Zhang, Michael. *Chinatown After September 11th, An Economic Impact Study.* New York, NY: Asian Federation of New York, 2002.

Simon, Paul (D-IL), Senator. *Interviews by Birgit Zinzius*, 1990, 1992.

Sit, Elaine. *Interview by Birgit Zinzius*, September 12, 1989.

Sit, Ma. *Interviews by Birgit Zinzius*, 1989-1991.

Smith, Robert F. *Celebrating Cultural Diversity Through Children's Literature.* November 17, 2002. "Chinese Americans," <http://www.multiculturalchildrenslit.com/chinesewel.html> (April 4, 2003).

Sobel, Henry. *Interview by Birgit Zinzius*, October 24, 1989.

Statutes at Large of the United States of America 22-65. Washington, DC.

Steinberg, Laurence, Brown, Bradford, and Dornbusch, Sanford. *Beyond The Classroom.* New York, NY: Simon & Schuster, 1996.

Stevenson, Harold W., and Stigler, James W. *The Learning Gap: Why Our Schools Are Failing And What We Can Learn From Japanese And Chinese Education.* New York, NY: Simon & Schuster / Touchstone Books, 1994 (Reprint).

Studwell, Joe. *The China Dream. The Elusive Quest for the Greatest Untapped Market on Earth.* London: Profile Books, 2002.

Sue, Derald W. and Sue, Stanley. Counseling Chinese Americans. In: *Understanding and Counseling Ethnic Minorities.* Henderson, George (Ed.). Springfield, Ill.: Charles C. Thomas, 1979, 392-404.

Sue, Stanley. "Personality and Mental Health." *Amerasia Journal*, 2 (Fall), 1974, 173-177.

————, Sue, Derald W. and Sue, David W. "Asian Americans as a Minority Group." *American Psychologist*, September, 1975, 906-910.

————, and Zane, N. "Academic achievement and socioemotional adjustment among Chinese university students." *Journal of Counseling Psychology*, 32, 1985, 570-579.

Sung, Betty Lee. *The Story of the Chinese in America.* New York, NY: Collier Books. A Division of Macmillan Publishing Co., Inc., 1971.

————. *A Survey of Chinese American Manpower and Employment.* New York, NY: Praeger Publishers, 1976.

————. *The Adjustment Experience of Chinese Immigrant Children in New York City.* New York, NY: Center for Migration Studies, 1987.

————. *Chinese American Intermarriage.* Staten Island, New York, NY: Center for Migration Studies, 1990.

Supreme Court Reporter 13. 149 U. S. 698, 1893.

Sutter, Robert G. "Taiwan and the Killing of Henry Liu: Issue for Congress." *Congressional Research Service*, Report No. 85-42F, February 1, 1985.

Synovate. *Asia Pacific Market Handbook 2003.* Hong Kong: Synovate, 2003.

Sweatshop Watch. "The Garment Industry." 2001, <http://www.sweatshopwatch.org/swatch/industry> (March 14, 2002).

Taft, William. *The United States and Peace.* New York, NY: C. Scribner's Sons, 1914.

Taiwanese Government Information Office. "The Republic of China – Taiwan Yearbook 2002." July 2002, <http://www.roc-taiwan.org> (December 10, 2002).

Takagi, Paul and Platt, Tony. Behind the Gilded Ghetto: An Analysis Of Race, Class and Crime in Chinatown. *Crime and Social Justice.* 1978, 2-25.

Takaki, Ronald. *Iron Cages: Race and Culture in Nineteenth Century America.* New York, NY: Alfred Knopf, 1979.

————. *Strangers from a Different Shore: A History of Asian Americans.* Boston, MA: Little Brown, 1989a.

————. *Interview by Birgit Zinzius*, September 19, 1989b.

————. *A Different Mirror: A History of Multicultural America.* Boston, MA: Little Brown & Co., 1994.

————. *Debating Diversity. Clashing Perspectives on Race and Ethnicity in America.* New York, NY: Oxford University Press, Third Edition, 2002.

Tamayo, Bill. Broadening the „Asian Interest" in United States Immigration Policy. *Asian American Policy Review*, Vol. II, Spring 1991, 65 - 81.

Tan, Amy. *The Joy Luck Club*. New York, NY: Ballantine Books, 1989.

———. *The Kitchen God's Wife*. New York, NY: G.P. Putman's Sons, 1990.

———. *Interviews by Birgit Zinzius*, 1991.

———. *The Hundred Secret Senses*. London: HarperCollins Publishers, 1996.

———. *The Bonesetter's Daughter*. New York, NY: Putman Publishing Group, 2001.

Tan, Gloria. *Interview by Birgit Zinzius*, February 15, 1991.

Tan, Mely Gick-Lan. *Social Mobility and Assimilation: The Chinese in the United States*. Taipei: The Orient Cultural Service, 1973.

Thernstrom, Abigail M. *"Whose Votes Count?; Affirmative Action and Minority Voting Rights."* Cambridge, MA: Harvard University Press, 1987.

Thernstrom, Stephan. "The Demography of Racial and Ethnic Groups." In: Thernstrom, Abigail M., and Thernstrom, Stephan (Eds.). *Beyond the Color Line: New Perspectives on Race and Ethnicity in America*. Stanford, CA: Hoover Institution Press, 2002, 13-36.

Tien, Chang-lin. *Interviews by Birgit Zinzius*, 1991.

Timberlake, E., Triplett, W., and Triplett W. II. *Year of the Rat: How Bill Clinton Compromised U.S. Security for Chinese Cash*. Washington, DC: Regnery Publishing, 1998.

Tong, Benjamin. *Interview by Birgit Zinzius*, January 25, 1990.

Tong, Sarah Yucting. *Foreign Direct Investment and Ethnic Chinese Networking*. Working Paper, Hong Kong Institute of Economics and Business Strategies, University of Hong Kong. April 2001, 1990.

Trasvina, John D. *Interviews by Birgit Zinzius*, 1990.

Tsai, Lisa S. "Emerging Power: A Study on Asian American Political Candidates." Cambridge, MA: Asian American Policy Review, Volume IX, 76-98, 2000.

Tsai, Shih-shan Henry. *China and the Overseas Chinese in the United States, 1868-1911*. Fayetteville, AR: University of Arkansas Press, 1983.

———. *The Chinese Experience in America*. Kimball, Warren F. and Harrell, David E. Jr. (Eds.). Bloomington, IN: Indiana University Press, 1986.

Tung, William Ling. *The Chinese in America 1820-1973. A Chronology and Fact Book*. Dobbs Ferry, New York, NY: Oceana Publications, 1974.

Underwood, Robert A. "Building a National Community." *Asian Week*, August 11, 2000.

United Nations. *International Monetary Fund International Financial Statistics (IMF/IFS)*. 2002. <http://unstats.un.org/unsd/cdb/cdb_source_xrxx.asp?source_code=26> (December 4, 2002).

U.S. Bureau of Security and Consular Affairs, Department of State. *Reports of the Visa Office*. Washington, DC: U.S. Government Printing Office, 1965.

U.S.-China Peoples Friendship Association. *China Now: Reports & Appraisal*. New York, NY: U.S.-China Peoples Friendship Association, 1992.

U.S. Commission on Civil Rights. *Civil Rights Issues of Asian and Pacific Americans: Myths and Realities*. Washington, DC: Government Printing Office, 1980.

U.S. Commission on Civil Rights. *Recent Activities Against Citizens and Residents of Asian Descent*. Washington, DC: U.S. Government Printing Office, 1986.

U.S. Commission on Civil Rights. *Recent Activities Against Citizens and Residents of Asian Descent*. Clearing House Publication No. 88, 1988.

U.S. Commission on Civil Rights. *The Economic Status of Americans of Asian Descent: An Exploratory Investigation*. Washington, DC: Clearinghouse Publication 95, 1988.

U.S. Department of Commerce. Bureau of the Census. *Public Use Samples of Basic Records from the 1970 Census. Description and Technical Documentation*. Washington, DC: U.S. Bureau of the Census, 1972.

———. *Statistical Abstracts of the United States. 1957 - 2001*. Washington, DC: U.S. Government Printing Office, 1957-2001.

———. *A Public Use Sample of Basic Records from the 1960 Census. Description and Technical Documentation*. Washington, DC: U.S. Bureau of the Census, 1975.

———. *1980 Census of the Population. General Social and Economic Characteristics.* Washington, DC: U.S. Government Printing Office, 1981.

———. *Race of the Population by States: 1980.* Washington, DC: U.S. Government Printing Office, 1982.

———. *Census of Population and Housing, 1980: Public Use Microdata Samples, Technical Documentation.* Washington, DC: U.S. Bureau of the Census, 1983.

———. *Asian and Pacific Islander Population by State: 1980.* Washington, DC: U.S. Government Printing Office, 1983.

———. *Population of Asian Pacific Islanders, 1990.* Washington, DC: U.S. Government Printing Office, 1993.

———. *General Population Characteristics.* Washington, DC: U.S. Government Printing Office, 1983.

———. *Ancestry of the Population by State: 1980.* Washington, DC: U.S. Government Printing Office, 1983.

———. "Foreign-Born Immigrants: Chinese-Tabulations from 1980 U.S. Census of the Population and Housing." *mimeographed report,* Washington, DC, 1984.

———. *Statistical Abstract of the United States, 1985 through 2002.* Washington, DC: U.S. Government Printing Office, 1985 through 2002.

———. *We, the Asian and Pacific Islander Americans.* Washington, DC: U.S. Government Printing Office, 1988.

———. *Foreign Economic Trends and their Implications for the United States, Hong Kong.* Washington, DC: October 1992.

———. *We the Americans: Our Education.* WE-11. Washington, DC: September 1993.

———. *1997 Economy Census. Minority- and Women-Owned Businesses.* Economic Census 1997. March 1999, <http//:www.census.gov/epcd/mwb97/us/us.html> (December 16, 2002).

———. *Overview of Race and Hispanic Origin: 2000.* Census Brief, C2KBR/01-1. March 2001, <http//:www.census.gov/population/www/cen2000/briefs.html> (December 10, 2002).

———. *The Asian Population: 2000.* Census Brief, C2KBR/01-16. March 2001, <http//:www.census.gov/population/www/cen2000/briefs.html> (December 10, 2002).

———. *Historic Income Tables – Households.* Table H-5. June 28, 2001, <http//:www.census.gov/hhes/income/histinc/h05.html> (December 10, 2002).

———. *The Asian and Pacific Islander Population in the United States (Update). March 2000.* PPL-146. Yax, Laura K. June 28, 2001, <http//:www.census.gov/population/www/socdemo/race/ppl-146.html> (November 26, 2002).

———. Racial Statistics Branch. Yax, Laura K. (Population Division), August 1, 2002 <http://www.census.gov/population/www/socdemo/interrace.html> (December 16, 2002).

———. *Residential Segregation.* U. S. Census Bureau, Housing and Household Economic Statistics Division. February 12, 2002, <http//:www.census.gov/hhes/www/housing/resseg/ch1.html> (November 27, 2002).

———. *Home Computers and Internet Use in the United States.* P23-207. September 2001, <http//:www.census.gov/population/www/cen2000/briefs.html> (December 15, 2002).

———. *The Big Payoff: Educational Attainment and Synthetic Estimates of Work-Life Earnings.* P23-210. July 2002, <http//:www.census.gov/population/www/cen2000/briefs.html> (December 15, 2002).

———. *Historical Census Statistics on Population Totals By Race, 1790 to 1990, and By Hispanic Origin, 1970 to 1990, For The United States, Regions, Divisions, and States.* Gibson, Campbell, and Jung, Kay. Working Paper Series No. 56. September 2002, <http//:www.census.gov/population/www/documentation/twps0056.html> (December 15, 2002).

U.S. Department of Education. "Introduction: No Child Left Behind." January 10, 2003, <http://www.nclb.gov/next/overview/index.html> (January 21, 2003).

U.S. Department of Health. *Asian American Reference Data Directory.* Washington, DC: U.S. Government Printing Office, 1976.

U.S. Department of Health and Human Services. *An Annotated Bibliography on Refugee Mental Health.* Washington, DC: Government Printing Office, 1989.

U.S. Department of Homeland Security. *2003 Yearbook of Immigration Statistics.* Washington, DC: Government Printing Office, September 2004.

U.S. Department of Justice. Immigration and Naturalization Service. *Annual Reports, 1897-1928.* Washington, DC: U.S. Government Printing Office, 1928.

———. *Percentage of Legal Immigrants 1961-1977.* Washington, DC: U.S. Government Printing Office, 1977.

———. *1978* through *2001 Statistical Yearbook of the Immigration and Naturalization Service.* Washington, DC: U.S. Government Printing Office, 1979 through 2002.

———. *Report of the Attorney General to the Congress of the United States on the Administration of the Foreign Agents Registration Act of 1938, as amended, for the Calendar Year 1987.* Washington, DC: U.S. Government Printing Office, 1988.

———. *Estimates of the Unauthorized Immigrant Population Residing in the United States: 1990 to 2000.* Washington, DC: January 2003.

U.S. Department of Labor. *The Effects of Immigration on the U.S. Economy and Labor Market.* Washington, DC: Bureau of International Labor Affairs, 1989.

U.S. Embassy Beijing. "Bringing the PRC Students Home: Why They Stay, Why They Return." Beijing: February 1997.

U.S. Immigration Policy and the National Interest. Staff Report of the Select Commission of Immigration and Refugee Policy. April 30, 1981, 372.

United Press International. "Amnesty's Report on China's Executions." *San Francisco Chronicle,* September 13, 1990, A23.

University of California. "New Directions for Outreach: Report of the University of California Outreach Task Force." July 1997. <http://www.ucop.edu/acadaff/otf/otf.html> (June 19, 2002).

Vialet, Joyce. *U.S. Immigration Law Policy: 1952-1979.* Washington, DC: U.S. Government Printing Office, 1979.

———. Education and Public Welfare Division. "Immigration Legislation - Questions and Answers." In: *CRS Report for the Congress.* June 4, 1991.

Vodak, Jessica. "Tenants and Chinatown Community Development Center Save Affordable Housing for Seniors." May 14, 2002 <http://www.chinatowncdc.org> (December 12, 2002).

Wah, Tom Wing. *Interviews by Birgit Zinzius.* 1990.

Waldinger, R., and Bozorgmehr, M. *Ethnic Los Angeles.* New York, NY: Russell Sage Foundation, 1996.

Waley, Arthur. *The Opium War through Chinese Eyes.* London: Allen & Unwin, 1958.

Walsh, Joan. "A new racial era for San Francisco schools." *Salon.* February 18, 1999, <http://www.salon.com/news/1999/02/18news.html> (December 22, 2002).

Waltz, Kenneth N. "International Structure, National Force, and the Balance of Power." *Journal of International Affairs,* Vol. 21.2, 1967.

Wang, L. Ling-Chi. "Lau v. Nichols: History of a Struggle for Equal and Quality Education." In: *Counterpoint: Perspectives on Asian America.* Gee, Emma et al. (Ed.). Los Angeles: Asian American Studies Center, Resource Development and Publications, University, 1976, 240-263.

———. *Post-War Developments in the Chinese American Community.* 1980 (Unpublished).

———. "Meritocracy and Diversity in Higher Education: Discrimination Against Asian Americans in the Post-Bakke Era." *The Urban Review,* Vol. 20, No. 3, 1988, 189-209.

———and Chan, Sucheng. *Racism and the Model Minority: Asian Americans Higher Education.* Berkeley. 1988 (Unpublished).

———. *Interviews by Birgit Zinzius,* 1989-1991.

———. "Being Used and Being Marginalized in the Affirmative Action Debate: Re-envisioning Multiracial American from an Asian American Perspective." *Asian American Policy Review,* Volume VI, 1996a, 49-58.

———. "The John Huang Controversy – A Wake-up Call for Asian-American Activists." *JINN,* October 23, 1996b, <http://www.pacificnew.ord/jinn/stories/2.22/961023-lobby.html> (February 5, 2003).

————. "The closing Chapter of the Opium War—Why I am Going to Hong Kong." *JINN,* June 25, 1997, <http://www.pacificnew.ord/jinn/stories/3.13/970625-transition.html> (March 15, 2003).

————. "Asian Americans and the Campaign Finance Scandal: New Analysis." *Amerasia Journal,* Vol. 24:1, 1998.

————. "Letter to President Clinton Regarding When Ho Lee Case." October 6, 2000. <http://www.gateway2china.com/report/clinton_letter.htm> (May 12, 2002).

————. "Elaine Chao: Conservative, But How Compassionate Will She Be?" *Asian Week,* January 19, 2001.

Wang, Sharon. *Interview by Birgit Zinzius,* 2003.

Wang, Y. C. *Chinese Intellectuals and the West.* Chapel Hill, NC: University of North Carolina, 1966.

Waxman, Sarah. „The History of New York City's Chinatown." Harken, Avery, and David, Sam, Interactive Insights, 2002, <http://www.ny.com/articles/chinatown.html> (December 8, 2003).

Webster's Third New International Dictionary. Springfield, MA: Merriam–Webster, 1993

Wei Min She Labor Committee. *Chinese Working People in America: A Pictorial History.* San Francisco, CA: United Front Press, 1974.

Whiting, Allan S. "PRC-Taiwan Relations, 1983-93." *SAIS Review,* 3:1 (Winter-Spring), 1993, 131-145.

Wing, Yung. *My Life in China and America.* New York, NY: Henry Holt and Co., 1909.

Wong, Benjamin. *Interviews by Birgit Zinzius,* 1989.

Wong, Bernard P. *Patronage, Brokerage, Entrepreneurship and the Chinese Community of New York.* New York, NY: AMS Press, 1988.

Wong, Bernhard P. *Ethnicity and Entrepreneurship: The New Chinese Immigrants in the San Francisco Bay Area.* Upper Saddle River, NJ: Pearson Education, 1997.

Wong, Cheryl. *Interviews by Birgit Zinzius,* 1991.

Wong, Chester. *Interview by Birgit Zinzius,* February 18, 1990.

Wong, Fred. *Interview by Birgit Zinzius,* 1991, 2001.

Wong, Jade Snow. *Fifth Chinese Daughter.* New York, NY: Harper & Row, 1950.

————. *No Chinese Stranger.* New York, NY: Harper & Row, 1950.

Wong, John.. *Interviews by Birgit Zinzius,* 1989-1991.

Wong, Morrison G. "Changes in Socioeconomic Status of Chinese Population from 1960-1970." *International Migration Review,* 14, 1980, 511-524.

————. "Chinese Sweatshops In The United States: A Look At The Garment Industry." *Research in Sociology of Work: Peripheral Workers,* 2, 1983, 357-379.

Wong, Nellie. Broad Shoulders. In: *Making Waves. An Anthology of Writings by and about Asian American Women.* Asian Women United of California (Ed.). Boston, MA: Beacon Press, 1989, 260-265.

Wong, Peter. *Interview by Birgit Zinzius,* February 21, 1990.

Wong, Say-ling Cynthia. "Necessity and Extravagance in Maxine Hong Kingston's The Woman Warrior: Art and the Ethnic Experience." *MELUS,* 15:1, 1990, 3-26.

Wong, Say-ling Cynthia. *Interview by Birgit Zinzius,* February 28, 1990.

Wong, Stella Lee. *Interview by Birgit Zinzius,* February 26, 1990.

Wong, Ted. *Interviews by Birgit Zinzius,* 1991.

Wong, Y.H., and Leung, Thomas K.P. *Guanxi. Relationship Marketing in a Chinese Context.* Binghamton, NY: International Business Press, 2003.

Woo, Deborah. The Gap between Striving and Achieving: The Case of Asian American Women. In: *Making Waves. An Anthology of Writings by and about Asian American Women.* Asian Women United of California (Ed.). Boston, MA: Beacon Press, 1989, 185-197.

Woo, Henry. *Interview by Birgit Zinzius,* March 6, 1990.

World Health Organization. "WWW Virtual Library. Country-Specific WHO Data on Public Health." Wenzel, 2002, <http://www.ldb.org/iphw/index.htm> (January 17, 2003).

Wright, Lawrence. „One Drop of Blood." *The New Yorker,* July 24, 1994.

Wu, Cheng-Tsu. *Chinese People and Chinatown in New York City*. PhD. dissertation, Clark University, 1969.

———. *"Chink!"*. New York, NY: World Publishing, 1972.

Wu, Frank H. *Yellow: Race in America Beyond Black and White*. New York, NY: Basic Books, 2001.

Wu, Winfried. "Asian Americans Charge Prejudice Slows Climb to Management Ranks." *Wall Street Journal*, September, 1985.

Wu, Yuan Li. *Interview by Birgit Zinzius*, November 8, 1989.

Xingci, Wu and Chen, Li. "Gum San Haak in the 1980's: A Study on Chinese Emigrants who return to Toishan County for Marriage." *Amerasia Journal*, 14:2, 1988, 27-35.

Yao, Esther Lee. "A Comparison of Family Characteristics of Asian American and Anglo American High Achievers." *International Journal of Comparative Sociology*, XXVI, 3-4, 1985a, 198-208.

———. "Adjustment needs of Asian immigrant children." *Elementary School Guidance and Counseling*, 19:3 (Fall), 1985b, 222-227.

Yee, Norman and Yu, Wu. *Interview by Birgit Zinzius*, November 1, 1989.

Yep, Laurence. *Dragonwings*. New York, NY: Harper&Row, 1975.

———. *Child of the Owl*. New York, NY: Harper&Row, 1977.

———. *The Rainbow People*. New York, NY: Harper&Row, 1989.

———. *Dragon's Gate*. New York, NY: HarperCollins Juvenile Books, 1993.

———. *Thief of Hearts*. New York, NY: HarperCollins Juvenile Books, 1995.

———. *The Magic Paintbrush*. New York, NY: HarperCollins Juvenile Books, 2000.

Yen Ching-hwang. *The Ethnic Chinese in East and Southeast Asia. Business, Culture and Politics*. Singapore: Times Academic Press, 2002.

Yee, Lauren D. "Lowell High School accepts fewer minorities for Class of 2004." The Lowell on the Web, March 14, 2000, <http://www.thelowell.org/news/1999-00/mar14-admit.html> (December 22, 2002).

Yi, Jeannie J., Ye, Shawn X. *The Haier Way: Making of a Chinese Business Leader and a Global Brand*. Dumont, NJ: Homa & Sekey, 2003.

Yochum, Gilbert and Agarwal, Vinod "Permanent Labor Certifications for Alien Professionals, 1975-1982." *International Migration Review*, 22, 1988, 265-281.

Yoki, Stan. *Interview by Birgit Zinzius*, February 28, 1990.

Yu, Connie Young. *Chinatown, San Jose, United States*. Muller, Kathleen (Ed.). San Jose, CA: San Jose Historical Museum Association, 1991.

———. *Interviews by Birgit Zinzius*, 1989-1992.

———. *Profiles in Excellence. Peninsula Chinese Americans*. Palo Alto, CA: Stanford Area Chinese Club, 1987.

Yuan, D. Y. "Voluntary Segregation: A Study of New York Chinatown." *Phylon*, XXIV, 1963, 255-265.

Yung, Judy. *Chinese Woman of America. A Pictorial History*. Seattle, WA: University of Washington Press, 1986.

———. *Interviews by Birgit Zinzius*, 1989-1992.

———. *Unbound Feet: A Social History of Chinese Women in San Francisco*. Berkeley, CA: University of California Press, 1995.

———. *Unbound Voices: A Documentary History of Chinese Women in San Francisco*. Berkeley, CA: University of California Press, 1999.

Zelnick, Robert. "The Battle for Color-Blind Public Policy." In: Thernstrom, Abigail M., and Thernstrom, Stephan (Eds.). *Beyond the Color Line: New Perspectives on Race and Ethnicity in America*. Stanford, CA: Hoover Institution Press, 2002, 405-414.

Zhang, Wei-hua. "Fred Ho and Jon Jang: Profiles of Two Chinese American Jazz Musicians." *Chinese America: History and Perspectives*. San Francisco, CA: Chinese Historical Society of America, Vol 8, 1994.

Zhou, Min, and Portes, Alejandro. Chinatown: The Socioeconomic Potential of an Urban Enclave (Conflicts in Urban and Regional Development). Philadelphia, PA: Temple University Press, 1995.

Zhu Rongji. "Zhu Rongji Proud of Chinese Economy." *People's Daily*, September 20, 2001.

Zinzius, Birgit. *Die chinesisch-amerikanische Familie in der ersten Einwanderungsphase 1848-1882.* Magisterarbeit, München, 1988.

———. *Sino-Amerika: Stereotyp und Wirklichkeit.* Frankfurt: Peter Lang Verlag, 1995.

———. *Der Schlüssel zum Chinesischen Markt.* Wiesbaden: Verlag Dr. Th. Gabler, 1996.

———. *Das kleine China-Lexikon.* Darmstadt: Primus Verlag, 1999a.

———. *China entdecken.* München: Beck, 1999b.

———. *China Business. Der Ratgeber zur erfolgreichen Unternehmensführung im Reich der Mitte.* Berlin: Springer Verlag, 2000.

———. *Doing Business in the New China.* New York, NY: Praeger Publishers, 2004.

Zweig, David, Chen, Changgui, and Rosen, Stanley. *China's Brain Drain to the United States: Views of Overseas Chinese Students & Scholars in the 1990s.* Berkeley, CA: University of California, Institute of East Asian Studies, 1995.

SELECTED INTERNET SITES

Statistical Sources:

<http://www.census.gov/main/www/cen2000.html> (Census results)
<http://factfinder.census.gov/> (Facts and maps about the Census)
<http://members.aol.com/chineseusa/> (Facts about Chinese Americans)
<http://www.arthurhu.com/> (Facts about Asian Americans)

Organizations:

<http://www.acp-atlanta.org/> (Many links to Chinese American sites)
<http://www.asianam.org/links.htm> (Links to Chinese American sites)
<http://www.caasf.org/> (Chinese for Affirmative Action)
<http://www.capa.org/> (Chinese American Political Organization)
<http://www.capal.org/apanationalorgs.htm> (Links to organizations)
<http://www.committee100.org/> (Chinese American leaders)
<http://www.oca.com/> (Organization of Chinese Americans)
<http://www.ocanatl.org/> (Organization of Chinese Americans)
<http://www.leap.org/> (Leadership Education for Asian Pacifics)
<http://www.nyjpw.org/> (Chinese American Arts & Culture Association)

General and political interest:

<http://aad.english.ucsb.edu/aa.html> (Resource on affirmative action)
<http://www.asianamerican.net/> (General website on Asian Americans)
<http://www.asian-nation.org/> ("Asian Americans 101 online")
<http://www.asianweek.com/> (Premier Asian American weekly)
<http://www.chsa.org/> (Chinese Historical Society of America)
<http://www.goldsea.com/index.html> (Asian American "Supersite")
<http://www.modelminority.com/> ("Asian American empowerment")
<http://www.momao.com/> (Chinese American art)
<http://www.sfchinatown.com/about1.html> (Chinatown-information)

INDEX

M